Dangerous Crossings

When Asian immigrants, African Americans, or Native people in the United States harm animals in their (cultural) practices, controversy is sure to follow. *Dangerous Crossings* offers a compelling analysis of three of these impassioned disputes: the battle over the live animal markets in San Francisco's Chinatown, the uproar over the conviction of NFL superstar Michael Vick on dogfighting charges, and the firestorm over the Makah tribe's decision to resume whaling in the Pacific Northwest after a hiatus of more than seventy years. Moving beyond simplistic explanations about "culture clashes" and "double standards," Claire Jean Kim shows that in each dispute, race and species operate as conjoined logics, or mutually constitutive taxonomies of power, fashioning the animal, the Chinese immigrant, the Black man, and the Indian in the white imaginary. In each dispute, too, the optic of cruelty and ecological harm, evoked by animal advocates, confronts the optic of racism and cultural imperialism, evoked by race advocates. The answer to this conundrum, she argues, is a multi-optic approach to social justice, one that takes multiple forms of domination seriously and encourages an ethics of avowal among different justice struggles.

Claire Jean Kim is a Professor of Political Science and Asian American studies at the University of California, Irvine, where she teaches classes on Asian American politics, Black politics, comparative race studies, social movements, and human-animal studies. Her first book, *Bitter Fruit: The Politics of Black-Korean Conflict in New York City* (2000), won two awards from the American Political Science Association – the Ralph Bunche Award for the best book on ethnic and cultural pluralism and the Best Book Award from the Organized Section on Race and Ethnicity. Dr. Kim has also written numerous journal articles and book chapters. She coedited, with Carla Freccero, a special issue of *American Quarterly* entitled "Species/Race/Sex" (2013). She is the recipient of a grant from the University of California Center for New Racial Studies, and she has been a Fellow at the Institute for Advanced Study in Princeton, New Jersey, and the University of California Humanities Research Institute.

Dangerous Crossings

Race, Species, and Nature in a Multicultural Age

CLAIRE JEAN KIM
University of California, Irvine

CAMBRIDGE
UNIVERSITY PRESS

32 Avenue of the Americas, New York, NY 10013-2473, USA

Cambridge University Press is part of the University of Cambridge.

It furthers the University's mission by disseminating knowledge in the pursuit of education, learning, and research at the highest international levels of excellence.

www.cambridge.org
Information on this title: www.cambridge.org/9781107622937

© Claire Jean Kim 2015

First published 2015

Printed in the United States of America

A catalog record for this publication is available from the British Library.

Library of Congress Cataloging in Publication Data
Kim, Claire Jean, author.
Dangerous crossings : race, species, and nature in a multicultural age / Claire Jean Kim, University of California, Irvine.
   pages   cm
Includes bibliographical references and index.
ISBN 978-1-107-04494-4 (hardback) – ISBN 978-1-107-62293-7 (pbk.)
  1. Animal welfare – United States.   2. Human-animal relationships – United States.   3. United States – Race relations.   I. Title.
HV4764.K56   2014
179.308900973–dc23   2014032780

ISBN 978-1-107-04494-4 Hardback
ISBN 978-1-107-62293-7 Paperback

For Astyanax

Contents

Figures and Tables

Acknowledgments

My sincere thanks to the following:

Friends, colleagues, and interlocutors whose support and (sometimes highly skeptical) feedback made a difference, including: Emma Johnson, Suzanne Tebbetts, Ellen Radoviç, George Lipsitz, María Elena García, José Antonio Lucero, Jared Sexton, Kim Tallbear, Jane Junn, Dorothy Solinger, Naomi Murakawa, Sarah Banet-Weiser, Adolph Reed Jr., Kenneth Warren, Carla Freccero, Janelle Wong, Taeku Lee, Paul Watanabe, Cathy Cohen, Michael Dawson, Roger Waldinger, Lisa García Bedolla, Helen Marrow, Kristen Monroe, David Schlosberg, Richard Twine, David Meyer, James Fujii, Fiona Probyn-Rapsey, Dinesh Wadiwel, Marti Kheel, Lori Gruen, Paul Frymer, Alexandra Isfahani-Hammond, Wayne Pacelle, Joyce Tischler, Keith Topper, James Lee, Greg Gerrard, Margaret Perret, and George Ioannides.

Graduate students and faculty who commented on presentations at University of California, Berkeley; University of Washington; University of California, Santa Barbara; University of Chicago; and University of California, Los Angeles.

Participants in the University of California Humanities Research Institute research group "Species Spectacles: Locating Transnational Coordinations of Animality, Race, and Sexuality" (Mel Chen, Carla Freccero, Jack Halberstam, Tamara Ho, Kyla Schuller, Lu Tonglin); the conference on "The Wild" organized by Erica Fudge and the British Animal Studies Network at the University of Strathclyde; the conference on "Critical Animal Studies and Intersectionality" organized by Margaret Perret and the Institute for Critical Animal Studies at the University of California, Berkeley; the conference "Life in the Anthropocene" organized by Fiona Probyn-Rapsey, Dinesh Wadiwel, and the Human-Animal Research Network at the University of Sydney; and the special workshop on my work in the Department of American Studies at University of Texas, Austin (Nhi Lieu, John Hartigan,

Elizabeth Engelhardt, Janet Davis, Nicole Guidotti-Hernández, Kim
Tallbear).
The interviewees for this book. Special thanks to Virginia Handley for
sharing her files, Patricia Briggs for sharing photographs, and Eric
Mills for sharing news articles and other materials.
The anonymous reviewers for Cambridge University Press, as well as
Elizabeth Janetschek at Cambridge University Press, for assistance
with figures and tables.
Teresa Ojeda of the San Francisco Planning Department for allowing me
to use two figures (Figure 4.2 and Figure 4.3) that she created.
Robert Dreesen, my editor at Cambridge University Press, for his guid-
ance and friendship.
Joe Wood, who is here.
My family, for believing in this book.

PART I

TAXONOMIES OF POWER

I

Impassioned Disputes

In July 1996, the San Francisco Commission on Animal Control and Welfare held a much-anticipated meeting. For nearly a year, the Commission, an advisory board to the city's legislative body, the Board of Supervisors, had held heated public hearings on whether to ban the sale of live animals for food in the city, a move that would especially affect the merchants in Chinatown who sell turtles, frogs, birds, fish, and other animals. It was finally time for the Commission to hold a vote. The meeting room at the Taraval Police Station was full and an overflow crowd of hundreds gathered outside. On the street, animal activists held up signs condemning "cruelty" toward animals in Chinatown's live animal markets, while Chinese Americans held up signs condemning the "cultural imperialism" of their critics. The crowd waited, murmuring. The air was thick with tension. The Commissioners passed the ban with a vote of 7 to 3, with one abstention. When the vote was announced, the crowd roared and police officers escorted Commissioners out of the back of the building for their personal safety.

This turned out to be yet another skirmish in the battle that raged for more than a decade and a half starting in the mid-1990s over the sale of live animals for food in the City on the Bay. After the Commission on Animal Control and Welfare voted, the Board of Supervisors declined to implement the proposed ban, which was, in the trenchant words of one local activist, "a political hot potato." So, over the next decade and a half, in a long and tortuous journey marked by victories and setbacks alike, animal advocates took their case against the live animal markets to the San Francisco Superior Court, the California legislature, the California Fish and Game Commission, and the public. This protracted struggle generated an occasionally vitriolic and always illuminating discourse in the public sphere about race, species, nature, and culture. It raised vital questions about what constitutes culture; which cultural traditions deserve protection and which do not; who belongs; whether animals are morally considerable; which animals are morally considerable and how much consideration they are due; what constitutes cruelty to animals, environmental damage, and racial harm; how to think about nature; and who has the standing and authority to decide these matters.

Bemused reporters covering the story remarked, "only in San Francisco," referencing the city's renowned progressivism on many issues, including animal welfare and immigrant rights. In some ways, this is indeed a local story about the town that Richard DeLeon (1992) famously dubbed the "Left Coast City." Many of the city's unique features shape this story: the multiplicity of small-scale animal advocacy groups in the Bay Area, residents' pride in the Franciscan tradition of compassion for animals, the prominence and influence of the San Francisco SPCA (Society for the Prevention of Cruelty to Animals), the city's distinctive history as the hotbed of anti-Chinese activism in the nineteenth century, the city's current racial and ethnic diversity and shift toward becoming less white and Black and more Asian and Latino, the continuing symbolic significance of the country's oldest and most storied Chinatown, the spatial and organizational reorientation of Chinese American politics in the city, and the recent growth of local Chinese American political power, culminating in the election of Mayor Ed Lee in 2011. San Franciscans engage in politics with passion, ardently advancing their respective visions about what the city should be and how it might realize its destiny. These visions show up in this story, as do some of the most colorful and controversial characters in local politics.

At the same time, this is a story that goes beyond San Francisco. It is a story about some of our central contradictions as a nation – our official embrace of and actual suspicion toward nonwhite immigrants and cultural difference; our simultaneous touting of colorblind norms and continued investment in racial domination; our growing interest in the status of animals and environmental protection and seeming acquiescence in neoliberalism's progressive instrumentalization and commodification of humans, animals, and the earth. In this sense, the Chinatown live animal market story is an American story, a story about a nation caught up in the new millennium in powerful currents of racial, cultural, economic, and environmental change.

The Chinatown case is indeed one of many impassioned disputes that have sprung up in the United States in recent years over how racially marginalized groups (nonwhite immigrants, Native peoples, native-born racialized minorities) make use of animals in their cultural traditions. Battles have been joined over horse-tripping and cockfighting by Mexican immigrants, dog-eating by Asian immigrants, whale hunting by Native peoples, dogfighting by urban Black folks, and animal sacrifice by the Santería, among other practices.[1] In addition to the Chinatown case, this book briefly examines two other conflicts:

[1] When these disputes traverse national boundaries, they become additionally weighted with questions about foreign (specifically Western) domination and control. The efforts of European and American activists to stop dog-eating in South Korea, bear bile farming in China, and whale hunting and dolphin slaughter in Japan have elicited fierce nationalistic responses that seem, perhaps inevitably, to have more to do with global history and politics than with a sober assessment of the animal practices in question.

the controversy over the decision by the Makah, a Native people in northwest Washington State, to resume whale hunting in the mid-1990s after a hiatus of seventy years; and the uproar over the arrest and conviction of NFL superstar quarterback Michael Vick, who is African American, on dogfighting charges in 2007.

Looking at these three cases together helps us to think clearly about the difference that difference makes. Despite the disparate nature of the cases, they manifest a shared script whereby animal/environmental advocates charge the racialized group with "cruelty" and/or "ecological harm," and the response is a countercharge of "racism" and "cultural imperialism." How and why social actors craft and advance these competing discursive and interpretive frames (which I will call "optics") and with what implications are topics I explore seriously in this book. At the same time, the three cases differ in that they emerge out of three distinct group histories of oppression that are shaped in part by the three groups' different relations to the nation (immigrant, indigenous, native-born minority) and different positions in the American racial order (Asian, Native, Black). It also matters that each case involves a different category of animal: the Chinatown case involves "lesser" animals that are "food" animals in Chinese but not American culture; the Makah case involves the charismatic gray whale; the Vick case, "man's best friend."[2]

These impassioned disputes over animal use cast a revealing light on three triumphalist stories that form part of the American mythos at the dawn of the twenty-first century. All three stories – about multiculturalism, colorblindness, and environmental consciousness, respectively – depict the nation on a long but successful journey from darkness to light, ignorance to understanding, conflict to accord. They fit neatly within the centuries-long tradition of glorifying the United States as a uniquely dynamic, forward-moving, progressive nation. The first story says that we have achieved meaningful multiculturalism in the United States. Post-1965 immigration diversified the population dramatically along racial and ethnic lines, the story goes, and the dictum "When in Rome, do as the Romans do" has given way over the past several decades to a robust cultural accommodation of immigrant minorities. Having overcome our history of intolerance and ethnocentrism, we now celebrate and affirm cultural difference. Having set aside racial quotas in our immigration laws and abandoned

[2] I have benefited from sharing this work with several audiences over the past few years. At one talk, I was asked if I was reproducing an imperialist orientation, as it were, by focusing on minority animal practices and not on white/majority animal practices. The marking or denaturalization of white practices is an important task, but that is not the book I wanted to write. If I were advancing a direct critique of minority animal practices, I would think it important to consider white animal practices as well, or at least explain why I am not addressing them. But my point is not to critique minority practices per se but to interpret the controversy swirling around them – the social, cultural, political struggle over their meaning. What it means to call animal advocates' criticism of these minority animal practices imperialist and whether the charge is fair are precisely the matters I seek to explore. In any case, there is a powerful argument to be made that the majority's animal practices are at least as morally troubling as minority practices.

forced Americanization classes, we now embrace the joys of Mariachi and dim sum. This is what Nathan Glazer grudgingly and ruefully concedes in the title of his book *We Are All Multiculturalists Now* (1998).

The second and closely related story has us moving unerringly toward a "colorblind" or "postracial" society. This tale, crafted in the crucible of civil rights era activism and policy, involves both retroactively interpreting all of U.S. history as a journey of racial transcendence and announcing a future where racism is no longer an issue. Martin Luther King Jr.'s memorable words at Selma – "The arc of the moral universe is long, but it bends toward justice" – have been recuperated in service of the idea that the nation has moved inexorably toward colorblindness. Barack Obama's campaign rhetoric and his election to the U.S. presidency in 2008 gave this story new life, and today it is common to hear declarations of "how far we have come," even if these are sometimes accompanied by qualifiers about "how far we have to go." Having overcome racism, for all intents and purposes, we still face the task of perfecting the dream, which partly involves taking precautions against "reverse racism." In recent media coverage of the events commemorating the fiftieth anniversary of the 1963 March on Washington, commentators lamented that the dream was not yet fulfilled and thus remained faithful to this story's narrative structure and teleological thrust.[3]

Finally there is the story of how the United States has come to see the light on animal and environmental issues. As a nation, we have traveled the road from ignorant recklessness to compassionate and wise stewardship. Brought along by Rachel Carson's *Silent Spring* (1962) and the animal liberation and environmental movements of the 1970s, and progressively enlightened by science, we have left behind our wildlife-decimating, coal-burning, forest-leveling past and assumed the position of global park ranger on matters of animal exploitation and ecological degradation. Although we are still figuring out how to make farming practices more humane and how to reduce the emission of greenhouse gases at home, we are confident in our positions on other nations' practices (e.g., Chinese shark finning, ivory consumption, and industrial pollution). President Obama's Executive Order "Combating Wildlife Trafficking" (July 1, 2013) exemplifies the United States' performance as a champion of animal and environmental protection on the global stage.[4]

The impassioned disputes I examine in this book give the lie to these triumphalist stories in many different ways. Multiculturalism, it turns out, is far from a settled issue: the standing of nonwhites to practice their cultural traditions remains hotly contested, and open ethnocentrism and intolerance persist in the general population, brought out into the light during these conflicts. Colorblindness is nowhere in evidence either. Indeed, these disputes evoke centuries-old racial tropes (about Chinese cruelty, Indian savagery, Black bestiality)

[3] See, for example, "Martin Luther King's Dream Partly Met" (2013) and Barbara Raab (2013).
[4] http://www.whitehouse.gov/the-press-office/2013/07/01/executive-order-combating-wildlife-trafficking.

that function in each case to displace attention from structural racialized exclusion onto the supposed character flaws of these groups. The Chinese immigrant's resistance to adopting humane American ways, the Makah's stubborn rejection of modernization, the Black man's refusal to overcome his animal nature – these "facts" take center stage, while persistent ethnocentrism against nonwhite immigrants, ongoing relations of colonial domination with Native Americans, and the violence inflicted by the carceral state and neoliberal policies upon Black communities go unrecognized.

The animal/environmental consciousness story gets sent up, too. What comes across in these impassioned disputes is how profoundly neoliberal policies, language, and values have pervaded American culture and society.[5] In the broader society, growing environmental awareness notwithstanding, the commodification and instrumentalization of animals and the earth intensifies, from the expansion of industrial animal farming to the continued destruction of endangered species' habitats in the name of development to the genetic engineering of animals for food production and medical research. And in the cases examined here, the profound commodification of the racial/animal/natural other and the pervasion of market practices and values into myriad realms are strikingly apparent. In the Chinatown case, the California Fish and Game Commission describes wild animals as "living natural resources" that must be husbanded so that the maximum number of people now and in the future can use them. The animal-centric and earth-centric arguments advanced by parts of the early U.S. animal and environmental movements are but a memory now, and conservation and environmental protection are understood as projects aimed at protecting natural resources (living and otherwise) for the sake of maximizing human utility. In fact, environmental language has become a legitimating cover for the advancement of economic interests, as when the California Fish and Game Commission deploys the "invasive species/native species" trope, wherein native species are almost always proxies for humans whose economic interests are adversely impacted by "invasives."

If these triumphalist stories are cast in doubt, what are we to think about race, species, nature, and culture in the millennial United States? My sense is that the war metaphor serves us better than the journey metaphor. The journey metaphor is as misleading as it is comforting. It suggests that "we" are moving along together as a nation and that history is a teleological process tending toward the good. Conflicting interests, struggle, violence, and domination are elided. Injustices are cast as vestigial difficulties that will be resolved with time (if only people could understand that change is slow and difficult). The war

---

[5] *Neoliberalism* refers to a set of practices, ideologies, and values that have been globally ascendant since the 1970s (Duggan 2003; Brenner and Theodore 2002). Its central tenet is that markets should be allowed to operate freely and competitively and with minimal interference from states or other public entities. Neoliberal policies championed by institutions such as the International Monetary Fund, the World Bank, and the World Trade Organization emphasize fiscal austerity, deregulation, privatization, and market liberalization.

metaphor rudely disabuses us of these fantasies. It forces us to think clearly about the disharmony of interests that "we" have, rips away the comfort of teleological thinking, and confronts us with the fact that the stakes are nothing less than life and death, both human and nonhuman. Neoliberalism did not originate it, but it has escalated the war on racialized others, animals, and nature in the name of concentrating wealth and privilege in the hands of a tiny elite. This war is the larger backdrop against which the Chinatown, Makah, and Vick disputes play out. If we can give up our attachment to this idea of a collective journey to the promised land – if we can understand it as hortatory ideology and not sociohistorical analysis – and consider seriously that U.S. racial, animal, and environmental histories reflect a war without end fought on shifting terrain and by shifting coalitions of interests, we will gain in understanding whatever we lose in comfort.

My purpose in this book is, first, to give a persuasive interpretation of what is going on in these impassioned disputes over animal use; second, to read them as windows onto our contested and contradictory imaginings about and struggles over race, species, nature, and culture in the United States at the start of the twenty-first century; and third, to suggest how we might begin to think through, ethically and politically, the competing sets of moral claims being advanced. Studying these conflicts instructs us about how power in its many dimensions is articulated, expressed, and engaged in the contemporary United States, and it just may give us some insight into the possibilities of resistance as well. But first, a brief detour to examine and critique how scholars have explained these kinds of disputes.

THE "CLASH OF CULTURES" EXPLANATION

The most common interpretation of these conflicts over animal use, favored by political theorists working on multiculturalism, is that they are best read as "clashes" between the majority culture and minority cultures. The core question, according to this view, is whether the majority's accommodation of troubling minority cultural traditions is necessary, desirable, or even possible. Theorists have come up with a range of responses to this question, with some arguing for a great deal of accommodation and some arguing for very little. I highlight a few of these responses here. Some discuss controversial animal practices specifically; all discuss the question of whether and how to respond to vexing minority traditions more generally.

Alison Renteln's *The Cultural Defense* (2004) makes the most far-reaching case for the accommodation of minority traditions. In fact, she endorses the establishment of a formal "cultural defense" to be recognized by the courts and other governmental entities. Beginning with the premise that culture "shapes the identity of individuals, influencing their reasoning, perceptions, and behavior" (10) and the observation that the right to culture is guaranteed in Article 27 of the International Covenant of Civil and Political Rights, Renteln asserts a strong minority right to cultural expression. In her chapter on controversial animal practices, where she briefly mentions the San Francisco Chinatown case, she unequivocally dismisses criticism of minority cultural traditions as biased, ethnocentric, and tainted by the "presumption of assimilation" (6). Critics of minority practices employ a "double standard," she charges, inasmuch as they "often appea[r] to be more concerned with the unacceptable practices of minority groups than with those of the dominant culture" (112). What government should do, Renteln avers, is follow a "principle of maximum accommodation" (15) unless minority traditions cause "irreparable physical harm to others" (19).

In *Multicultural Citizenship: A Liberal Theory of Minority Rights* (1995), Will Kymlicka, too, advocates extensive protections for minority cultures. Against conventional liberal thinking, he contends that multicultural rights are not only not antithetical to individual rights in a liberal democracy but in fact necessary to secure them. Culture, for Kymlicka, makes individual freedom possible inasmuch as the latter consists of making choices among options about the good life and it is culture that provides us these options and makes them meaningful to us. Except in cases where there is a gross violation of basic rights, he advocates the use of persuasion and supporting internal reforms as alternatives to coercing minority cultures into change. The rub, however, is that Kymlicka thinks only "national minorities" – that is, those who were previously self-governing, occupy a given territory or homeland, and share a language and history – deserve cultural protection. The Makah nation in the Pacific Northwest qualifies here, but neither Chinese immigrants nor Black people in the United States do. The Chinese, in Kymlicka's view, effectively waived their right to their own culture by being voluntary migrants to the United States.

Like Kymlicka, Bhikhu Parekh views cultural rights as facilitative of individual rights. In *Rethinking Multiculturalism* (2000), Parekh argues that a commitment to equal rights entails granting not identical rights but rather differentiated rights, which provide culturally different individuals with comparable opportunities to enjoy their rights. Opportunity, Parekh avers, is a "subject-dependent concept" (241), meaning that an individual can only be said to possess a particular opportunity or right if s/he possesses a cultural disposition, capacity, or knowledge that enables him/her to access it. Culture is constitutive of an individual's identity and self-respect and plays a vital role in enabling the enjoyment of individual rights, Parekh argues, so societies should respect and accommodate minority cultures whenever possible. However, he takes seriously those instances where the majority feels compelled to speak out against minority practices that it perceives to be violating its fundamental values. Parekh considers, among other issues, the exemption of kosher slaughter from British animal welfare regulations. He argues that on these kinds of issues, the majority should initiate a cross-cultural moral dialogue with the minority, one that avoids the trap of cultural imperialism to the extent that the majority both gives reasons for its criticism and opens up its own values and practices to scrutiny and criticism. If such a "bifocal" moral dialogue fails to produce a consensus, Parekh suggests, the majority should prevail because its values are integral to the society's cohesion, because it has no final obligation to accommodate minorities to the detriment of its own way of life, and because minorities, needing the support and goodwill of the majority, should defer to it in the last instance.

At the opposite end of the accommodation spectrum from Renteln, we have Brian Barry. In *Culture & Equality* (2000), Barry argues that equal treatment in a liberal democracy means identical treatment for all under the law. Where multiculturalist advocates argue for exemptions or special treatment for minorities under the law on the grounds that uniform laws have unequal impact, Barry denies that unequal impact is unfair or something the law should seek to remedy. Countering Parekh's notion of opportunity, Barry insists that "the critical distinction is between limits on the range of opportunities open to people and limits on the choices that they make from within a certain range of opportunities" (37). Barry, too, turns to the argument over exempting kosher slaughter from general animal welfare regulations that require the stunning of the animal prior to killing. It is not the animal welfare law requiring the stunning of animals before slaughter that prevents Jews from eating meat, Barry argues, but rather the religious restrictions of Judaism that prohibit them from eating nonkosher meat. Jews have the same opportunity and right to eat meat under the law as non-Jews, and if their religion limits the choices they make from among available opportunities, that is not a disparity the law must alleviate. Since Jews do not have to eat meat to be observant, it cannot be argued that the animal welfare law restricts their religious liberty either. Barry bristles at the notion that culture is ever its own justification, remarking that saying something is part of one's culture is not a moral statement but an anthropological one. He writes: "*Culture is no excuse.* If there are sound reasons against doing something, these cannot be trumped by saying – even if it is true – that doing it is a part of your culture. The fact that you (or your ancestors) have been doing something for a long time does nothing in itself to justify your continuing to do it" (258).

Susan Okin's *Is Multiculturalism Bad for Women?* (1999) also takes multiculturalism to task for infringing upon equal rights. Okin's particular concern is the rights of women who are treated unequally to men in minority cultures. In Okin's view, a liberal society that accommodates and protects a minority culture wherein men subordinate women is guilty of aiding and abetting that project. Because the cultural defense endorsed by Renteln and others actually facilitates the violation of women's equal protection under the law, Okin argues that "[i]t is by no means clear, then, from a feminist point of view, that minority group rights are 'part of the solution'" (22). In a provocative turn, Okin concludes that "[i]n the case of a more patriarchal minority culture in the context of a less patriarchal majority culture, no argument can be made on the basis of self-respect or freedom that the female members of the culture have a clear interest in its preservation" (22). The idea that the minority culture's exercise of systematic domination might weaken its claim to multiculturalist protections from the majority has interesting implications for the exploration of the impassioned disputes examined in this book (with the caveat, of course, that women, unlike nonhuman animals, are widely if not universally recognized to have certain fundamental rights).

These works on the question of cultural accommodation share, to varying degrees, two important shortcomings. First, they employ a problematic notion of culture. Cultures here are fixed, bounded entities that map neatly onto particular groups and particular spaces. They are like material objects in physical space – they can collide, they can be objectively measured for traits (consider Okin's observation that Western culture is demonstrably less sexist than non-Western cultures), they can be destroyed or lost. This essentialization and reification of culture, this treatment of culture as both self-evidently coherent and an explanatory cause in and of itself, is untenable because it effaces the social and political processes by which certain actors, under specific historical conditions, shape how some practices and not others emerge, develop, and get tagged as "culture" in the first place, as Uma Narayan (1997) has eloquently explained in her work. There are many divergent practices between the majority and minorities, so how is it that a few and not others, on some occasions and not others, become flashpoints for intergroup conflict? Who benefits from making certain kinds of cultural claims? Who loses? What is at stake?

Second, these works, with the partial exception of Okin's, oversimplify the workings of power. Everything is reduced to a single dyad: the powerful majority and the powerless minority. There is little room here to reckon with the multidimensionality of power and the complex, ambiguous positionality that groups can hold in this context. Okin's work raises the question of male domination over women, but none of these works, even the ones that explicitly discuss animal practices, pauses to consider human domination over nonhuman animals. Disputes like the Chinatown market conflict are taken by these theorists to raise issues about group domination *between human groups* but human domination over animals, thoroughly naturalized, remains invisible. It is the elephant in the room, so to speak. Consider Renteln's dictum that minority traditions should be protected unless they cause "irreparable physical harm." Since all of the minority animal practices she defends cause animals to suffer and die, we are pressed to conclude that she sees "irreparable physical harm" to animals – and indeed animals themselves – as morally irrelevant in a categorical sense (i.e., so absolutely that this requires no elaboration or argument). Renteln also argues that a chicken would rather be killed in a religious ritual than end up in a bucket of Kentucky Fried Chicken. This is a peculiar assertion because it suggests that chickens have phenomenal world(s) and that they have a sense of dignity – both claims that Renteln's implicit denial of animal considerability seems to contradict.

Matters become much more complicated – and much more interesting – once we grapple with power's multidimensionality and, specifically, with the question of human domination over animals and how it intersects with the question of racial or cultural domination among humans. Paula Casal's "Justice Across Cultures: Animals and Accommodation" (2004) – originally entitled

"Is Multiculturalism Bad for Animals?" as a riff on Okin's title – suggests the fruitfulness of this direction. Like Okin, Casal calls out and objects to the harm done to the powerless (in this case, nonhuman animals) under the protective cover of multiculturalism. Responding to the "double standard" argument advanced by Renteln and others, Casal writes: "[T]he fact that many murderous dictators have escaped the punishment they deserve is no good reason not to try other dictators whenever feasible – let alone to create legal exemptions for other individuals engaging in comparable activities" (256). Such a position, she suggests, would invalidate all existing prohibitions and render impossible incremental reforms of any kind. Against this notion of "comparative desert," she invokes the priority of the "principle of noncomparative desert," which holds that restricting a particular inhumane activity is worth doing in and of itself whether or not other equally or more inhumane activities are being challenged at the same moment. By this principle, Casal would disallow any exemptions from anticruelty legislation, even for those practicing Santería, a religion that specifically requires its practitioners to engage in animal sacrifice. Many Santería practitioners are Afro-Caribbean immigrants of little means, but their disadvantaged status does not give them license, in Casal's view, to harm nonhuman animals. By addressing the elephant in the room, Casal moves us toward a more honest, meaningful discussion of power's complexity and multidimensionality.

THE "RACISM/CULTURAL IMPERIALISM" EXPLANATION

The second most common interpretation of these impassioned disputes is that they are the latest expression of the centuries-long pattern of Western contempt toward racialized others. These scholars, writing in diverse fields such as anthropology, law, geography, philosophy, ethnic studies, and women's studies, denounce animal advocacy in these conflicts as racist and imperialist projects. They are frank partisans concerned to defend minority cultures from external assault. By emphasizing the constructedness of racial and other meanings, scholars writing in this vein avoid the trap of essentializing and reifying "culture." However, like most of the political theorists discussed earlier, they, too, misapprehend the workings of power by focusing exclusively on one hierarchical relationship (majority over minority) and ignoring the other hierarchical relationship (human over nonhuman) that is at issue. Racial and cultural meanings are denaturalized and deconstructed but species meanings – what it means to be human, what it means to be animal – are naturalized once again. While these works are often rich in critical insight, then, they tell only half of the story.

Anthropologist Olga Nájera-Ramírez has written extensively on the Mexican rodeo (*charreada*), produced a film on the topic (*La Charreada: Rodeo a la Mexicana*, 1996), and testified at a governmental hearing on behalf of Mexican cowboy (*charro*) organizations. The *charreada* is a site of controversy because certain of its events, *los manganas*, which involve lassoing the legs of a running horse and bringing it crashing to the ground, have provoked accusations of cruelty. Animal advocates fighting "horse-tripping" have lobbied successfully for laws outlawing such practices in numerous states including California. Nájera-Ramírez valorizes the *charreada* as a deeply rooted historical practice that expresses and bolsters Mexican identity on both sides of the border in the face of white/American hostility – that is, "as a [transnational] master symbol" of "lo mexicano (literally, 'Mexicanness')" (1994, 1) and "a counterdiscourse of resistance against Anglo domination, cultural erasure, and the demeaning portrayal of Mexicanos" (n.d., 2). In "The Racialization of a Debate: The *Charreada* as Tradition or Torture" (1996), Nájera-Ramírez characterizes opposition to the *charreada* as a racist/cultural imperialist project. Conceding that animal advocates target the American rodeo as well, she nevertheless declines to explore their stated objections to the *charreada* and focuses instead on the mainstream media's coverage of the issue, which, she argues, trades in enduring anti-Mexican imagery. It is her responsibility as a "cultural expert," she avers, to "point out the subtle, insidious, and often unspeakable ways in which racism operates" (510) on this issue.

Whale and seal hunting by Native peoples have also found passionate and openly partisan defenders in the academy. In "The Makah Whale Hunt and Leviathan's Death" (2004), Rob van Ginkel states his intention to comprehensively "inventory and analyze the debate" (59) over the Makah tribe's decision to revive whaling in the mid-1990s. He sympathetically discusses the claims of the Makah Tribal Council that whaling will restore the tribe's cultural identity and pride. Yet instead of examining the substantive moral claims of the environmental and animal activists who were involved in the conflict – why they believe gray whales deserve protection from hunting – Van Ginkel lists random anti-Makah quotes from Internet fora and letters to the media. These he labels as "Indian-bashing" (72). The depth of anti-Indian sentiment exposed here is an important topic, but Van Ginkel's conflation of environmental and animal activists with the authors of these sentiments and his decision to ignore the historically grounded and thoughtful moral arguments of the former raises concerns about the integrity of his "inventory." Indeed, he barely conceals his contempt for environmental and animal activists, whom he charges with "anthropomorphizing" whales, using them as fundraising mascots, and demonstrating "normativism, cultural imperialism and ethnocentrism" (80). Against such malicious aggression, the Makah are cast as heroic resistance fighters: "By transgressing a taboo of mainstream Western society, the Makah showed the world without that they are 'different.' In doing so, they found their 'true selves' and reinvented themselves as Makah" (83).

In *Animal Rights, Human Rights: Ecology, Economy and Ideology in the Canadian Arctic* (1991), George Wenzel declares that he is engaged in "advocacy anthropology," which he defines as "interced[ing] on the side of indigenous groups" against those trying to "civilize" (8) them. Wenzel's specific concern is with the controversy over seal hunting by the Inuit in Canada. During the 1980s, as the European Economic Community voted to issue a ban on the sale of seal products, the Inuit faced an onslaught of global criticism from EEC leaders, Canadian officials, and animal advocates about the cruelty of their seal hunting practices. Wenzel characterizes animal advocacy here as the culmination of "a colonial process in the Canadian North" (8) begun by the government, fur traders, and economic interests centuries earlier: "In the history of Euro-North American colonial encroachment into the Arctic, there has never been a southern challenge so directly aimed at the physical and biological base critical to Inuit culture" (5). Like Nájera-Ramírez and Van Ginkel, Wenzel accounts for how an animal war unfolds in the context of a specific imperial history and how groups mobilize identity and cultural meaning (and in this case, a specific way of life) around a particular animal practice. However, like these authors, too, he omits consideration of the substantive moral arguments made by animal advocates. In a sense, the ready adoption of a colonial framework for understanding these conflicts predisposes scholars to engage in just such omissions. What is to be explored when the motives of animal advocates are already accounted for a priori?

Of course, it is logically possible to be attuned to *both* racial/imperial histories and the history of human domination over animals – as well as the many political and moral issues raised by their intersection. Marcie Griffith, Jennifer Wolch, and Unna Lassiter's "Animal Practices and the Racialization of Filipinas in Los Angeles" (2002) gestures in this direction. It discusses how whites racialize Filipinos/as in Southern California through attention to the latter's practice of dog-eating and how Filipino/as defend dog-eating as a form of "resistance" to racialization and cultural imperialism. It concludes with this observation: "Perhaps only by confronting the subjectivity of animals, and seeing the connections between people and animals rather than the species divide, will we be able to stop the violence toward animals" (243). Similarly, in "*Le Pratique Sauvage*: Race, Place, and the Human-Animal Divide" (1998), Glen Elder, Jennifer Wolch, and Jody Emel discuss how these disputes over animals "construct racial difference by casting the Other as 'savage' or uncivilized" and conclude with a call for "a radically inclusive politics which considers the interests and positionality of the enormous array of animal life and lives, as well as the lives of diverse peoples" (88) – a tantalizing hint of what a more multidimensional account of these conflicts might look like. The disputes examined in this book showcase power in its multilayered, fragmented, contradictory complexity and forcefully disrupt simple oppositions of good and bad, victim and oppressor. They invite us to move beyond half of the story.[6]

---

[6] Greta Gaard's (2001) work on the Makah is one of the few works I have found that takes this imperative seriously. She grapples with both the perspective of the Makah and the perspective of animal and environmental advocates.

THEORETICAL PREMISES, ADJUSTMENTS, ARGUMENTS

I begin my analysis where the second set of scholars discussed earlier leaves off (with the denaturalization of culture and race and the focus on racial/imperial histories) and suggest that we should also denaturalize *species* difference and consider the history and contours of *human* supremacy if we are to understand the events in question. I do not mean by this that we should replace the focus on race with a focus on species. This is not an either/or choice. To the contrary, my argument is that our interpretive success depends on our ability and willingness to engage with these two taxonomies of power, race and species, at once – *and to understand their connectedness*. All three cases in this book are situated both in a narrative history of racial and cultural persecution and in a narrative history of human domination over the animal, and these two narratives are interwoven in important ways.

I begin with two theoretical premises. The first premise is that categories of difference – race, species, culture, sex – are historically and socially constructed rather than given by nature. Michael Omi and Howard Winant's *Racial Formation in the United States* (1994) shaped a generation of scholarship with its insistence on viewing race as an "unstable and 'decentered' complex of social meanings constantly transformed by political struggle" (55) rather than as a fixed and heritable biological essence. Nature, of course, has always offered up a great deal of visible human variation by way of skin color, hair texture, facial features, and so forth, but "race" is a historically and culturally mediated way of reading, classifying, and ranking bodies, of assigning some more worth than others on the basis of physical variation. It is a means of producing and disciplining different and inferior bodies.

Cultural difference, too, is actively made. Akhil Gupta and Jim Ferguson point out that twentieth-century anthropology's "implicit mapping of the world as a series of discrete, territorialized cultures" has given way to a new vision that sees cultures "as less unitary and more fragmented, their boundedness more of a literary fiction ... than as some sort of natural fact" (1997, 3). The accelerated flow of bodies, capital, and ideas across borders in the age of globalization contributes to this shift in thinking. In the impassioned disputes examined here, questions of culture – what is culture, what constitutes an "authentic" cultural tradition, and what kind of consideration is it due – are contested not just between groups but within them. Cultural difference triggers these disputes, but disputatious politics in turn drives the further elaboration of cultural difference, which is to say that culture gets constructed through fluid, dynamic, and contingent political processes. As Uma Narayan writes, "Cultures are not pre-discursively individuated entities to which 'names' are then bestowed as simple 'labels,' but entities whose individuation depends on complex discursive processes linked to political agendas" (1998, 93).

Species difference tends to be deeply naturalized, its constructedness unrecognized even by scholars keenly interested in domination.[7] Much of the academy resists engaging the question of the animal and historicizing the formation of the hierarchy between "human" and "animal." Instead we defer to scientists of centuries past, who encountered a dizzying array of physical variations among living beings and labored to corral them into classificatory boxes, hierarchically arranged (Thomas 1983; Ritvo 1987, 1998; Dunayer 2001). Humans do differ from chimpanzees, of course, but it is human classification that has read momentous political and moral meaning into these differences, placed humans and chimpanzees into discontinuous, unequal categories of beings, and bestowed upon the former the right to dominate the latter. It is human classification that insists that humans stand alone, apart from and above all other "animals" – an assemblage taken to contain beings as wildly disparate as gorillas, wombats, and mosquitoes. As Barbara Noske (1997) writes, the modern academy enshrines this hierarchical thinking with its separation of biological science (animals are simply bodies) from social science (humans alone have mind, culture, and society). It is also human classification that rank orders "types" of animals, resulting in the differential valorization of "charismatic megafauna," companion animals, and so-called food animals.

My second theoretical premise is that differences are co-constituted or produced as effects of power in a profoundly interdependent way. Kimberlé Crenshaw's (1989) concept of "intersectionality" in legal theory has been enormously influential in thinking through the connectedness of forms of domination. Building on the work of earlier Black feminist theorists, she writes: "[T]he intersection of racism and sexism factors into women's lives in ways that cannot be captured wholly by looking at the race or gender dimensions of those experiences separately" (1994, 94). Many legal theorists have built upon Crenshaw's work in the last few decades, introducing new substantive forms of difference for analysis or otherwise attempting to deepen the analysis of intersectionality (Kwan 2000; Hutchinson 2001; Ehrenreich 2002; Deckha 2006).

Ecofeminism, which Noël Sturgeon characterizes as "a feminist rebellion within radical environmentalism" (1997, 31), has been plowing related theoretical ground. Val Plumwood (1993), for instance, argues that power produces difference through structuring dualisms such as master/slave, male/female, human/animal, white/black, reason/nature, culture/nature, civilized/savage, mind/body, subject/object. These dualisms are, according to Plumwood, "interlocking" and "mutually reinforcing." Thus the beast is made not just as animal but as savage, nature, other, body, object, alien, and slave. Similarly, Greta Gaard writes: "the ideology which authorizes oppressions such as those based on race, class, gender, sexuality, physical abilities,

---

[7] While the scientific demarcation of nonhuman animals into distinct species is itself a classificatory act deserving of scientific and moral scrutiny, I use "species" more generally to refer to the impassable divide Western culture has erected between humanity and animality, as well as the differential valuation of "pets," wildlife, farm animals, and other categories of animals.

and species is the same ideology which sanctions the oppression of nature"
(1993, 1; see also Gruen, 2014, 2011 and Kheel 2009). According to many
ecofeminists, it is this ideology, this aspiration to control and transcend
nature through instrumental rationality, that has led us to the brink of ecological disaster (Plumwood 2001).

Building upon these premises, I offer some adjustments and arguments to
orient the reader for the chapters to come. The adjustments emerge out of
my keen sense that theory is imperfect and incorrigibly so: no matter how
complex, thoughtful, and sophisticated the concepts, they not only fall short
of capturing reality, they inevitably do violence to it in some way. Consider
Plumwood's notion of "interlocking" dualisms. If we focus on this overarch-
ing structure and on the parallelism or connectedness of these dimensions of
power, the specificity of each dimension goes out of focus. We miss the trees for
the forest. Of course, we always lose specificity when we generalize, but sometimes we lose so much that the whole interpretive project is imperiled. If we
focus on the historical uniqueness of each form of domination, alternatively,
the larger structure and dynamics of interdependence go out of focus. We miss
the forest for the trees. Concepts can present these tensions and contradictions
but cannot resolve them.

With this in mind, I propose two modest adjustments to the notion of "interlocking" dualisms. The first is that we think in terms of taxonomies rather
than dualisms – complex classification systems instead of simple dyads. Race
is not expressed as a binary of white over black (or white over nonwhite) but
as a complex, fluid set of multiple positions (Kim 1999, 2000). The taxonomy concept encourages us to ask questions about relationality, positionality,
and multidimensionality that are obscured by the dualism concept – for example, how to move beyond the presumptive homogenization of nonwhite group
experiences and toward an explanation of their differential proximity to and
participation in racial power (Sexton 2010).

Similarly, the concept of species cannot be reduced to a dualism (human/ani-
mal) but rather expresses itself as a taxonomy or complex hierarchical ordering
of different animal kinds. Biological science, always culturally inflected, elaborates a classification system for ordering animal bodies *qua* species, even as
culturally variable systems of worth further delineate which animals are good
to use in which ways, based on factors such as intelligence, beauty, similarity to
humans, affinity with humans, wildness, susceptibility to training, utility, and
potential for affecting human economic interests positively or adversely (Ritvo
1998). In the United States at the start of the twenty-first century, we see dogs
and cats as possessing special qualities that make them ideal for domestication;
elephants and whales as "charismatic mega-fauna" who should be admired
and protected out there in the wild (although they may be kept in circuses and
aquariums precisely because their grandeur is so entertaining and educational);
cows, pigs, and chickens as unremarkable and thus suitable for being farmed
and eaten; rodents, coyotes, wolves and insects as threatening and suitable for
extermination. Animal kinds matter differently to us, and some matter much

more than others. In the Chinatown and other stories examined here, we see
the explosive confrontation of race and species, two elaborated taxonomies of
power whose respective drives to discipline different types of bodies are intertwined in deep and enduring ways.

The second modest adjustment is to think of forms of domination as synergistically related rather than "interlocking." Anne McClintock (1995) admonishes us not to think of formative cultural categories as "armatures of Lego"
(5) and urges us instead to consider how they "converge, merge and overde-
termine each other in intricate and often contradictory ways" (61–2). Indeed,
the mechanical language of "interlocking" predisposes us to think of axes of
power as standardized, fungible units that fit together in some predetermined
fashion. The dangers of this kind of mindless pluralism are profound: we may
find ourselves casually presuming (as opposed to being able to demonstrate)
a universal equivalence among various forms of domination, x=y=z (that they
are all equally salient and of equal moral importance), and presuming that the
dynamics of co-constitution are everywhere and at all times the same and pre-
dictable. If we think of oppressions as synergistically related rather than "interlocking" – that is, if we substitute an energy metaphor for an architectural
one – we are less likely to fall into the trap of mindless pluralism and more
likely to remain attuned to the unevenness, messiness, complexity, fluidity, and
unpredictability that actually mark the dynamics of difference production.

The synergistic taxonomies of race and species are my particular concern in
this book. Much of the exclusionary work of defining the human in American
culture is done at precisely this juncture.[8] Animalization has been central
not incidental to the project of racialization, and Blackness, Indianness, and
Chineseness have been articulated on U.S. soil for centuries in continuous and
intimate relationship with notions of animality and nature – all of which forms
part of the historical backdrop for the impassioned disputes I examine. Race
has been articulated in part as *a metric of animality*, as a classification system
that orders human bodies according to how animal they are – and how human
they are not – with all of the entailments that follow. The historically enduring
taken-for-grantedness of animality, dating back more than two millennia, renders it a ready resource for those seeking to elaborate racial (or other) meanings. Sometimes, as we shall see in the following chapters, the flow of meanings
is reversed and certain nonhuman species get racialized or imbued with negative meanings associated with despised human groups. The less-than-humanity
of one type of being reverberates across time and space with the less-than-
humanity of the other. In contemporary American life, the taxonomies of race
and species continue to shape what Ruth Wilson Gilmore (2007, 28) describes
as "group-differentiated vulnerability to premature death" and do a great deal
of the work of defining who is a grievable life and who is not (Butler 2004).

---

[8] See García and Lucero (2008) for an excellent discussion of the logics of race and species in a
Latin American (Peruvian) context.

The theoretical arguments I wish to make concern the kinds of discursive and political moves that get made when two justice struggles collide. In each of the cases examined here, it seems we are being asked to choose: Who is more important, racially subordinated humans or nonhuman animals/nature? Which is more serious, racism or animal cruelty/environmental harm? Suddenly, forms of domination thought of as parallel or even co-constituted are linked to the generation of competitive and incommensurate claims. If we reject a mindless pluralism that renders all oppressions presumptively fungible and equivalent, where are we? How do we begin to think through these entanglements in an ethically coherent and responsible manner?

The question of which form of oppression – racism or speciesism – is more fundamental, important, and urgent runs like a powerful current through the disputes examined in this book. The position I assume is that the question should be asked and will be asked but that it is (at least provisionally) irresolvable. The question must be asked in order to resist the temptation of mindless pluralism and its elision of differentials in power, position, and privilege among subordinated groups. But it is irresolvable because no consensual set of metrics has emerged either in scholarship or politics for determining an answer. Nor is it likely to, given the myriad stakes different groups have in the posing and/or suspension of the question. In a profound and discomforting way, the question *will* be left open.

The theoretical arguments, concepts, and arguments I advance here assume a context of (provisional) irresolvability. In the impassioned disputes examined here, each side embraces what I call *single-optic vision*, a way of seeing that foregrounds a particular form of injustice while backgrounding others. Looking through a single optic or lens – cruelty to animals, ecological harm, racism, or something else – these parties see *but they also do not see*, and these two facts are of course connected. Every act of illumination also obscures. For reasons having to do with economies of affect as well as institutional incentives, most social justice struggles mobilize around a single-optic frame of vision. The process of political conflict then generates a zero-sum dynamic whereby single-optic vision leads predictably to what I call a *posture of mutual disavowal* – an explicit dismissal of and denial of connection with the other form of injustice being raised. This posture, I will argue, is both ethically and politically troubling.[9]

In the analysis of each case, I engage in and demonstrate a practice of *multi-optic vision*, a way of seeing that takes disparate justice claims seriously without privileging any one presumptively. Jeremy Bentham's Panopticon erected a single privileged external vantage point from which to surveil inmates, patients, and other powerless wards of the state. Multi-optic seeing, by contrast, entails seeing *from within* various perspectives, moving from one vantage point to another, inhabiting them in turn, holding them in the mind's eye at once. By

---

[9] There are interesting potential connections to explore here between what I am arguing and Timothy Pachirat's argument about the "politics of sight" (2011).

decentering all claims, at least initially, this method of seeing encourages us to move beyond the seductive simplicity of a single-optic storyline and to grapple with the existence and interconnectedness of multiple group experiences of oppression.

Multi-optic vision encourages a reorientation toward an *ethics of mutual avowal*, or open and active acknowledgment of connection with other struggles ("This matters to me and relates to me" instead of "That has nothing to do with me.") If disavowal is a closing off, a repudiation, a turning away from, avowal is an opening, a recognition, a turning toward. Developing such an ethics would not rule out the practice of critique – in fact, it might well generate or intensify critique aimed at countering particular manifestations of domination – but it would transform the contours and spirit of critique. If we develop an ethics of mutual avowal in relation to other justice struggles, we not only reduce the chance we will reinscribe other forms of oppression (even inadvertently), but also open ourselves to new ways of imagining ourselves in relation to others. Drawing on the work of Bruno Latour and Isabelle Stengers, María Elena García advances a cosmopolitical approach that calls upon us to pay attention to other life worlds and be attentive to "a wider range of potentially intersecting fields of subjectivities, power, and resistance" (2013, 507). I see this project, and specifically the argument about disavowal and avowal, as moving in this direction.

If single-optic vision generates a Manichean opposition of oppressor and victim, multi-optic vision begins with and in turn reinforces a sense that positionality is a very complicated thing indeed. In a dense web of relationships structured by multiple forms of difference, simple oppositions such as powerful/powerless, good/bad, over/under have limited purchase. Positionality is better imagined as fractured, contingent, and continually disputed. The Chinese merchants who attended hearings held by the Commission on Animal Control and Welfare or the California Fish and Game Commission are disadvantaged by many measures – they are first-generation, nonwhite immigrants with limited English proficiency and modest incomes. Yet in their stores on the commercial avenues of San Francisco's Chinatown, these merchants are in a position of undisputed mastery over the animals they keep and kill. Disadvantaged by race, nativity, language, and class, they are advantaged by being human. And while the animals in these markets are powerless by any measure, recognition of their disadvantage (a morally fraught term) is complicated by the fact that their moral standing relative to humans is contentious and the fact that they are often "represented" in these disputes by activists who are white and middle class. Nothing is straightforward in these stories. There is no obvious cast of heroes or villains, no easy assignment of moral virtue or blame.

An ethics of avowal is ultimately about constructing a reimagined "we" in resistance to the neoliberal elites waging war against racialized groups, animals, nature, and others. Race, species, and other taxonomies of power structure how we see, think, feel, and act, and as long as they remain intact, the dominative practices that grow out of them will flourish. It may be that only a ruthless deconstruction of these synergistic taxonomies will move us in the direction of social justice and ecological salvation. We hear a lot about particularized forms of justice – justice for Black people, justice for women, justice for workers, justice for immigrants. But can we imagine a world wherein one form of supremacy has been eradicated but all other supremacies persist? Would we want to? The answer to neoliberalism's destructive practices and values is not to marginally broaden the category of beneficiaries of this destructiveness but rather, through a critical and transformational politics, to radically restructure our relationships with each other, animals, and the earth outside of domination.

RESEARCH NOTES/CHAPTER OUTLINE

I draw upon a wide variety of primary and secondary sources in this book. I conducted personal interviews (13) with the major actors in the San Francisco Chinatown controversy. These included animal advocates, Chinatown business advocates, Chinese American community leaders, attorneys, a retired warden from the California Department of Fish and Game, and members of the San Francisco Commission on Animal Control and Welfare. All interviews were loosely structured, open ended, and conducted in person and in English in the San Francisco/Oakland area. They lasted from one to three hours and were recorded and transcribed. All interviews are excerpted in the book. (Interview excerpts are single-spaced.)

Other primary sources include: transcripts of public hearings held by local and state commissions; local and state legislative records (including legislative histories and transcripts of committee hearings); municipal reports on public health, demographics, and neighborhood profiles; federal and international commission reports; foundation reports; reports by animal advocacy and environmental organizations; historical texts; visual culture (trade cards, drawings, paintings, cartoons); legal briefs from state and federal courts; judicial rulings; correspondence on the part of activists and public officials; newspaper and magazine stories from the English- and Chinese-language media;[10] newsletters of governmental bodies and animal and environmental advocacy groups; data from the U.S. Census and American Community Survey; Web sites (governmental, nonprofit, and other); blogs; video clips; and more.[11]

Secondary sources included work by scholars in fields such as anthropology, English, sociology, law, geography, ethology, ecology, philosophy, political theory, human-animal studies, feminist theory, history, cultural studies, American studies, Asian American studies, African American studies, Native American studies, and political science.

[10] A Cantonese native speaker translated Chinese-language newspaper articles into English for me.
[11] Virginia Handley generously shared her files on the Chinatown conflict with me.

The chapter outline is as follows. Chapter 2, "Animals, Nature, and the Races of Man," shows that Blacks, Native Americans, and the Chinese were all constructed historically in the American cultural imaginary in continuous and intimate relationship with animals and nature. I start with the colonial period and end with the 1800s, when modern racial ideas, given the imprimatur of science, crystallized in Western thought.

Chapter 3, "The Optic of Cruelty: Challenging Chinatown's Live Animal Markets" begins a multi-optic reading of the San Francisco Chinatown controversy by exploring how animal advocates advanced an optic of cruelty to challenge the practices of Chinese live animal vendors. I start with a brief discussion of how the American public views animal welfare issues and animal activists generally and then trace animal advocates' decade and a half struggle from the Commission on Animal Control and Welfare through succeeding venues of conflict.

Chapter 4, "The Optic of Racism: Mobilizing the Chinese American Community," continues the multi-optic reading of the Chinatown case by examining how Chinese American activists in San Francisco advanced the optic of racism as a countercharge against animal advocates. After looking briefly at how white Americans have historically imagined Chinese culture as cruel and transgressive, a trope that helped to shape this dispute, I show how Chinese American activists, with the help of the Chinese-language media, used the conflict to construct a sense of community in a diverse and growing population fractured by class, national origin, language, and politics.

Chapter 5, "The Optic of Ecological Harm: Protecting 'Nature' in a Neoliberal Age," extends the multi-optic reading of the Chinatown case by examining how animal advocates transposed the battle from San Francisco venues to the California Fish and Game Commission in Sacramento and shifted to an optic of ecological harm accordingly. I discuss Fish and Game's neoliberal discourse about nature being a global commons managed by scientific experts in the public interest and then examine how the Fish and Game Commission dealt with the proposal to ban the importation of live turtles and frogs for food.

Chapter 6, "Vision/Critique/Avowal," concludes the analysis of the Chinatown case. I show how animal advocates moved from focusing on cruelty to disavowing race and how Chinese advocates moved from focusing on racism to disavowing species, and I advocate for a reorientation toward an ethics of avowal on both sides.

Chapter 7, "Makah Whaling and the (Non) Ecological Indian," explores the controversy that greeted the Makah nation's decision to resume whale hunting in the Pacific Northwest in the mid-1990s after a hiatus of seventy years. Animal and environmental activists advanced optics of ethical and ecological harm, while Makah activists pushed back with an optic of ecocolonialism. The centuries-old trope of the "ecological Indian," evoked by the Makah's critics, pointedly raised the question of the Indian's relationship to nature. One distinctive feature of this conflict was that the Makah advanced an alternative Native ontology wherein animals give themselves to worthy hunters in a reciprocal exchange. In this ontological framework, reverence and respect for the whale are consistent with killing the whale for food. Animal and environmental protectionists, on the one hand, and Makah leaders, on the other, dismissed each other's moral, political, and ontological claims in the course of political conflict.

Chapter 8, "Michael Vick, Dogfighting, and the Parable of Black Recalcitrance," examines the controversy over NFL quarterback Michael Vick's dogfighting conviction in 2007. While animal advocates read Vick's actions through an optic of cruelty, race advocates read the prosecution and public condemnation of Vick through an optic of racism. As in the other two cases, a powerful and persistent racial trope – here, about Black men as violent beasts impervious to improvement – structured the conflict. Again, I document the mutual disavowal of animal advocates and race advocates and suggest that an ethics of avowal would do more to advance social justice broadly understood.

Chapter 9, "We Are All Animals/We Are Not Animals," briefly examines a PETA exhibit comparing animal exploitation to slavery, as well as arguments of Black commentators who cast the reaction to Hurricane Katrina (2005) and the George Zimmerman verdict (2013) as evidence that whites value animals more than they do Black people. This epilogue offers some concluding thoughts on the themes raised throughout this book.

2

Animals, Nature, and the Races of Man

> Race as a natural-technical object of knowledge is fundamentally a category
> marking political power through location in "nature."
>
> – Donna Haraway, *Primate Visions*

Racialized groups have been likened to animals for centuries in Western culture, and because such comparisons have enabled extreme violence, they are
considered today to be "dreaded" or even "inadmissible."[1] The conventional
wisdom is that powerful groups have used animalization to "dehumanize"
less powerful groups, demoting them from category A (humans) into category
B (animals) and thus stripping them of the entitlements, rights, and protections distinctively owed to humans. Of course, this argument assumes an a
priori state in which racialized groups were accepted as fully human. I argue
in this chapter that racialized groups were never seen as fully human to
begin with, so they did not have this status to lose. They were always already
animal or animal-like. Animality and nature have been integral not incidental to the production of racial difference (Haraway 1989). Constructed
in intimate relationship with animals and nature, Blacks, Indians, and the
Chinese in the United States have been located for centuries in a borderlands between human and animal, a fraught zone of ambiguity, menace, and
transgression.

As a taxonomy of power, race lumps and splits. First, it places all nonwhites
into a borderlands between human and animal. The concept of "borderlands"
can mean an area around a border and/or an indeterminate area where units
overlap, that is, an area demarcated by borders or an area that gives borders the

---

[1] See Spiegel (1997). A conference entitled "Inadmissible Comparisons" was held at New York
University Law School in March 2007. Cosponsored by United Poultry Concerns and the New
York University Student Animal Legal Defense Fund, it brought together activists from various
movements (gay/lesbian, workers' rights, peace, animal liberation, Black liberation, feminist) to
discuss connections among their struggles.

lie.[2] Here I use it to suggest an imaginative space where both liminal humans and the most human-like animals are located – testimony to both humans' powerful drive to distinguish themselves hierarchically from other humans and animals and their failure to do so in any permanently successful way. It is a space wrought by power but illustrative of power's indeterminacy. Whites, seen as quintessentially human, have never been located in this borderlands – they transcend the body and nature, they are progressive, they move forward through history, they have civilization and a history. Animals and animal-like humans, on the other hand, are untranscendent, tethered to the body and nature, incapable of civilization and progress, and lacking history.

At the same time, the taxonomy of race differentiates nonwhite groups according to how animal they are or how closely associated with nature they are. Western ethnological frameworks in the 1800s generally placed the Mongolian/Asiatic between the European and the African. Thus the Chinese were imagined as less human and more animal than whites, but also as more human and less animal than Blacks and Indians, and as having a history and a civilization (albeit a decadent one well past its zenith). Indians, also placed between Europeans and Africans, were seen as barely distinguishable from various kinds of wild animals with which they shared the forest and plains, and Black people were most persistently identified with a single type of animal (primates) as the medieval notions of gradation and hierarchy continued to hold sway. These two racial dynamics of lumping and splitting appear contradictory but they function together to make race flexibly adaptive as a structure of power: sometimes racial domination is better served by emphasizing similarities among nonwhite groups, sometimes by emphasizing dissimilarities.[3] Either way, race is forged in the crucible of ideas about animality and nature.

In this chapter, I begin by looking at a particular visual image from California in the Reconstruction era and asking what it can tell us about racial dynamics in that time and place. I then take a brief look at the construction of animality as a repository of meaning in Western culture before turning to examine the construction of Blackness, Indianness, and Chineseness in the United States with reference to animality and nature. I start with the colonial period but focus primarily on the nineteenth century because that is when the Black, Indian, and Chinese "questions" came to the fore and converged in a powerful way in the national consciousness. The abolitionist challenge to slavery and the Civil War; the Indian wars and "removal"; the legal persecution and exclusion of Chinese immigrants; white westward migration under the banner of Manifest Destiny – all of these dramatic events, coupled with the advent of

---

[2] This notion has been used by geographers (Wolch and Emel 1998) to describe both the imaginative nature/culture border and physical spaces where people and animals meet. It has been elaborated by Gloria Anzaldúa (2012), too, who uses it to describe the U.S.-Mexico border as a place of indeterminacy whose inhabitants are forbidden and abnormal.

[3] Different Asian groups, too, were sometimes lumped together, sometimes differentiated in the American imagination, depending on the exigencies of the situation.

scientific racism in the transatlantic field, made the 1800s a critical period in the history of U.S. racial dynamics. All three of these racialized groups were seen as deficient in reason, culture/religion, and civilization, and thus as unfit for social or political membership. All three were imaginatively located in the human-animal borderlands. At the same time, they were differentiated from one another in ways that were contingent upon the region, time period, and issue at hand. These complex understandings of race, species, and nature made their way into the Western (and specifically, American) cultural and imaginative lexicon, where their citationality is obvious even today.

"SAY, GORHAM! PUT THIS BROTHER UP"

This picture, "Reconstruction" (Figure 2.1), is a satirical cartoon published during the 1867 California gubernatorial race. It is the Reconstruction period and the topic is the debate over extending voting rights to Blacks in California – a hot topic with the Thirteenth Amendment having just passed, the Fourteenth Amendment undergoing ratification, and the proposal of the Fifteenth Amendment only a few years away. In the cartoon, George Gorham, the Union Party candidate who favors Black suffrage, is shown bearing the weight of a Black man, a Chinese man, and an Indian man (one on top of the other) as Brother Jonathan (a predecessor to Uncle Sam) admonishes him that suffrage was meant to be an exclusively white privilege: "Young Man! read the history of your Country, and learn that this ballot box was dedicated to the white race alone. The load you are carrying will sink you in perdition, where you belong, or my name is not Jonathan."

In the image, the Black man says dubiously to Gorham, whom he addresses as "Massa": "I spose we'se obliged to carry dese brudders, Kase de'se no stink-shun ob race or culler any more, for Kingdom cum." Gorham replies: "Shut your mouth Cuffy ... here's the way I express it – The war of authority, and 'Manhood alone' shall be the test of the right to a voice in the Government." The Chinese man is gleeful at the prospect of voting: "Boss Gollam belly good man. He say chinaman vo-tee all same melican man – Ketch – ee mine all same – no pay taxee – belly good." The Indian, too: "Chemue Walla! Ingen vote! plenty whisky all time – Gorom big ingin." From the right, a white man approaches from the side with a leashed ape and urges, "Say, Gorham! put this Brother up."

This richly layered text speaks to the fact that the late 1860s were a watershed historical moment in U.S. racial dynamics. The biologization of racial ideas was well under way in the transatlantic discursive and ideological field (Gould 1996). Racial difference, which had been thought of through the 1700s as possibly environmentally induced and thus environmentally correctible, was nailed down in the mid-nineteenth century as immutable biological fact. Scientists in various fields demonstrated race's fixity by comparative studies of cranial capacity, facial angle, cranial folds, and more. The hierarchical categories created by ethnologists varied in some of the details, but virtually all

FIGURE 2.1. "Reconstruction". Courtesy of the Library of Congress.

confirmed the superiority of the European and the inferiority of the African, who came in just above the ape in scientific rankings. The physical, mental, and cultural inferiority of colored races, determined as it was by nature itself, meant that various programs of uplift, Christian or other, were for the most part doomed to ultimate failure, raising vexing questions about the terms on which such beings were to live in the same society with whites.

These questions acquired greater urgency because of dramatic political and economic events on the ground. The legal abrogation of U.S. slavery starting in 1865 and the introduction of the Reconstruction amendments ending slavery and promoting equal protection and voting rights sent aftershocks throughout the nation. What would be the impact of freed slaves living as equals among whites? Would Black suffrage undermine American institutions and principles and destroy the American way of life? Although California entered the Union as a free state in 1850, rejecting the institution of African slavery in favor of a free-labor ideology promising white economic mobility, Blacks in the state were excluded from political and social membership in various ways, including the denial of suffrage.

In the minds of white Californians, the question of whether to grant Black suffrage in the late 1860s was intimately tied to the question of whether to grant it to that other "degraded" nonwhite group in their midst, the Chinese.[4] Demographics shaped the perception of relative threat. From 1860 to 1870, the Chinese population in San Francisco grew from 2,719 to 12,022, whereas the Black population rose from 1,176 to 1,322, rendering the "Chinese question" foremost in white Californians' minds.[5] With the acceleration of Chinese immigration into California, anti-Coolieism became both a powerful movement uniting white labor, newspapers, and other nativist interests and an all-but-obligatory position in state politics. The late 1860s saw a potent mix of hardened, scientifically sanctioned ideas about racial hierarchy and political and demographic changes that were posing the race question in new and urgent ways. It was a historical moment of uncommon indeterminacy and anxiety.

Enter George Gorham and the 1867 contest. When the Anti-Coolie Association asked Union Party gubernatorial candidates for their thoughts on the "Chinese question" that year, Gorham alone repudiated the Association's agenda, writing,

I believe in the Christian religion, and that rests upon the universal fatherhood of God and the brotherhood of man. I am as emphatically opposed to all attempts to deny the Chinaman the right to labor for pay, as I am to the restoration of African slavery whereby Black men were compelled to labor without pay.[6]

---

[4] In *People v. George Hall* (1854), the California Supreme Court decided that an 1850 state law prohibiting courtroom testimony by Negroes, Mulattoes, and Indians against whites also applied to the Chinese.
[5] Skjeie (2005).
[6] Tinkham (1915), 212–13.

In making these arguments in defense of Chinese immigrants, arguments that echoed abolitionist critiques of slavery in the South, Gorham alienated important interests. Although he later succumbed to pressure by taking a stand against Chinese suffrage, this did not stop the press and opponents from the Democratic Party from excoriating him as an advocate of equality for nonwhites. The Democratic candidate Henry Haight prevailed over George Gorham in the election because the Democrats' anti-Reconstruction, anti-Black, and anti-Chinese platform spoke to the hearts and minds of many white Californians.[7] During this period, the California legislature, dominated by Democrats, refused to ratify both the Fourteenth and Fifteenth Amendments.

In this satirical picture, we see a rhetorical strategy long favored by opponents of social change – the "What's Next?" or "slippery slope" strategy. When Mary Wollstonecraft published *A Vindication of the Rights of Women* (1792), Thomas Taylor responded by publishing *A Vindication of the Rights of Brutes* (1792), which purported to show the preposterousness of Wollstonecraft's argument by indicating that it could apply as much to animals as to women. The issues in play in 1867 were Black suffrage and racial equality, so the image asks, What's next? Chinese suffrage? Indian suffrage? Ape suffrage? Each step seems more unthinkable than the one before, which makes the first step seem not only illegitimate but dangerous and destabilizing. Granting Black suffrage, it is suggested, would be like pulling on the thread that holds civilization together.

Of course, Gorham's comment about "Manhood" being the key to voting only begs the questions posed in the cartoon: Who counts as a man? Who is man enough to be a citizen? The ascent up the human ladder in the picture is an inversion of true racial hierarchy, reversing the journey from savagery to semi-barbarity to civilization. The subservient Black man is closest to the white man physically and his mode of dress, Christianity, and shared concern about the implications of universal suffrage all explain why he is positioned this way. Despite being seen as wholly inferior to whites and undeserving of meaningful citizenship, Blacks were seen as less foreign than the Chinese and Indians – as reflected in the Naturalization Act of 1870, which permitted free Blacks to become citizens and explicitly prohibited Chinese immigrants from doing so.[8] Thus the Black man here (in anticipation of Kipling) shares the white man's burden.

The Chinese man, whose heathenism is displayed through his queue, mode of dress, cultural activity (the firecracker he holds), and accent, makes clear his lack of civic capacity by openly celebrating suffrage as a means to greater wealth. From the mid-1800s to today, the notion of the Asiatic as overly concerned with money and unconcerned with citizenship as the performance of

[7] Skjeie (2005).
[8] When the 1850 California law prohibiting nonwhites from courtroom testimony was revisited in 1863, lawmakers decided to permit Blacks to testify but upheld the ban on the Chinese and Indians (Shaffer 2005).

civic duty has persisted. At the top of the human ladder, the Indian stands on the frontier between civilization and savagery. Nearly naked and waving a bow and arrows that signal his warlike nature and his primitivism, the Indian shows himself to be even less capable in a civic sense than the Chinese. Where the Chinese man has culture and is part of the industrial labor force, the Indian is wild and indolent and shows a childlike glee that suffrage is likely to boost his liquor supply. The image of the "drunken Indian" was exceptionally enduring, having first emerged in colonial discourse on the Eastern Seaboard in the late 1600s.

Essentializing the Chinese as venal and apolitical, whites elided their own historical agency in denying the Chinese the right to naturalize; essentializing the Indian as a drunkard, whites elided their own historical agency in introducing alcohol to North American Indians and using it as a tool of political and economic control.[9] The cartoon asks of these ridiculous figures: Are these really candidates for suffrage? What's next? Is Gorham going to claim the ape as his "Brother"? Is he going to attribute "Manhood" to the ape as well? The ape in the picture is walking upright and smiling; he looks semi-human. However, he is the only figure in the picture who says nothing, which apparently reflects his lack of consciousness or will. He is on a leash, following orders.

This picture captures succinctly the way racialized groups in the nineteenth century United States were both lumped together and painstakingly distinguished from one another. They were all imaginatively located in the borderlands between full humanity and animality – in this picture, literally between Gorham and the ape, were the latter to take his rightful place at the top of this inverted hierarchy. At the same time, they were defined relationally, in contradistinction to whites and to one another. These distinctions were exquisitely fine-tuned so as to generate specific, shifting grounds for othering and exclusion as historical exigencies required. In 1867, the pressing question for white Southerners was whether freed slaves would go back to Africa, die out from disease and hereditary weakness in the face of competition with whites, or be virtually re-enslaved as sharecroppers. To white Californians, however, Blacks seemed distinctly more familiar and American than the Celestials, and the latter, because of their numbers, posed a far greater threat in terms of labor competition. Although the Chinese were bearers of an ancient and accomplished civilization, that civilization had decayed, and it was their very cultural fixity – as opposed to the infinite plasticity of the culture-less Black man – that sealed their fate as unassimilable (Kim 1999). If the Indian question was being resolved in the rest of the nation through military conquest, "removal," and the reservation system, it found temporary resolution in California in

---

9 Alcohol was first introduced to North American Indians in the 1500s by European traders and quickly became a commodity for trading. Despite complaints about the "drunken Indian," moralistic handwringing, and sporadic legislation to restrict the provision of alcohol to Indians, U.S. business and government interests regularly encouraged Indian consumption of alcohol for the sake of both profits and political control (Duran 1996).

the establishment of Indian slavery at mid-century.[10] In California in 1867, reflecting the exigencies of the time and place, the Chinese and the Indian were depicted as more animal than the Black man, closer to the ape without speech in the corner. The relative placement of these racialized groups varied, as we shall see, depending on which was seen as the greatest threat to white privilege in any given time and place.

THE ANIMALIZED ANIMAL

It is not surprising that an ape shows up as the exclamation point in the Reconstruction cartoon. As historian Erica Fudge (2000) notes, the question of human identity – what precisely is it that makes us human? – is continuously posed and never fully answered in the Western imagination. And no figure has been evoked in these speculations more often than the ape, seen as the most human-like animal and located in the imaginative borderlands between human and animal. More generally, the idea of the animal has been a vital prop in the project of defining the human. Virginia Anderson (2006) points out that seventeenth-century Algonquian-speaking Indian tribes had no single word for "animal," suggesting that they perceived a great diversity of creatures rather than lumping them together into a single category whose defining character-istic was that it was subhuman or not human. For English colonists, however, animality was constructed as an explicit counterpoint to humanity. What Keith Thomas writes about England was true for English people in the United States as well: "Men attributed to animals the natural impulses they most feared in themselves '– ferocity, gluttony, sexuality. ... It was as a comment on *human* nature that the concept of 'animality' was devised."[11]

But animals have proven an imperfect foil. The search for *the* single trait distinguishing all humans from all animals has been as fruitless as it has been relentless over the past few millennia. Reason, language, self-consciousness, a sense of time and the future – all of these have been tried on and found lack-ing. Bodies are, as a matter of course, unruly and resistant to the classificatory regimes that produce them. The borderlands concept here captures the inde-terminacy, contestation, and anxiety that attends such boundary failure. In the borderlands between human and animal, where animalized and raced bodies meet as joint transgressors and joint captives, one of the central contradic-tions of Western culture makes itself known – that humans have for millennia asserted their superiority to animals even as they are ambivalent and insecure

[10] California entered the Union a free state in 1850 and ratified the Thirteenth Amendment in 1865; during this period and beyond, Indian slavery was thriving in the state (Rawls 1984, Almaguer 1994).

[11] Thomas (1983), 40–1. While most of this chapter discusses the role that animality plays in con-structing race, it is also true that animals have been racialized. See, for example, Harriet Ritvo (1992) on the Chillingham cattle in eighteenth-century Britain, who were identified as "ancient Britons" and constructed as white both discursively and practically (through the slaughter of Black calves). I discuss the racialization of animals in Chapters 5 and 8.

about whether the difference between the two is one of kind or degree and about what forms of mastery such difference might authorize (Thomas 1983; Fudge 2000; Steiner 2005).

In ancient Greek mythology, although gods, humans, and animals were distinct groups, the boundary between gods and humans, on the one hand, and animals, on the other, seemed quite porous. Gods regularly went undercover as beasts (usually for nefarious purposes) and often turned disobedient men and women into beasts as punishment. In Homer's epic poem, *The Odyssey*, the goddess Circe delights in turning Odysseus' men into pigs. Pre-Socratic thinkers such as Pythagoras and Empedocles wrote of metempsychosis, the idea that souls transmigrated from human to animal bodies and vice versa. Although they believed in human distinctiveness, they also thought that humans shared a basic nature with animals.[12] At the same time, the notion of heroism in Greek mythology was inextricably tied to mastery over animals. The Greek hero – whether Perseus slaying Medusa and then the sea dragon, or Theseus slaying the Minotaur, or Herakles slaying all manner of beasts in his Twelve Labors – becomes a hero and a founder of civilization through the highly specific act of killing fearsome beasts. Slaying animals is a performance of mastery that establishes order, however tenuously. Without the Minotaur, there could be no Theseus.

As Gary Steiner argues, it is in ancient Greek philosophy that we see the beginnings of the "long and complex historical turn against the notion of natural continuity" between humans and animals.[13] In his discussion of the tripartite human soul, Plato argues that the rational and soldierly parts of the soul need to gain control over the lowest or appetitive or animal part of the soul, giving rise to the notion that a human must master the beast within himself. Aristotle's enshrinement of "reason" as the faculty marking superior types of beings, as well as his ideas about natural slavery, helped to sculpt the argument that animals were created by nature to serve human purposes.[14] However, it was the Stoics – Epictetus and Seneca among them – who raised the dividing line between humans and animals "to the status of a cosmic principle."[15] They insisted that animals existed entirely for the sake of humans, who achieved humanness by freeing themselves from bodily needs in order to contemplate God.

The Bible (Old and New Testaments) reinforced the idea that humans were distinct from and superior to other animals in crucial ways that justified their domination over the latter. Here it was not reason but rather the possession of a soul that rendered humans unique. Consider this famous passage from Genesis 1:26: "And God said, Let us make man in our image, after our likeness: and let them have dominion over the fish of the sea, and over the fowl of the air,

[12] Steiner (2005).
[13] Ibid., 52.
[14] See Plato's *Republic* and Aristotle's *Politics*.
[15] Steiner (2005), 77.

and over the cattle, and over all the earth, and over every creeping thing that creepeth upon the earth."[16] In the Garden of Eden, Adam and Eve are apparently vegetarian and their "dominion" seems like thoughtful stewardship, but after the Fall, that "dominion" takes on a harsher cast. Animals' relations with one another become cruel and wild and the eating of animals by humans is divinely sanctioned, as when God says to Noah and his sons after the Flood, "And the fear of you and the dread of you shall be upon every beast of the earth, and upon every fowl of the air, upon all that moveth upon the earth, and upon all the fishes of the sea; into your hand are they delivered" (Genesis 9:2) and "Every moving thing that liveth shall be meat for you" (Genesis 9:3).[17] Writing in the Middle Ages, Saint Thomas Aquinas relied on Scripture to argue both that humans were superior to animals in that they were created in God's image and had immortal souls, and that animals existed for the sake of humans. Men should avoid being cruel to animals, according to Aquinas, but only because mistreating animals would cultivate a habit of cruelty toward humans.

Rooted in Platonic thought, the notion of the Great Chain of Being emerged in the Middle Ages and became a governing imaginative framework by the eighteenth century. It is easy to understand the appeal of an idea that purported to arrange everything from God to the angels to man to various beasts to the smallest stone in a single, unbroken hierarchical ladder. Man was located between the angels and the beasts, his soul being composed of both angelic and beastly parts, which were always warring. As Michael Walzer writes: "Angels moved by perfect intelligence and animals by perfect instinct; but men possessed neither ... they walked always on the very brink of chaos and disorder."[18] Interestingly, the Chain of Being codified man's superiority to animals but at the same time cast doubt upon the hard boundary that the Stoics and Aquinas had asserted. Arthur Lovejoy points out two aspects of the Chain idea that potentially counteracted ideas of human supremacy. First, all species were created for the sake of the completeness of the Chain, which testified to God's power and splendor; none was created for the utility of another species. Second, the Chain exemplified the principles of continuity and gradation: "every one [link] of them differing from that immediately above and that immediately below it by the 'least possible' degree of difference."[19] As John Locke wrote on this matter:

In all the visible corporeal world we see no chasms or gaps. All quite down from us the descent is by easy steps, and a continued series that in each remove differ very little one from the other. ... There are some brutes that seem to have as much reason and knowledge as some that are called men ... that if you will take the lowest of one and the highest of the other, there will scarce be perceived any great difference between them.[20]

---

[16] King James Bible, Cambridge edition. See Matthew Scully (2003) for a softer reading of "dominion."
[17] King James Version.
[18] Walzer (1965), 158.
[19] Lovejoy (2009), 59.
[20] *Essay Concerning Human Understanding*, III, Chap. VI, § 12, cited in Lovejoy (2009), 184.

Hierarchy suggested difference but continuity and gradation mitigated that difference. Humans were above animals in the Chain, closer to God, but there was no strict divide between humans and animals. Rather, there was an ambiguous borderlands where the basest man and the most exalted animal met. Not surprisingly, the early modern period in Europe was one marked by what Erica Fudge (2000) calls "anxious anthropocentrism," a felt need to continuously reassert human superiority through brutal performances of mastery (animal baiting, hunting, etc.).

Writing in the 1600s, Descartes had no patience for such ambiguity. His writing played a critical role in enshrining the dualisms that structure Western thinking and in drawing an impassable line between humans and animals. For Descartes, "Embodiment is a sign of imperfection. ... Any being that is wholly corporeal is of the lowest order of being. ... Nature is taken in its essence to be pure corporeality."[21] Humans were defined by soul, mind, thought, and language: *Cogito, ergo sum* (I think, therefore I am). Animals, on the other hand, were machines, pure matter, bodies unencumbered by souls or minds. When they cried out upon being dissected while fully conscious, Descartes insisted that they were not feeling or expressing pain but making mechanical noises like a clock might make if certain mechanisms within it were triggered. Thus was the "long and complex historical turn" against the notion of natural continuity accelerated. When utilitarians Jeremy Bentham and John Stuart Mill pointed to animal sentience to argue for the moral considerability of animals – recall Bentham's quote, "The question is not, Can they *reason?* Nor, Can they *talk?* But, Can they *suffer?*"[22] – they were swimming against the tide of Western theology and philosophy. Most thinkers of the eighteenth century agreed rather with Kant, who asserted that animals were not rational, morally autonomous beings, which meant that they had no intrinsic moral worth.

If there was a semblance of philosophical consensus on animals, there was a good deal of ambivalence felt by nonphilosophers at every stage. As Harriet Ritvo puts it, "A lot of evidence suggests that when people are not trying to deny that humans and animals belong to the same moral and intellectual continuum, they automatically assume they do."[23] Writing about eighteenth- and nineteenth-century animal breeders in Britain, Ritvo observes that in talking about resistant bitches and dull cows, "they would not have made the same claims about the nature of their animals ... if they had not implicitly assumed an identity between human nature and animal nature – an identity they would certainly have denied if they had been asked about it directly."[24] Through the eighteenth and nineteenth centuries, various developments – including the articulation of less anthropocentric taxonomic systems (such as the Linnaean one in *Systema Naturae*, 1735–68); the emergence of urban middle-class pet

---

[21] Steiner (2005), 135.
[22] Bentham (1948), 310–11.
[23] Ritvo (1991), 70.
[24] Lovejoy (2009), 81.

keeping; urbanization and industrialization and the distancing from rural life; and the expansion of fields such as astronomy, geology, botany, and zoology – all worked together to increase a sense of human-animal continuities and generate new ways of relating to, thinking about, and feeling for animals.[25] By the early 1800s, animal advocacy was emerging in Britain, where Parliament passed a number of anticruelty provisions. And in a watershed event, Charles Darwin argued in *On the Origin of Species* (1859) that humans and animals shared a common ancestor, that both were subject to the laws of evolution, and that there was a human-animal continuum in terms of cognitive and emotional abilities. Although Darwin's work was vigorously resisted in many circles, including religious ones, it gave the imprimatur of science to the argument that the human-animal divide needed rethinking.

THE NEGRO BEAST

The positioning of man over beast in the Great Chain of Being settled one question but raised others: Which type of man ranked the lowest among humans and closest to beasts? And following the principles of continuity and gradation, what type of creatures constituted the link between the lowest men and the highest beasts? The man-ape interval was the focus of "especial zeal" on the part of scientific observers and philosophers from the Middle Ages forward.[26] It was the Negro, seen as base, lowly, and inferior in intelligence and civilization, who was imaginatively located between man and ape. In fact, the Negro was frequently characterized *as an ape*, a notion that emerged in the West as early as the start of the sixteenth century, won the support of leading scientific minds by the mid-nineteenth century, and peaked in the late nineteenth century as a justification for lynching in the Jim Crow South.

Winthrop Jordan (1968) cautions that the insistence and ubiquity of the ape comparison should not blind us to the fact that whites' Christianity compelled most of them to believe in the unity of man and reject the notion that Negroes were a different species. Whites did not literally think of Negroes as beasts despite their language, he chides. Yet the historical record suggests that the ape comparison was more than just a forceful metaphor meant to denigrate or express difference; it was an indicator of whites' uncertainty and ambivalence about how to think about the Negro and their imaginative placement of him in the human/animal borderlands where he was variously seen as subhuman, not quite human, almost animal, actually animal. It was an indicator that they thought of beings, at least in part, as being related through continuity and gradation, a la the Great Chain, rather than being neatly separable into dichotomous categories such as "human" and "animal." This idea of the Negro as beast waxed and waned and shape-shifted depending on historical and geographical

[25] Thomas (1983).
[26] Lovejoy (2009), 233.

context, and it coexisted with other ideas, some of which contradicted it, but it remains part of the fabric of racial meanings in the United States today.

Jordan traces this "extraordinarily pervasive and enduring" association of Africans and apes to the early 1500s when British explorers first encountered both of them at the same time and began describing Africans as apes who were tailless and walked upright.[27] From the start, the English viewed Africans as "brutish," "bestial," and "beastly." Some observers speculated that Africans were the offspring of apes; they pored a great deal over the likelihood of copulation between Africans and apes and apes sexually assaulting African women – "Sexual union seemed to prove a certain affinity without going so far as to indicate actual identity."[28] The Negro-ape comparison depended, of course, on the ongoing imaginative construction of the ape (Spiegel 1997). It was only because naturalists such as Edward Topsell already imagined the ape as "lustful" and "venerous" in *The History of Four-Footed Beasts* (1607) that the comparison worked to highlight the African's putative hypersexuality. One cannot but notice the prurience in the traveler's accounts. As Anne McClintock notes, "For centuries, the uncertain continents – Africa, the Americas, Asia – were figured in European lore as libidinously eroticized. Travelers' tales abounded with visions of the monstrous sexuality of far-off lands, where, as legend had it, men sported gigantic penises and women consorted with apes. ... Africa and the Americas had become what can be called a porno-tropics for the European imagination."[29]

Many European scientific observers from the 1600s forward posited that the so-called Hottentots (Khoikhoi of South Africa) were the connecting link between man and ape. An English essayist in 1713 wrote in this representative tract:

> The Ape or the Monkey that bears the greatest Similitude to Man, is the next Order of Animals below him. Nor is the Disagreement between the basest Individuals of our species and the Ape or Monkey so great, but that, were the latter endow'd with the Faculty of Speech, they might perhaps as justly claim the Rank and Dignity of the human Race, as the savage *Hotentot*, or stupid native of Nova Zembla.[30]

The effort here, *pace* Descartes, is to question the human-animal boundary and suggest the virtual indistinguishability of borderland denizens. Some commentators posited that Negroes occupied a midpoint between Europeans and apes. In *Notes on the State of Virginia* (1781), Thomas Jefferson indicated this when he said Negro men preferred white women to the same measure that the "Oran – ootans" (chimpanzees) preferred Negro women, the males of each species reaching up the Chain of Being in their sexual desires.[31] Others were torn between locating Negroes close to apes and rendering them

---

[27] Jordan (1968), 238.
[28] Ibid., 32.
[29] McClintock (1995), 22.
[30] Blackmore and Hughes, *The Lay Monastery* (1714), 28, cited in Lovejoy (2009), 234.
[31] Jordan (1968), 490.

apes. Jamaican journalist Edward Long – whose writings were excerpted and reprinted as "Observations on the Gradation in the Scale of Being between the Human and Brute Creation. Including Some Curious Particulars Respecting Negroes" (1788) – divided the genus *homo* into three categories: Europeans and other humans, Blacks, and "Oran-outangs" (chimpanzees). Of the last he said they had a "much nearer resemblance to the Negro race than the latter bear to white men" and that they "did not seem at all inferior in the intellectual faculties to many of the negroe race." Long's conclusion: "I do not think that an oran-outang husband would be any dishonour to an Hottentot female."[32]

The Enlightenment's emphasis on reason, progress, and the universal perfectibility of man ensured that for much of the eighteenth century the Negro was seen as theoretically improvable. Despite the entrenchment and expansion of African slavery in the United States and the British Empire during this period, the transatlantic literati continued to speculate that the Negro's baseness, inferiority, and even his skin color might be a product of environment, broadly construed as climate, living conditions, diet, and institutional context. This left open the possibility that these processes might be reversible, leading to the Negro's improvement. But by the start of the nineteenth century, European and American scientists were moving away from environmentalism and in the direction of biological determinism, and in this context, the discursive practice of linking of Negroes and beasts found new life. If the hallmark of humanity was perfectibility, progress, and history, Negroes seemed to lack it. To the Western eye, Africa remained "a fetish-land, inhabited by cannibals, dervishes, and witch doctors" and "a land perpetually out of time in modernity, marooned and historically abandoned."[33]

Virtually every ethnological framework created from the dawn of the nineteenth century forward placed Blacks at the very bottom of the human hierarchy of races and somewhere between man and ape. In *An Account of the Regular Gradation in Man, and in Different Animals and Vegetables; and from the Former to the Latter* (1799), English surgeon Charles White posited, after inspecting facial angles in his colleague's skull collection, that the downward gradation dictated by nature was Europeans/Asiatics/American Indians/Negroes/Orang-outangs/Monkeys. Having examined skeletons of Europeans, Negroes, "orang-outangs" (chimpanzees), and monkeys, as well as living white and Black bodies, White concluded that the Negro was more similar to the ape than was the European.[34] These ideas were shared by the leading minds of the day. George Cuvier, a founder of geology, paleontology, and modern comparative anatomy, described Africans as "the most degraded of human races, whose form approaches that of the beast," and Charles Lyell, a founder of modern

---

[32] Pieterse (1992), 41; Jordan (1968), 492–3.
[33] McClintock (1995), 41 characterizing Hegel's view of Africa.
[34] Jordan (1968), 500–1.

geology wrote, "The brain of the Bushman ... leads toward the brain of the *Simiadae* [monkeys]."[35]

If naturalists and comparative anatomists focused on the Negro-ape interval, another comparison animated and was in turn reinforced by the discursive and material practices of Southern slavery. This was the link between Negro slaves and domesticated animals, specifically livestock. Winthrop Jordan writes, "Slave traders in Africa handled Negroes the same way men in England handled beasts, herding and examining and buying."[36] New slaves off the ships were described as "well-fleshed," "strong-limbed," "lusty," "robust," "unblemished," making it clear that "Negroes, just like horses, were walking pieces of property."[37] Indeed, as Marjorie Spiegel (1997) and Charles Patterson (2002) point out, slavery saw the redeployment of the very technologies of domination and control originally developed for use in animal husbandry – including chaining, whipping, branding, and selling at auction. Some slave owners described slavery as an institution that transformed the Negro "from the 'savage' (best understood through the metaphor of the wild animal) to the slave (best understood through the metaphor of the domestic animal)," even as opponents of slavery decried slavery's treatment of men as dumb beasts.[38]

The image of Sambo, the docile, childlike, plastic slave, was meant to shore up this notion of slavery as benevolent toward Black people. The slave imagined as Sambo would have been lost without white protection. That the Negro was supposedly improved by slavery and civilized and Christianized by his contact with whites provided a moral justification for the institution even as it reassured whites anxious about slave rebellion. The Sambo image coexisted with the "Negro as beast" belief and was theoretically compatible with it, as in the common argument made by Southerners that Negroes could be partially civilized by slavery but would revert back to bestiality at the first taste of freedom.[39] The Negro might be emancipated from slavery but never from his own nature. He could only ever be, under the best conditions, a semi-civilized brute, not a civilized man. Because the "Negro as beast" idea coexisted with the Sambo image, Southerners in the mid-1800s were ambivalent as to whether "the model for the ideal slave was taken from the realm of the subhuman, with the slave as a high type of domesticated animal to serve as the white man's tool like another beast of burden" or whether the slave was a child in a patriarchal relationship with his master.[40]

It was in this intellectual and political context that one abolitionist author in 1804 felt the need to devote a chapter in his book to "Whether the African Negroes be a part of the Human Species, capable of intellectual, moral, and

---

[35] Gould (1996), 66–9.
[36] Jordan (1968), 28.
[37] Ibid., 233.
[38] Jacoby (1994), 96.
[39] Fredrickson (1971), 54.
[40] Ibid., 56.

religious Improvement, no less than the other Nations of Mankind; or, an inferior Order of beings, occupying a middle Place between Men and Brutes?"[41] According to George Fredrickson, abolitionists' direct challenges to slavery ironically led to the hardening and tightening of proslavery arguments. He writes, "It took the assault of the abolitionists to unmask the cant about a theoretical human equality that coexisted with Negro slavery and racial discrimination and to force the practitioners of racial oppression to develop a theory that accorded with their behavior."[42] Summoned in defense of slavery, arguments about permanent, biologically determined Negro inferiority gained traction as the nineteenth century progressed. Richard Colfax, in a pamphlet entitled *Evidence Against the Views of the Abolitionists, Consisting of Physical and Moral Proofs of the Natural Inferiority of the Negroes* (1833), concludes that Negroes "are so inferior as to resemble the brute creation as nearly as they do the white species." Crucially, Colfax makes the additional point that this status is immutable as demonstrated by the fact that in thousands of years Negroes had "never even *attempted* to raise themselves above their present equivocal station in the great zoological chain."[43]

The "American School" of anthropology emerged at this time, with Samuel George Morton, George Gliddon, and Josiah Nott using data from craniometric investigations to not only rank races (whites on top, Blacks on the bottom, Indians in the middle) but argue that they were different species altogether. Christian orthodoxy held that mankind was created at one time and in the image of God even if it had differentiated or degenerated into separate varieties or races since Creation. Bucking this orthodoxy about a single origin (monogenism), Morton and colleagues advanced the notion of polygenism: that different races were different species created at different times. This was a momentous shift in thinking: "The difference between a variety and a species meant also, in theory at least, the difference between a Black man who was inferior to the whites but akin to them ... and a Black man who was more animal than human and could, for most purposes, be treated as such."[44] Taken from Nott and Gliddon's *Types of Mankind* (1855), Figure 2.2 shows the imaginative location of the Black man between the white man and the ape.

Although polygenism never became a majority viewpoint, it was eagerly embraced by defenders of slavery and resurrected by Southerners during Reconstruction. In 1867, Buckner Payne, writing under the pseudonym "Ariel," published *The Negro: What Is His Ethnological Status?*, in which he claimed that Negroes were created as a separate species before Adam and Eve and related to "higher orders of the monkey."[45] Of course, polygenists in the

---

[41] Jordan (1968), 505.
[42] Fredrickson (1971), 43.
[43] Ibid., 49–50.
[44] Fredrickson (1971), 84.
[45] Ibid., 188.

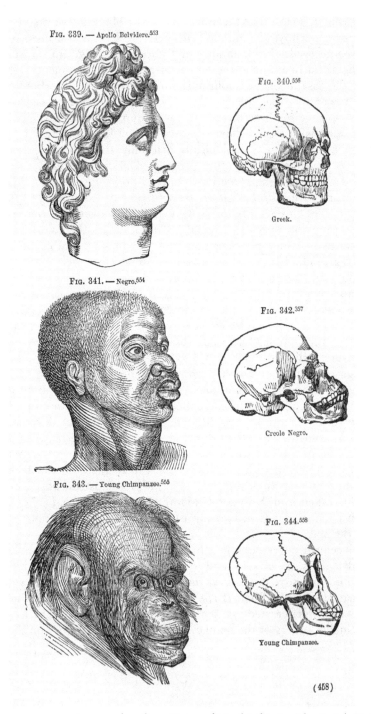

FIGURE 2.2. Image taken from *Types of Mankind* (1855) by Josiah Nott and George Gliddon. Courtesy of the Library of Congress.

mid-1800s had no monopoly on the Negro-ape comparison, which was a fixture of scientific analyses grounded on the principles of continuity and gradation. Charles Darwin, whose theory of evolution placed him squarely in the monogenist camp, wrote of his anticipation of a time when the gap between human and ape would be clearer "instead of as at present between the negro or Australian and the gorilla."[46]

In the late 1800s, new images of the Negro were added to the old. Since the antebellum period, minstrel show characters like Jim Crow had presented Negroes as incompetent, posturing buffoons unfit for equality with whites. However, the "Negro as beast" image "came to the surface in a new and spectacular way around the turn of the century."[47] Released from the civilizing and constraining shackles of slavery, the Negro was now a roaming, mortal threat to the white woman and the nation. The national craze over "coon" songs from 1890 to 1910 – which replaced unthreatening, buffoonish characters from the earlier period with hypersexual "razor-wielding savages"[48] – marked this shift. Lynchings of Black men, which peaked in the South during this period, were routinely characterized by participants and/ or the press as the proper punishment for Negro beasts who had dared to besmirch the purity of white women. All of this was memorialized in literature by Thomas Dixon, whose novels *The Leopard's Spots* (1902) and *The Clansman* (1905) gained great popularity by traducing in the "Negro as beast" image.[49]

In *"The Negro a Beast"...or..."In the Image of God"* (1900), Charles Carroll argues on the basis of Scripture and studies of comparative anatomy that the Negro is literally a beast. Winthrop Jordan may have been too sanguine in his conviction that Christianity protected the Negro from this type of degradation, or he may have underestimated the willingness of some commentators to reimagine Christianity as supportive of their anti-Black ideas. Carroll ridicules both the "athetistic theory of Natural Development" (Darwinism) and "Enlightened Christianity," which together teach that although there are five varieties or races of man, they are all part of a single human species. This is heresy, Carroll contends, because it tears down the barriers that God set up between man, whom He made in His image, and the ape, and brings man down to the level of the ape by saying that he descended from the latter. The Negro, Carroll insists, was formed separately from the white man, is not part of the Adamic family, and is an ape. The crucifixion of Jesus Christ was made necessary precisely because man forgot this fact about the Negro, for the Savior "came to destroy man's social, political and religious equality with the Negro

---

[46] Gould (1996), 69.
[47] Fredrickson (1971), 277.
[48] Dormon (1988), 455. Negroes were associated with raccoons, whom they were said to be fond of hunting and eating. The word "coon" was used as a racial epithet well into the civil rights era.
[49] In 1915, the latter was made into the film *Birth of a Nation*.

and mixed-bloods and the amalgamation to which these crimes inevitably lead, and to rebuild the barriers which God erected in the Creation between man and the ape" (269).

Carroll sets forth various contrasts – the "short, broad skull" of whites versus the "long, narrow skull" of Negroes; the "short, narrow jaw" of whites versus the "long, broad jaw" of Negroes; the "prominent chin" of whites versus the "retreating chin" of Negroes; the "long, slender neck" of whites versus the "short, thick neck" of Negroes; the "highly developed calves" of whites versus the "thin calves" of Negroes; the "short, narrow heel" of whites versus the "long, broad heel" of Negroes, and so forth (46–58) – and concludes: "All scientific investigation of the subject proves the Negro to be an ape; and that he simply stands at the head of the ape family. ... [T]he Negro is the only anthropoid, or man-like ape; and ... the gibbon, ourang, chimpanzee and gorilla are merely negro-like apes" (87). The costs of ignoring the Negro's ape nature are high, Carroll insists, and many catastrophic events (in addition to the crucifixion of Christ) can be traced to this root cause.

Three years later, Reverend W. S. Armistead published *The Negro Is a Man: A Reply to Professor Charles Carroll's Book* (1903). Armistead's indignation at Carroll's heterodox interpretation of the Bible is apparent in his frequent use of exclamation marks. Point by point, referring to Scripture, Armistead offers a refutation of Carroll's argument. The Negro, he writes, "is of Adamic offspring, Noachic origin, Hamitic descent, a blood relation of whites, reds, browns, yellows and copper colors – a human being, and therefore has a soul" (xv). That the Negro, like the white man, has dominion over animals and eats meat is further proof of his humanity (526). Not to be outdone by Carroll's mobilization of scientific data, Armistead has a chapter on each of the following topics: skin, hair, skeleton, muscles, digestive organs, thorax and heart, organs of voice and respiration, urinary organs, nervous system, organs of sense, organs of circulation, lymphatics and articulations, brain. His conclusion is that "from bone to skin, the Negro is a *fac simile* of the white man"(161). For the reader innocent enough to infer by the end of the 582-page volume that Armistead is a defender of the Negro – as opposed to being a defender of Christian orthodoxy – the concluding chapter provides a surprise twist. Here Armistead explicitly states his commitment to preventing social equality and intermingling between Negroes and whites, which would be bad for both groups and would violate God's design (why else would He separate them by continents?). In closing, Armistead denounces:

the practice of the Blacks in *assaulting* white females. A more *dangerous practice* could never have been *started by the Blacks*. ... For a strong man to meet an unprotected female in some lonely place, seize her person, choke her to insensibility and rape her person, and then, in most instance, murder her to prevent detection, argues a *beastliness*, a *cold-blooded, murderous heart*, a *depth of criminality* that *demonstrates fitness for equalization with beasts, rather than with human beings.* ... *Let the Blacks beware*!

As sure as there is a God in heaven, a *continuation* of such outrages on Southern females, is *digging the grave* of *their race*. To continue such practices is to *invite* and *make certain their extermination!*" (540–2)

Thus does the Reverend who sets out to argue that *The Negro Is a Man* reduce the Black man to a beast.

A couple of years after the Carroll-Armistead exchange, the Congolese man Ota Benga was exhibited in the Bronx Zoo in a cage with an orangutan. The sign above the cage read "THE AFRICAN PYGMY, 'OTA BENGA.' AGE, 23 YEARS / HEIGHT, 4 FEET 11 INCHES. WEIGHT, 103 POUNDS. / BROUGHT FROM THE KASAI RIVER, / CONGO FREE STATE, SOUTH CENTRAL AFRICA / BY DR. SAMUEL P. VERNER. / EXHIBITED EACH AFTERNOON DURING SEPTEMBER." *The New York Times* ran stories about Benga, asking "Is it a man or a monkey?"[50] In the same vein, filmmaker Martin Johnson planned a movie on "African Babies" in 1922 that would show "elephant babies, lion babies, zebra babies, giraffe babies, and Black babies," suggesting that "African human life had the status of wildlife in the Age of Mammals."[51]

Indeed, when African humans attempted to transcend nature and assert mastery over animals in the presence of whites, matters were promptly set straight. Donna Haraway (1989) recounts the story of the white scientist/hunter Carl Akeley going on an African safari in the early 1900s with his African servant, a Kikuyu known as Bill. Bill shot at an elephant he thought was charging Akeley, and Akeley, not realizing what had prompted the shooting, slapped Bill. Haraway notes: "The African could not be permitted to hunt independently with a gun in the presence of a white man ... Bill's well-meaning (and well-placed) shot was pollution, a usurpation of maturity."[52] It was no accident that in the period of African decolonization at mid-century, Western primatologists working in Africa were white and female – they had to be, Haraway argues: "People of color could not mediate the required touch with nature that could reassure 'man' within the myth and science system of National Geographic ... because they were still implicitly (if no longer officially) assigned to a lower rung on the chain of being, insufficiently differentiated from the nonhuman primates. ... Black people *were* the beast."[53]

THE INDIAN SAVAGE

If it was the Negro's lowliness that linked him to apes, it was the Indian's savagery that linked him to wild animals and the wilderness itself. Coming in above the Negro on ethnological scales, the Indian was not imagined, with a few exceptions, as the missing link between man and ape but rather as someone located in a space of antecedent time and ahistoricity, a primitive as incapable

[50] Baker (1998), 72.
[51] Haraway (1989), 45.
[52] Ibid., 53.
[53] Ibid., 153.

of cultural development as the wolves and trees he lived among.[54] At the start of contact, and at moments thereafter, whites discussed Indians as civilizable and assimilable as equals, perhaps through intermarriage and amalgamation – notions that were almost never expressed about Blacks. But the assimilation impulse toward Indians, when implemented, was done coercively, and it gave way over time to a much harsher posture.

Just as ideas about Blacks emerged in engagement with the institution of slavery, ideas about Indians emerged in engagement with the centuries-long white land grab initiated by English colonists in the 1600s. Rendering Indians wild beasts of the forests proved crucial first, to constructing an account of why English colonists and other Europeans had a right to appropriate the land, and second, to constructing an account of why they had a right to clear the Indians out, much as they killed wolves and cleared forests, in order to make way for civilization. When whites characterized Indians as savages and likened them to wild beasts, they were not simply using strong metaphors to express a sense of distance; nor were they strategically dehumanizing them to further their material agenda. They knew Indians were men but they thought them animal-like men, and being inclined to thinking in terms of continuity and gradation rather than dichotomy, they imagined them into the human-animal borderlands in ways that decisively shaped white-Indian relations into the twenty-first century.

By the time English colonists began to settle on the Eastern Seaboard, they knew that the Spanish had already resolved that the Indians of the New World were in fact human, but only barely. After Columbus named the natives "Indians" in a moment of geographical disorientation, his compatriots assessed all those they lumped together under this label and found them deficient from the standpoint of both Christianity and civilization. In 1550, the famous debate between Bartolomé de las Casas and Juan Ginés de Sepúlveda transpired, in which the former argued that the Indians were human and that the Spanish subjugation of them was unjust, and the latter argued that they were subhumans deserving Spanish domination. Through the 1500s, the English, who prided themselves on being less cruel than the Spanish, used "savage" and "Indians" interchangeably.[55] Travel narratives in the 1500s depicted the Indian as "a fierce, cannibalistic creature" and as "less than human – naked, violent, warlike, and frequently, more animalistic than human"; they warned travelers against being "seduced into savagery" by the "unrestrained sexuality and immorality" of the Indian.[56]

From the 1500s onward, we see the coexistence of "two fundamental but contradictory conceptions of Indian culture" – the good Indian who is friendly, hospitable, brave, handsome, dignified, and innocent; and the bad Indian who

---

[54] See McClintock (1995).
[55] Berkhofer (1979).
[56] Bataille (2001), 2.

is brutal, cruel, warring, lecherous, dirty, lazy, and thieving.[57] Encouraged by the Crown to Christianize and civilize the Indians, English colonists in Jamestown, judging from the written record, started with good intentions at the dawn of the seventeenth century. Unlike the merciless Spaniards, they would gently instruct the Indians how to behave in terms of food, clothing, arts, and skills and bring them into the community, whether by adopting Indian children into white families or building a college to civilize and convert Indian youth to Christianity.[58] For a while at least, these benevolent impulses coexisted with the tendency to see Indians as beasts who were occupying land to which they had no claim. So the Virginia Indians "live and lie up and downe in trouples like heards of Deare in a Forrest" and "have no particular proprietie in any part or parcell of that Country, but only a generl recidencie there, as wild beasts have in the forest."[59] Operating with the Roman legal concept of *res nullius* – "empty things" – the Virginia colonists believed that the land remained common property until its use led to specific rights of ownership.[60] The rub lay in what constituted proper and genuine use. Because Indians lived as "wild" animals on the soil, hunting and gathering, they had no claim to it. By tilling the land, growing crops, and establishing animal agriculture, the English developed a legitimate claim to the land. The fact that Virginia Indians did grow crops, particularly corn, which they sometimes offered to save the lives of starving colonists during particularly inclement winters, did not interfere with this dichotomous notion in the minds of the colonists between the "savage" life of the Indians and the "civilized" life of Englishmen.

At mid-century, the Virginia colonists came up with a scheme to use domestic beasts to reward beast-like men for subduing and killing wild beasts. Thus in 1656, the House of Burgesses, keen on protecting livestock from wolves, decided to give Indians one cow for every eight wolf heads they produced. This bounty was smaller than that which whites received for the same number of wolf heads: the Indian was invited to kill wolves but this move, a product of exigency, was not to be mistaken for an acknowledgment of full humanity. The idea behind the plan was that animal agriculture, and, specifically, individual property in livestock, would civilize Indians, turning them into industrious, God-fearing, peace-loving farmers. However, "the cows proved no more successful as missionaries than the few ministers who tried their hand at it."[61] Before long, as Virginia Anderson writes, "the expansion of livestock-based agriculture ceased being a model for Indian improvement and instead served almost exclusively as a pretext for conquest."[62] Colonists' livestock encroached on Indian land and invaded Indian cornfields, which prompted Indians to kill

[57] Berkhofer (1979), 28.
[58] Morgan (1975).
[59] Anderson (2006), 78–9.
[60] Ibid.
[61] Morgan (1975), 232.
[62] Anderson (2006), 7.

the animals, which prompted colonists to initiate hostilities in defense of their "property." Livestock became a major flashpoint for conflict between Indians and colonists in Virginia and New England, and the need for more grazing land became an important driver in territorial expansion and the seizing of Indian lands in both areas.

Powhatan's successor, Opechancanough, decided to try to eliminate the Virginia colony in one concerted assault in 1622, killing hundreds of colonists and launching an all-out war. This was a historical turning point, after which the victorious colonists segregated Indians within certain territorial boundaries and established a tributary relationship with them. Images of the Indian took a hard turn, too, as suggested by this poem written in the aftermath of the massacre:

> ...For, but consider what those Creatures are,
> (I cannot call them men) no Character
> of God in them: Soules drown'd in flesh and blood;
> Rooted in Evill, and oppos'd in Good;
> Errors of nature, of inhumane Birth...
> Sprung up like vermine of an earthy slime...
> What feare or pittie were it, or what sin...
> To quite their Slaughter, leaving not a Creature
> That may restore such shame of Men, and Nature.[63]

These were no longer the friendly natives whom the Crown directed colonists to bring into the fold; these were merciless, monstrous beasts beyond the pale of humanity. Laws in the colony increasingly reflected this shift in thinking. In 1670, the Virginia legislature had distinguished Indians from African slaves, categorizing the former as indentured servants, but in 1676, it determined that enemy Indians could be made slaves for life. Edmund Morgan argues that this move lumped Indians and Negroes together legally and clarified the racial foundation of slavery. Why did the English colonists not enslave Dutch captives of war? Morgan writes: "There was something different about the Indians. Whatever the particular nation or tribe or group they belonged to, they were not civil, not Christian, perhaps not quite human."[64]

Further north, during this same period, the Puritans of the Massachusetts Bay Colony showed a special inclination to associate Indians with wolves, who were invested with Satanic significance in their theology and posed an ever-present threat to livestock. A 1638 Massachusetts law held that "[W]hoever shall shoot off a gun on any unnecessary occasion, or at any game except an Indian or a wolf, shall forfeit 5 shillings for every shot."[65] Cotton Mather, in rousing soldiers to fight the Indians in 1689, exclaimed: "*Vengeance, Dear Countrymen! Vengeance upon our Murderers ... Beat* them small as the *Dust before the Wind*, and *Cast them out*, as the *Dirt in the Streets* ... those Ravenous howling

[63] Berkhofer (1979), 20–1.
[64] Morgan (1975), 233.
[65] Emel (1998), 102.

Wolves."[66] Similarly, when Reverend Solomon Stoddard recommended to the governor of Massachusetts in 1703 that dogs be used to track Indians, he justified this departure from Christian practice thus: "*If the Indians were as other people are* and did manage their warr fairly *after the manner of other nations,* it might be looked upon as inhumane to pursue them in such a manner. ... [But] they act like wolves and arc to be dealt withall as wolves."[67] Just as the Negro-ape association relied on a particular constructed notion of apeness (as hypersexual and violent), the Indian-wolf association, too, relied on a particular constructed notion of wolfness in the Puritan mind (as cruel, merciless, bloodthirsty, and evil).

During the 1700s, Enlightenment optimism about the unity and perfectibility of mankind warred with and eventually succumbed to the image of the Indian as an irredeemable savage standing in the way of the civilizing mission in the New World.[68] Many American commentators, influenced by Enlightenment thinking, were environmentalists in the sense that they believed that climate, diet, living conditions, and the state of organizational development shaped a people's physical bodies, cultural traits, and level of civilization. As such, "[M]any fully believed that Indians could progress rapidly through the three stages of society from savagism to barbarism to civilization – if the conditions under which they lived were changed."[69] Thomas Jefferson, in *Notes on the State of Virginia* (1781), characterized Indians as brave, manly, eloquent, and the physical equals of white men, expressing hope they would amalgamate with the white population.[70] He was not as generous to the Negro. In a letter to the Marquis de Chastellux in 1785, Jefferson wrote: "I am safe in affirming that the proofs of genius given by the Indians of N. America, place them on a level with whites in the same uncultivated state. ... I believe the Indian then to be in body and mind equal to the white man. I have supposed the Black man, in his present state, might not be so."[71]

Of course, Jefferson had a horse in this race, so to speak. Incensed by French naturalist Buffon's claims that the American environment was inferior to the European one and that it had produced smaller animals and a savage who is "feeble" and shows "no ardor whatever for his female," Jefferson was determined to demonstrate the Indian's worth as an index of the quality of the American environment.[72] At the same time, another luminary and Jefferson's contemporary, Hugh Henry Brackenridge, wrote about "the animals, vulgarly called Indians" in this striking passage:

---

[66] Axtell (1972), 348–89.
[67] Ibid., 343–4.
[68] Although the *philosophes* in Paris used the "noble savage" idea during this period to criticize the corruption and decadence of European society, this notion of the Indian did not become popular in the United States until the 1800s, when the Indian question had been largely resolved.
[69] Bieder (1986), 9.
[70] Jordan (1968), 480.
[71] Takaki (1990), 58.
[72] Jordan (1968), 480.

What use do these ring, streaked, spotted and speckled cattle make of the soil? Do they till it? Revelation said to man, "Thou shalt till the ground." This alone is human life. It is favorable to population, to science, to the information of a human mind in the worship of God. Warburton has well said, that before you can make an Indian a christian you must teach him agriculture and reduce him to a civilized life. To live by tilling is more human, by hunting is *more bestiarum.* I would as soon admit a right in the buffalo to grant lands, as in Killbuck, the Big Cat, the Big Dog, or any of the ragged wretches that are called chiefs and sachems. ... I am so far from thinking the Indians have a right to the soil, that not having made a better use of it for many hundred years, I conceive they have forfeited all pretence to claim, and ought to be driven from it.[73]

Brackenridge echoes the century-old notion that Indians are beasts who exist on the land rather than cultivators who through their labor develop a rightful claim to it. His angry contempt at the notion of Indian land rights indicates that this was still, to some extent, a live issue at the time of his writing. Within several decades, this issue would be settled once and for all, and not in favor of the Indians.

Enlightenment thinkers, viewing history as progressive, saw Indians as primitives, men in the state of nature who had not progressed toward civilization as Europeans had. What emerged in the early part of the nineteenth century was the conviction that Indians could *never* progress beyond their primitive state. Like the wild beasts of the forest, Indians were static and without history, in pointed contrast to dynamic, progressive whites. Ann McClintock writes of the colonial view of the native:

The colonial journey into the virgin interior reveals a contradiction, for the journey is figured as proceeding forward in geographical space but backward in historical time, to what is figured as a prehistoric zone of racial and gender difference. ... Since indigenous peoples are not supposed to be spatially there – for the lands are "empty" – they are symbolically displaced onto what I call *anachronistic space* ... [where] they do not inhabit history proper but exist in a permanently anterior time within the geographic space of the modern empire as anachronistic humans, atavistic, irrational, bereft of human agency – the living embodiment of the archaic "primitive."[74]

Once it was decided that Indians could not be induced to make progress toward civilization through conversion, education, or other environmental changes – that they were forever marooned in "anachronistic space" – their fate was sealed. Like the wolves in the forests and the buffalo on the plains, they had to give way in the face of advancing white civilization. In "Removal of the Indians" (1830), Lewis Cass, President Jackson's secretary of war, averred that Indians had not advanced despite two centuries of contact with whites: "Like the bear, and deer, and buffalo of his own forests, an Indian lives as his father lived, and dies as his father died. ... His life passes away in a succession of listless indolence, and of vigorous exertion to provide for his animal wants,

73 http://www.ankn.uaf.edu/curriculum/ANCSA/Claims/book2.html#THE%20ANIMALS,%20 VULGARLY%20CALLED%20INDIANS.
74 McClintock (1995), 30.

or to gratify his baleful passions … he is perhaps destined to disappear with the forests."[75] Clearing the land for white civilization reflected the unfolding of both God's will and nature's laws; it was necessary, moral, and inevitable.

One sees during the late 1700s and early 1800s how closely American nationalism and exceptionalism were tied to this idea of conquering the wilderness and establishing civilization. As Klaus Lubbers shows, Fourth of July orations during this period, delivered by local men of prominence, were rhapsodic paeans to the nation's greatness and singularity. In them, Indians were often tightly linked with animals of the wilderness as obstacles overcome in the journey of progress. In 1791, William Linn said in his oration:

Less than two centuries ago, what was this now pleasant country? A dismal wilderness; the habitation of wild beasts, and of savage men. Where now the populous city lifts its spires, the solitary wigwam stood; where commerce spreads it sails, was seen the bark canoe; and where the sound of industry is heard, and all the arts of civilized life flourish, indolence, rudeness, and ignorance, held a gloomy reign.[76]

Similarly, in 1800, Matthew Livingston Davis recalled "when these fair and extensive domains were rude and inhospitable wilds … when wild and ferocious animals divided the empire of this continent with human savages, still more barbarous and intractable than themselves." And in 1809, John Treat Irving spoke triumphantly of "the glad ray of knowledge [that] shall burst upon these dark recesses, where the wandering savage holds dominion, the mighty mammoth thunders thro' the forest, and the rattling serpent wreathes his folds among the herbage."[77]

The Indian Removal Act of 1830 forcibly moved most Indian tribes from the Eastern portion of the nation westward beyond the Mississippi River. Continued expansion westward on the part of whites necessitated a second phase of Indian removal farther west during the 1840s and 1850s and the establishment of reservation systems. As the "Indian question" found resolution in this way, and as Indian wars on the Great Plains began to subside, whites felt a surge of nostalgia and pity for the "dying Indian" (Berkhofer 1979), some of which was memorialized in literature such as James Fenimore Cooper's *The Last of the Mohicans* (1826) and George Caitlin's portraits of the "vanishing race" through the 1800s.

There was not much sentimentalization of the Indian in California, however, where Indian slavery was thriving in the mid-nineteenth century. California Indians were compared to simians and put up for consideration as the missing link between man and ape. (Recall that the Indian in the Reconstruction picture with Union Party gubernatorial candidate George Gorham is indeed the link between man and ape.) California Indians were seen as darker than their Eastern counterparts (as almost Black), and their diet, manner of eating,

---

[75] Takaki (1990), 83.
[76] Lubbers (1994), 32.
[77] Ibid., 30, 39.

dwellings, and behavior were all likened to animals, both domestic and wild. The epithet "Digger" conveyed an image of a filthy animal grubbing for roots. Decimated by disease and warfare between 1848 and 1870, the California Indians who survived were subjected to state legislation (1850) that authorized forced "apprenticeships," "vagrancy" statutes that permitted the practically unlimited coercion of labor, and outright kidnapping and sale as slaves for the Californio rancheros as well as small farmers and frontiersmen (Rawls 1984). The fact that Indians were sometimes paid in liquor and then arrested and forced to labor under "vagrancy" statutes forbidding intoxication lends a special irony to the depiction of the liquor-loving Indian in the Reconstruction picture.[78]

The biologization of race at mid-century and the monogenism/polygenism debate that arose then involved the Indian as much as it did the Negro. Based on his study of Indian crania, polygenist Samuel George Morton rejected environmentalism as an explanation for racial difference and concluded that Indians' small brains meant that they were biologically incapable of becoming civilized.[79] That Indians ranked higher in craniometric studies than Blacks – Morton offered a mean of ninety-two cubic inches for Caucasians, seventy-nine cubic inches for Americans (Indians), and seventy-five cubic inches for Hottentots and Australian Bushmen[80] – did them little practical good because they were likely to be lumped with Blacks even as they were being distinguished from them, as we see in Josiah Nott and George Gliddon's *Types of Mankind* (1855):

Lofty civilization, in all cases, has been achieved soley by the "Caucasian" group. Mongolian races, save in the Chinese family, in no instance have reached beyond the degree of semi-civilization; while the Black races of Africa and Oceanica no less than the *Barbarous* tribes of America have remained in utter darkness for thousands of years. ... Furthermore, Certain savage types can neither be civilized or domesticated. The *Barbarous* races of America (excluding the Toltecs) although nearly as low in intellect as in the Negro races, are essentially untameable. Not merely have all attempts to civilize them failed, but also every endeavor to enslave them. Our Indian tribes submit to extermination, rather than wear the yoke under which our Negro slaves fatten and multiply. ... The pure-blooded savage still skulks untamed through the forest, or gallops athwart the prairie.[81]

This statement concisely demonstrates how race both lumped and split non-white groups in reference to animality and nature. Whites, the Chinese, Indians, and Negroes are ranked according to their degrees of humanity/animality. Only the fully human whites reach the apex of civilization, and the Chinese come in second, while the Negro slaves merely "fatten and multiply" and the Indian savages "skulk" and "gallop" through the wilderness.

[78] Almaguer (1994).
[79] Bieder (1986), 73.
[80] Berkhofer (1979), 58.
[81] Ibid., 58–9.

Jody Emel notes that the Indians' fate was intertwined with and paralleled that of the wolf and buffalo during the 1800s. At one time, wolves lived in almost every part of North America, particularly in the forests and on the plains, but bounties were issued for wolf heads in the East starting in the mid-1600s. By the mid-1800s, a trade in wolf pelts had been established so that buffalo hunters picked off the wolves who came to eat the buffalo carcasses left after the hunters had taken only the hams, tongue, and skin. The buffalo were decimated between 1850 and 1880, with some 75 million killed, in large part because of the leather trade.[82] The result: "Native Americans and wolves, who had been dependent upon the buffalo herds, resorted to other means of survival ... [and] became semi-starved reservation dwellers or died fighting."[83] When General Philip Sheridan of the U.S. Army said, "Let them kill, skin, and sell until the buffalo is destroyed ... it is the only way to bring lasting peace and allow civilization to advance," he understood well that the viability of independent Indian tribes depended on the survival of the buffalo.[84] The slaughter of wolves on the plains peaked just after, from 1875 to 1895, as cattlemen hired wolfers to use every available means, including strychnine, to eliminate the wolf. An estimated one to two million wolves were slaughtered in the second half of the nineteenth century on the Great Plains by a coalition of government agencies, ranchers, and sportsmen. By 1925, the wolf ceased to be a major presence in the Southwest and a decade later, the wolf had been eliminated from the Great Plains and Montana and Wyoming.[85] Emel writes: "Reading the military journals of officers tracking the last small groups of free Comanches along the canyons of the Llano Estacado in West Texas is remarkably like reading the accounts of government hunters tracking the last remaining southwestern wolves."[86]

John Gast's 1872 painting, *American Progress* (Figure 2.3), suggests how inevitable and right all of this seemed to many white Americans. The painting depicts white westward expansion under the banner of Manifest Destiny. Columbia, as the personification of America, is a white goddess in classical robes with the star of empire on her forehead, carrying a schoolbook and a telegraph wire. Her expression is serene as she leads the white settlers, who advance on horseback, by wagon, by stagecoach, and by train. White farmers till the land with oxen and plough in the foreground, and ships are visible in the harbor to the east. Fleeing westward before Columbia are a number of wild animals and Indians, who look back in horror and fear. Golden light suffuses the sky from the east, gradually illuminating all but the westernmost region.

---

[82] Emel (1998).
[83] Ibid., 97.
[84] Moore (2001), 63.
[85] Emel (1998), 98–9.
[86] Ibid., 113. In recent times, forty-one Native American tribes have been working together to rebuild buffalo herds through the Intertribal Bison Cooperative, which Moore (2001) reads as an audacious rewriting of the national narrative regarding the elimination of Indians and buffalo.

FIGURE 2.3. American Progress. Courtesy of the Library of Congress.

All that is savage and wild retreats before the march of civilization, and this is necessary and good. The history of violence against racialized humans (Blacks, Indians, Mexicans, the Chinese) and nonhuman animals in westward expansion is elided. The driving agent of change is neither white desire nor white power but progress itself.[87]

THE CHINESE PESTILENTIAL MENACE

Virtually every comparative anatomist and ethnologist of note ranked the Chinese just below Europeans on a hierarchical scale of intelligence and civilization, clearly superior to Indians and especially Blacks. As such, there was no discernible talk of the Chinese constituting the missing link between man and ape and little discussion of their being actual beasts. Nevertheless, whites resisted seeing the Chinese as fully or truly human and thus located them in the human-animal borderlands, too. In the late 1800s, the practical problem, plainly stated, was that the Chinese were living in ever larger numbers in

---

[87] This idea was reprised, of course, in historian Frederick Jackson Turner's 1890 address, "The Significance of the Frontier in American History," wherein Turner portrays native peoples, according to Huhndorf, as "casualties of progress rather than of violence" (2001, 58).

places like San Francisco, where they competed with white working-class men for jobs. As economic conditions worsened in the 1870s, white Californians increasingly cast the Chinese as a degenerate race encroaching on and invading white spaces, posing a moral, medical, and economic threat to the nation. Menacing, swarming, pestilential animal images became stitched indelibly into the body of the Chinese. The only answer was to expel the pests from the body politic and keep them out.

When the Chinese first arrived in significant numbers in Gold Rush California, they were a racial wild card of sorts. The writings of diplomats, travelers, and others had long furnished Americans with images of China itself but there was uncertainty about where Chinese immigrants fit into the specific racial landscape of California in the mid-nineteenth century. On the one hand, naturalists and ethnologists had a rough consensus on the location of the Chinese in the hierarchy of human races. In the early 1860s, Pierre Gratiolet, arguing that higher mental functions were associated with the front of the brain, offered a schema dividing humans into *"races frontales"* (whites with anterior and frontal brain lobes most highly developed), *"races pariétales"* (Mongolians with parietal or mid lobes most developed), and *"races occipitales"* (Blacks with the back of the brain being most developed).[88] Paul Broca, an eminent craniometrist and founder of the Anthropological Society of Paris in 1859, was embroiled in a bitter debate with Gratiolet about the correlation between brain size and intelligence, but he concurred with his erstwhile opponent about the ranking of these three racial groups.

On the other hand, the Chinese were culturally fixed and thus permanently unassimilable. What marked the Chinese as different from whites was their ancient civilization, which was once glorious but had fatally degenerated, even as Anglo-Saxon culture was advancing, thrusting forward, dynamic, and energetic. Chinese culture was at once an index of relative superiority (to other nonwhite groups) and the eternal barrier to assimilation with whites. Whites placed the Chinese, too, into "anachronistic space": where Indians remained mired in static primitivism, the Chinese had progressed, but then peaked and degenerated. As much as Indians, then, they were impervious to further progress. Thus Charles Wolcott Brooks, former U.S. consul to Japan, testified to the Joint Congressional Committee Hearings on Chinese Immigration in 1879 that "The Chinese are non-assimilative because their form of civilization has crystallized."[89] To be impervious to history and progress was to be incompletely human, animal-like. An 1874 drawing in *Thistleton's Jolly Giant* shows a progression of images in which a monkey evolves into John Chinaman, who then degenerates into a pig. The commentary gives props to Darwin, describes the processes of evolution

[88] Gould (1996), 129.
[89] Spoehr (1973), 198–9.

and degeneration captured in the picture, and concludes with, "Any further comment would be useless."

Where whites encountered nonwhite peoples seems to have shaped, at least in part, *how* they viewed them, whether it was the English coming across Africans in a land overrun with apes and other wildlife, colonists encountering Indians in the forests of Virginia, or white Californians beholding the strange denizens of San Francisco's Chinatown (Anderson 1987). Although Chinatown was produced by white exclusionary practices – residential segregation, immigration restrictions, discriminatory labor legislation – it was taken to be all that was essentially Chinese. Thus the overcrowding, poverty, lack of health care, female prostitution – all of these were proof, in the minds of whites, of immutable Chinese traits such as clannishness, degeneracy, lustfulness, and filthiness. The rankings that preoccupied ethnologists (and privileged the Chinese, relatively speaking) did little to mitigate whites' impressions of the Chinese in Chinatown as alien, decaying, repulsive bodies who threatened whites' bodies, health, labor, and way of life. Degeneracy attached not only to Chinese bodies but to Chinatown itself. Nayan Shah notes the contrapuntal images of "decaying, regressive Chinatown" and "growing, progressive San Francisco," and notes that the former was thought to be "impervious to progress" and "unaffected by the forces of modernity."[90]

Chinese immigrants living in Chinatown were, in the eyes of whites, more like domesticated animals or vermin than human beings. The newspaper *The Daily Alta* described Chinese living quarters as "dirty, filthy dens" where the Chinese "piled together like pigs in a pen."[91] Reports from a series of government-sponsored investigations of Chinatown between 1854 and 1885 also read Chinese bodies as filthy, less than human, and animal-like. One municipal report from 1869–70, for example, described them thus:

> The portion of the city occupied by the Chinese is situated between Kearny and Stockton, and California and Jackson streets, within which district Chinese life in all its phases (which in general is but little better than that of the brute creation) may be seen. As a class, their mode of life is the most abject in which it is possible for human beings to exist. The great majority of them live crowded together in ricketty, filthy and dilapidated tenement houses, like so many cattle or hogs.[92]

Echoing this theme, an 1880 Board of Health report on Chinatown described Chinese men and women "huddled together in beastly promiscuousness," and an 1885 municipal report concluded that the "mode of life among the Chinese here are not much above 'those of the rats on the waterfront.'"[93] By the time the Chinese were characterized as "satisfied with the bare necessities of their

[90] Shah (2001), 43.
[91] Ibid., 21.
[92] "Municipal Reports of San Francisco 1869–1870."
[93] Shah (2001), 35, 42.

brute-like lives" during a conference on Chinese exclusion in 1901, the Chinese had been imaginatively located in the human-animal borderlands for decades.[94] Although the Chinese were a decaying race who could not vanquish the mighty Anglo-Saxons head on, there was always the possibility that Chinese degeneracy could insidiously undermine white civilization from below. This sense of threat registered on numerous levels. There was, to begin with, acute concern about dirt and disease. As Nayan Shah (2001) argues, San Francisco health officials and politicians routinely referred to Chinatown as a "plague spot" and a "cesspool" and blamed Chinese immigrants' supposedly filthy and degraded lifestyle for outbreaks of syphilis, smallpox, and bubonic plague.[95] *Chinatown Declared a Nuisance!*, an 1880 pamphlet produced by the Workingmen's Committee of California, opined about "this laboratory of infection – situated in the very heart of our city, distilling its deadly poison by day and by night and sending it forth to contaminate the atmosphere of the streets and houses of a populous, wealthy and intelligent community." That the Chinese "should so pertinaciously and willfully disregard our sanitary laws … so maliciously pursue that course of conduct which they know is bringing distress upon our city, by destroying the lives of our citizens … can only be accounted for on the supposition that they are enemies of our race and people."[96] The Chinese threat was frequently sexualized as well, just as with Negroes and Indians. Nefarious Chinamen luring virtuous whites into opium dens, Chinese houseboys molesting little white girls, Chinese prostitutes infecting white boys with syphilis – these imaginings made the sense of a Chinese menace at once more acute and more titillating.[97] Chinatown was, simply told, a hidden alien space where inscrutable Asiatics engaged in the unspeakable. Efforts to move Chinatown from the heart of the city to the outskirts, although unsuccessful, were continuous during this period, reflecting the fear that the Chinese threat would cross over the boundaries of Chinatown into white San Francisco.

And then there was the threat to white labor. Alexander Saxton (1975) shows that the construction of white working-class identity and solidarity in this period of California history depended heavily on the cultivation of anti-Chinese feeling. In every area of work (railroads, mines, factories, fields), the "coolie" was seen as degraded labor like the slave and as a threat to the very promise of America for the white working class – namely, economic mobility.[98] That white employers used a dual wage labor system to divide white and

[94] *Proceedings and List of Delegates, California Chinese Exclusion Convention* (1901), 58.
[95] Shah (2001), 1–2.
[96] *Chinatown Declared a Nuisance!* (1880), 5–6.
[97] Shah (2001), 79, 89.
[98] There were Chinese coolies (servants indentured for life who were often auctioned off like slaves) in the Caribbean and elsewhere, but Chinese immigrants in the United States were not coolies. Typically, they labored for a certain number of years in order to pay back money for their passage from China. After repaying their passage, they were free labor.

Chinese workers and sometimes brought the Chinese in as scabs when white workers went on strike only deepened the sense that "coolie" labor was incompatible with a free labor. In this context, Union Party gubernatorial candidate George Gorham's defense of Chinese labor was both brave and politically suicidal. An 1882 drawing from *The Wasp* periodical, "What Shall We Do With Our Boys?" forcefully expresses white labor's fear and loathing toward the Chinese.[99] On the left, a Chinese man is shown as a crazed octopus-like creature with multiple arms, each one working at an inhuman speed to monopolize a distinct trade such as laundry work, shoe manufacturing, cigar production, and so forth. On the right, a group of white young men stand idle from lack of employment; jails are visible in the distance. It was the subhumanity of the "coolie," readily depicted as animality, which enabled him to undercut the proud Anglo-Saxon worker and threaten the American way of life.

What the Chinese did and did not eat became an index of their humanity/animality as well. In *MEAT vs. RICE: American Manhood against Asiatic Coolieism, WHICH SHALL SURVIVE?* (1908), Samuel Gompers and Herman Gutstadt of the American Federation of Labor assert: "[Y]ou cannot work a man who must have beef and bread alongside a man who can live on rice. In all such conflicts, and in all such struggles, the result is not to bring up the man who lives on rice to the beef-and-bread standard, but it is to bring down the beef-and-bread man to the rice standard."[100] Whiteness, masculinity, nationalism, and human supremacy are all interwoven here: eating animals makes one not just a man but a full human being. As rice eaters, the Chinese were questionable on both counts.[101] The authors of the pamphlet also criticize the Chinese for their "gratification of the animal proclivities" and "animal passions" (17–18), and for "living literally the life of vermin" (16).

As J. A. G. Roberts notes, the Western tradition of expressing disgust at Chinese eating habits dates back at least to Marco Polo's *Travels* in the late thirteenth century, wherein the adventurer notes: "They [the Chinese] eat all sorts of flesh, including that of dogs and other brute beasts and animals of every kind which Christians would not touch for anything in the world."[102] As early as 1855, just six years after the Gold Rush began, minstrel show singers in California regularly performed "John Chinaman," which featured this verse about the Chinese diet: "I thought of rats and puppies, John / You'd eaten

[99] http://content.cdlib.org/ark:/13030/hb938nb337/?query=the%20wasp&brand=calisphere.
[100] Cited in Shah (2001), 167.
[101] In the Irish musical play *Mulligan's Silver Wedding* (1881), washerwoman Honora Dublin complains about Hog Eye, the Chinese laundryman who competes with her business, by questioning his manhood and humanity at once: "You're not half a man. You're a nagur, you eat your dinner with drumsticks. You're a monkey, you have a tail growing out of your head. ... You're a mongrel Asiatic. ... Why don't you have whiskers on your face like a man you baboon you ... walking around in your petticoats and calling yourself a man." Cited in Moon (2004), 53.
[102] Roberts (2002), 28.

your last fill; / But on such slimy pot-pies, John / I'm told you dinner still."[103] In the 1850s, the *Alta California* newspaper ridiculed the "no ways partickler Celestial" for his addiction to rats and lizards and his general willingness to eat anything.[104] Various performers lampooned the Chinese for eating dogs, cats, rats, and mice in the following years. In 1873, Jason Johnson of Hooley's Minstrels sang a version of "The Heathen Chinee" which contained these verses:

> Lady she am vellie good, makie plenty chow chow,
> She live way up top side house
> Take a little pussey cat and a little bow-wow.
> Boil em in a pot, slew wit a little mouse.
>
> Some say pig meat makie goodie chow chow
> No muchie largie too muchie small,
> Up sky, down sky, down come chow chow
> Down come a pussy cat, Bow wow and all.[105]

Only cruel, transgressive people eat pussy cats and puppy dogs. An 1870s trade card for a rat poison called "Rough on Rats" shows John Chinaman about to drop a rat into his open mouth.[106] The caption "They must go" echoes the Workingmen's Party slogan, "The Chinese Must Go!" There is deliberate ambiguity here – who is it who must go? The Chinese, as supposed rat eaters, are "rough on rats" but they are also like rats and deserving of the same end. Both are pestilential vermin to be dispatched without mercy.

The Wasp, a late nineteenth-century San Francisco weekly known for its pungent political commentary and satire, produced unforgettable images of the Chinese in the human-animal borderlands.[107] Although the *Wasp* cartoonists caricatured most everyone, "the Chinese bore the brunt of *The Wasp*'s venom."[108] They were depicted as almost every kind of animal – frogs, camels, horses, elephants, vipers, vermin, tigers, among others. But two of the most salient types of images were of the Chinese as swarming and pestilential beasts or insects, and the Chinese as dragon-like monsters. Both types of creatures are of no use to humans; both are unmitigated threats that must be exterminated. The theme of these cartoons taken together is quite clear: The Chinese, heedless and transgressive, pose a mortal threat to the American nation, and if Americans stand idly by, the Chinese will supplant American civilization with their own.

---

[103] http://www.columbia.edu/itc/history/baker/w3630/edit/chinpoem.html.
[104] Roberts (2002), 136.
[105] Moon (2004), 47–8.
[106] http://www.flickr.com/photos/meaghancourtney/2380779257/.
[107] All of *The Wasp* images discussed here (except "The Question of the Hour") are accessible online through the Bancroft Library's Web site. http://bancroft.berkeley.edu.
[108] Brechin (n.d.).

FIGURE 2.4. "Uncle Sam's Farm in Danger". Courtesy of The Bancroft Library, University of California, Berkeley.

In "Who Will Make The Chinese Go?" (1879), Uncle Sam stands (holding a gun labeled "Congress") with apparent unconcern as crows swarm over a scarecrow wearing tattered U.S. military dress.[109] The crows have Chinese faces and queues sticking straight up out of the tops of their heads. There are many more of them on their way, darkening the sky. In "Uncle Sam's Farm in Danger" (1877–8) (Figure 2.4), an apparently infinite number of grasshoppers with Chinese faces and queues swarm on Uncle Sam's farm as he and another white man try to beat them back. A shadowy Chinese pagoda can be seen in the left rear where the grasshoppers originated; the sun is setting on a Western capitol-type building in the right rear; and a Satanic figure labeled "Famine" hovers behind the Chinese insects. The caption reads: "Seventy Millions of People Are Starving in the Northern Provinces of China. All Who Can Do So are Making Preparations to Come to the United States. Look Out for the Grasshoppers, Uncle Sam!"

Finally, "Devastation" (1880) shows countless wild boars with queues crashing through a gate labeled "Burlingame Treaty" and laying waste to a cornfield.[110] The ears of trampled corn bear the names of different industries, and the pole holding up the scarecrow says "The Chinese Must Go." Uncle Sam stands in the

---

[109] http://content.cdlib.org/ark:/13030/hb8c6005vx/?query=who%20will%20make%20the%20chinese%20go&brand=calisphere.

[110] http://content.cdlib.org/ark:/13030/hb2779n51w/?query=devastation&brand=calisphere.

FIGURE 2.5. "Immigration East and West". Courtesy of The Bancroft Library, University of California, Berkeley.

farmyard and Eureka, the classical personification of California, leans out of the farmhouse window; both look on in horror. Again, the Chinese pagoda on top of the gate on the left contrasts with the American farmhouse on the right.

In the cartoons that feature the Chinese as monsters, civilizational struggle and the transgressiveness of the Chinese are once again the central themes. "Immigration East and West" (1881) (Figure 2.5) is a splitscreen drawing with the caption "Westward, the course of empire takes its way. Eastward, the march of national decay." In the left half of the cartoon, New York asks Eureka to take her immigrants, who are disembarking from ships and heading westward carrying shovels, hoes, and signs saying "labor," "industry," "capital," and "agriculture." In the right half, Eureka is menaced by a serpent-like monster who is labeled "Chinese immigration," has a caricatured Chinese visage, and wears a queue that extends outward to spell "Asia."

In "The Rescue," (1882), the Greek hero Perseus symbolizing the Board of Health saves the chained maiden San Francisco from a three-headed hydra monster labeled "smallpox."[111] The hydra heads have Chinese faces and queues. White supremacy, male supremacy, and human supremacy come together with explosive force in this image. Similarly, in "Our Foreign Relations" (1883), the classical female figure of San Francisco is attacked by a Chinaman/vampire bat labeled "leprosy," while other figures labeled "opium" and "smallpox" menace her.[112]

---

[111] http://content.cdlib.org/ark:/13030/hb78700564/?query=the%20rescue&brand=calisphere.

[112] http://content.cdlib.org/ark:/13030/hb2n39n5b5/?query=our%20foreign%20relations&brand=calisphere.

Perhaps the most memorable image is "The Question of the Hour" (1893).[113]
Here Uncle Sam stands over an enormous and peculiar creature who is tied to
a post and ponders, "Gosh I've got this critter lassoed right enough but how in
thunder am I going to get him over thar to China?" The creature has Chinese
features, Black skin, and a dragon's tail and wings; it is part beast, part human.
Lying on its stomach with its chin cupped in its hands, it smiles broadly at Uncle
Sam's consternation. What is to be done with this repulsive beast? Any further
comment would be useless.

As a taxonomy of power, race has been elaborated in the United States in intimate connection with species and nature. From the 1600s to the 1800s, Blacks,
Indians, and the Chinese in the United States were imaginatively located in
a human-animal borderlands where they were at once lumped together and
painstakingly differentiated, depending on the exigencies of the situation.
Remarkably, the racial stories crafted during these centuries – that Blacks are
bestial, Indians part of nature, the Chinese cruel and transgressive like animals and with animals – continue to structure the American cultural imaginary today. They play a key role in the impassioned disputes examined in the
remainder of this book.

---

[113] http://homepages.uwp.edu/martinmo/Summer2007/HUM103/raceimage4.htm.

PART II

THE BATTLE OVER LIVE ANIMAL MARKETS
IN SAN FRANCISCO'S CHINATOWN

3

The Optic of Cruelty

Challenging Chinatown's Live Animal Markets

> The issue is not culture but a degrading human tradition, from Ming Lee to KFC, that ... needs to be changed.
>
> – United Poultry Concerns

Animal advocates in San Francisco have challenged the way Chinatown's live animal vendors keep and kill animals, arguing that cruelty is something "you know when you see it." Positing the prohibition against cruelty as a universal value and appealing to a least common denominator of public belief are strategies that date back at least to the American Society for the Prevention of Cruelty to Animals in the 1830s, the first organized animal advocacy group to emerge in the United States. What becomes clear in the course of struggle in San Francisco is the difficulty of reaching a legally and politically actionable consensus on what constitutes cruelty toward animals, in large part because there is little formal institutional acknowledgment of the notion that animals are morally considerable at all. The argument from the universal, in any case, promptly triggered a counterargument from the particular, as Chinese American business advocates and community leaders claimed that they were being targeted because they are racially different. The optic of cruelty foregrounds animal suffering and backgrounds questions of racism, and the optic of racism (discussed in the next chapter) does the reverse.[1]

In this chapter, I begin with a brief discussion of what Americans make of animals, animal usage, and animal activists at the turn of the millennium. I then turn to the Chinatown live animal market campaign and trace its development from approximately 1995 to 2006, paying particular attention to how the optic of cruelty was articulated and deployed and to what effect. By looking closely at the origins of the campaign, we can evaluate the charge made by many Chinese American activists that the campaign was racially motivated. The

---

[1] Throughout this book, single-spaced quotes are excerpts from personal interviews conducted by the author.

overall narrative of the campaign also speaks to the complications involved in advocating for "lesser" animals like birds, fish, turtles, and frogs; the dynamics of cooperation and conflict among animal advocacy groups; and the challenges of negotiating the institutional terrain of San Francisco politics. Unlikely and hard-fought victories are won again and again by animal advocates in different venues, but a confluence of political and institutional factors ensures that little changes in the actual lives of animals as a result.

AMBIVALENT ANTHROPOCENTRISM (AND THE SUSPECT ANIMAL ACTIVIST)

As a nation, we are not quite sure what we think about animals. The belief that humans and animals are discontinuous and hierarchically ranked orders of beings remains strong, not only because of the philosophical and religious traditions discussed in the previous chapter but also because of the energetic ideological, political, and legal labor of industries heavily vested in this belief. Humans are, the story goes, rational, intelligent, morally autonomous, self-aware beings with advanced cognitive and emotional capacities, the ability to communicate through language, and complex social relations. Animals operate from instinct, have limited intelligence and no self-consciousness, show only lower-order cognitive and emotional capacities, and do not communicate through language. But if many of us accept some version of this story, we are not Cartesians: most of us believe that the dog crying out during dissection is not a machine but a feeling being. And as long as we are not Cartesians, there is a nagging possibility that nonhuman animals might in fact deserve some, perhaps a good deal of, moral consideration.

In the United States over the past several decades, there has been, simultaneously and contradictorily, an intensification in the instrumental usage of animals, driven by consumer demand and enabled by technological innovation, *and* a widening and deepening discussion over whether animals have the intrinsic right to be protected from such usage. "Animal capital" (Shukin 2009) is more salient than ever in the U.S. economy: scientists are genetically engineering "biopharm" animals to produce specific substances like human insulin; "xenotransplant" animals to be harvested for cells, tissues, and organs for transplantation into humans; "food" animals like fast-growing salmon, pigs whose meat contains omega-3 fatty acids, and the "Enviropig" whose manure contains less phosphorus (Adams 2009). In its ruthless single-mindedness, the neoliberal instrumentalization of animal bodies has reached the level of science fiction.

But there is little doubt that affective interest in the capacities and moral standing of animals is growing as well, judging from the expanding genre of blockbuster animal escape movies (*Chicken Run, Babe, Babe 2, Madagascar 1, Madagascar 2, Madagascar 3, Madagascar 4, Free Willy, Free Willy 2, Free Willy 3*), the explosion of stories about institutionalized animal exploitation in mainstream newspapers over the past several years, the success of a number of prominent animal welfare campaigns, and the dramatic increase in academic and legal attention to animal issues. If we have always been "anxious" anthropocentrists (Fudge 2000), we have now become ambivalent ones as well, worrying quite openly about whether we should be treating animals as we do. The recent decision by the National Institutes of Health, the primary funder of scientific research in the United States, to move decisively away from the use of chimpanzees in scientific research is a watershed moment in the struggle against vivisection. Yet NIH Director Francis Collins's words – "Chimpanzees are very special animals. We believe they deserve special consideration as special creatures" (Brumfield 2013) – are as important for what they do not say as for what they say. Chimpanzees are uniquely deserving of exemption from scientific usage, but other species (namely rats and mice, who make up more than 90 percent of laboratory animals) are not. In the taxonomy of species, humans are at the top, and chimpanzees and other Great Apes (bonobos, orangutans, gorillas) are positioned fairly close to them, along with a few other favored animals such as whales, dolphins, elephants, and dogs. But almost all other species are seen as much less "special."[2]

The paradox of intensifying usage and growing ambivalence can be seen clearly with factory farming. In the past few decades, industrial concentration in the U.S. meatpacking, poultry processing, and dairy industries has created an "intensely consolidated landscape" where a "few giant agribusinesses" exercise unprecedented power over independent producers.[3] The result has been a dramatic increase in both the size of farming facilities and the concentration of animals therein as producers struggle to maintain or increase their profit margin in this context. According to Food & Water Watch's report *Factory Farm Nation* (2010), a dramatic shift occurred between 1997 and 2007 in U.S. food production, with large-scale operations in a few areas replacing dispersed small and medium-sized farms. This is confirmed by a General Accounting Office study showing that the number of large livestock operations in the United States tripled from 3,600 to 12,000 between 1982 and 2002.[4] As of 2008, the four largest firms controlled 83 percent of beef packing, 66 percent of pork packing, 58 percent of poultry processing, and 43 percent of fluid milk processing.[5] Using USDA Census of Agriculture data from 1997, 2002, and 2007, *Factory Farm Nation* shows that the total number of livestock on the largest farms rose by more than 20 percent between 2002 and 2007 – with a 93 percent increase in dairy cows from 1997 to 2007, a 17.1 percent increase in beef cattle, a 36.3 percent increase in hogs, an 87.4 percent increase in broiler chickens, and a 23.6 percent increase in egg-laying hens.[6]

---

[2] See Donaldson and Kymlicka (2011) for a philosophical argument for making distinctions among animal species in terms of how close they are to us and what our obligations to them are.
[3] Food & Water Watch, *Factory Farm Nation*, 6.
[4] "United States Facts."
[5] Food & Water Watch, *Factory Farm Nation*, 24.
[6] Ibid., 5.

Concentration and growth have vaulted animal production to historic levels: roughly 10 billion land animals are killed for food every year in the United States alone. Supported by federal policies that reduce the two main costs of livestock production (purchasing feed and managing manure), and by various technological advances (artificial insemination, the use of hormones and antibiotics, improvements in slaughterhouse assembly lines), agribusinesses profit while independent farmers struggle and everyone else loses out.[7] Consumers get relatively inexpensive meat, dairy, and eggs, but the externalized costs of raising animals for food this way are staggering: animals suffer from intensive confinement; rural communities suffer adverse health effects related to the pollution of the water, soil, and air; workers suffer from pollution-related conditions and injuries; the public suffers from increased antibiotic resistance and foodborne illnesses like *e. coli* and salmonella; and the environment suffers from pollution, topsoil erosion, and the release of greenhouse gases such as methane.

The plight of the egg-laying hen is emblematic of animal suffering under this regime. The chicken coop of the family farm has been replaced by the battery cage, a wire cage approximately the size of a file cabinet drawer. Battery cages are stacked one on top of the other, several cages high, and crammed into industrial sheds large enough to hold up to 100,000 birds each. Hatched in an incubator, each hen is placed into a battery cage along with several other birds for the duration of her adult life. The overcrowding in battery cages is extreme. Each hen has approximately a single piece of paper's (8" x 11") worth of space in which to exist. Hens are "debeaked," a painful procedure in which the front of the beak is cut off without anesthetic, to prevent them from pecking at each other in these conditions of stressful confinement. Some birds perish because they cannot reach food or water on the other side of the cage. None of the birds can engage in preferred behaviors such as scratching in the dirt and dust-bathing; indeed, none has the room to stretch her wings. Some farmers practice "forced molting," which involves depriving hens of food for extended periods in order to shock them into producing more eggs. Through genetic manipulation, hens are made to lay significantly more eggs than they would naturally, which leads to severe osteoporosis as their bodies use available calcium to make more eggs. After a year or so, the hen's productivity declines and she is sent to slaughter, her body sufficiently damaged that she can only be used for potpies or pet food. (The natural lifespan of a hen is approximately ten years.) The hen is not a grievable life. She is not just vulnerable to premature death but certain to meet it, although it is not culturally legible to talk about her death as premature. She has the ontological status of an instrument in the profit-making venture of industrial farming.

But with the intensification of mastery has come the intensification of doubt. As major animal advocacy groups like the Humane Society of the United States (HSUS) and People for the Ethical Treatment of Animals (PETA) turn their

---

[7] Ibid.

attention to factory farming, there are intimations of a shift in public attitudes. Books like Eric Schlosser's *Fast Food Nation* (2002) and Jonathan Foer's *Eating Animals* (2009), as well as movies like *Earthlings* (2005) and *Food, Inc.* (2008), have made Americans more aware of what goes on inside of industrial farms and slaughterhouses. Grocery chains and restaurants increasingly offer organic, cage-free, free-range, or grass-fed animal products to the environmentally conscious and/or cruelty-conscious consumer.[8] The HSUS has developed a highly successful strategy of bypassing state legislatures – where food industry lobbyists exercise significant clout – and taking the issue of farm animal welfare straight to the people in the form of ballot initiatives. And the people have responded. In 2002, Florida was the first state to outlaw the use of gestation crates to confine sows. In 2006, Arizona banned both gestation crates and veal crates. In the next few years, Oregon banned gestation crates and Colorado banned both gestation and veal crates through legislative action.[9] In 2008, Californians passed Proposition 2, which alleviates overcrowding for egg-laying hens, sows, and veal calves.

All of this indicates that many Americans think that even lowly "food" animals, who occupy a much lower taxonomic status than "pets" or "charismatic mega-fauna," deserve some consideration. A recent poll by Oklahoma State University and the American Farm Bureau Federation found that 75 percent of the public favors government mandates for basic animal welfare measures.[10] Another survey of Ohioans showed that 92 percent agreed or strongly agreed that it is important for farm animals to be well cared for, 85 percent agreed or strongly agreed that the quality of life for farm animals is important even when they are used for meat, 81 percent agreed or strongly agreed that the well-being of farm animals is just as important as that of pets, and 75 percent agreed or strongly agreed that farm animals should be protected from feeling physical pain.[11] The food industry knows what is at stake if this shift in public thinking goes too far. In addition to launching commercial campaigns intended to salve the public's conscience – such as the California cheese producers' advertising campaign, "Happy Cows come from California" – agribusinesses have fought hard to pass "food libel" laws at the state level (making it easier for food producers to sue animal activists) and "ag gag" laws at the state and federal levels intended to hamper animal activism such as undercover investigations of farming and slaughterhouse facilities.[12]

---

[8] Sales of organic meat and poultry grew from $33 million in 2002 to an estimated $121 million in 2004 in the United States (Holcomb et al., n.d.).

[9] Humane Society of the United States, *Factory Farming in America*, 30.

[10] *Putting Meat on the Table*, 31.

[11] Rauch and Sharp (2005).

[12] "Food-Disparagement Laws." When Oprah Winfrey said that guest Howard Lyman's remarks on feeding rendered cow remains to other cows "stopped [her] cold from eating another hamburger" in April 1996, Texas beef producers sued Winfrey and Lyman under the state's food libel law, which criminalizes criticisms of food production. The lawsuit, *Texas Cattlemen v. Howard Lyman and Oprah Winfrey*, did not succeed. http://www.madcowboy.com/01_BookOP.000.html.

The recent formation of a Pew Commission on Industrial Farm Animal Production signals the mainstreaming of concerns about modern industrial farming. The Commission, composed of fifteen experts in animal agriculture, public health, animal health, medicine, ethics, public policy, and rural sociology, conducted public hearings, collected technical information, and visited facilities. It then issued the report *Putting Meat on the Table: Industrial Farm Animal Production in America* (2008), which plainly states: "The present system of producing food animals in the United States is not sustainable and presents an unacceptable level of risk to public health and damage to the environment, as well as unnecessary harm to the animals we raise for food" (viii). Significantly, the report discusses the powerful economic interests who strive to keep the public in the dark about animal farming. It notes the obstructionism the Commission encountered – "while some industrial agriculture representatives were recommending potential authors for the technical reports to Commission staff, other industrial agriculture representatives were discouraging those same authors from assisting us by threatening to withhold research funding for their college or university" (viii) – and, in a self-conscious echo of Eisenhower's warning about the military-industrial complex, identifies and warns against "the agro-industrial complex – an alliance of agriculture commodity groups, scientists at academic institutions who are paid by the industry, and their friends on Capitol Hill" (viii).

Public discussion about the moral considerability of animals is not only widening but deepening. Where advocates in the early twentieth century aimed to reduce cruelty and alleviate animal suffering, the modern animal liberation movement that began in the 1970s introduced the argument that nonhuman animals should be emancipated from all forms of domination and exploitation. The U.S. animal movement today, a complex amalgam of these welfarist and abolitionist arguments, is being energized by myriad factors – genetic studies showing humans share 98.7 percent of their DNA with chimpanzees; ethological studies showing the tremendous cognitive, emotional, and moral capacities of nonhuman animals (Savage Rumbaugh 1996; Fouts 1998; Moss 2000); legal and philosophical arguments urging justice toward animals (Wise 2003; Nussbaum 2007; Francione 2009; Donaldson and Kymlicka 2011); and investigative journalism shedding light on concealed farming and slaughtering practices (Eisnitz 2007). There has been an explosion of scholarly interest in human-animal studies in the past decade, reflected in the emergence of new think tanks, journals, anthologies, book series, conferences, and list serves. Harvard and Georgetown law schools offered the first classes in animal law in 1999; as of 2011, 121 U.S. law schools, including the top ten, offered them.

A May 2003 Gallup Poll shows that 96 percent of Americans think that animals deserve some protection from harm and exploitation, with a full 25 percent saying they deserve "the exact same rights as people to be free from harm and exploitation," and only 3 percent saying they do not require much protection "since they are just animals." A significant majority (62 percent) support strict laws on the treatment of farm animals. At the same time, large majorities reject bans on medical research, product testing, and hunting.[13] However, more recent polling by the Pew Research Center suggests that even views on medical research – that last outpost of valorized animal usage – may be moving. Fifty-nine percent of respondents in 2010 said they thought medical testing on animals was morally acceptable (34 percent said it was morally wrong), whereas the numbers in the same poll taken nine years earlier were 65 percent/26 percent.[14] Moreover, a 2009 poll showed that 39 percent of 18–29-year-olds favored animal research and 58 percent opposed it, while 61 percent of those 65 and older supported it and 33 percent of this group opposed it.[15] Attitudes on animals are shifting.

Views of animal activists, on the other hand, seem to have hardened. In contemporary U.S. public discourse, animal activists are routinely condemned as rabid, overzealous, unbalanced, irrational, absurd, and morally out of joint (Girgen 2008). Indeed, they have gone from being ridiculed as misanthropists to being prosecuted as terrorists. As Will Potter recounts in *Green Is the New Red: An Insider's Account of a Social Movement Under Siege* (2011), a fire set by the Animal Liberation Front (ALF) at a UC Davis veterinary diagnostic lab in April 1987 marked a turning point after which the federal government began labeling animal and environmental activism as "terrorism" – indeed the FBI described it as the "number one domestic terrorism threat." For their part, animal industry groups hired public relations firms to generate campaigns whose explicit aim was to "insert eco-terrorism into the national security dialogue."[16] In 1992, responding to animal industry lobbying, Congress passed the Animal Enterprise Protection Act (AEPA), which created the term "animal enterprise terrorism" and applied it to anyone who a) "travels in interstate or foreign commerce, or uses or causes to be used the mail or any facility in interstate or foreign commerce, for the purpose of causing physical disruption to the functioning of an animal enterprise" or b) "intentionally causes physical disruption to the functioning of an animal enterprise by intentionally stealing, damaging, or causing the loss of, any property (including animals or records) used by the animal enterprise."[17] Suddenly, anyone engaged in the time-honored protest tactic of disrupting business as usual could, as long as their target was an "animal enterprise," be prosecuted as a "terrorist."

The AEPA mandated the production of a governmental report on "animal enterprise terrorism," and the report's findings, issued a year later, cast doubt upon the need for the law in the first place. Put together by the USDA and the Department of Justice, the "Report to Congress on the Extent and Effects of Domestic and International Terrorism on Animal Enterprises" (1993) states: "In order to present as reliable a profile of animal rights extremism as possible,

---

[13] "Public Lukewarm on Animal Rights."
[14] Russell (a) (2011).
[15] http://www.people-press.org/2009/07/09/section-5-evolution-climate-change-and-other-issues/.
[16] Potter (2011), 58.
[17] http://www.nal.usda.gov/awic/legislat/pl102346.htm.

representatives from entities that have been victimized by animal rights extremists, including government agencies, private industry, and organizations representing the interests of targeted industries or professions, were interviewed."[18] Without a trace of irony, the report thus suggests that a full understanding of animal activism can be gleaned by talking exclusively to those targeted by it. The implication is that animal "extremists" are irrational, pathological, and malevolent – they do not have a bona fide viewpoint to explore. Constrained by the historical record, in any case, the report concedes: "Despite the severely destructive nature of some of these activities, none of the extremist animal rights-related activities analyzed for this report is known to have resulted in the injury or death of another individual." According to the report, between 1977 and June 1993, a total of 313 incidents were recorded; of these, 51 percent involved vandalism (minor property damage), 25 percent the theft/release of animals, 9 percent threats against individuals, 8 percent vandalism (major property damage), 7 percent arson, 5 percent bomb threats, 4 percent firebombing, 3 percent bomb hoaxes. The incidents peaked in the late 1980s and declined thereafter. If there was a case to be made for denoting animal activism as the "number one domestic terrorism threat" in the United States, the report did not make it.

The process by which the state labels certain actors "terrorists" is, of course, deeply politicized. Currently, animal activists are domestic "terrorists" and anti-abortion activists – who committed eight murders between 1977 and 2009 and whose actions also include bombings, arson, vandalism, and death threats – are not.[19] In 2005, U.S. Representative Bernie Thompson, a ranking member of the House Committee on Homeland Security, issued a report along with some other committee members criticizing the Department of Homeland Security for focusing on "eco-terrorism" and ignoring right-wing threats such as anti-abortion activists, militia groups, and white supremacists.[20] Could it be that those who threaten major corporate interests in the United States get labeled as "terrorists" whereas those who do not remain mere "criminals"? Documents obtained through Freedom of Information Act requests show that in 2003 an FBI Joint Terrorism Task Force surveilled activists doing undercover investigations on farms and recommended prosecuting them as "terrorists."[21] These activists posed a real and present danger to the profit margins of the farms involved, but it is straining credulity to suggest that they threatened national security. Consider, too, the placement of animal activist Daniel Andreas San Diego on the FBI's Most Wanted Terrorist list.[22] San Diego is wanted in connection with bombings at a biotechnology corporation and a nutritional products

[18] http://www.naiaonline.org/articles/archives/terrrpt.htm.
[19] Potter (2011), 46.
[20] Ibid., 237.
[21] http://www.greenisthenewred.com/blog/fbi-undercover-investigators-animal-enterprise-terrorism-act/5440/#more-5440.
[22] http://www.fbi.gov/wanted/wanted_terrorists/@@wanted-group-listing.

corporation in 2003 – actions in which no one was injured or killed. The other individuals on the list are wanted for charges such as "Conspiracy to Kill U.S. Nationals," "Conspiracy to Murder U.S. Employees," "Conspiracy to use Weapons of Mass Destruction Against U.S. Nationals," and the like.

In 2006, Congress upgraded the AEPA into the AETA or Animal Enterprise Terrorism Act. The AETA closed a loophole that the AEPA had left open. Animal activist groups like Stop Huntingdon Animal Cruelty (SHAC) had effectively pressured so-called tertiary targets, or businesses doing business with their main corporate target. The AETA, therefore, prohibited intentionally damaging not only an animal enterprise, but any entity having a connection to an animal enterprise. It also prohibited "intentionally plac[ing] a person in reasonable fear of" death or serious bodily injury "by a course of conduct involving threats, acts of vandalism, property damage, criminal trespass, harassment, or intimidation."[23] This broad and vague language was intended to have a chilling effect on animal activism. Anticipating free speech objections, the law states that nothing shall be construed "to prohibit any expressive conduct (including peaceful picketing or other peaceful demonstration) protected from legal prohibition by the First Amendment." Yet in 2009, four activists were indicted under the AETA for peacefully protesting on public property outside of the homes of university faculty engaged in animal research. By the time charges were dismissed, the defendants had been under house arrest for almost a year.[24] On December 15, 2011, five activists filed a lawsuit in U.S. District Court in Massachusetts claiming that the AETA violates First and Fifth Amendment guarantees to free speech and due process.[25]

The driving force behind the passage of the AETA was the American Legislative Exchange Council (ALEC), a group of conservative corporate and legislative leaders working together behind the scenes to advance a corporate agenda through governmental (primarily state level) action. ALEC's corporate members, who include many food industry representatives, were determined to move against the threat of animal activism. In 2003, the group issued a report, "Animal & Ecological Terrorism in America," which called for a federal law to crack down on this phenomenon through various measures, including expanding the definition of "terrorism" to include journalists taking undercover footage of animal facilities and creating a federal "terrorist registry."[26] ALEC was

[23] http://www.govtrack.us/congress/bills/109/s3880/text.
[24] Order Dismissing Indictment Without Prejudice and Denying as Moot Other Pending Motions http://cldc.org/PDFs/aeta4_dismissal.pdf.
[25] Complaint for Declaratory and Injunctive Relief, *Sarah Jane Blum et al. v. Eric Holder*. Plaintiff attorneys are from the Center for Constitutional Rights and a private firm. Plaintiffs argue that the AETA violates the First and Fifth Amendments and is unconstitutional because a) it is overbroad and includes speech protected by the First Amendment; b) it is vague so citizens do not know which actions violate law; and c) it discriminates on the basis of the content of speech and conduct (3). In March 2013, the District Court granted the defendant's motion to dismiss on the grounds that the plaintiffs lacked standing to bring the suit. Plaintiffs are appealing.
[26] Potter (2011), 128. ALEC has also been instrumental in getting state legislation passed on this issue. In April 2006, a Pennsylvania law aiming to include "ecoterrorism" in the state criminal

also the animating force behind Arizona's SB 1070 and Alabama's HB 56 (two controversial anti-immigrant state laws), the "stand your ground" laws rendered infamous by George Zimmerman's killing of Trayvon Martin in Sanford, Florida in February 2012, as well as various antiunion and antienvironment statutes.

ALEC's modus operandi has been to operate by stealth. They have sought to influence state and federal legislation anonymously rather than publicly. As a result, few Americans know that ALEC exists. It has been called "the most influential corporate-funded political force most of America has *never* heard of."[27] Few Americans know that the organization spearheaded Arizona's SB 1070 – or, more specifically, that it was a specific subset of ALEC's members, a set of private prison companies who stood to gain economically from this anti-immigrant measure, who drafted the legislation and pushed it through the state legislature. But the veil of secrecy has been slipping lately, and a series of exposés has laid out the remarkable influence this organization has had on American politics in recent years. As an organization that labors to intensify the domination of the poor, nonwhites, immigrants, nonhuman animals, and the earth in the service of a corporate agenda, ALEC is a powerful reminder of the silent war that neoliberal elites are waging on the most marginalized and vulnerable among us. Journalist Bill Moyers's chilling assessment of its reach is reflected in the name of his documentary, *United States of ALEC* (2012).

Despite the growing public discussion about the moral status of nonhuman animals, animal activists remain distinctly unpopular, widely depicted by animal industry types as "a universal threat impinging on the interests of all Americans."[28] The specter of the human-hating, destructive animal extremist has worked its way into the American cultural lexicon. Although animal activists in the Chinatown controversy were not, as we shall see, called "terrorists" or prosecuted under the AETA, they had to contend with the general suspicion and disparagement that attaches to animal advocacy in the United States today, even in an animal-friendly city like San Francisco.

THE BEGINNING: WITNESSING CRUEL PRACTICES

The Chinatown story begins in the mid-1990s with Pat Briggs. Pat Briggs had lived in San Francisco for forty-nine years, and for much of that time she had been a part-time activist on animal issues, including spay and neuter, the circus,

---

code passed both houses overwhelmingly. The law makes the obstruction of commercial activity involving animals or plants a felony, and the penalties are up to forty years in prison or a fine of up to $100,000, as well as restitution up to triple the amount of damages. The American Civil Liberties Union opposed the bill as "a threat to the First Amendment rights of all Pennsylvanians who wish to express their views on matter of public policy" and stated that "classifying people who trespass or engage in disorderly conduct as terrorists is unwarranted." Rutmanis (2006), 4.

[27] http://www.theunitedstatesofalec.org.
[28] Girgen (2008), 118.

fur farming, hunting, and rodeos. She was an animal rescuer and a member of Animal Protection Institute, In Defense of Animals, PETA, and Sierra Club. In the mid-1990s, Briggs was working at the Wax Museum at Fisherman's Wharf. On her way to work each day, she passed vendors at the Wharf putting live crabs and lobsters into pots of boiling water. Her visceral experience of anguish at this daily sight led her to approach the vendors:

I was going down to Fisherman's Wharf every day to the Wax Museum. … [T]his crab stand was right there. I had to go past it. They had a big tank with, I could swear sometimes the crabs were like, probably, maybe this is an exaggeration, but not a very big one, there would be, like, crabs 20 deep. And then they'd throw them in the boiling vats of water. … And then I went down one night and I talked to the vendor and said, "Can't you find a more humane way?" And he said, "The meat is more tender." So for your taste, you're putting this animal through horror. And then they say, "Well, how do you know they feel pain?" Absence of proof is not proof of absence. If you can't prove that that animal has a nervous system and feels pain, you still can't prove that they don't, and you have to give it the benefit of the doubt.

Around the same time, Briggs noticed a Chinese market in her neighborhood, the Richmond district of San Francisco:

One day I was walking by Clement Street and I went by Wing Hing market. And I noticed there was, like, a bin on the floor, and my curiosity took me in there, and I swear to God, when I walked in that store, I nearly lost it. The sights and the smells were just so overwhelming. … I saw this bucket on the ground of turtles that were red-eared slider turtles, no water, they're aquatic turtles, semi-aquatic. They need water. There was not a drop of water in there. They were piled on top of each other, pitifully trying to crawl over each other. They had cracks in their shells. And then we went on to see horrors like fishhooks in their mouths. … And then I went in there and the frogs were in a tank that was – again, you know, frogs are aquatic, no water in there, or just residual water, filthy. Filthy. I mean, you could smell it a mile away. And then I went on to go back in there repeatedly, and it started opening up, going into other markets and seeing horrors like you would not believe. I mean, they would take the turtles and either lay 'em down flat on the counter and cut around the carapace and you see their feet kicking wildly or they would stand them up on end and hack between the shells. It was very disturbing to see that. You don't forget, ever. It puts a cloud over your head.

Briggs wrote a letter in 1994 to Mayor Brown, the California Assembly, and the San Francisco Commission on Animal Control and Welfare, asking them to address the cruelty she had observed toward "live food" in various locales, including large supermarkets, Fisherman's Wharf, and Chinatown. In two subsequent letters, entitled "Observations on the Selling of Live Food" and "Why Live Food Markets Should Be Regulated or Outlawed," she broadened her focus to other live animal vendors in the city including the farmers' markets at the Civic Center and Alemany, Chinese markets in the Richmond and Sunset districts, and restaurants throughout the city.[29] During this same period, she

---

[29] Both letters are undated but were written in the mid-1990s, around the start of the live animal market campaign.

wrote letters to the managers of Lucky supermarkets objecting to the cruelty of their seafood tanks, and contacted experts in marine biology and invertebrate zoology about humane methods of killing crabs and lobsters.

Place structured this story in critical ways. It was in the course of Briggs's spatially embedded daily routine that she observed and attached meaning to killing practices at Fisherman's Wharf and Clement Street. Being forced to observe emplaced practices (over and over again) led to moral evaluation and political action. Place also gave Briggs both a sense of responsibility and a sense of standing on this issue. A witness is someone who has seen and is then called upon to provide evidence. Briggs felt this way – that having seen, she was morally obligated to testify to what she had seen, to try to persuade others to take another look at these naturalized and normalized forms of violence. María Elena García (2013) writes that animal suffering is "invisibilized." What Briggs sought to do in this case was bring it out into the light.

As someone who had lived in the city for nearly five decades, Briggs also had a stake in the place and the sense of standing that comes with that. Unlike animal advocates who work in the headquarters of national organizations like the Humane Society of the United States, where they brainstorm about what national campaign to develop next, animal advocates in the Bay Area are locally oriented and reactive. They usually work in small local groups or as individuals, and even when they are affiliated with national organizations, they tend to organize around local events and practices as they arise. Their resources consist mainly of time, energy, and commitment; their activities consist mainly of attending meetings, lobbying, and letter writing. When other animal advocates questioned the live animal market campaign's importance, Briggs's response had something to do with place:

[P]eople would come to us sometimes and they'd say, "Why aren't you working on factory farming?" I'd say, "You know, I have worked on that, and by the way" – this is not what I told them, but this is what I would say today – "By the way, what are you doing? You're criticizing me, and all you're doing is mouthing off. Let's all work together. You pick your issue that has to do with making the world a better place, and I work on my issue, and together we're going down the same road, and together we're going to make for a more compassionate world. It's all related." But there's some of these people that just want to attack you. Hey, we've worked on all those issues. Virginia's worked on veal calves. She's been in Sacramento for 30-plus years. She's gone to all the meetings. She goes religiously to all the meetings. So does Eric. The Fish and Game. And factory farming is one of our big issues. So we've been there. Chinatown is happening right in your own backyard. It's extreme cruelty, and on a large scale.

Locally grown activism, responding to place-specific practices and events, might not pass a decontextualized assessment of issue urgency, but the notion of a "backyard" – of a place to which one belongs and in which one has standing and responsibility – remains a powerful force in activism.

For generations, of course, live food has been largely "out of place" in U.S. cities. Nicole Shukin recounts that in 1903, Swift & Company provided public tours of its Chicago slaughterhouse in order to interest consumers in meat consumption. But the risk of such tours was apparent to all, and company representatives handed out Visitor's Reference Books meant to be read after the tour to manage and shape recollections and ensure that visitors' affect would not "revert into counterproductive forms of metabolic and political revolt."[30] Because of concerns about hygiene and disease, as well as urban dwellers' squeamishness about animal suffering and violence, slaughterhouses throughout the United States eventually went the way of their counterparts in England and France and moved out of the cities into surrounding areas. Those few live food vendors who remain in cities like San Francisco sell birds, fish, crustaceans, turtles, and frogs rather than larger farm animals, and they often cater to an exclusively immigrant clientele. Most San Franciscans now purchase meat and fish at the grocery store.

Food questions are of course, "profoundly cultural questions."[31] Cultures have distinct rules about which foods are permissible and which foods are taboo, and there can be intense emotional investment in these demarcations. For this reason, foodways are often "instrumental in marking differences between cultures"[32] and in grounding group identity (García 2013). As mentioned in Chapter 2, nineteenth-century white Californians derided Chinese immigrants for their food choices as a way of marking them as unassimilable others. In the live animal market dispute, Chinese community leaders suggested that Briggs and other animal advocates were continuing this historical pattern of expressing racism through food complaints. Yet Briggs's primary targets included non-Chinese entities such as Fisherman's Wharf and local supermarkets. She neither focused on Chinese eating habits in particular nor sought to apply culturally specific norms about which animals are edible and which are not. She did not argue that turtles and frogs are not suitable for sale in live animal markets because they are not "food" animals to most Americans. Rather, she expressed concern about the suffering of all animals in all "live food" establishments in the city.

Briggs found herself swimming upstream, so to speak, by focusing on the animals found in "live food" markets. In the scientifically and culturally defined taxonomy of species, crustaceans, fish, turtles, frogs, and fowl are lowly indeed. They are not loved like "pets," admired like "charismatic mega-fauna," or loathed like rodents and insects – they are simply unremarkable, not considerable, morally invisible. Animal advocates and scholars in human-animal studies have responded to these complex hierarchical distinctions in disparate ways. Legal scholar Steven Wise (2003) seeks to codify the taxonomy by assigning different species numerical rankings that reflect their intelligence and dictate the amount of consideration they are due. Peter Singer (2009), Tom Regan (2004), and Carol Adams (1995, 2010), on the other hand, advance

---

[30] Shukin (2009), 96.
[31] Ashley et al. (2004), 187.
[32] Lupton (1996), 25.

philosophical arguments meant to broaden our concern significantly beyond the most valued animals, although the outer limits of this concern are not always clear. Sue Donaldson and Will Kymlicka (2011) reject a hierarchy of worth among species but recuperate the principle of differentiation to help us think through our duties of justice toward differently situated categories of animals. Activists are no less divided on the issue. Historically, most general animal advocacy organizations have focused on "pets" and "charismatic mega-fauna" because this is what works, in terms of getting the public to pay attention and make donations. The Great Ape Project, too, works with the grain of the species taxonomy, seeking legal personhood for Great Apes and only them. On the other hand, in the past few decades, the extreme scope of industrial farming has prompted groups like HSUS and PETA to turn their attention to lowly "food" animals. But the kinds of animals found in San Francisco's live animal markets have remained largely invisible, even to animal activists.

In her letter "Observations on the Selling of Live Food," Pat Briggs notes that animal advocates have shown little inclination to fight for "lesser creatures" like crustaceans. Writing to Jennifer Holdt of Animal Legal Defense Fund, she says: "This would be a most valuable case, because it starts people looking at the 'lesser' animals (which they are not) and even amongst animal welfare groups, there's much inertia in starting to look at crabs, frogs, lobsters and the like."[33] And in a letter to Virginia Handley, who was to become one of the leaders of the campaign, Briggs writes:

> Someone mentioned that they don't care about fish, but that would make us sound specie-sist as we're (at least) trying not to draw bounds, at least not with those that have nervous systems. Also, many people have been very upset with the supermarkets' tanks. I think it's time ALL the animal welfare groups … enlist in this field. Purely and simply, it would be as cruel to throw a crab or lobster into boiling water as it would be a turtle. I think it's important to also include F. Wharf as well as supermarkets because this is live food and it gets it away from being a "cultural" issue and then the opposition could not treat it as such. But that's not the point – the issue, of course, is to call attention to all live food. We may lose with the [Board of] Supervisors … but we're not losing if we let the public at large become aware that the lesser creatures are suffering, too.[34]

Far from discouraging her, it was the indifference of the public and animal advocates to "lesser creatures" that helped to motivate Briggs to act.

Briggs turned to her local network of activist colleagues – in particular, Virginia Handley of the Fund for Animals and Animal Switchboard and Eric Mills of Action for Animals – for help.[35] She had known each of them for

---

[33] The letter is dated February 11, 1995.

[34] The letter is dated February 24, 1995.

[35] Eric Mills started Action for Animals (AFA) twenty-five years ago with a handful of friends. AFA has had an anticruelty focus from the start. As one of the key leaders of the live animal market campaign, Mills lobbied commissioners, supervisors, and state legislators; wrote letters to officials and the media; built coalitions to support particular bills; attended public hearings; visited the markets and called in violations to CALTIP (Fish and Game's hotline), and more. Virginia Handley, another key leader in the campaign, was with the Fund for Animals until it

more than thirty years and had built a relationship of deep trust with them by working on various animal issues together. The San Francisco Society for the Prevention of Cruelty to Animals (SFSPCA) and American Tortoise Rescue also got involved, and there were occasional contributions from organizations like HSUS, In Defense of Animals, United Poultry Concerns, and Animal Legal Defense Fund over the years, but Mills, Handley, and Briggs coalesced into the core leadership of the live animal market campaign.[36]

None of the three wanted the campaign to be thought of as an "animal rights" action because of the denigration associated with that term. If the animal "rights" person or liberationist is despised as fanatical and misanthropic, the animal "welfarist" or "protectionist" is seen as more reasonable, precisely because s/he is not trying to undermine the human-animal divide. Pat Briggs comments on this:

[T]he only reason I call myself a welfarist is because if you say "animal rights," all of a sudden you're like a fanatic, you're one of the confrontational PETA types. The funny thing is, everyone knows PETA because they are so activist. But there's a difference. Animal welfare says, for example, you can eat animals as long as you kill them humanely. But you're taking their life. Whereas animal rights says, no, you can't eat them. They have intrinsic interests of their own. They want to live as much as you do. They have a right to life as much as you do. So I am more an animal rights [advocate]. ... I'm somewhat a vegan. It's hard to be a vegan unless you're cooking all the time. I'd say I'm about 65 percent, 75 percent vegan.

And Eric Mills:

You talk animal rights and right away you're a kook in this country. I don't believe in God-given rights for humans in the universe. It's something that civilized people do. But animal rights? Most people think it's a joke. Animals have a right to drive, to vote, and all that nonsense? ... [I]n my work, I never say "animal rights." I always say "animal welfare," "animal protection," "environmental protection," "human health." I want to do what works. "Animal rights" really doesn't work very well.

To maximize their public appeal, therefore, Mills and his colleagues framed the live food campaign as an animal protectionist (and later environmental protectionist) campaign. On more than one occasion, Eric Mills scolded a journalist for referring to it as an "animal rights" campaign. The optic of cruelty

merged with HSUS. She is now with Animal Switchboard and PawPAC. She has been an animal activist for forty years and specializes in lobbying for animal protection laws at the state level. She has shepherded through laws prohibiting painful animal experiments in elementary and high schools, banning killing in decompression chambers at local pounds, and banning the introduction of greyhound racing. At various times, she has worked on humane slaughter, the facebranding of cattle, whale hunting, traveling animal shows, fur, laboratory animals, feral cats, and wildlife.

[36] Karen Benzel of In Defense of Animals organized some early meetings in the fall of 1996 involving IDA, HSUS, and local activists. The HSUS sent representatives to speak at public hearings occasionally and also paid for necropsies on some frogs and turtles. Animal Legal Defense Fund provided legal advice. United Poultry Concerns helped with the lawsuit animal advocates brought against Chinatown markets.

fit naturally with this orientation – the point being to reduce animal suffering rather than to radically transform human-animal relations.

There was a good deal of discussion initially over how to delimit the campaign – both in terms of how to define the targets and what kind of animals to include. The two were related, of course, because including Fisherman's Wharf meant including crustaceans. Briggs recalls:

I remember Virginia [Handley] saying at one point that if we brought in the crabs at Fisherman's Wharf, that instead of – how did she put it? She put it very eloquently. She said. ... "We may end up bringing all the animals down if we bring in the fish and the crabs, because people don't relate to them."

Despite her initial resolve, Briggs started to think that perhaps

[P]eople weren't ready for crabs. People would write letters to the editor and make a mockery of us, saying, "Why don't you get a life?" My first media contact was when this guy came out to ... [interview me]. ... And they were kind of – not making fun of it, but in a subtle way.

Handley recalls her own concerns about feasibility:

[T]here was always the fear that Fisherman's Wharf is so powerful, they'll just come in and kill the whole thing. ... But I think most of the animal people were very democratic in our efforts in that we don't care who's doing it. It's about the animals. So whether it's Fisherman's Wharf or the pet trade, our preference would be to do something about it. The problem is, what is doable?

Mills, too, wanted to include Fisherman's Wharf in the campaign but thought it politically impracticable. Of course, leaving Fisherman's Wharf out of the campaign presented another political problem, the appearance of targeting the Chinese. Mills comments:

Here's where politics and money get involved. Can you imagine on Fisherman's Wharf, if the restaurants couldn't sell crab or lobster? They would all go belly up. There's no way in hell that was going to fly. ... [T]here were 11 Supervisors, and I met with nine of them, one to one, to talk about this issue. They were all supportive, but nobody wanted to touch Fisherman's Wharf because of the restaurant trade and tourism that bring billions of dollars into San Francisco. I mean, the city would go belly up without Fisherman's Wharf. So money is always involved in there. We as a species are quite happy to trade morality and ethics for money, whatever it is. So that was dropped out of the equation, and then the backers of the Asian markets rightfully said, "This is not fair. This is discrimination. You're letting Fisherman's Wharf, which is almost all white, off the hook while you pick on Chinatown." And I agreed. And I also am quite aware of the horrendous treatment that Asians have gotten in San Francisco over the centuries, where they used to cut off pigtails and burn Chinatown to the ground a number of times, put women into prostitution, they died of syphilis, illegal trade. It's a nightmare.

Here Mills grants the point that there is no moral distinction between Fisherman's Wharf and Chinatown markets, only a distinction in money and political clout. The Chinatown markets were low-hanging fruit, relatively speaking.[37] When Pat Briggs approached the San Francisco Commission on Animal Control and Welfare, she included Fisherman's Wharf and crustaceans in her request for action, but the Commissioners, as we will see later in this chapter, self-consciously excluded the Wharf from their considerations, which left the campaign to focus on the other major institutional player in the city's live food industry, Chinatown. The targeting of the Chinese was not racially motivated in the sense of reflecting special animus toward the Chinese – the activists' initial focus was broader and they went to some lengths to avoid targeting only the Chinese or giving the appearance of racial targeting – but the campaign was shaped by political exigencies, and Handley's question, "What is doable?" was inextricably tied to questions of relative vulnerability and disadvantage.

THE ANIMAL COMMISSION HEARINGS: CRUEL PRACTICES SHOULD BE BANNED

The San Francisco Commission on Animal Control and Welfare (CACW) makes recommendations on animal issues to the Board of Supervisors, the legislative body of San Francisco city and county.[38] It is strictly advisory and has no enforcement powers. The CACW is composed of eleven members – seven who are appointed at large and four who represent the city's Departments of Animal Control, Public Health, Police, and Parks and Recreation. All serve as volunteers with no compensation. The CACW holds monthly meetings that solicit public comment on all matters animal from the treatment of stray dogs and cats to dog licensing to animal cosmetic surgery to the use of animals at UCSF for research. In the mid-1990s, according to Commissioners who served then, the CACW was a somewhat obscure, ad hoc, disorganized affair. It was, in fact, the Chinatown controversy that thrust the CACW into the spotlight for the first time, baptizing it through fire. Once the Commissioners decided to take up the live food issue, Chinese American community leaders got involved and the media was not far behind.

After Pat Briggs brought the issue to the CACW in 1995, the Commission formed the Live Animals for Food Consumption Subcommittee to investigate. For nearly a year, the subcommittee held public hearings, examined photographs of the markets, researched laws and regulations in California and other states, and consulted various experts, including people in Hialeah, Florida who had been involved in the Santería animal sacrifice controversy there.[39] During this process, animal advocates gave public testimony, provided evidentiary material, lobbied, wrote letters, and talked to the media. The argument they made focused squarely on cruelty: the live animal markets keep animals in cruel conditions (there is severe overcrowding, many are injured and sick, they

---

[37] My thanks to Kenneth Warren for insight on this issue.
[38] The city and county are exactly coterminous.
[39] Golden (1996).

are often deprived of food and water), and they kill them cruelly (by hacking or beating them to death or skinning them alive).[40] Something needed to be done. Eric Mills recounts:

The overriding issue for everybody, first off, was the animal cruelty. Because much of it was avoidable. Just kill an animal and then eat it, big deal. But no, these animals were tortured to death quite often. … So it was the animal cruelty, seeing turtles hacked up while fully alive, seeing them stacked this deep and the ones on the bottom being crushed to death. I saw frogs with missing body parts. Almost all of them had abraded noses from rubbing on the wire trying to get out of the cage, with no water in there.

Eyewitness testimony was a recurrent feature of the public hearings, as animal advocates tried to make these animals visible, both literally and morally, to the CACW and the public.

The San Francisco SPCA entered the picture at this point, conducting an undercover investigation and submitting its report, "Statement on San Francisco's Live Animal Markets" (September 12, 1996), to the CACW. Elaborating on the optic of cruelty, the report condemns conditions in the markets as "deplorable and inhumane" (2) and provides this summary statement on the cover page:

The conditions we witnessed included intense overcrowding, failure to provide for the animals' most basic needs, and inhumane methods of slaughter. … [T]he fact that animals in San Francisco's markets are sold to be killed and eaten does not mean these creatures don't feel and can't suffer. And the fact that markets sell them to be killed and eaten does not mean these dealers have a license to inflict *needless suffering* on the animals beforehand (italics added).

On page 1, the report lists "Conditions Observed in San Francisco Live Animal Markets":

- An eighteen-inch turtle having its shell sliced from its body, while the animal was fully alive. We believe this is akin to skinning or scalping a person alive.
- Chickens crammed into rusted wire cages with less than eight-by-five inches of floor space per bird – an area smaller than half a sheet of normal typing paper.
- Fish packed into tanks so severely overcrowded that even those who remained alive were pinned upside down and sideways, unable to move or right themselves. We estimate the crowding in these tanks was equivalent to shoving seventy-five people into an eight-by-eight-foot elevator.

---

[40] In addition, animal advocates raised two other dangers – the potential threat to public health (necropsies on market frogs and turtles turned up diseases and parasites that can infect humans, such as salmonella, pasturella, giardia, and roundworms) and the potential threat to local ecosystems (as imported frogs and turtles who find their way to the wild endanger local species through competition, predation, and disease). But the main focus at this stage of the campaign was cruelty.

- Two geese – a bird whose average height is two and a half feet with a wing-span up to four feet – forced to remain hunched down in a single wire cage a little more than one foot high and about two feet long.
- Frogs piled one on top of each other, crushing those at the bottom, in bare wire cages and open plastic bins smeared with black slime.
- Quail jammed so tightly together in tiny cages they were unable to move or turn around. These birds, like others we saw, were made to stand on wire over a layer of encrusted feces and other debris.
- Turtles, whose natural habitats include quiet lakes and rivers, stacked up to five layers deep, some turned defenselessly on their backs and half buried beneath others.
- Fish, flailing and gasping, left to suffocate slowly in shallow dry pans.
- A turtle, vainly struggling to retreat into its shell, hacked and pounded at least six times on and about the head with a dull knife before finally being decapitated and cut apart.

What the report deems cruelty is not the keeping and killing of animals for food per se, or even the infliction of suffering, but rather the infliction of "needless suffering" on these animals. The term "cruelty" is usually only invoked when suffering is seen to be unjustifiable and gratuitous, whether it is caused negligently or maliciously. When suffering is inflicted for the sake of the sufferer (e.g., medical treatment) or for the sake of some higher good, however defined, the label of cruelty is typically not applied. The report continues:

We heard no testimony whatsoever that the conditions we witnessed were in any way necessary to produce fresher, more palatable, or healthier food. ... Nor did anyone come forward to testify that keeping geese or other birds hunched down in small wire cages, unable to spread their wings or stretch their necks, was a necessary component of any religious practice or cultural tradition. In fact, the only justification given for the inhumane and unsanitary conditions in our City's live animal markets was that it was cheaper: To do any better – to improve conditions for the animals and for the public – would cut into business profits (2–3).

The suffering of animals in the markets is "needless," the report suggests, because its only justification is greater profits.

Veterinarian Lexie Endo presented forensic evidence to the CACW that reinforced the theme of cruelty, while also raising public health concerns. In a July 19, 1996 letter, Endo recounts that she examined 200 turtles, mostly red-eared sliders rescued from Chinatown markets. Thirty percent arrived dead or died within ten days because of "deplorable health"; another fifteen percent were chronically ill. Most of the turtles were dehydrated and starved, and many had bacterial shell and skin infections in addition to being "riddled with parasites, primarily roundworms, giardia and flukes as well as blood parasites like hemogregarines." Endo writes: "If these same animals were presented to me as a dog or cat, the owner of the stores would be reported to authorities for animal cruelty. ... I ask that you give serious consideration to the health and treatment of turtles both from a humanitarian aspect as well as that of the consumer."

Using the optic of cruelty to defend animals is a centuries-old strategy in the United States. When the ASPCA (the parent organization of the SFSPCA) first opened its doors in New York City in the 1830s, members chose to condemn the "cruelty" of animal practices (such as the beating of carriage horses), which was both radical in that it demanded recognition of animals as morally considerable and conservative in that it demanded only the amelioration of animal practices rather than their cessation (Beers 2006). Since the advent of the modern animal liberation movement in the 1970s, animal advocacy has been divided between "abolitionists" calling for an end to the institutionalized exploitation of animals (e.g., PETA) and "welfarists" calling for more humane treatment and a reduction in animal suffering (e.g., HSUS) (Francione 1996).[41] The live animal market campaign in San Francisco, which deployed a cruelty optic to mobilize public support, belongs in the latter category, although its leaders hold abolitionist views on some issues.

Significantly, animal advocates did not argue that Chinese culture was singularly cruel or more cruel than American culture. Rather, they chose to make a universalist argument that cruelty is wrong *no matter what group is engaged in it*. In a magazine article, Eric Mills wrote:

There can only be one standard of decency, regardless of the impressive array of cultural influences in the United States. ... We must have the courage of our convictions in declaring that practices that are harmful, destructive and cruel are unacceptable – in any language. In a letter I received in December, 1990 from Cesar Chavez, he writes: "Kindness and compassion towards all living things is a mark of a civilized society. Conversely, cruelty, whether it is directed against human beings or against animals, is not the exclusive province of any one culture or community of people. Racism, economic deprivation, dog fighting and cock fighting, bullfighting and rodeos are cut from the same fabric: violence. Only when we have become nonviolent towards all life will we have learned to live well ourselves."[42]

Mills is not making an anti-multiculturalist argument (that the Chinese are more cruel than whites and are thus an inferior and unassimilable other) but rather an argument about the proper limits of multiculturalism (that cruelty and injustice cannot be allowed to continue in the name of respecting cultural differences).

Still, the use of the optic of cruelty should give us pause because it seems to rely on the mobilization of cultural antipathies to work, regardless of activists' intentions. Animal advocates presented facts about the live animal markets on the assumption that "you know cruelty when you see it" – that people recognize cruelty viscerally and instinctually because of a universal human sensibility. But it is almost certainly true that our judgments about cruelty are strongly culturally inflected – that acts become legible to us as cruel or not cruel through

---

[41] This distinction is much cleaner in theory than in the real world.
[42] Mills (1999).

a cultural lens. This means that the concern about cruelty can easily become (and has often been) a vehicle for ethnocentrism and even imperialism (Ritvo 1987; Davis 2013; Deckha 2013). In addition, the cruelty optic – again regardless of the intentions of activists – cannot help but reverberate with the culturally embedded trope of Chinese cruelty and transgressiveness. This is not to say, however, that there is no *there* there when it comes to cruelty. That we are culturally predisposed to evaluate certain practices as cruel and not others does not change the fact that humans engage in practices that inflict intense and prolonged suffering on animals.

As the CACW deliberations over the live food ban proceeded, the Commissioners made the explicit decision to exclude crustaceans and therefore Fisherman's Wharf from consideration. Althea Kippes, a member of the Live Animals for Food Consumption Subcommittee, comments:

Everyone gets worked up over the gorilla, but no one really cares about a lab rat. And it was like, crabs, no one is going to take banning the sale of crabs seriously. There's Pat Briggs supporting the crabs and everybody else, it was like, people don't think crabs is the same thing. I know there are frogs in Chinatown. When Pat brought the issue up, and I think Eric [Mills], too, it covered crabs and everything. But we told them, you've got to pick your battles and draw the line. No one's going to get worked up over crabs. People – it will just make them hungry – this has no chance in hell of ever passing.

Richard Schulke, the chair of the Subcommittee, elaborates:

Was there a pretty open discussion about whether to include the crabs and lobsters?

Oh, it went back and forth all the time. Patricia Briggs was really big on trying to add crabs and lobsters. ... Some of the other Commission members were okay with it and some were not. So it seemed it would be better if we left them out if we could get a consensus vote.

Although the Commissioners and animal advocates continued to talk about the issue as one of "live animal markets" generally, it was clear to everyone that the campaign would focus thenceforth on Chinatown, which, like Fisherman's Wharf, held a concentration of such markets.

At this point, Chinese American community leaders and organizations got involved in an attempt to forestall the ban.[43] The Chinese Consolidated Benevolent Association (or "Six Companies") invited Commissioners to their headquarters in Chinatown for discussions. Julie Lee and Rose Tsai of the San Francisco Neighborhood Association used their Chinese-language radio program to mobilize people to turn out at the CACW hearings. Julie Lee comments on the hearings:

First of all, this Commission is just six animal lovers. What do you expect them to do? And how they can fix a law to tell the rest of us how to live? That is wrong, I think. They're not even willing to talk. ... They keep a very – they never go to the community. They never go talk to people. Because I go on radio every day, we have call-in every day, we talk with hundreds, thousands real people every day. We don't just close door and have, you know.

---

[43] Chapter 4 explores relations among these Chinese American activists and organizations.

Because my business, I know a lot people, we talk about everything what's going on. ...
There were no Asians on the board. There were no colored people on the board. And they
all animal lovers, okay? That's fine. You can love your animal. I don't have a thing against
them. But they cannot tell us how to eat, how to live. That is wrong.[44]

Rose Pak, a consultant with the Chinese Chamber of Commerce (CCC), organized Chinatown merchants (clients of the CCC) in response to the campaign.
Pak was widely recognized as a major powerbroker in San Francisco politics,
a close ally of Mayor Willie Brown, and a liaison of sorts between Chinatown
and City Hall. (She would help to arrange the ascension of Ed Lee to the may-
or's office in 2011.) At one Subcommittee meeting at the Chinatown Public
Library in August 1996, an animal activist held a sign saying, "Rose Pak I hope
you're reincarnated as one of those frogs in the tanks," to which Pak responded,
"You come back as a fly and I'll eat you up!"[45] Her take-no-prisoners attitude
was legendary. Pak attended the CACW hearings even though she thought they
were ridiculous:

Can you tell me what you remember about the Commission hearings back in '95, '96?

Oh, those? Well, they wasted a lot of time for our small businesses, because people usually
are family-owned, small stores, and the owners have to take time off to participate. That's
their living. So then people like me had added pressure to represent them, to go to those
hearings. It never ceased to amaze me, where did those people [animal rights activists] find
the time? It's not a legitimate cause when you're talking about food on tables versus pets
or whatever. ... They freak you out, because they're very vocal. They're very belligerent ...
The animal rights activists. Their messages are very confrontational, and they make up in
noise, as I said, they're belligerent, and they are vocal, and they carry signs and so it's – for
our people, it's intimidation. So they call you names, they do all kinds of stuff. ... [A]ll the
media was there, and there's a circus. And our people get intimidated. So then I feel the
burden, like, how do you fight them without letting them wear you down and not let your
people suffer.

*They [the CACW] voted to recommend the ban to the Board of Supervisors. The Board of
Supervisors didn't do anything.*

No, no, I was not surprised. They [the Commissioners] were cowed. They were all – and
they were ignorant, cowed, they were just so scared of them [animal rights activists] because
of their tactics. And so they don't want to be harassed. ... I knew that the Mayor [Brown]
would support us, because it doesn't make any sense.

How many of the merchants who were actually involved went [to the CACW hearings]?

I just make them sign and then we represented them. They have to make a living. They
can't shut down the business. So we always had a handful that rotated, the 40, 50 stores
that would send each hearing three or four as a representative, and then I'll go to each and
every one.

Did you go to a lot of those hearings?

I went to every hearing.

44 Vickie Ho Lynn, a Chinese American, was a member of the CACW during this period.
45 Golden (1996), 4.

Pak invokes negative tropes about both animal activists ("belligerent" and "confrontational") and animals ("not a legitimate cause when you're talking about food on tables") to construct a narrative sympathetic to the Chinese merchants.

Pak's assessment that Mayor Brown would protect the Chinatown merchants, in part because of his close alliance with her, was widely shared by the CACW Commissioners. Richard Schulke recounts:

You mentioned the phrase "political hot potato." Can you talk about that? Was this an open discussion within the subcommittee and within the larger Commission that this was a politically tricky issue?

Of course it was an open discussion that it was a politically tricky issue. It was more of our discussion amongst ourselves where the city department people [Commissioners from city departments] were like, "What are you, crazy?" ... [and] "This is a very tough issue. It's a very hard political issue here in the city." And it certainly was. I sure realized it.

Althea Kippes elaborates:

Was there sort of behind-the-scenes discussion that this was a political hot potato?

Oh, that was obvious. ... It was pretty apparent, because at the time the mayor was Willie Brown, and he got a tremendous amount of political support from Chinatown merchants, and they didn't want any kind of ban, any restriction. Yeah, actually, I do remember, because I remember that before the vote, I had gotten a call from the city attorney's office telling me that the Mayor had removed me from the Commission. I think it was, I guess Lorraine [Lucas] and Richard [Schulke], too. ... I thought it was very interesting, because we were appointed by the Board of Supervisors and not the Mayor, I just remember it struck me as something he would do, because he just thinks he's God.

According to Schulke, the Commissioners who worked for city departments never considered voting for the ban:

It always shook down pretty much that I knew the city people on the Commission were not going to vote for this. They pretty much told me that. ... I could tell when we finally got to the full Commission hearings on it that I wasn't going to change anybody's mind, even if they agreed with me. I had several of them tell me under the table that the Mayor was not going to allow this to happen, nor was the Board [of Supervisors] president, Barbara Kaufman. They were adamantly against it, so they [the Commissioners] weren't going to vote for it.

As the CACW hearings went on, they became dramatic and intense, filled with charges, countercharges, and emotional testimony. The city's very identity seemed to be on the line. As one reporter put it: "What's an animal-respecting, multiculturally sensitive, compulsively democratic city to do?"[46] Richard Avanzino, who was president of the SFSPCA, comments:[47]

---

[46] Golden (1996).

[47] Richard Avanzino was president of the SFSPCA until 1999, when he became the director of Maddie's Fund.

We knew that this was a controversy of major significance. One out of every three house-holds in San Francisco supported the San Francisco SPCA. That's a huge market penetration for a not-for-profit charity, especially in a community that is very liberal and very fond of charitable causes. … At the same time, we knew that the Chinese American community had a very, very strong backing of San Franciscans because San Franciscans believed in diversity. This was always of huge import to city hall, but to the people of San Francisco as well, that we were one that respected all cultures, that we admired the contribution of the Chinese American community, and that this was a group that was actually revered. So if we put a clash of culture versus animal rights, that this was going to be an uncertain outcome, because there was divided loyalties. Many of our members who were animal lovers, some to the extreme, were also very much aligned with protecting all minorities in San Francisco, and particularly the Chinese American community. So it was a clash of titanic proportion in terms of allegiances and cross-allegiances. There were many in the Chinese American community, especially the younger generations, that were very much in favor of what we were trying to accomplish, but some of the older members of the community and some of the people of more recent immigration to the city had very strong committed feelings about these practices and traditions that had come from the old country.

Richard Schulke recounts how suddenly the live food ban became a big media story:

We [Commissioners] were doing a variety of things, really just trying to figure out how the Commission worked. We used to have our meetings over in the auditorium of the state building. It was sparsely attended, I would say. A big auditorium, and I was looking around saying, "Wow, there's nobody here." A few people in the front row. But a couple of people in the front row mentioned the live animal markets. They looked around and said, "Let's form a subcommittee," and I volunteered to chair the subcommittee. And that's kind of what got everything rolling. … [I]n the beginning, the subcommittee, hardly anybody came except the same faces, Patricia Briggs, Eric Mills sometimes, a few other people. We were about to wrap up the testimony, taking some testimony. And then word got out somehow. It was pretty funny, a local TV station, Channel 5, maybe … [T]here were so few people at this subcommittee that we had to move around the table, we'd all be in different locations to make it look like there were more people there. But that story broke, and all of a sudden now everybody wants to come testify on this issue. It really got big. So now I can't close the subcommittee, because now I have – the more we'd have meetings, the subcommittee, the more people wanted to testify. … So when we go to the full Commission hearings on it, it's packed. It was crazy packed, you know? We had to make public comment a couple of minutes just because every meeting there was 100 people that wanted to get up and give public comment. … I'll be quite honest with you, I had no idea the firestorm that this would create, and the media firestorm that it would create. We hardly had – we'd get the local radio, KCBS guy, in the beginning once in a while. [By the end], you couldn't fit the television trucks, crews were in there, people were getting made up before they came out on the Commission because they wanted to look good on CNN.

As things heated up, Richard Schulke, chair of the Subcommittee, faced accusations of racism from the Chinese American community:

After the Commission hearings some people would pull me aside and say – and it was quite often from the Six Companies – "You're giving the Asian community a black eye. We don't need that." … It looked bad. I said, "Gee, that's certainly not what's driving this." … I was in law school at the time, or I had just graduated, so I was getting a lot of the, you know, the famous case about the Chinese laundromat [*Yick Wo v. Hopkins*], "It's just another version of that, you're doing that."[48] ... [W]e all started to be called "racist" or "anti-Chinese" or "anti-Asian." For me it was weird, I'd never been accused of being anti-anything. I always thought I was kind of a very liberal kind of guy. So it was – it took me aback a little bit. But I also realized that some of it was just political tactics from the people that didn't want the markets closed down. They essentially played the race card, which was difficult to deal with. But I don't think that it swayed any of the Commissioners.

At times, Schulke was afraid for his personal safety:

And then there were the death threats. Boy, I started getting death threats like crazy. ... Mostly by phone. Really, really angry Chinese people, sometimes in Chinese, sometimes in English, sometimes in a mix of both. ... [Y]ou know, very angry, bad things. I can't really repeat them. They were going to "fuckin' kill me," all this kind of stuff. I basically contacted the police and they said, not super-reassuring, "These kind of people are either hunters or howlers," as they called them, "And the people that howl generally never hunt. And the people who hunt you aren't going to let you know. So don't really worry about it." But it was a little bit in the background. I only got them randomly, it wasn't like I was getting them every day. But it was enough to make you think. ... At one point in time, I am living in the Sunset. The advice [from police] was, "Look out for angry young Asian males." ... I said, "I live in a neighborhood filled with Asian males. Who am I looking out for? The angry ones? Maybe they're having a bad day, it has nothing to do with me, you know?" So that was a little bit of pressure, not much, but it was just a little bit disconcerting to think that I was in a volunteer position and people would threaten my life.

The vote turned out largely as predicted, with the seven at large Commissioners voting yes on the ban, three of the city department people voting no, and one city department person abstaining. On December 9, 1996, Matt Kaplan, the chair of the CACW, wrote a letter to the Board of Supervisors declaring that the CACW had passed a motion recommending that the Board enact an ordinance to "Prohibit the keeping and selling of live mammals, birds, fowl, reptiles, and amphibians intended for human consumption within the City and County of San Francisco." Crustaceans as well as fish were excluded by this language.

Schulke recalls that he would have preferred regulating the sale of live animals to banning it, but that he had decided that regulation was impossible:

---

[48] In *Yick Wo v. Hopkins* (1886), the U.S. Supreme Court ruled that a law that is facially neutral with regard to race but applied in a racially discriminatory manner violates the Equal Protection Clause of the Fourteenth Amendment. The case dealt with a San Francisco ordinance that required laundry operators housed within wooden buildings to secure a permit from the city. Most of those who fell into this category were Chinese immigrants and when they applied for permits, they were denied. Much of the legislation against the San Francisco Chinese in the 1800s was race neutral on its face, including the Sidewalk Ordinance of 1870 (outlawing the Chinese method of carrying laundry and peddling vegetables with poles), the Cubic Air Ordinance of 1871 (requiring 500 cubic feet of living space per adult), and the Queue Ordinance of 1873 (requiring prisoners to have their hair cut within an inch of their scalp). See Bernard Wong (1998).

I think the reason we went finally for banning was that we felt it was such a political hot potato that the local agencies wouldn't regulate it even if we appointed a law for regulation. It just was not going to happen. So since it was not going to happen, we decided we should go for the ban. It was very difficult for me, to be honest with you. … Just an outright ban just seemed to be too harsh for me if we weren't banning crabs and lobsters over at Fisherman's Wharf. I was much more for the regulation, but if anything, I changed my mind, because I can speak for myself, when I realized that it wouldn't be enforced. … Animal Care and Control said, "Look, we don't have the budget and the people." Carl [Friedman] said, "Between you and me, we don't have the budget and the people and the Mayor don't want it, we're not doing it." And the Health Department said, "No, it's Animal Care and Control that has to do that. We can't."

Nor did the Commissioners expect the Board of Supervisors to act on their recommendation. According to Schulke, the Board of Supervisors heeded the CACW's recommendations about 10 percent of the time – and only on basic municipal issues like dog licensing rather than on general animal welfare issues like this one:

Would it be fair to say that those of you who voted for the ban didn't expect the Supervisors to accept it?

Absolutely fair to say that.

What was the purpose of doing it then?

I guess more than anything else to try to get the word out there about what was going on, get everybody involved in thinking about it. I just want to – I realized that the best thing we could do was get people to think about it, and perhaps to get the state legislature involved, which eventually it did, it got to the point where, because I knew that on the local level, again, just because it's such a political hot potato, that the Board wasn't going to do anything.

Lorraine Lucas, another Subcommittee member, comments:

We didn't think it [the ban] was going to pass the Board, I didn't think so. Maybe some of the others thought it might, but from dealing with city hall on the zoning issues, I didn't think it was going to pass, there was too much of a political thing. Chinatown is very powerful with money and votes, so I didn't think it was going to pass. I just thought that maybe if we did this, there would be some sort of compromise, that if we banned it, we could have compromised and said, "OK, we're not going to ban it, but we're going to do some enforcement."

The political fallout of the CACW vote could be observed the following year when the Board of Supervisors refused to renew the terms of two of the Commissioners who had voted for the ban, including the sole Chinese American, Vickie Ho Lynn. Schulke recounts: "It was very under-the-table. Some aides of Supervisors came to me and said, 'Hey, there's going to be blood money for that.'"

What happened with the CACW is a modern urban politics tale. It is a story about city officials passing the buck in dealing with problems, budget shortfalls disabling the enforcement of regulations, and issues falling through the cracks of jurisdictional lines. It is a story of how public hearings staged by local or state commissions are more often about mobilizing opposing constituencies than they are about discussion and consensus building (although the former may be no less democratic than the latter). It is a story of the influence of political contributions on local elected officials. It is a story about behind-the-scenes politicking and machinations, how intensely personal these can be on the local level, and how configurations of political clout set the parameters for what is thinkable in terms of political action. Finally, it is a story about the role of symbolic politics – how actions are taken even when or sometimes precisely because they will have minimal if any material impact on the issue at hand. With the CACW drama concluded, both sides to the conflict moved forward, negotiating the complex grid of local and state institutions and looking for points of maximum influence.

THE LAWSUIT: CRUEL PRACTICES VIOLATE THE LAW

According to animal advocates, Chinatown live animal markets violated numerous city health codes and animal welfare laws, but the problem was enforcement. Baron Miller, attorney for the animal advocates, said: "We didn't see the DA, the district attorney, getting involved in prosecuting anybody for violating these penal code sections. We went through all that. We tried. I remember talking to the district attorney at the time, trying to get him interested in this, and they weren't."[49] With Mayor Brown on the other side of the issue and the Board of Supervisors refusing to get involved, the next step was to take the matter in front of a judge. In 1997, Baron Miller filed a lawsuit in the California Superior Court of the City and County of San Francisco on behalf of animal advocates against twelve Chinese-owned live animal markets, including nine in Chinatown, two in the Richmond, and one in the Sunset.[50]

Before filing the lawsuit, Baron Miller talked with Eric Mills, Virginia Handley, and others about how broadly to define the targets. Once again, the issue of Fisherman's Wharf came up and once again, it was set aside. Miller explains:

Originally I took the position that we weren't going to – I was not going to be involved in suing live animal markets in Chinatown unless we also sued the restaurants in Fisherman's Wharf that were boiling crabs alive, killing them by boiling them. And then once we got into the preparation stage of the lawsuit, I discovered how difficult if not impossible it was going to be to establish physical or mental suffering by the crabs, as opposed to establishing it for the animals in the stores that were mostly in Chinatown. I realized that it was probably going to be a loser, it almost certainly would be a loser against the Fisherman's Wharf stores. ... I wasn't happy about it. I wasn't happy about people in the Chinese community

[49] Baron Miller has practiced law in San Francisco since 1973.
[50] Baron Miller worked on the lawsuit pro bono for a time and then took a much-reduced fee. United Poultry Concerns and Animal Legal Defense Fund helped to raise money for the lawsuit; individual donations were also received from all over the country.

feeling that they were being singled out. It was disturbing to me. It was disturbing to a lot of people in the coalition. We didn't want that. We didn't want to hurt people's feelings. We didn't want to single them out. And I can fully understand why they felt that they were being singled out. And they were being singled out. But I can understand why they felt they were being singled out for their race or for their culture. Because realistically what was going on in Chinatown is no worse than what's going on at any factory farm anywhere in the state. And it's just that we felt we could do something about this. We couldn't do anything about the factory farms. That was the reality.

Crustaceans would have been a hard sell not only because most people do not see them as morally considerable but also because it is harder to "prove" scientifically that they suffer. Again, the main consideration was what was doable.

The Plaintiffs' Trial Brief (April 1998) argued that the business practices of the named stores were "unlawful" because they violated portions of the city Health and Safety Code (prohibiting the keeping of live animals where food is stored and sold) and the California Penal Code (prohibiting the cruel treatment of animals and mandating the provision of adequate exercise, food, and water to animals) and requested that the court enjoin these practices. While Penal Code 599c explicitly states that anticruelty provisions are not meant to interfere with the right to kill animals for food, the plaintiffs' brief avers that this only precludes the claim that the act of killing animals for food is itself cruel and illegal. Plaintiffs do not make this claim; instead they argue that the keeping of food animals in inhumane conditions and the killing of food animals in an inhumane fashion are cruel and illegal.

Baron Miller followed the animal liberation movement's controversial practice of linking the animal issue to slavery and the Holocaust.[51] The Plaintiffs' Trial Brief stated:

Historical cruelty in so-called civilized societies, e.g. the Holocaust in Europe or the American institution of slavery, were made possible because what we now perceive as cruelty was then rationalized as necessary and acceptable. Society teaches us daily not to perceive animals as the sentient, conscious, feeling beings that they are, but as objects for us to exploit in order to enhance our lives. It is due to this conditioned attitude that the defendants are able to come into court and argue that the atrocities they are committing and the misery they are creating are neither extraordinary nor consequential, and should be ignored (6).

In another brief, Miller states: "That we live in an anthropocentric world is no more justification for inflicting misery on other species than the racism of American society was justification for the Dred Scott case" (7–8).[52] Miller, who describes himself as a vegan committed to "animal rights," says that he used animal liberationist language to appeal to the judge's affect and conscience:

[51] See Chapter 9 for further discussion of this practice.
[52] "Memorandum of Points and Authorities in Opposition to Defendants' Motion for Summary Judgment," February 20, 1998.

[T]he argument is made by me as a way ... to reach the judge, as a way to get the judge to maybe have a light bulb go on in his head where he says, "Oh, yeah, we're doing the same thing to animals that the Nazis did to Jews or that – " So I'm not suggesting that animals suffer as Jews suffer. ... I'm trying to educate the judge. The judge obviously has defenses built up through a lifetime of living in our society, and so to win a case like this, you can't just present the facts of the law and say, "Now rule in our favor." You have to educate the judge. You have to make the judge want to rule in your favor. You have to make the judge understand why you're doing what you're doing.

Eric Mills later expressed skepticism about this strategy, wondering whether they would have been better off with a lawyer who "didn't give a damn about animals."

Attorney Paul Wartelle, hired by Rose Pak to represent the defendants, argued that the market practices in question were "customary community practices" (2) that were already intensely regulated. Because the "defendants' practices fall well within the law and custom of the industry" (5), plaintiffs' charges about overcrowding and other issues were, according to Wartelle "farcical, fanatic, and fantastic" (4), "lunacy" (5), and "outlandish" (5).[53] He also argued that the markets' manner of keeping and killing animals was an integral part of Chinese cultural tradition.

As Wartelle understood quite well, the legal definition of cruelty to food animals in the United States hinges on the question of whether given practices are "customary" or not. U.S. courts do not assess cruelty in farming based on whether a particular practice is intrinsically horrifying but rather by looking at whether it is standard practice in the industry, in which case it is deemed not cruel. Cruelty, again, means the infliction of wanton, gratuitous suffering, and the courts have ruled that just about any amount of animal suffering is non-gratuitous and permissible in farming if the practice is customary and thus presumably related to business success (Francione 1996). No matter how stomach churning a practice is and how much suffering it produces, it is not cruel if enough people are doing it. In one Pennsylvania case, a defendant was convicted of cruelty for starving horses to be sold for meat not because he inflicted suffering by starving the horses, but because his attorney "could not prove that enough people were doing the same thing."[54]

This legal state of affairs – where animals raised for food are radically unprotected by law – is a result of concerted lobbying on the part of U.S. agribusiness interests. As Wolfson and Sullivan explain, agribusinesses have "persuaded [state] legislatures to amend criminal statutes that purport to protect farmed animals from cruelty so that [they] cannot be prosecuted for any farming practice that the industry itself determines is acceptable, with no limit whatsoever on the pain caused by such practices."[55] There are no federal laws regulating the

---

[53] "Memorandum of Points and Authorities in Support of Defendants' Motion for Summary Judgment," March 6, 1998.

[54] Wolfson and Sullivan (2004), 215.

[55] Ibid., 206.

treatment of farm animals, either, and the one federal law that regulates slaughter, the Humane Slaughter Act of 1958, is virtually unenforced by the USDA
(Eisnitz 2007).

Whether or not a farming practice is customary, as long as there is no cost-
effective alternative that is more humane, the courts are likely to deem it not
cruel. In HBO's *Death on a Factory Farm* (2009), a documentary about an
undercover animal investigator working on a Midwest hog farm, the court
admits that it finds the farm's practice of killing sows by hanging to be offensive (as well as not customary), but concludes that it does not violate the anticruelty statute because there is no way to kill a sow that is feasible and more
humane. This is similar to what happened in the live animal market case, where
in his Tentative Opinion of July 20, 1998 Judge Carlos Bea ruled that the
markets' practices did not constitute "cruelty," defined in Penal Code 599b
as physical pain and suffering, inflicted unnecessarily or unjustifiably, caused
by gross negligence or omission, such that it causes danger to an animal's life
(6). He wrote: "[A]s distasteful as is the shell removal method of slaughter [of
turtles], there presently is no reasonable alternative. As a result, there is no 'cruelty' because the physical pain inflicted is neither unnecessary nor unjustified
within the meaning of Penal Code section 599b" (11–12). On the significance
of this statute, Bea wrote:

By making this the law of California in 1905, and refusing to amend it since then, the
People have spoken: humans have the right to kill all food animals. If they can reasonably
kill the animals with little or no physical pain, they should choose that method. However,
if the slaughter involves physical pain to the animal that is not reasonably avoidable, food
animals can still be killed by people even though the animal suffers physical pain (19).

Bea traces this view of animals back to Genesis 1:28 (where God grants man
"dominion over the fish of the sea, and over the fowl of the air, and over the
cattle, and over all the earth, and over every creeping thing that creepeth upon
the earth")[56] and concludes: "Whether the plaintiff is correct in its world-view
of what are desirable relations between humans and animals is a matter which,
in a democracy based on the separation of powers, must be addressed to the
People's Legislature" (20).[57]

In the "Plaintiff-Appellant's Reply Brief" (August 1999), Baron Miller challenged Judge Bea's reasoning, arguing that it would

[A]llow the most egregious acts of cruelty on animals used for food as long as they
were done often enough. It would allow those in control of the animals, whose main

[56] King James Bible, Cambridge edition. See Matthew Scully (2003) for an alternative, more animal-friendly reading of "dominion."
[57] Bea also took a moment to declare his distaste for multiculturalist arguments on behalf of the
Chinese: "Some time and effort has been devoted by defendants to justify their conduct on the
basis of their shared Chinese 'culture.' Claims have been made that what defendants do in their
markets is what has been done in China for thousands of years. This 'culture' argument is not
only irrelevant, it is bothersome and is rejected. Defendants' markets are in San Francisco, not
China. The laws which apply here are Californian, not Chinese" (3).

considerations are necessarily cost and efficiency, to decide for themselves what level of cruelty is acceptable. ... Letting the industry decide what is or is not cruel is to metaphorically allow the fox to guard the hen house. Cruelty should not become legal simply because it occurs on a massive scale. Such a result would defeat the statutory purposes of protecting animals and promoting public morals (20).

Here Miller spoke to the core of the problem – that legal and statutory definitions of animal "cruelty" are structured so that business interests will decisively trump animal interests every time. There are anticruelty laws on the books, but they do more to give animal industries protective cover and to salve our collective conscience than they do to protect animals from suffering (Francione 1996). In the "Defendants-Respondents' Brief" (June 30, 1999), Wartelle ridiculed Miller for overreaching in this case: "In this action, Appellant ... sought to achieve a revolution in the law of animal husbandry: the virtual liberation of live seafood and poultry from commercial sale" (1). Months later, the Court of Appeals, First Appellate District, Division One, ruled against the plaintiffs, and an editorial in the *San Francisco Chronicle* (February 11, 2000), entitled "A Win for Chinatown Markets," declared the markets were now "safe from animal rights zealots." Victorious in court, Wartelle was rebuked at home: "My main critic was my [eight-year-old] daughter. She said, 'Daddy, you should start that case over and do it on the other side!'"

THE JOINT GUIDELINES AND THE KUEHL BILL: ON "HUMANE" CARE AND KILLING

Animal advocacy groups who made common cause during the CACW hearings found themselves in conflict after the hearings concluded. Eric Mills, Virginia Handley, and Pat Briggs initiated the lawsuit with Baron Miller and went to both the California legislature (seeking legislation on the humane treatment of animals in live markets) and the California Fish and Game Commission (seeking a ban on the importation of turtles and frogs for food). Meanwhile, Richard Avanzino of the SFSPCA decided to negotiate an agreement with the Chinese Six Companies. These "Joint Guidelines" laid out certain parameters for the "humane" care and killing of animals in the Chinatown markets. The campaign's core activists thought the agreement was meaningless – it was strictly voluntary and did not include enforcement provisions – and believed that Avanzino had sold them (and the animals) out for his own glory. Eventually, Mills and his colleagues persuaded the California legislature to pass the Kuehl Bill, AB 2479, which was almost identical to the "Joint Guidelines" except that it had the force of law. However, the Kuehl Bill has not been enforced.

Avanzino pursued a separate agreement with the Chinese Six Companies not because he had philosophical differences with the other animal advocates about how animals should be treated – they had all coalesced consensually around an anticruelty theme – but because he differed with them in his assessment of what was possible, what counted as progress, and how to achieve it.

Conceding the strength of the opposition, Avanzino believed that moderation and compromise were in order. Here he contrasts the behind-the-scenes, conciliatory approach of the SFSPCA with the more militant approach of other animal advocates:

[The SFSPCA] never got involved in public controversies if there was a way to get the job done without making it a matter of public spectacle. There is a separation between us and some of the other animal rights groups in that regard. They were – their first agenda, I think, was to bring public awareness to a controversy and try to get the public on their side to bring about change, either through outreach or through legislation, but basically create a controversy. Our style was to approach all issues initially by trying to reach a win-win situation without anybody being aware of it other than the principals.

It was the SFSPCA's reputation for moderation and discretion that gave them leverage to be effective negotiators, Avanzino claimed. Furthermore, according to Avanzino, discretion required him to conduct the negotiations in this case privately, without the other animal advocates knowing:

When we negotiate, we let the other party pretty much declare the ground rules. We at no point wanted to keep anybody out, but many times when we're negotiating, the other party decides who they want in the room and who they don't want in the room. My recollection, and this is imperfect, so I don't want you to consider it a fact, was that Virginia and Eric had taken some rather strong statements, tried to – I don't know how to say it – villainize? Anyway, they were certainly very critical of the live animal markets. We had been less outspoken than they had been, and therefore my recollection was that Pius Lee was more comfortable trying to see if he could work something out with us. I believe that we had the stronger hand. We had the best market penetration, the best access to a broad section of the San Francisco community. But knowing full well that their hand was also extremely strong because of the reverence for the Chinese American community and for Chinatown and for their political influence. They had the Board of Supervisors very much in their hand.

The SFSPCA and the Chinese Six Companies were the soft liners in their respective assemblages of organizations: both favored behind-the-scenes conciliation and compromise. This made it easier for the two to come together and broker an agreement, at least on paper. Implementing the agreement over the resistance of hard-liners was a different matter.

The timing of the announcement of the Joint Guidelines on April 1, 1998 could not have been more dramatic. For months, the core activists had been pressing the California Fish and Game Commission to pass a ban on the importation of turtles and frogs for food, on the grounds that these animals escape (or are released from) the markets and endanger local wildlife through predation, competition, and disease (see Chapter 5). Such a ban would have effectively ended the sale of turtles and frogs in Chinatown markets, which import turtles from the southeastern U.S. and frogs from Taiwan. The Fish and Game Commission was on the verge of passing a ban at its April 1, 1998 meeting in Long Beach when Avanzino stood up during public comment and announced the agreement on the Joint Guidelines.

JOINT STATEMENT OF PRINCIPLES AND GUIDELINES

Subscribed to by The San Francisco Society for the Prevention of Cruelty to Animals and Representatives of San Francisco's Live Animal Markets

The San Francisco SPCA and the representatives of San Francisco's live animal markets agree that cultural, religious, and ethnic diversity are vital to our community's success and well-being. We also recognize that all people benefit when different traditions, beliefs, and practices are allowed to flourish in an atmosphere of tolerance and goodwill. To further our mutual respect and understanding, the San Francisco SPCA and the representatives of San Francisco's live animal markets are committed to working together to preserve traditional practices and foster kindness and compassion throughout our community. Towards this end, the following guidelines have been agreed upon and will be adhered to in a spirit of cooperation, respect, and compassion:

1. All animals that are to be killed will be killed humanely.
2. No animal will be dismembered, flayed, cut open, or have its skin, scales, feathers, or shell removed while the animal is alive.
3. No injured or diseased live animal, or carcass of any such animal, will be sold or offered for sale.
4. No live animals will be confined, held, or displayed in a manner that results, or is likely to result, in injury, starvation, dehydration, or suffocation.
5. No live animals will be confined, held, or displayed in a manner that results in the animal being crushed, attacked, or wounded by any other animal.
6. No live animal will be confined, held, or displayed in a manner that prevents the animal from lying down, standing erect, changing posture, and resting in a normal manner for that species.

During public comment, Virginia Handley tried to control the damage, pointing out that she and other activists had also met with Chinese merchant representatives, who had refused to negotiate guidelines unless Handley and her colleagues backed off of the Fish and Game ban:

It came down to, "Either you go to the [Fish and Game] Commission and oppose this ban or you can forget anything happening in San Francisco on these markets." We were absolutely threatened that nothing would happen unless we opposed this ban. We said, "No, we will not oppose this ban." At that point, all those guidelines are tossed in the can. All that's out the window now, and Mr. Avanzino sat down with them, and the guidelines, I don't know how long it took them to write it up, with absolutely no specificity to them at all, absolutely no enforcement to them at all. No, we are not – we would just be sickened to think that this Commission would accept that as though now the problem is solved.

Handley's suggestion was that Chinese merchant representatives cynically manipulated the SFSPCA and that the latter let themselves be used, to the detriment of the cause. Eric Mills comments:

[A] number of us felt betrayed at that meeting when Avanzino got up and spoke, because he hadn't told us ahead of time that that's what he was going to do, and the Commissioners all about peed in their pants, fell all over themselves. "Oh, what a great idea, let's go for that. We don't have to do a ban. Now nobody's going to shoot me!" So that's what happened, and of course, nothing came of it, nothing was enforced, nothing changed, business as usual. I just think Avanzino sold out. He'd done a lot of terrific work before then. Maybe he thought he was doing the right thing, that he didn't think we were going to win the whole caboodle. But you didn't know that at the time. He should have pushed for it, I thought, and then come up with some kind of a compromise, perhaps. I hate that word, "compromise." It always means the animals lose.

Upon hearing about the Joint Guidelines, the Fish and Game Commission postponed consideration of the ban. It would be another twelve years of deliberation before they voted to pass the ban in 2010.

The Joint Guidelines revealed a dramatic fracture among Chinese American groups. As discussed in the next chapter, two groups competed to organize the Chinese American community's response to the live animal market campaign: Pius Lee and the Chinese Six Companies (CCBA), on the one hand, and Rose Pak and the Chinese Chamber of Commerce (CCC), on the other. Pius Lee and the Chinese Six Companies had negotiated the Joint Guidelines, so Rose Pak and the CCC wanted nothing to do with them. Although the Chinese Six Companies, the CCC, and the SFSPCA met several times to discuss implementation of the guidelines through the summer and fall of 1998, the meetings were unproductive and eventually came to a halt. In personal correspondence dated July 22, 1998, Paul Wartelle, attorney for the CCC, chastised Richard Avanzino for believing that the Chinese Six Companies represented the Chinese merchants and could command their cooperation – when, in fact, Wartelle had made it quite clear that the merchants were his own clients. He wrote: "You negotiated with the wrong parties. You got what you negotiated for – an empty agreement that nobody needed to implement."

A few months later, the SFSPCA formally declared the Joint Guidelines a failure. In its "Statement Regarding Live Animal Markets" (September 29, 1998), the SFSPCA recounts that it made good-faith efforts to "find a harmonious and nonadversarial resolution" and to promote a "voluntary, community-based effort" based on "mutual respect and understanding" (1). Although the Chinese merchants had agreed to an October 1 deadline for implementation, they had stopped coming to meetings and had made no changes in their practices despite the arrival of the deadline. The statement closes with: "We must now conclude, however, that our attempt to forge a resolution based on mutual trust and understanding has failed, and that further controversy in our community would appear to be inevitable" (2).

As the drama of the Joint Guidelines came to a close, the action shifted to Sacramento. There the legislature, responding to heavy lobbying from both sides, simultaneously passed two bills related to the live animal market issue, the Honda Bill (AB 238) and the Kuehl Bill (AB 2479). Chinese American community leaders pushed for the first bill and declared its passage a victory; animal advocates pushed for the second bill and declared its passage a victory. Sponsored by Assemblyman Mike Honda, a prominent advocate for Asian American issues, AB 238 originally sought to prohibit the Fish and Game Commission from banning the importation of turtles and frogs into the state for food.[58] Tying the hands of the state-level body proved politically infeasible, however, and AB 238 became greatly diluted through the legislative process. In its final iteration, it simply "permit[ted]" a city or county to "regulate the disposition" of such animals in various ways. Because it mandated no action and only allowed for something that the Board of Supervisors showed no inclination to do, it seemed of mostly symbolic value. Its pronouncements that the selling of turtles and frogs for food had gone on in California "since the days of the Gold Rush," that wholesalers and retail restaurants in the state purchase an estimated one million pounds of these animals per year, and that many small markets and restaurants depended on this commerce to stay in business were gestures of support for the Chinese merchants' position.

The passage of AB 2479 also raised questions about what counts as a legislative victory. Eric Mills explains why he and Virginia approached Assemblywoman Sheila Kuehl in the first place:

I wanted to shut [the live animal markets] down. I think everybody else did, too, but we knew that that was not politically realistic. People are going to eat animals, regardless, even if it kills them, and it probably will before it's over with. But we wanted at least the basics taken care of. No butchering of live animals, no animals kept out of water that lived there, basic stuff. … We went to Sheila Kuehl, and Virginia and I co-sponsored a bill.

The initial version of the Kuehl Bill was almost identical to the Joint Guidelines.

KUEHL BILL/AB 2479

Original Version, as Introduced in the California Assembly on February 24, 2000

1. Animals are to be killed humanely.
2. No animal will be dismembered, flayed, cut open, or have its skin, scales, feathers, or shell removed while the animal is still alive.
3. Take reasonable care to offer for sale only those animals or carcasses that are free of injury or disease.

(continued)

---

[58] As originally introduced by Assemblyman Mike Honda into the California Assembly on January 28, 1999.

4. No live animal will be confined, held, or displayed in a manner that results, or likely to result in injury, starvation, dehydration, or suffocation.
5. No live animal will be confined, held, or displayed in a manner that results in the animal being crushed, attacked, or wounded by any other animal.
6. No animal will be confined, held, or displayed in a manner that prevents the animal from lying down, standing erect, changing posture, and resting in a normal manner for that species.
7. Provides that the standards outlined in d, e, and f are met, in the case of frogs and turtles, when the animals are held and kept according to internationally accepted standards for the transport of live animals.

This bill, too, became watered down in the legislative process: only items (2) and (4) were left standing in the final iteration, and the penalties were weakened. Virginia Handley, who had fought hard for the Kuehl Bill, was nevertheless overjoyed at its passage:

I cried when it passed, I was so happy. I thought, "Thank God, at last, something!" Even though it was heavily compromised. ... [A] lot of people say, "Don't bother with the bills, because they don't get enforced." But I say, get them on the books, and enforcement is a whole other issue.

In Handley's view, the Kuehl Bill was a step in the right direction: it was an act of symbolic importance as the declaration of a legislative body, and it had the potential to change conditions on the ground were it to be enforced. But others disagreed. Miles Young, a warden with the Department of Fish and Game (DFG) who later worked as an investigator for animal advocates in this case, explains why he would not tell his squad to enforce the bill:

Eric [Mills] let me look at the [Kuehl] bill. I was at that time one of the senior members on the policy procedures team for the Department of Fish and Game. We reviewed all legislation, all laws, from our viewpoint. Is it going to work? Is it not going to work? Is it applicable? Is it practical? Is this just showpiece? Can we afford it? Do we have the manpower? ... I looked at it and I went, "You know, this doesn't look right. I want to see the penalty section. If there's no penalty section, it doesn't mean anything." ... Eric's one of my best friends, but we're at totally opposite ends on some of this stuff. ... I've got 36 years of law enforcement [experience]. And I kind of have an idea of what gets through the courts and what doesn't and how politics works. They never consulted me. ... So they came out with this bill and he calls me up one day and says, "Oh, you're going to love this. This is great. It's out. We need you to go enforce it. Here's a copy." He sends me an email version. I went right to the penalties section. The penalties section says if they're mishandling the animals, you have to give them a verbal warning. I'm thinking, "That's useless right there." The second time, if you catch them a second time, they can pay up to a $250 fine. Has to be the same person. And I went, "Eric," I'm talkin' to him on the phone, he's all excited, "Eric, calm down. This is useless. I'm not going to send my squad into San Francisco for that." "What are you talking about?" "Eric, if you look at it, the second time might be a

$250 fine, but it has to be the same person. Do you think we're going to remember months later which person in one of these Chinese markets was the same one that was butchering? Not only that, they have an option [of taking a class on animal welfare provided by law enforcement instead of paying a fine]." ... And I said, "That's what I want to do. We're shorthanded, we don't have enough people, and I want to send somebody in there and have them do that and have them cite somebody and then we have to put a class on? We lose money in the deal and time." They fought me for – they thought I wasn't doing my job. As good friends as we were and everything, they thought I wasn't doing my job for a long time. I said, "Eric, I'm not sending my squad in."

The bill was simply unenforceable, from Young's perspective, especially in a time of budget constraints and reduced manpower for the Department of Fish and Game:

Do you think with the Kuehl bill, do you think it's worse to have it on the books than not to have it at all?

Yeah, because once it came out, the merchants said, "We were nice." Pius [Lee] was great: "We supported your bill." Once they found the penalty section, they said, "We support it. You've got a law. Don't complain about it. If there's a law, enforce it if we're doing something wrong." And we're going, "Yeah, right."

So that's sort of a permanent loophole for them?

Exactly. If it wasn't there, we'd be better off, we at the enforcement agency. Understand, San Francisco couldn't enforce that itself. Have you gone to the markets and have you seen the health inspection numbers up there? Next time you go to Chinatown, next time you're up here, I'll walk you through and show you this stuff. They've got these little green stickers that say "health inspection." You go to some of their finest restaurants and they've got a reading of 78 or 80 or something. This frickin' market's got 88, 92, 94. There's flies floating around, people walking out with frog guts on their feet.

Because they're bought off?

Absolutely. It's a joke to everybody.

Because the merchants pay them a little bit?

I can't – all I know is that it's a lie. You just have to go there and look at it. They can't rate a 90 something. Hell, the Safeway in Nob Hill doesn't get that.

Young's point was that laws get written in the way that they do because they represent compromises among competing interests, but they do not take into account what is practical and enforceable on the ground. Thus legislators can earn credit for taking action even though the laws don't actually work. Enforcement is then stymied by a mix of factors, including budget problems (leading to understaffing) and corruption.[59] Responding to queries about the nonenforcement of the Kuehl Bill years later, L. Ryan Broddrick, director of the DFG, wrote in an April 25, 2006 memorandum to John Carlson Jr., executive director of the Fish and Game Commission: "With current staffing levels

[59] See Miles Young (2004) for his critique of AB 2479.

the same as in the 1960s and with the increased demands on enforcement, live animal market cases don't make our enforcement priority list."[60]

This part of the story ends where it began – with the San Francisco Commission on Animal Control and Welfare. Even after the conclusion of the CACW hearings in 1996, animal advocates continued to attend the CACW's monthly meetings and to raise the live food issue there. In 2001, CACW Commissioners once again considered a ban on the sale of live animals for food. Dr. Thelma Lee Gross, a veterinary pathologist at the School of Veterinary Medicine at University of California, Davis, gave a presentation on the suffering of "lower vertebrates" at the March 14, 2002 CACW meeting. In words that echoed Pat Briggs's early ruminations on crustaceans, Dr. Gross stated: "Pain is often neglected in lower animals because of a lack of knowledge and an inability to recognize pain in those species. But the inability to recognize pain does not mean that it doesn't exist." Her words were to no avail. Despite energetic discussion of the matter, the CACW did not propose another ban.

Americans are ambivalent anthropocentrists at the start of the new millennium, and they are thoroughly skeptical of animal advocacy. Against this backdrop, animal advocates in San Francisco challenged Chinatown's live animal vendors using an optic of cruelty that traces back to the first stirrings of animal advocacy in the United States. Although they did not set out to target the Chinese only, and in fact went to some lengths to avoid doing so, the question of what was doable ultimately shaped their decisions, and this question was in turn related to which animal species are morally considerable and which human groups are relatively vulnerable. While their arguments for the most part scrupulously respected multiculturalist and colorblind norms, the optic of cruelty inevitably mobilized ethnocentric and anti-Chinese feeling among some part of the public, as I discuss in later chapters. Animal advocates won victories at the CACW and the California state legislature, but these came to naught in large part because Chinese Americans had enough political clout to counter these moves. The next chapter looks at how Chinese American groups countermobilized around the optic of racism in a moment of broader Chinese political ascendancy within San Francisco.

---

[60] The relationship between the Department of Fish and Game and the Fish and Game Commission is discussed in Chapter 5.

4

The Optic of Racism

Mobilizing the Chinese American Community

> When you target just Chinese merchants, you have to be out of your mind not to
> see it is racially motivated.
>
> — Supervisor Leland Yee

The live animal market conflict emerged just as the Chinese American community in San Francisco was reaching for meaningful political power. A significant presence in the city for a century and a half, the Chinese community survived the Exclusion era (1882–1943) to be reinvigorated by post-1965 waves of immigration from throughout the Chinese diaspora. Global political and economic developments powerfully influenced Chinatown and Chinese San Francisco more broadly during this period, shaping the flow and composition of migration as well as the circulation of capital and goods (including animals and animal parts). By the mid-1990s, Chinese San Francisco was vibrant, diverse, and complex, fractured by class, national origin, language, and politics even as it was stitched together by an enduring identification as a distinct cultural and racial group. With dramatic population growth and dispersal beyond Chinatown into the far reaches of San Francisco, Chinese Americans made significant gains in terms of political representation at both the local and state levels, securing the ultimate prize of the mayor's office in 2011.

The live animal market campaign was one of several issues Chinese American leaders used during the late 1990s and early 2000s to build community or mobilize their fractious population into a reliable political base. Advancing the optic of racism – uniquely resonant in San Francisco because of its distinctive history of anti-Chinese persecution – Chinese leaders argued that the animal campaign was racially motivated and thus threatening not only to Chinese live animal vendors and Chinatown residents but to *all* Chinese Americans throughout the Bay Area and indeed the nation. The appropriate response, they insisted, was community mobilization, self-defense, and empowerment – that is, to circle the wagons around the live animal vendors and understand that what happened to them happened to the whole Chinese American community.

Intent on casting the vendors as innocent victims of racism, Chinese American activists openly declared their belief in human supremacy and peremptorily dismissed the issue of animal cruelty. The optic of racism cast shadows even as it illuminated.

CRUELTY AND TRANSGRESSION: IMAGINING CHINESE CULTURE

In Chapter 2, I argued that white Americans in the late 1800s imagined the Chinese as cruel and transgressive *like* animals and *with* animals. This trope did not abate during the Exclusion era. Consider Dr. Fu Manchu, the enormously popular character created by British novelist Sax Rohmer in 1913 and immortalized in books, film, television, radio, and comics for decades thereafter. Fu Manchu, the evil genius bent on world domination, was the very embodiment of cruelty and transgressiveness (and the very embodiment of Chineseness for American and British audiences for several decades). In Rohmer's novels, he is always imagined as animal-like, associated with animals, in the borderlands between human and animal. In the first novel, *The Insidious Dr. Fu Manchu* (1913), Fu Manchu is described thus: "Imagine a person tall, lean and feline, high-shouldered, with a brow like Shakespeare and a face like Satan, a close-shaven skull, and long magnetic eyes of true cat-green."

Fu Manchu hides his emerald cat eyes and claw-like hands through various contrivances in an attempt to disguise his true animal nature. But that nature always reveals itself, in part because of his predilection for deploying venomous animals – including swamp adders, centipedes, spiders, scorpions, pythons, and wasps – as weapons against his enemies. In *The Return of Dr. Fu Manchu* (1916), Fu Manchu plans to torture his enemy by placing him in a cage where his body parts are exposed to Cantonese rats, "the most ravenous in the world." Fu Manchu uses his laboratory to make animals even more deadly than they are naturally, to elicit their poisons, even to make human-animal hybrids. He is a brilliant scientist, but his intimacy with animality, his "cruel cunning," marks him as baser than whites. His is the brilliance of an exceptionally skilled predator, unleavened by human/civilized feelings of compassion or remorse. It is what he does to/with animals that marks him as cruel and it is his boundless cruelty that makes him animal.

This trope about Chinese culture as cruel and transgressive has proven remarkably enduring, structuring how events involving the Chinese and Chinese Americans become culturally legible to us. (Of course, the trope has coexisted with other notions about the Chinese, including the model minority myth that emerged in the postwar period, valorizing the Chinese and other Asian Americans as intelligent, hardworking, family-oriented, thrifty, and respectful of authority.) In recent years, perceiving China's ascendancy as a global financial, military, and manufacturing power with a combination of fascination and anxiety, the American media talk about China as a foil to the humane, rights-respecting, law-abiding, democratic nation they perceive the United States to be – that is, as selfish and ruthlessly exploitative toward animals and the environment (using endangered animals in traditional Chinese medicine, generating high levels of pollution), selfish and reckless regarding the health of others (manufacturing poisoned pet food and lead-painted children's toys, engendering and spreading SARS and bird flu), and cruelly indifferent to human rights (the one-child policy, infanticide, Tiananmen Square, political prisoners).

Consider a *San Francisco Examiner* article entitled, "Lust for Tiger Parts Whittles Away Species" (June 1, 1997), published at the height of the live animal market controversy, which reports that only a few thousand tigers remain in the wild, in part because of an increase in the illegal trade in tiger bones, skin, and other parts for use in traditional Chinese medicine.[1] The Chinese believe, according to the article, that tiger brain can be used to treat laziness and pimples and tiger fat can be used for vomiting, dog bites, and hemorrhoids.[2] The reporter's language and tone suggest much that she does not state directly: that the Chinese have an unbridled hunger for animal parts; that this hunger is misguided because it is based on unscientific, backward ideas about medicine; and that it is transgressive, selfish, and destructive because it harms endangered species and the environment, which belong to all of us. This proprietary sense about a global or universal commons explains the article's subtly indignant tone. The Chinese are so rapacious toward animals that they are practically animal themselves.

As Jeff Yang observes, "What one might call 'food libel' has long been an aspect of a larger fear of China. The association of Chinese with dubious edibles has insinuated itself into our [U.S.] cultural consciousness in small and seemingly trivial ways – in schoolyard taunting, in sitcom gags about takeout food, in standup monologues about puppy chow mein."[3] In his 1988 book about his journey through China, British travel writer Colin Thubron observes "an old Chinese mercilessness toward their surroundings" and recounts the items on a Guangzhou restaurant menu with bemused horror: "Steamed Cat, Braised Guinea Pig (whole) with Mashed Shrimps, Grainy Dog Meat with Chilli and Scallion in Soya Sauce, Shredded Cat Thick Soup."[4] A recent T-Mobile television ad strikes the same tone.[5] Seated in a Chinese restaurant, NBA greats Charles Barkley and Dwyane Wade watch in disbelief and horror as the waitress presents them with "Yao's favorite" dish – a bowl of live, crawling shrimp.

---

[1] Bulman (1997), a7.

[2] Chinese traditional medicine also prescribes tiger bone for clearing colds and stimulating blood circulation, tiger penis as an aphrodisiac, tiger whiskers for relieving toothache, and tiger eyes for curing malaria and epilepsy. Tigers are nearing extinction in China, India, Sumatra, and the former Soviet Union because of loss of habitat, poaching, and the use of tiger parts. No more than 5,000 exist in the wild today, and their numbers have fallen 95 percent since the start of the twentieth century. See Bert Eljera (1998).

[3] Yang (2007). Many Chinese acknowledge this "anything goes" approach to animal eating when they repeat the southern Chinese saying that Chinese people "will eat anything with four legs except a table, and anything that flies except a plane."

[4] Cited in Roberts (2002), 129.

[5] http://www.youtube.com/watch?v=VdHdIR8OS50.

Yao Ming calls Barkley's cell phone and asks how he likes the shrimp. Barkley complains that it is moving, has eyes, and is still alive. Yao responds, "That's the best part" and "don't be a baby." As Barkley and Wade conspire on how to make it look like they ate the shrimp, the waitress, chef, and Yao Ming chant a crescendoing chorus of "Eat the head! Eat the head!"

The tracing of the Severe Acute Respiratory Syndrome (SARS) epidemic of 2003 to live animal markets in southern China – where a viral disease of animal origins (the civet cat) jumped the species barrier to infect humans – created a media firestorm in which the tropes of Chinese cruelty, transgressiveness, backwardness, and recklessness were given full play.[6] With headlines like "Noxious Nosh: In China, People Are Hungry for a Taste of the Wild" and "Chinese Taste for Exotic Flesh," news accounts vividly described live animal markets in southern China as entangling human and animal bodies in strange and filthy ways.[7] Mei Zhan recounts that the media blamed SARS on the animal appetites of the Chinese people:

> At play in the frenzies surrounding the "zoonotic origin" is the translocal scientific and media representation that the Chinese, in indulging their appetites for exotic "wild animals," transgressed proper barriers between human and animal, the domestic and the wild, and culture and nature. In other words, the story of "zoonotic origin" did not blame nature itself for the SARS outbreak; what went wrong was the Chinese people's uncanny affinity with the nonhuman and the wild. This affinity was enabled not only by the highly mutable virus that was crafty enough to move between Chinese bodies of both human and nonhuman sorts but also by the visceral act of consumption. (2005, 37)

Was SARS the realization of centuries-old white fears that the spiritual, economic, and medical threat posed by the Chinese would spill over all boundaries to infect Western civilization? When the Chinese government lifted the ban on the sale of civet cats in August 2003, just four months after imposing it, many thought the move was premature and showed a reckless disregard for public health. The title of one *Associated Press* news article – "Chinese Economic Concerns Trump Safety" – said it all.[8]

Western animal protection groups have paid a good deal of attention to China in recent years, rhetorically linking concerns about animal welfare with progress, modernity, and democracy. In July 1997, the International Fund for Animal Welfare (IFAW) launched an initiative entitled "A New China: A New Era for Animal Welfare" that aimed to persuade practitioners of traditional Chinese medicine to stop using endangered animals and to reduce the number of animals they use overall. In his article, "Break the Engagement with Cruelty-Prone China," published in *Friends of Animals* magazine (Spring

---

[6] The first reported cases of Severe Acute Respiratory Syndrome were in December 2002; three and a half months later, the Chinese government admitted what was happening, and in March 2003, the World Health Organization formally issued a worldwide alert about a new disease known as SARS. See Zhong and Zeng (2006).

[7] Beech (2003); York (2003).

[8] Ang (2003).

1999), Ze'ev Boded writes: "The horrific cruelties to animals in China are not intrinsic to the Chinese people. They are, however, intrinsic to the authoritarian communist system." Noncommunist Taiwan, he notes, has a political culture that permits animal protection organizations to do their work. Even among Asian nations, China has lagged behind, observes an Animals Asia Foundation position paper entitled "Friends ... or Food? Why Dogs and Cats Deserve Better" (March 2006). While the Philippines, Taiwan, and Hong Kong have all passed laws banning the killing of dogs and cats for food, China has yet to follow suit.[9]

Since the 1990s, both the Chinese government and the Chinese people have become attuned to animal welfare in new ways, in part because of Western animal activism.[10] The efforts of Jill Robinson of IFAW to curtail bear bile farming in China, for example, have led to the rescue of some bears, the closing of a few farms, and stricter regulations on remaining farms.[11] Peter Singer's *Animal Liberation*, the so-called bible of the U.S. animal liberation movement, was translated into Chinese during this period. Several animal welfare conferences have been held in China, and international NGOs like IFAW and World Wildlife Fund (WWF) have been allowed greater freedom of operation there (Li 2006). In June 2004, the state-controlled China Central Television company broadcast a documentary on "animal welfare," and legislators have debated animal protection legislation.[12] Public opinion surveys of Chinese college students from 2002, 2003, and 2005 all show the same results: that more than 90 percent agree that animals feel pain and suffering, agree that animals deserve respect and consideration, and support the work of animal protection organizations.[13]

At the same time, there is resistance to animal advocates because they are seen as purveyors of a Western bourgeois lifestyle and agents of Western imperialism. Qiao Xinsheng condemned the anticruelty law being debated by Chinese legislators in the early 2000s as Western in origin and contrary to Chinese traditions. He opined:

Highly educated people in China are knowledgeable about the outside world, including outside criticisms of aspects of Chinese culture. ... Being knowledgeable, they can cite examples of foreign practices to counterattack foreign criticisms of Chinese practices. Being nationalistic, they have the tendency to equate foreign criticisms with a wholesale assault on the Chinese culture. Like educated South Koreans, educated Chinese detest their

---

[9] In 1998, the Philippines banned the killing of dogs and cats for food; Taiwan banned dog eating in 2003.

[10] In February 2002, university student Liu Haiyang threw sulphuric acid and caustic soda onto black and brown bears housed in the Beijing Zoo. The incident shocked the Chinese people and stimulated discussion about the need for anticruelty legislation.

[11] In this practice, bears are kept for years in extreme confinement with catheters implanted in them to regularly extract gall bile for use in traditional Chinese medicine.

[12] Littlefair (2006).

[13] Zu, Li, and Su (2005); Davey (2006).

motherland being portrayed as a barbaric nation because of dog eating or other practices criticized by Westerners.[14]

In response to calls for gradual animal welfare reforms, Zhao Nanyuan wrote an article, "The Essence of the Animal Rights Argument Is Anti-Humanity," in which he argues that there is no animal welfare problem in China: non-human animals are not sentient or conscious, and talk of animal welfare is "foreign trash" imposed by Westerners and their Chinese accomplices in a "neoimperialis[t]" move (Li 2006, 113).

Some American animal advocates caution against the imperialist trap of seeing the United States as good and China as bad on animal issues. In 2008, *Animal People*, a prominent newspaper in the U.S. animal movement, published an editorial entitled "National Image & the Quality of Compassion":

> Nearly every cruelty commonly observed and cited by some animal advocates in appeals for a boycott of the forthcoming 2008 Olympic Games in Beijing has a parallel in the U.S., albeit taking a superficially different form. Even when U.S. laws nominally prohibit the cruelty, enforcement is often so sporadic that the laws serve more to shield animal use industries from criticism than to bring offenders to justice. ... [T]he Chinese people could scarcely be accused of broadly enjoying or accepting violent abuse of animals as entertainment, even to the degree that Americans do. ... Despite the recent rapid rise of Chinese meat consumption, Americans still eat about twice as much meat per capita. ... The U.S. is far ahead of China in paying legal lip service to eradicating cruelty, especially to dogs and cats, but the gap in animal advocates' perceptions of the U.S. and China is unfortunately more a matter of image than reality.[15]

The editorial likens the Chinese practice of skinning dogs for fur to the American practice of skinning cattle for leather, and the Chinese practice of farming bears for bile to the American practice of confining pregnant sows to gestation crates. And it reminds us that for all of their fabled bloodthirstiness, the Chinese have never shown interest in the venerable Western traditions of bullfighting, rodeo, cockfighting, and dogfighting.

CHINATOWN: THE GLOBAL IN THE LOCAL

From its politics to the composition of its population to the languages heard on its streets to the goods proffered in its markets, San Francisco's Chinatown is a product of the global (see Figure 4.1). Chinatown was from the start what Yong Chen (2002) calls a "transpacific" community wherein the Chinese government exercised powerful influence over the Chinese Consolidated Benevolent Association (CCBA, also known as the Chinese Six Companies), the leading organization representing Chinatown to the broader society. From 1878 to 1911, the Chinese consulate in San Francisco appointed CCBA board directors and considered the organization an extension of the consular service, a

---

[14] Zu et al. (2005), 84.
[15] http://www.animalpeoplenews.org/08/4/textpercent20files/editorialfeature_0408.txt.

FIGURE 4.1. Chinatown in San Francisco, California.

situation that Chinese San Franciscans, eager for the protection of the Chinese government, accepted (Lai 1999). The Chinese government viewed Chinatown as an outpost of China whose inhabitants were, like all of the emperor's subjects, deserving of guidance and protection. Anti-Chinese practices in the United States were thus taken as an insult to the Chinese nation.

During the Cold War, Chinatown became a site of intense political struggle between those favoring the Communists (PRC), who had taken control of the mainland after the Chinese Civil War, and those favoring the Kuomintang (KMT), who had lost to the Communists and fled to Taiwan. The KMT worked with the FBI and INS to weaken PRC supporters in Chinatown in the early years of the Cold War, and its Cell for Direction of Overseas Activities bent its energies to bringing Chinese American organizations into the KMT fold (Yeh 2008). As a result, during the 1950s, "a large part of the community acquiesced to the conversion of many community institutions to KMT-controlled tools to be used in Taiwan's struggle with the PRC."[16] Every year on October 10, National Day, the CCBA issued a proclamation calling for the community

---

[16] Lai (1999).

to "support the fight against communism and restore the nation" (Lai 1999). Politically speaking, the CCBA got something out of taking sides. As Yeh notes, the CCBA "manipulated the anticommunist hysteria to enhance their power in the community."[17]

Organizations in San Francisco's Chinatown have steadily warmed toward the PRC during the past few decades. Nixon's visit to China in 1972 opened the door to family visits, trade, and cultural and educational exchanges, and the normalization of relations between the United States and China in 1979 accelerated these developments. The PRC began openly courting Chinatown associations, which led in some cases to the formation of parallel community organizations and in other cases to open conflict within organizations between pro-KMT and pro-PRC factions (Lai 1999). Ed Liu, a Chinese American attorney and community leader in San Francisco, explains: "[E]ach government has an executive office that is strictly dedicated to ethnic Chinese overseas affairs. Beijing has one, Taipei has one. They all have their outreach. ... So it becomes an extraterritorial rivalry." Liu points out that the annual flying of the flags in Chinatown is an indisputable index of who is faring better in this rivalry:

Every year, October 1st is PRC national day. October 10 ... is Republic of China. ... The flags, the raising of the flags now has shifted towards Beijing and the PRC. ... If you go down to Chinatown, late summer, you will notice that the flags – it's what they call the battle of turf. All of these community organizations, with the family associations and so forth, will generally, by the time it rises to a crescendo, will raise the flags. Every single year I observe what association is flying what flag, the PRC flag or the ROC flag. ... Every single year, you're seeing that the shift is happening. Ah, so-and-so organization suddenly now has a majority of pro-PRC members and the officers now have decided that this year on October, they will fly the PRC flag in lieu of the ROC flag. As a matter of fact, the PRC now, every October, they get to go to City Hall. San Francisco City Hall now has a flag-raising ceremony. No longer the ROC flag, but the PRC flag.

In 2004, in a sign of the times, the new CCBA president Daniel Hom refused to go along with tradition – which involved singing the Taiwanese national anthem and swearing an oath under the Taiwanese flag – and opted instead to hold a banquet at a Chinese restaurant under the PRC flag. Some Chinatown elders boycotted the banquet and others filed suit to remove him as president, alleging that his snub of Taiwan "created chaos" within the community (Tam 2004). According to Chinatown elder and CCBA leader Raymond Mah, Chinatown was 70 percent pro-KMT ten or twenty years ago and is now 70 percent pro-PRC.

Chinese San Francisco was once a community composed mostly of merchants and low-skilled laborers from southern regions of China. This is no longer true. Although the United States granted a token number of visas to Chinese immigrants during World War II in recognition of China's status as a wartime ally, the turning point for Chinese immigration was the passage

[17] Yeh (2008), 25.

of the Hart-Celler Immigration Act of 1965. This act, a self-conscious public relations move by the United States in the context of the Cold War, dismantled the national quota system that had preserved the whiteness of the nation for four decades and put in its place a system emphasizing family reunification and professional skills. The subsequent flow of Chinese immigrants diversified Chinese San Francisco by class, educational background, occupational status, and income.

Then, starting in the late 1970s, Chinese from Hong Kong, anticipating the return of the former British colony to China in 1997, entered the United States as part of what Ed Liu calls "yacht immigration" – people coming with "bagfuls of money" to buy real estate and make other investments in San Francisco's Chinatown. These immigrants, who came to the United States "to seek safe havens for their families and investments in American cities and suburbs," were part of a bifurcated Chinese immigrant stream, which also contained unskilled, uneducated, poor immigrants with limited English capacity arriving from mainland China.[18] Diversification of national origins has also been a striking trend, with immigrants coming from not only mainland China but throughout the Chinese diaspora – from Hong Kong, Macau, Taiwan, Vietnam, Cambodia, Malaysia, the Americas, and elsewhere (Zhou 2011). This complexity generates centrifugal pressures, as Ed Liu notes:

[W]ith the influx of immigration from all over now – you have Chinese coming in from Nicaragua as a result of the Somosa regime, you have Chinese coming in from Latin America, from Southeast Asia, from Indonesia, from Malaysia, in my case from the Philippines, you have Chinese coming in from Vietnam – it muddles up the dynamic of the community. So instead of coalescing, we are diversifying.

Driven by increased immigration from certain regions of the mainland, there has also been a perceptible shift from Cantonese to Mandarin during the past few decades. A 1986 survey showed that almost 70 percent of Chinese households in the San Francisco area spoke Cantonese and 19 percent spoke Mandarin. A 2002 survey showed that 53 percent spoke Cantonese and 47 percent spoke Mandarin.[19]

Demographics are an important part of the Chinatown story. Asian Americans are the fastest-growing minority and immigrant group in the United States as a whole.[20] Asian Americans now make up almost 6 percent of the U.S. population, with Chinese Americans, who are 23.2 percent of all Asian Americans, constituting the single largest national origin group.[21] The Chinese

---

[18] Li (2005), 36.

[19] "Chinese Communities Shifting to Mandarin."

[20] This would include those who are fully and partially of Asian descent. The rapid growth of the Asian American population is expected to continue. The U.S. Census Bureau projects that Asian Americans will grow by 161 percent between 2008 and 2050, compared with a projected 44 percent increase in the overall population, and that Asian Americans will constitute 9 percent of the total U.S. population by 2050. http://www.census.gov/newsroom/releases/archives/population/cb08–123.html.

[21] Pew Research Center, "The Rise of Asian Americans."

American population alone grew thirteen-fold between 1960 and 2006 (Zhou 2011). Within California, the Asian American population grew 31.5 percent (to 12.8 percent) between 2000 and 2010, faster than any other racial/ethnic group. In San Francisco, the Asian American population grew by 11 percent from 2000 to 2010; by comparison, Latinos also grew by 11 percent but whites shrank by 12.5 percent and Blacks shrank by 22.6 percent (Fagan 2011).[22] Asian Americans are expected to surpass whites, who are now 42 percent of the city's population and the single largest racial/ethnic group, by 2020 (Geron and Lai 2011).

San Francisco has the second largest Chinese American community in the nation, second only to New York City. One out of three San Franciscans today is Asian American, and most of them are of Chinese descent. Chinese are the single largest Asian national origin group at 21.4 percent of the city's population, with Filipinos at 4.5 percent, Vietnamese at 1.6 percent, Japanese at 1.3 percent, Asian Indians at 1.2 percent, and Koreans at 1.2 percent.[23] As of 2011, according to David Lee, executive director of Chinese American Voters Education Committee (CAVEC), approximately 18 percent of the San Francisco electorate is Asian, and 80 percent of that group is Chinese.[24] San Francisco, in sum, has experienced dramatic growth in its Asian population and is now significantly more Asian and Chinese than California or the United States as a whole (see Figures 4.2 and 4.3).[25]

Since 1965, the growing Chinese population of San Francisco has dispersed spatially across the city. Historically, Chinatown was created and actively maintained as a site of racial exclusion. However, as exclusionary measures such as restrictive covenants stopped being enforced during World War II, more and more Chinese immigrants opted to move out of Chinatown into areas such as the Richmond and the Sunset, as well as suburbs farther out.[26] The influx of Chinese immigration after 1965 accelerated this trend. Some arrived in Chinatown and stayed there briefly before moving; others had the financial means and wherewithal to bypass the Chinatown entry point and go

---

[22] Between 1970 and 2000, as San Francisco's Asian and Latino populations grew, its white and Black populations declined. The most significant losses of white population occurred in the Sunset and Excelsior neighborhoods, with corresponding Asian and Latino growth in these areas. The most significant losses of Black population occurred in Oceanview, Merced, and Ingleside, with corresponding Asian growth in these areas (Willis 2004).

[23] "GCT-PH1 – Population, Housing Units, Area, and Density: 2010 – County – Census Tract." 2010 *United States Census Summary File 1*. United States Census Bureau. Retrieved July 11, 2011.

[24] Gordon, "SF Asian Americans Ascending in Halls of Power" (January 11, 2011).

[25] San Francisco Planning Department, *San Francisco Neighborhoods: Socio-economic Profiles*, 1.

[26] Moving into the suburbs did not always go smoothly for Chinese Americans. See Cheng (2006) for the story of Sing Sheng, who tried in 1952 to move into the Southwood suburb of San Francisco. He requested that the residents take a popular vote about whether to allow him to move into the neighborhood, counting on the ideology of Cold War democracy to work in his favor. The residents voted against him.

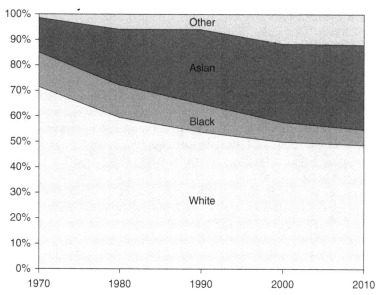

FIGURE 4.2. San Francisco Change in Racial Composition, 1970–2010. Courtesy of the San Francisco Planning Department.

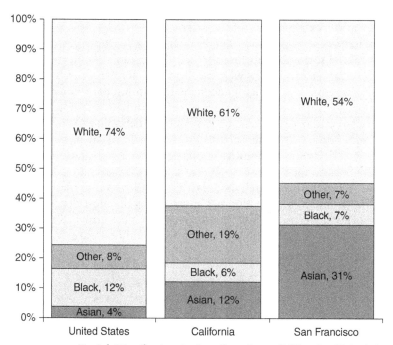

FIGURE 4.3. Racial Distribution in San Francisco, California, United States, 2010. Courtesy of the San Francisco Planning Department.

directly to these other neighborhoods. Michel Laguerre (2005) refers to these new areas of Chinese settlement that emerged in the 1960s in San Francisco and elsewhere as "new" Chinatowns or "ethnoburbs."

The Richmond district of San Francisco, for example, which used to be mostly Irish American, became a favorite choice for Chinese immigrants in the 1960s because the housing was larger, of better quality, and cheaper than in Chinatown and because several bus lines allowed for direct and easy transit to Chinatown. Chefs trained in Chinatown could open new restaurants in the Richmond and still access Chinatown for shopping, visiting friends and family, and securing Chinese language instruction for their children. Chinese American real estate agents advertised housing in the Richmond to diasporic Chinese before they arrived in the United States, and before long, a thriving Chinese middle-class community replete with restaurants and markets – a "new" Chinatown – emerged in the Richmond district (Laguerre 2005).

While Chinese immigrants of means have moved into areas like the Richmond, those who are older, uneducated, and have limited English proficiency and few skills and resources have had to stay in Chinatown. Emphasizing the positive, Wong notes, "San Francisco's Chinatown is, in short, an acculturation agent for the new immigrants. The community has bilingual social service agencies, translation services, Chinese stores, familiar food supplies, Chinese mass media, and information networks, all of which cater to the needs of new immigrants."[27] Disadvantaged Chinese immigrants do benefit from these services, but they also lack a meaningful option to exit.

Thus what has emerged in Chinese San Francisco is a "pattern of geographic redistribution along socioeconomic lines."[28] Moving up and out has become a sign of middle-class success: those who can leave Chinatown do. Chinatown is marked by severe overcrowding, inadequate and substandard housing, and significant linguistic isolation. Ninety-five percent of Chinatown's housing was built prior to 1959 and 68 percent of it was built before 1939. It is overwhelmingly renter-occupied by those with low and/or fixed incomes.[29] Single room occupancy (SRO) hotels comprise about 60 percent of the housing stock and many date back to the late 1800s (Wright 2001). Chinatown's population density stands out even in a densely populated city: "With more than 16,000 residents living within 40 square blocks, Chinatown is the most densely populated neighborhood west of Manhattan; seven times more crowded than the typical San Francisco neighborhood."[30] Housing conditions are frequently

---

[27] Wong (1998), 18.

[28] Loo and Mar (1982), 97.

[29] Gee (2007), 35–6.

[30] Wright (2001), 72. In 2001, Wright observed "some 140 family associations, 38 social service agencies, 13 churches, 88 professional groups, 21 childcare facilities, 28 health centers, 8 youth organizations, 5 community development agencies, and 4 advocacy and tenant organizations" in San Francisco's Chinatown (2001, 72–3). There are associations by family name, region, district hometown, trade, kinship, and dialect, as well as alumni associations, labor unions, social service agencies, political organizations, and nonprofits (Wong 1997).

poor. According to one news report in 2005, 87 percent of tenants in Chinatown had reported at least one code violation, 62 percent had reported multiple violations, 35 percent had reported rodent or insect infestations, and most violations had gone unreported because of barriers like limited English proficiency (Hua 2005). In addition, Supervisorial District 3 (a rough proxy for Chinatown) has the highest rates of linguistic isolation – where all family members older than age fourteen have another primary language and speak English less than "very well" – in the city.[31] What Chalso Loo and Don Mar observed thirty years ago about Chinatown – that its residents are "disadvantaged by immigrant status, language, age, education, and income" – remains true today.[32]

A brief look at neighborhood socioeconomic profiles supports the idea of a roughly bifurcated Chinese San Francisco.[33] Chinatown's main socioeconomic indices are shown in Table 4.1, in comparison with those of the Richmond (Inner and Outer) and the Sunset (Inner and Outer). Because these data pertain to all residents of these areas (Chinese comprise 84 percent of Chinatown's population and Asians – mostly Chinese – comprise between 33 and 57 percent of the other areas), it is not a direct comparisons of the Chinese living in these areas.[34] Still, it is suggestive of a significant polarization in the Chinese community. Chinatown residents are less educated, are more likely to be foreign born, are less likely to own their home, are less likely to live in a single-family home, have lower median family incomes, and have higher rates of poverty and joblessness than (Chinese and other) residents of these other areas.[35] In addition, as indicated in Table 4.2, Chinatown residents are much more likely to hold service jobs and much less likely to hold managerial/professional jobs than residents of the Richmond and the Sunset.

Chinatown is a place that people leave behind and a place they return to. Julie Lee, a Chinese American activist who helped to start the San Francisco

[31] San Francisco Planning Department, *San Francisco Neighborhoods: Socio-economic Profiles*, 7.
[32] Loo and Mar (1982), 98.
[33] All figures are taken from San Francisco Planning Department, *San Francisco Neighborhoods: Socio-economic Profiles*.
[34] The Inner Richmond is 2 percent Black, 38 percent Asian, 51 percent white, 6 percent Latino (28–9). The Inner Sunset is 2 percent Black, 58 percent white, 33 percent Asian, 6 percent Latino (30–1). The Outer Richmond is 2 percent Black, 48 percent Asian, 44 percent white, 6 percent Latino (50–1). The Outer Sunset is 1 percent Black, 57 percent Asian, 35 percent white, 4 percent Latino (52–3). Chinatown is 84 percent Asian, 12 percent white, 2 percent Black, 2 percent Latino. Source: San Francisco Planning Department, *San Francisco Neighborhoods: Socio-economic Profiles*.
[35] For comparative purposes, here are the figures for San Francisco as a whole: 19 percent of the population is sixty and older; 34 percent are foreign born; 38 percent live in owner-occupied housing and 62 percent in renter-occupied housing; the median household income is $70,117; the median family income is $86,665; 11 percent live in poverty; and the unemployment rate is 7 percent. San Francisco Planning Department, *San Francisco Neighborhoods: Socio-economic Profiles*, 6–7.

TABLE 4.1. *Select Socio-Economic Indicators by Neighborhood, San Francisco, 2011*

	High School or Less	College Degree	Graduate/ Professional	Foreign-Born	Own Home	Single-Family Housing	Median Family Income	Poverty	Jobless
Chinatown	70	12	4	75	6	3	22,691	31	15
Inner Richmond	22	35	22	32	32	22	88,804	12	6
Outer Richmond	26	32	19	40	43	39	89,541	7	7
Inner Sunset	14	37	33	26	40	40	102,639	8	4
Outer Sunset	31	32	14	49	57	68	89,241	7	6

Source: San Francisco Neighborhoods: Socio-Economic Profiles, San Francisco Planning Department, May 2011.

TABLE 4.2. *Types of Employment by Neighborhood, San Francisco, 2011*

	Managerial/ Professional	Service	Sales/Office
Chinatown	22	41	23
Inner Richmond	52	14	26
Outer Richmond	49	16	26
Inner Sunset	66	9	19
Outer Sunset	46	17	23

Source: *San Francisco Neighborhoods: Socio-Economic Profiles*, San Francisco Planning Department, May 2011.

Neighborhood Association (SFNA) in the mid-1990s, explains why she lived in Chinatown for only three months before moving to the Richmond and then to the Sunset:

Chinatown is a shell. ... I found out it's not place for me. If I had to live in Chinatown, I rather go back to Hong Kong, because there's no future there. It's such a small – if you look at – if you standing on Grant Avenue, if you look around, what is going on here? This is like a – to me, honest to God, sometimes I feel it's like a zoo, you know? Everybody around in high-rise, beautiful development. Chinatown is so behind! Old structures, and they say, preservation, you cannot change a window. You cannot build. ... All right. That tells you. So no matter where you go in this country, every Chinatown, it is – it don't make me feel good. Some thing. Very behind, dirty, old.

For Lee, Chinatown is a place for poor Chinese immigrants and the community organizations who serve them – it is not a real neighborhood:

This association [CCBA], the people, the leaders in the association, they don't live there. Chinatown, the rest of them in Chinatown either very, very new immigrants who cannot survive once they leave Chinatown, they don't speak English at all, or a whole bunch of so-called nonprofit, nonprofit for low-income, they're still out there. The regular normal people don't live in Chinatown. Simple, there's not adequate school. ... So these people, they actually either the ones cannot leave or the ones just professionally have something to do with the area. Otherwise nobody want to go there. We just visit there, symbolic. It's not a town any more. It's not for average people to raise their children and live there.

On the other hand, Ed Liu, another SFNA activist, comments on the powerful connection Chinese San Franciscans living in other neighborhoods maintain with Chinatown:

When my parents were still alive, we'd come every weekend, we were down here – for a lot of Chinese families, even if it's a 10 cents difference, they will shop at a shop in Chinatown. The feeling over all is that number one, food is cheaper. Even if it's 10 cents cheaper, I will walk three blocks just to get my vegetables, because it's 10 cents cheaper. Number two, everybody has the feeling that the produce in Chinatown is more fresh, there's a lot more turnover, and there's more variety. So you like the idea of coming down here on a Saturday,

when the produce stores are packed full of people, you rub elbows. That's the idea of having the family get together.

Chinese San Franciscans' affective and imaginative ties to the place are clear:
they return there even if they never lived there. They go to restaurants there,
shop at markets there, socialize there, and attend cultural events there. Even
those who see it as a shell and hasten to leave it feel connected to it somehow,
so that what happens there affects them. Chinatown connects them to their
history and to each other.

Chinatown's reputation as a "center of cultural continuity"[36] is bolstered
by its multitude of traditional festivals – the New Year Festival, Dragon Boat
Festival, Mid-Autumn Moon Festival, Winter Festival, and more – that draw
tourists from around the world. These events essentialize Chinese culture
as a historically enduring object and commodity. Chinese business leaders
have always known that Chinese culture sells. When the 1906 earthquake
destroyed the original Western-style buildings of Chinatown, Chinese merchants seeking to attract tourists "paid white architects to come up with an
Oriental look that would be appealing and acceptable to a general public that
had come to view the Chinese with racist eyes."[37] The physical architecture
of Chinatown captures in a still frame the market's dynamic mediation of
cultural authenticity.

Chiou-ling Yeh's *Making an American Festival: Chinese New Year in San
Francisco's Chinatown* (2008) artfully demonstrates the contradictions that
beset the annual staging of the area's most famous and lucrative cultural event.
The first New Year festival in 1953 was planned by the pro-KMT Chinese
Chamber of Commerce as a display of American patriotism and a testament
to American racial diversity in the context of the Cold War. It "immediately
became a foreign policy weapon" (4), as the U.S. State Department recorded
and aired it on Voice of America radio in the PRC as a rejoinder to Soviet and
Chinese criticisms of racial discrimination in the United States. Since then, the
New Year Festival has grown into an internationally broadcast three-week-
long event that promotes Chinatown businesses as well as San Francisco tourism through the invention and selling of "a unified and fixed Chineseness"
(158). To create and maintain this fictive cultural unity, festival organizers must
suppress and deny tensions between the People's Republic of China and the
Republic of China, as well as intra-community divisions of class, gender, and
sexuality. Is Chinatown a real, living, breathing Chinese community or a site
for the performance of an imagined Chineseness? It is a product of global political struggles; the neoliberal and multiculturalist commodification and marketing of identity; the daily, material practices of new Chinese immigrants; and

[36] Wong (1988), 27.
[37] Tsui (2009), 21.

the felt longings of Chinese San Franciscans more generally. It is anything but straightforward.

THE OPTIC OF RACISM AND THE BUILDING OF COMMUNITY

During the 1990s, Chinese American activists in San Francisco sought to build a sense of community around several key issues, including proposed restrictions on the size of single-family homes, the rebuilding of the Central Freeway after the 1989 Loma Prieta earthquake, and the live animal market campaign. In the case of the live animal market campaign, Chinese activists used the optic of racism to mobilize Chinese San Franciscans and persuade the broader public of their position, arguing that the pressing moral issue at hand was not cruelty to animals but rather racism against the Chinese.

The mobilization of the diverse and fractious Chinese community was not automatic or guaranteed – the animal campaign targeted only live animal market vendors, after all. So activists worked hard to construct a sense of a common threat affecting *all* Chinese San Franciscans, their cultural traditions, their history. If it was not automatically apparent what a second-generation, affluent professional living in the Sunset had in common with an uneducated, low-income, non-English-speaking immigrant newly arrived in Chinatown, the proposed answer was that they were both Chinese and were being targeted for persecution as such. The imperative, therefore, was to close ranks and pursue political power. The optic of racism could not but resonate in the city that was once the leading site of anti-Chinese sentiment and action in the United States, a place where nativists persecuted the Chinese with a ferocious creativity still discussed in constitutional law classes today.

Organizations such as the Chinese Consolidated Benevolent Association (CCBA or Six Companies), the Chinese Chamber of Commerce (CCC), and the San Francisco Neighborhood Association (SFNA) began with the claim that selling live animals for food has been central to Chinese cuisine and culture for more than 1,000 years. The practice reflects the belief that freshly killed meat is not only more flavorful but also more energizing, more nutritious, and more medicinal (with healing properties for those suffering from arthritis and other ailments). The only way to know meat is fresh is to buy a live animal and kill it yourself or watch as it is killed at the market. May Chang, owner of a Chinatown market that sells turtles and frogs, recalls: "When I was a little girl in Shanghai, my mother always told me, 'When it's dead, you never know how long it's been dead.' I have been here 20 years, but I still sell everything live. It is healthier. If you offer people dead animals, they won't eat them."[38]

The multiculturalist narrative woven by Chinese activists called for the affirmation of racial and cultural difference. It imagined those of Chinese descent as

[38] Golden (1996).

a unified people, a distinct "we" with unbroken ties to the homeland, accumulated ancient knowledge about animal and human bodies, and traditions that reach back into the mists of time, unperturbed by migration and other disruptions. It also imagined a distinct "them" – a white majority that is at best ignorant and at worst ethnocentric and arrogant toward Chinese culture. Julie Lee of the San Francisco Neighborhood Association suggested that white Americans fail to recognize that cultures have different criteria for who is edible:

Here, we often see how people love pets, dogs. Dogs, man's best friend. I don't against that. But I see people sleep with dogs, they share ice cream. I thought that's kind of unsanitary. But they do that. But I'm not about to attack them. But in southern part of China, they eat dog meat. I went to China, and they sell them. My husband was so upset, he couldn't eat for one day, you see? That's cultural clash. I see your side of the story, I see that side of the story. Let's sit down and talk about it. We have to learn how to live together. Right?

Against the assertion of a universalist anticruelty narrative, then, Chinese activists argued that the definition of cruelty is shaped by one's cultural location. One man's pet is another man's dinner.

In a similar vein, Chinese activists argued that animal advocates were using a double standard – criticizing Chinese cruelty toward animals (which was hypervisible to them) while implicitly denying their own (which was invisible to them). Rose Tsai of the San Francisco Neighborhood Association wrote in to the *San Francisco Chronicle*'s Open Forum on January 10, 1997:

Are we so sure that if cameras were free to roam the slaughterhouses and meat factories that produce and supply the neatly packaged meat we buy at super-markets that the conditions there would not offend the sensitivities of many of us? Many in the Chinese community believe that traditional societies have a more honest attitude about our relationship to the animal world. We are reminded that our nourishment comes at the price of life. There is no need to hide that fact. ... Many raised in American society are squeamish about eating any food served in the form of the animals that became food. If San Francisco, as a city, wants to take on the issue of cruelty to animals, let it do so in a consistent manner. We should require certification and inspection of industries that supply meat for sale in the city. We should not focus only on the more visible targets.

Again, Chinese activists did not directly deny the charge of cruelty as much as they deflected it by raising the issue of cultural perspective. All cultures are cruel, they suggested, so it is unfair to call out Chinese culture in particular.

Prior to the Commission on Animal Welfare and Control's vote on the proposed ban on live food sales, the SFNA issued a flyer calling on the Chinese community (in both English and Chinese) to attend the hearing, suggesting that group rights, individual liberties, and community jobs were all in peril:

ALERT!!! ANIMAL RIGHTS ACTIVISTS DON'T WANT YOU EATING FRESH FOOD! Your right to choose fresh food is about to be taken from you. If the activists get their way, your choices at restaurants will be limited to frozen foods. Fishermen's Wharf will no longer be able to sell freshly cooked live crab. Markets which sell freshly-killed poultry and fish will be closed down. Hundreds of people will lose their jobs; all of this will happen if we let a few elitist activists succeed in imposing their standards on us with their proposed legislation. Show up at the last hearing to stop the unfair regulations.

Outside of the hearing, one Chinese American held a sign saying "Human Rights vs. Animal Rights," and another held a sign that said "Cultural Imperialism" with a line through the phrase.

Attorney Paul Wartelle made a statement at a CACW hearing that played to San Franciscans' sense of exceptionalism while reinforcing the notion of animal activists as misanthropic zealots. After waxing poetic about the "proud hardworking community of Chinese-Americans" who have "defined their cultural identity by their cuisine and their language since rice first began to grow in the Yangtze River Valley 4,000 years ago," Wartelle casts animal activism as a form of intolerance that violates San Francisco's spirit of openness:

The United States is riven apart today by many who seek, with earnest intensity, to enact their own deeply held concepts of personal virtue into law. One need only look to the intensity that causes right to life advocates to kill doctors in Pensacola abortion clinics or the intensity that urges religious fundamentalists to attack love between two men or two women as a sin to see that moral intensity itself is no substitute for wisdom. San Francisco was built on values of a different timber. We look back to Harry Bridges' longshoremen, who shut this town down to ensure that working men and women were included in its good life. San Franciscans followed Cesar Chavez and Martin Luther King with a special dedication when they struggled to include Blacks and Hispanics and people of all colors among those who are welcomed in our house. San Franciscans were inspired by Harvey Milk when he died so that gays and lesbians could live here as they chose. ... San Franciscans have built a unique open house with the broad rafter beams of openness, inclusion, diversity and mutual respect. ... Do not take this occasion to take up the narrow crooked timber of subjective and private virtue to board up our windows and doors. No one should think to post this house with signs saying: "CLOSED TO THE PUBLIC: HERE ONLY THE SAVED, CHOSEN, MORALLY PERFECT AND POLITICALLY CORRECT ARE WELCOME."

Wartelle later explained: "My approach to things like this has always been – you have to oversimplify. The way to fight a political campaign from the grass-roots is to get a big idea and define it, and that's what I tried to do. ... [The big idea here was] San Francisco is a crossroads of the world where we're tolerant."

At times, the multiculturalist exhortation to cultural affirmation gave way to direct charges of racism. Many Chinese activists argued that the professed concern about animals was actually a pretext for racial persecution. Bill Tam, executive director of the Chinese Family Alliance, wrote a letter to the editor of the *San Francisco Chronicle* on November 19, 1996 in which he defended Chinese live animal markets as providing the "most humane treatment of animals in the modern world" because "each animals' life is preserved to the fullest" and "there is no wastage or unnecessary slaughtering of extra animals for inventory purposes." Tam concluded "We consider the attempt to ban the slaughtering of live animals by Chinese merchants to be motivated by hidden agendas."

Citing prior efforts to regulate Chinatown food practices, Rose Pak of the Chinese Chamber of Commerce echoed this idea:

It's a constant battle. ... It seems we forever have issues with one group or the other. ... [A] lot of it has to do with food and culture. They tried to stop us from selling roast duck and roast pork. ... They demanded that all the roast duck, roast pork has to be heated in an oven certain degrees. You roast a duck in the oven for another half an hour and it will be burned. The pork will be completely dry. So we have to fight that, so to waive it. They tried to use health code. Then a bill was introduced to make it criminal to eat dog. And we go, "Huh? Why is that necessary?" ... Who the hell eats dogs? ... Every 10 years, another story, a stupid thing, surfaces like that.

What was their motivation, do you think, the animal activists?

Well, we are more vulnerable. ... They just think we are a more easy target. Why don't they go to the downtown fancy three-star, four-star restaurants. They were buying those things. What the hell do you think the French restaurants are serving? Turtle soup and frog legs. Why don't they go there? Why do they pick on these mom-and-pop stores, right? It's easier. They are racist. ... Well, they're not as blatant now. ... Only under certain circumstances the ugly head of racism will lift its head. They're not as blatant. But there still is a long ways to go yet. In San Francisco now we have three Chinese American Supervisors. First time in 160-some-odd years, in the history of the city. We don't have a mayor yet. ... And so we're still fighting, but at least they don't yank our hair and cut off our queue any more.[39]

Like Pak, other Chinese Americans explicitly located the animal campaign in a narrative of anti-Chinese persecution dating back to the 1800s. CCBA attorney Arnold Chin said at a CACW hearing on August 8, 1996 that the proposed ban on the sale of live food evoked memories of discriminatory anti-Chinese legislation from the past.[40] In his article, "Chinatown Butchers and Animal Rights" (September 20, 1996), *San Francisco Examiner* columnist William Wong wrote: "It doesn't take a great leap ... to come away with the impression that it's the heathen Chinese who are at the root of despoiling San Franciscan (and American) life." The following month, Supervisor Tom Hsieh held a press conference in which he stated:

I will fight any attempt to ban the sale of live animals in San Francisco markets. As a Chinese-American, I must take some offense at some of the short-sighted comments directed towards our community by some of the animal rights advocates. They self-righteously dismiss and show disrespect for our traditions, cultures and values. They may not be aware that their rhetoric is insensitive and divisive and perpetuates discrimination against our community.[41]

---

[39] Pak is referencing San Francisco's Queue Ordinance of 1873 requiring prisoners to have their hair cut within an inch of their scalp. Although facially neutral with regard to race, the ordinance was directed at Chinese immigrants, who wore queues as a matter of custom and to symbolize their loyalty to the Chinese Emperor.

[40] Lee (1996).

[41] Press Release from Supervisor Tom Hsieh's office, October 2, 1996.

Hsieh compared the animal campaign to the Chinese exclusion movement of the 1870s and handed out packets of photocopied materials that included San Francisco municipal reports from 1869–70 (describing the Chinese as "moral leper[s]"), as well as excerpts from scholarly writings on facially neutral but discriminatory legislation such as the Cubic Air Ordinance of 1870 (mandating that rented rooms must have at least 500 cubic feet of air/space per person) and the Queue Ordinance of 1873 (requiring prisoners to cut their hair short). Referencing these materials, Hsieh concluded: "During this ugly period of anti-immigrant sentiment, many of the same words were used by government officials to describe Chinatown as some of these animal rights activists today. I will be sure no further damage is done."

Eric Lin's *Chinatown* (1999), which was filmed during the live animal market controversy in San Francisco, voices the same perspective as Pak, Hsieh, and others. The story involves Jen, a mild-mannered Chinatown waitress, and Ender, her defiant male friend, responding to protests staged by strident white animal activists. While Jen is bewildered by it all and haunted by nightmares of eating human flesh or being eaten by humans, Ender is a hard-liner who rails about cultural domination and rejects all form of compromise as selling out. When his father's restaurant is vandalized by animal activists, he and his friends yank an animal activist into the alley and beat him up. Ender yells at him that he must have seen the movie *Chinatown* with Jack Nicholson – which depicts Chinatown as "a shithole of civilization" – many times even if he doesn't know it. In the meantime, Jen recalls that her parents used to complain during her childhood when tour guides depicted Chinatown as filled with brothels, hatchetmen, and shops selling rat meat. Eric Lin, who wrote and directed the film, said: "The attempt to control food practices in Chinatown was more of a symptom of representations of Chinatown, so as a result I looked at the deeper level. The decision to go against Chinatown rather than, say Fisherman's Wharf is a symptom of other issues. ... Asian Americans are an easy default villain" (Hsu 2000).

THE ROLE OF THE CHINESE-LANGUAGE MEDIA

Chinese-language media (including print media, television, radio, and online media) have grown rapidly since the early 1990s in areas with large Chinese American populations (Zhou and Cai 2002). With significant linguistic isolation in San Francisco's Chinatown and one-fifth of all San Franciscans older than age four speaking mostly Chinese at home (Tsai 2011), there is a large market for Chinese media in the city. A 1999 survey by the Chinese American Voters Education Committee (CAVEC) showed that 82 percent of respondents (Chinese living in the Bay Area) said they frequently read Chinese newspapers and 99 percent watch Chinese television. Four daily newspapers have local bureaus in the city, including *World Journal*, *Sing Tao Daily*, *China Press*, and *Epoch Times* – each one with a circulation of tens of thousands (Tsai 2011).[42]

---

[42] Chinese-language papers in San Francisco do not have audited circulation, so all of their figures are self-reported. Writing in 2004, Vanessa Hua reported that the *Sing Tao Daily* had a

Chinese radio stations such as Sing Tao Radio and Chinese television stations KTSF and KPST broadcast in the city as well, in both Cantonese and Mandarin. The Chinese media report on both homeland/diaspora issues as well as local issues of concern, thus keeping Chinese Americans informed about "their two social worlds."[43]

The Chinese media covered the live animal market campaign extensively, serving as a source of information, a forum for expression, and an instrument of political mobilization.[44] The *World Journal*'s news coverage provided a largely uncritical platform for Chinese leaders to advance their interpretation of events and call people to arms. The statements and actions of Chinese activists were frequently covered without mention of countervailing viewpoints. Sometimes the articles took on the hortatory tone of Chinese activists' pronouncements; sometimes they conveyed information (phone numbers to call, where to meet to be transported by bus to a public hearing) directly from Chinese activists to the public; sometimes they allowed Chinese American politicians to tout their accomplishments in the fashion of a campaign advertisement. While the mainstream English-language media's claims of "balanced" coverage may be more fanciful than true, the Chinese media's lack of concern for the appearance of objectivity is striking in comparison and suggests a different conception of how the media is supposed to relate to and serve the community.

The *World Journal*'s coverage helped Chinese leaders to advance these recurrent themes: that the live animal market campaign constituted a crisis with both racial and economic dimensions; that this was a slippery slope that could lead to more dire situations; that the Chinese community needed to come together, close ranks, and fight for its interests; and that political mobilization in the form of attending hearings, writing letters, and voting was essential. Together, these themes defined the problem, provided a solution, and clarified the need for action.

When the CACW voted to propose a ban on the sale of live animals for food, a *World Journal* article, "Mabel Teng: Anti-Asian Wind Blows for over Fifty Years" (November 19, 1996), reported that Chinese American Supervisor Mabel Teng denounced the CACW's action as "anti-Chinese" and "anti-Asian" and linked it to a pattern of discriminatory treatment that included the killing of Vincent Chin in 1983 and the prosecution of John Huang during the campaign finance scandal of 1996.[45] Arguing that the Chinese "must win" on this

circulation of 130,000 and the *World Journal* had a circulation of 65,000. Writing in 2011, Luke Tsai reported that the *World Journal* had a circulation of 50,000 daily and 60,000 on Sundays in Northern California. The readers of the *World Journal* are primarily immigrants from Taiwan and mainland China. Affiliated with the Taiwan News Company, it was perceived as anti-PRC until the 1990s, when it started to appear as more neutral toward the PRC. The *Sing Tao Daily*'s primary readership is immigrants from Hong Kong and mainland China, and the paper is seen as generally pro-PRC.

[43] Zhou and Cai (2002), 432.
[44] A native Chinese speaker assisted me by searching through the *World Journal* and *Sing Tao Daily* for articles on the live animal market controversy and then translating several articles into English.
[45] The author is Lu Shiwei.

issue lest it affect businesses in all U.S. Chinatowns, Teng urged the Chinese to register, vote, and fight to protect their rights. Similarly, when the lawsuit was filed against Chinese merchants, a *World Journal* article, "Anti-Chinese Wind Blows Heavily and the Chinese Need to Fight for Our Benefits" (April 19, 1997), reported on Supervisor Leland Yee's reactions.[46] According to Yee, the lawsuit showed that anti-Chinese and anti-Asian racism was "still rampant" and that events like this would recur if the Chinese did not "counterattack strongly." "We are actually still in their home as strangers," Yee declared, pointing to the Lowell High School controversy as proof that the Chinese in San Francisco were oppressed.[47] Anti-Chinese sentiment was greater now than at any time in his forty years in the United States, Yee claimed, as he urged "Chinese merchants to fight for their entitlements and ethnic Chinese voters to vote for their rights."

Like Chinese American elected officials, activists closer to the conflict used the Chinese media to achieve myriad goals at once – performing leadership, asserting ownership of the issue (against other officials or activists), and mobilizing the community to get involved. A *World Journal* article entitled "Killing Live Animals in Chinatown Leads to Another Anti-Chinese Action" (October 8, 1996) reports on a press conference called by Rose Pak and Paul Wartelle in Chinatown.[48] The story conveys Pak's claim that the animal campaign is racially discriminatory and lays out the slippery slope problem, quoting Pak: "San Francisco's Chinatown was their [animal advocates'] first war and if they win this battle, the war will spread to all California and even the whole United States, so success or failure has a great impact on the future." Pak's other comments – that City Administrator Bill Lee and others are creating disunity and doing Chinatown a disservice by seeking to negotiate with the other side, and that all Chinatown businesspeople should attend the last hearing before the CACW vote on the ban – are also reported. Here Pak forcefully stakes out her differences with other prominent Chinese – in this case, Bill Lee – in front of a Chinese audience. The same day, an article in *Sing Tao Daily*, "Chinatown Merchants Counterattack Animal Rights Activists over Issue of Selling Live Animals for Food," reiterated the statements made at the Pak-Wartelle press conference, including Wartelle's observation that the animal activists are "rabid racists" who treat people of color differently from whites.[49]

Rose Pak's competitors for the mantle of leadership in the live animal market conflict also spoke through the Chinese media. A *World Journal* article, "Chinatown Economic Development Group Supports Selling Live Animals"

---

[46] The author is Lu Shiwei.

[47] In the mid-1990s, a group of Chinese American parents brought a lawsuit against Lowell High School, one of the most prestigious public schools in San Francisco, alleging racial discrimination. Working within a consent decree imposed after a desegregation lawsuit brought by the NAACP, Lowell High School had placed caps on single ethnic groups in order to create a diverse student body. This had led to differential admissions requirements for Chinese students, who constituted the single largest ethnic group in the school.

[48] The author is Yu Ning.

[49] The author is Chen Tien-Shen.

(April 23, 1997), reports that community leader Pius Lee issued a public statement condemning the lawsuit against Chinese merchants as racially discriminatory and an attack on Chinese culture and calling upon the Chinese community "to be united to protect everyone's fundamental interests." Several days later, a *World Journal* article, "Facing a Lawsuit by Animal Protection Activists, CCBA Calls for All Chinese Americans' Support" (April 27, 1997), covered the CCBA's release of a statement in which its seven constituent organizations unanimously called for all Chinese to support the Chinatown shops and to "stand up and fight this lawsuit to the end."[50]

The SFNA, founded by Chinese Americans in the mid-1990s, used Chinese radio to mobilize the community around the live animal market conflict. By the 1990s, most of the Chinese living in the Bay Area were listening to Chinese radio.[51] During this period, SFNA activists Rose Tsai, Julie Lee, and Ed Liu hosted an hour-long radio show in Cantonese – first called "Voice of the Neighborhood" then "Community Forum" – five nights a week on KEST (AM 1450), a Chinese radio station that broadcast throughout the Bay Area. Rose Tsai explains, "We just decided that we should do our own show and we could talk about other issues, because it's such an effective tool. It was relatively novel, because back then, Chinese radio was also only just starting to take root in the city and in the Bay Area." Their goal was to inform and educate the Chinese community about salient issues as well as to encourage them to take part in politics, Tsai recalls:

[W]e talked about anything. Whatever happened to come up. We talked about current events. We'd talk about community issues and public hearings which are being held at City Hall. We were trying to get people to understand how the system worked. ... [T]he difference is that before, there wasn't a vehicle for people to voice their opinion, and many in the Chinese community just do not have the knowledge of how the system operates to be effective communicators and to advocate for their people. ... The Chinese are just not used to being activists. Being an activist is not an easy thing. It's pretty time-consuming, and you don't really see results for a long time. Many people in the Chinese community are just burdened with making a living.

The dynamism of talk radio opened up new possibilities for community discussion and action. Listeners tuned in, learned about issues from the hosts, heard the views of community leaders who came onto the show, called in to give their own opinions, and turned out at a public hearing that same night – all at a pace that traditional methods of mobilization (mailings, getting the word out through community organizations, newspaper stories) could not match.

According to Rose Pak, the Chinese media is indeed an important player in San Francisco politics, as reflected by Mayor Willie Brown's attitude toward it:

---

[50] The author is Xu Minzi.
[51] Chavez (1997).

I thought the Chinese media was instrumental in informing the public [on the live animal market issue]. They did a great service to the community, they always have. I've always maintained that our local media plays a very important role. That's why city government, when Willie Brown was the mayor, he every month met with the ethnic media, roundtable and hosted luncheons and discussion on every issue. His office had all monolingual staff. I remember him hiring one of our Chinese reporters to be the liaison in his Mayor's Office of Neighborhood Services, and I remember the director went to Willie Brown and said, "You hired this Chinese kid. His English is really poor." So Willie Brown looked at him, "What's your problem? I didn't hire him for his English. I hired him for his Chinese, because every person told me he speaks different dialects and he reads and writes, and that's why I hired him. I don't need him to speak English for me. I need him to speak Chinese for me. Move on."

There are indications that the Chinese media do facilitate formal participation in the political system. The aforementioned 1999 CAVEC survey of Chinese Americans concludes that "[Chinese] media use was related to perceived importance of voting"(24). Those who frequently partake of Chinese television and radio programming are roughly four times more likely than those who do not to think voting is "very important" for Chinese Americans, and households where everyone reads Chinese newspapers are four times more likely to say voting is "very important" for Chinese Americans as well (24).

WHO SPEAKS FOR CHINATOWN? OLD RIVALRIES, NEW CONFLICTS

Attorney Paul Wartelle marvels that Chinatown is an "unbelievably political place, with a 24-hour news cycle before anybody else had one." Politics in Chinatown, and in Chinese San Francisco more broadly, are thorny, complex, and dramatic. The live animal market conflict was shaped by and in turn shaped two salient dynamics in the political life of Chinese San Francisco. The first is a long-standing rivalry, both personal and political, between Rose Pak and the Chinese Chamber of Commerce, on the one hand, and the CCBA and Pius Lee, on the other, over who speaks for Chinatown. The second is the diversification of the political landscape, with economic stratification and spatial dispersal generating new types of organizations with new kinds of constituencies. On the live animal market issue, Chinese activists were less a coherent coalition than a loose, fractious assemblage of organizations and personalities jockeying for position around a common concern.

The CCBA in San Francisco has a centuries-old reputation of aiding Chinese migrants, mediating community disputes, and protecting the community from the broader society's discriminatory actions (Chen 2002; Wong 2006). Yet it has been the target of sustained criticism as well. Its zealous advocacy of the KMT and denunciations of the PRC have in the past invited the charge that it was turning community politics into a venue for the Taiwan-PRC conflict.

Its pronounced traditionalism gives the appearance that CCBA leaders are entrenched elites trying to protect their own privileges. Raymond Mah, former

president of the CCBA and current board member, describes the power structure in Chinatown, including the CCBA, as exclusive, closed, and static:

New immigration don't have any power in Chinatown anyway, because all are old organizations. ... That's why, like me, I have been there 40 years, so we have a lot of power in
the organization, something like that. So the new immigrant, mostly in south peninsula.
They all high-tech people. ... All those, they're not involved in Chinatown. Anyway, you
can't get in, because before, from the district, from China, the organization, always district.
From which district you come from, which family, surname family come from, university,
all those. Just like a network already set in Chinatown.

Echoing the Red Guards and other radicals of an earlier era, critics point out
that the CCBA's talk of "community" elides class conflict: "The CCBA always
claimed to be the spokesperson for the entire ethnic community and an organization devoted to the rights and welfare of Chinatown. Yet the CCBA and other
traditional groups were mainly concerned with the interests of factory owners,
merchants, and landlords, instead of the welfare of the working class."[52] The
CCBA has also been called an old boys' network: no woman has ever sat on
its board, or on the boards of the family and district associations of which it
is comprised.[53] In the eyes of its detractors, the CCBA is a vestige of the past,
composed of ceremonial figureheads who have no vision of the future and offer
no real leadership.

The Chinese Chamber of Commerce (CCC) formed more than a century
ago to promote small business interests in the wake of the 1906 earthquake.
Rose Pak joined as a consultant in 1984. Pak, who came from Hong Kong
in 1967, earned a BA from University of San Francisco and an MA from the
Columbia School of Journalism and worked as a lecturer at San Francisco
State University and a reporter with the *San Francisco Chronicle* before joining
the CCC. Pak dismisses the CCBA as irrelevant. The CCC has not competed
with the CCBA as much as it has stepped into the void left by the CCBA's lack
of leadership:

They're [the CCBA] very outdated, let me put it this way. ... They don't work on anything.
Yeah, that's why they're outdated. They just get together every month, have meetings and
they do banquets, they go to a lot of banquets and take pictures. That's all I know.

Pak also suggests that the two organizations represent different class interests,
with the CCBA promoting exploitative moneyed interests and the CCC protecting the little guys:

It's always been issues involving land use [in Chinatown]. The haves fighting the have-nots.
Landlords versus tenants. Who are our landlords? Our landlords are very precious few.
They're the family associations who own 30 percent of the real estate here. ... All they

---

[52] Yeh (2008), 89. As Morrison Wong (2006) points out, scholars differ on how much exploitation
exists within U.S. Chinatowns. Peter Kwong (1987, 1997) argues that Chinese small businesspeople exploit immigrant workers, whereas Min Zhou (1992) argues that these limited-English
workers are given employment and a foothold for upward mobility.

[53] Bishop (1990).

[the family associations, the landlords] do is spend on travel and food. They give very little back to the community. ... They don't maintain their properties. They keep on taking rents, gouging their high rents. Our rents are comparable to Union Square. ... Yet they don't spend – for every $100, they don't spend $1 on maintenance, keeping the building up to code. ... They don't paint the buildings. They don't upgrade the infrastructure of the buildings. But they take the money. Our SRO, the single room [occupancy], shared communal kitchen and bath, they are now $800 per month per single room. They're not cheap rent. ... sometimes whole families in one room. But they are at their mercy, with fixed income. The restaurants that they rent out, all of those commercial ground-floor space, they rent them for thousands of dollars. They don't make any improvements. They don't bring up the electrical code. They don't change the piping system. They don't change any of those. ... [W]e represent the businesses. But in the community, we're so small and tight-knit, everything is intertwined. Business suffers when our people suffer. So we now take on every issue, because if you don't care about your residents, they couldn't care less about your businesses. If we don't keep our street clean, if we don't pick up the garbage, that will have a profound effect on the economy also. So we end up doing everything. ... So we are involved with the tenants, with the land use, with the rent, commercial as well as residential. If you don't have stabilized tenants, your small businesses suffer.

In Pak's view, the CCBA exploits Chinatown small businesses while pretending to represent them. The CCC, on the other hand, rolls up its sleeves and takes on the dirty work of protecting the neighborhood's stores and residents.

By the mid-1990s, Rose Pak had established herself as a force to be reckoned with in San Francisco politics. She has acted as an old-style powerbroker, a liaison between her close ally, Mayor Willie Brown (1996–2004), and Chinatown interests. Paul Wartelle, whom Pak hired to defend the merchants in the live animal market lawsuit, explains:

[Rose] had a very tight alliance with Mayor Brown, and she was kind of his gatekeeper for Chinatown. I don't know if I should say that. She was alleged to be the gatekeeper. ... If you wanted access and you were from Chinatown or connected with the Chinese community, what people alleged, and I don't know if it's true, they said you had to go through Rose. And if you wanted to give money to Brown, you went through Rose. And the other leaders, like the Fangs and Pius [Lee], were deeply resentful.[54]

Ed Liu of the San Francisco Neighborhood Association echoes this characterization of Rose:

So people like Willie Brown or John Burton or any of these white politicians from Sacramento or the city would look to Rose Pak as what we call the gatekeeper. She's the go-to person. Makes things simple. If you want any money, you go to Rose, "Can you help me?" Rose will say, "OK, I can raise so much for you by Monday."

Pak's distinguishing characteristic, according to both fans and detractors, is her pugilistic and confrontational personality, her fight-to-the-death mindset. She relishes this reputation:

---

[54] The Fang family is prominent in San Francisco business and politics. They own *Asian Week* and many other media publications.

I'm different. I don't play your – how would I put it? I'm not your regular kind of turnover Chinese. ... I mean, we are law-abiding, we don't rock the boat. I don't conform to all the stereotypes. ... And I don't care about face. I don't care what people think of me. I'm never going to run for public office. I don't have the temperament nor the patience. I don't meet the diplomatic skill. I know I'm right, so I can be right at the top of my lungs.

Pak took an uncompromising stance on the live animal market conflict and expressed contempt for the CCBA's efforts at reaching a negotiated settlement.

The CCBA and the CCC were on a collision course from the start of the Commission on Animal Control and Welfare hearings (1995–6) on the proposed ban on live food sales. Both organizations got involved early on, attending and speaking at CACW hearings, and lobbying Commissioners and city officials. The Chinese merchants who would have been most affected by the ban were the CCC's clients, and Pak spoke on their behalf and organized their rotating attendance at hearings. As first-generation immigrants from throughout the Chinese diaspora (China, Hong Kong, Vietnam, etc.) who had little or no English proficiency, they relied on her to represent their interests to the CACW and the broader public. But the CCBA kept its hand in the game, too. Tensions over which organization spoke for the merchants, cared about their interests, and could deliver for them continued through the year of hearings. For the most part, the organizations worked on parallel tracks – the CCC went on to support the merchants in the lawsuit, for example, while those affiliated with the CCBA went to Sacramento to try to pass the Honda Bill (AB 238) and stop the Kuehl Bill (AB 2479) – but there were flashpoints of conflict between the two.

The CCBA's preference was to negotiate an agreement with various parties quietly and behind the scenes. Pius Lee, a businessman who was head of the Stockton Street Merchants' Association in Chinatown and had strong ties to the CCBA, assumed a leadership role in this effort. Together with City Administrator Bill Lee, Pius Lee organized several meetings with animal advocates Virginia Handley, Pat Briggs, and Eric Mills. When those talks fell through, Pius Lee worked with the SFSPCA's Rich Avanzino to draft the Joint Guidelines (discussed in Chapter 3). Pius Lee's tone when speaking at public hearings was consistently conciliatory rather than confrontational. He repeatedly characterized the problem as one of education: the Chinese merchants wanted to comply with the law but they weren't always aware of what the law required, so the solution was to step up educational efforts: "We have to keep their [Chinese] culture, but at the same time, they have to comply with the local law. They have to do both." Asked about Rose Pak, Lee declined to comment, instead turning the conversation to what he considered a major accomplishment – persuading legislators to water down the Kuehl Bill (AB 2479):

I'm going to give you how I negotiated to take away – that's important. Because if they approve the bill based on original one, the business dead in Chinatown. ... And then the [elimination of the] 90-day prison [requirement] is important. And also, later on we have to have some educational program, too.

Pius Lee later started the No-Ban Coalition that led the fight to dissuade the Fish and Game Commission from enacting a ban on the importation of live turtles and frogs for food (discussed in Chapter 5).

Rose Pak and Pius Lee were already famously at odds (Paul Wartelle: "I don't know if you picked up on it, but Pius Lee and Rose hate each other") and the live animal market conflict provided another stage for the playing out of this mutual animosity. If Lee was reticent about Pak, she was quite expressive about him:

The Chinese Six Companies [CCBA] do not understand politics and always want to reach agreements. … It was excruciatingly painful, because you've got idiots on your own side that don't even understand the issue – everything compromise, compromise, you know? … [The Six Companies] just want to show that they're doing something, so they jumped in in the last minute with one or two people from our own community, bananas, I call them … Pius Lee and Bill Lee. They're crooks! I'll go on record to call them crooks! They have no ethics. They have always been – Pius Lee would not do a thing without benefiting his own pocket. You can go down the street and ask anyone. … We don't like him. He's a man of no scruples. He only gives money to politicians so they make an appointment of him, that's all.

What makes them bananas?

Yellow on the outside, Bill Lee, white on the inside. He grew up in Baltimore. He never knew what being a Chinese meant. So he kisses ass with the whites and he knows even less about Chinese than the whites. Pius Lee is motivated – one thing that motivates him is money, and in which way he makes money, that's what motivates him. Community survival, a community's dignity, those things don't concern him.

What's the opposite of a banana? What do you consider yourself?

Chinese American. I'm Chinese first. Chinese American first. Community comes first.

Chineseness, for Pak, is not about descent, culture, or language, but passionate dedication to the interests of the community. Ironically, Pak had herself been accused of selling out Chinatown when she backed Mayor Art Agnos's decision to tear down rather than rebuild the Embarcadero Freeway – a main artery leading into Chinatown – after it was damaged in the 1989 Loma Prieta earthquake. According to Ed Liu of the San Francisco Neighborhood Association, Pak used the live animal market conflict as a vehicle for rehabilitating her reputation and resurrecting herself as Chinatown's preeminent leader after seven or eight years "in the wilderness." Attorney Paul Wartelle recalls Pak's attitude toward the lawsuit:

Rose was terrified during the trial, because she went out on a limb to say – Rose is a fighter. … I miss Rose. I hardly ever see her any more. She was tough as nails, and she was like, "Take 'em to the mat!" …

What was she terrified about?

That she would lose [the lawsuit]. That the stores would essentially be shut down. She'd lose face. Because Pius [Lee] kept up a steady stream of criticism of her. … He was always very hostile to her.

What was the substance of his criticism?

"Make a deal. Don't fight this thing" … [Pius Lee] and Bill Lee, who was the chief administrative officer at that time and was not Rose's friend. They were on one side and Rose was on the other.

For Pak, there was more at stake in this legal proceeding than the interests of her clients.

The SFSPCA and CCBA's surprise announcement about the Joint Guidelines in April 1998 created as much turmoil among Chinese activists as it did among animal activists. Caught off guard, the hard-liners on both sides felt undercut, but judged they could not afford to publicly reject the agreement. Wartelle recalls his reaction:

But the thing about the SPCA and the deal did completely blindside me. It hit right before the trial. That was another thing that was kind of dramatic. … And there wasn't really anything wrong with the agreement. But the fact that the Six Companies signed it right before the trial without consulting the businesses that they were supposedly – and then said, "We'll deliver the businesses." … The agreement said some things would be done by July. I figured I couldn't leave my guys hanging out with this agreement being shoved in their face and then refusing, because I didn't know what kind of judge I was gonna get and I didn't know whether this was gonna come in. And there was nothing about the principles that I couldn't say "okay." And so we signed it.

Although the CCC endorsed the Joint Guidelines before the general public, it voiced its displeasure behind the scenes and via the Chinese media. When he discovered that the CCBA had invited his clients but not him to meetings about implementing the Joint Guidelines, Wartelle wrote a letter to the CCBA's Raymond Mah (April 28, 1998):

The Chinese Chamber of Commerce had given unstinting support to the merchants throughout their long ordeal. At the same time the Chamber has not sought to dictate either strategy or tactics to my clients, but has simply encouraged my office to give them the best representation possible. While your organization and the Chamber do not always see eye to eye on every issue, when both are attempting to champion the interests of the same people, wouldn't it make sense to work cooperatively. Jostling to establish a separate position on so crucial and difficult a question can only have the effect of undermining the interests of the very people whom the whole community is eager to help (2).

Wartelle voiced dismay that the CCBA had his invited his clients but not himself to a meeting where they had contact with the animal activists with whom they were engaged in pending litigation. He concluded by saying he had instructed his clients not to attend any more meetings. Wartelle also published an open letter in the Chinese media stating that the Joint Guidelines would harm Chinese merchants and influence the court to rule against them.

In response, the CCBA held a press conference on May 2, 1998, reported in a *World Journal* article entitled "CCBA Will Not Harm the Interests of

Chinatown Businessmen."[55] The article reports that Raymond Mah issued a "formal rebuttal" of Wartelle's charges at the press conference. Pius Lee is quoted defending the CCBA and calling on the Chinese to stop their infighting and unite against a common foe. Several days later, on May 8, 1998, Douglas Chan, attorney for the CCBA, fired back a letter to Wartelle, in which he stated that the CCBA was not obligated to share information with the CCC and credited the Joint Guidelines with forestalling a Fish and Game Commission ban on importing turtles and frogs. He wrote:

My client is extremely disappointed that you and your taskmasters at the Chinese Chamber of Commerce have sought to distort the public's perceptions of the role of the Six Companies and to impugn the motives of other concerned citizens in drafting the Joint Statement. ... We do question whether the Chinese Chamber of Commerce (whom you took special care to praise in your letter to the press at the expense of my client), and the community is ably served by your baseless, public pronouncements that the Six Companies is "jostling" to undermine the interests of the merchants. ... We ask whether you and the Chamber's consultant, Rose Pak, simply want to position yourselves to assure that 1) you and Rose can exercise the option to discredit the Six Companies if you lose the pending litigation, or 2) take credit in the Chinese community for successfully defending the merchants? ... The interests of the Six Companies and the Chinese Chamber of Commerce have been, and are, congruent on a wide range of issues affecting the Chinese American community in San Francisco. ... [T]he Six Companies will reiterate that it is ready, willing and able to work cooperatively with all members of the Chamber, but it will not permit you or Rose Pak to perpetuate the fallacy that the objectives of the organizations are in conflict. We hope that the community will deem the alleged differences between the organizations to be nothing more than a mere artifice by Rose to capitalize politically on perceived divisions within the Chinese community (2–3).

A few months later, the CCBA and CCC came together to sign an open letter in which Chinese merchants expressed their commitment to implementing the Joint Guidelines. A *World Journal* article (July 10, 1998) drily remarked: "This is the first cooperation between the two representative Chinese organizations in many years."[56]

THE SFNA: CHINESE ACTIVISM OUTSIDE OF CHINATOWN

In addition to stoking tensions between established Chinatown organizations, the live animal market conflict provided a focal point for the coalescence of a new Chinese organization, the San Francisco Neighborhood Association. The SFNA formed to address the quality of life concerns of Chinese homeowners living outside of Chinatown (in the Richmond, the Sunset, and surrounding areas) – concerns overlooked by Chinatown organizations serving businesses, tenants, workers, and new immigrants.[57] It was, as such, the direct product of

[55] The author is Yu Ning.
[56] The author is Liu Kaiping.
[57] SFNA members were from the Richmond and the Sunset as well as Excelsior, Oceanview, Outer Mission, and Bay View-Hunter's Point.

the economic diversification of Chinese immigrant flows into San Francisco and the spatial dispersal of this population within the city. Interestingly, two of the three founders of the SFNA, Rose Tsai and Julie Lee, are women. Women, who have been excluded from the traditional power structure of Chinatown's old associations, are asserting political leadership in new venues just as the Chinese community stands on the brink of achieving significant political power.

Ed Liu, one of the founders of SFNA, says he is part of the "ethnic Chinese diasporic experience." His grandfather emigrated from China to the Philippines, where Liu was born and raised before coming to the United States for school. Attending Hastings Law School in San Francisco in the late 1970s raised his political and racial consciousness:

I remember going through a constitutional law class and suddenly things opened up. In those days, Asian American studies, ethnic studies was still at its very formative stage. The concept of identity, you know, with the early activists who were involved in the '60s civil rights movement, we were sort of the Johnny-come-lately. ... I'd heard about all this fervor in UC Berkeley and the ethnic Chinese studies movement. I was engaged in contemporary Chinese studies with Mao Zedong and the Chinese revolution. In those days you had the Vietnam War. So there was intellectual fervor. But something sparked my interest when I began to study constitutional law. And lo and behold, the spate of constitutional law cases ... and the civil rights cases, the right of citizenship and even the *People v. Hall* about the non-person status of a Chinese in the criminal court system, where they cannot testify against a white man. So something sparked. The light bulb went on, and I became fascinated with the whole subject. So lo and behold, when I was on my second year of law school, I began to think that my future will be in terms of practicing law in the community that I can identify with. ... [T]here were very few Asian law firms at the time, a smattering, very, very few. ... So when I graduated in 1981, there was no doubt in my mind I was going to practice in San Francisco Chinatown. That's where I've been. Our practice started out as a little hole in the wall on Grant Avenue, where the heart of Chinatown is.[58]

The other two founders of the SFNA are also immigrants and established professionals. Rose Tsai moved to the United States from Hong Kong when she was a child and grew up in New York City; later, she came to California to earn a law degree, hosted a show on Chinese talk radio, and ran for the Board of Supervisors. Born and raised in Shanghai, Julie Lee moved to Hong Kong and then to the United States. She owns a real estate firm in the Sunset.

Place was central to the SFNA's formation and mission. Like animal activists, SFNA members were moved by issues that emerged out of their spatially embedded daily lives. The organization formed in 1995 as a response to the city's hearings on the proposed Residential Conservation Act (RCA), a law that sought to limit so-called Richmond specials – single-family homes that had been replaced with multi-unit structures or built out to accommodate larger

---

[58] *People v. George Hall* (1854) was a California Supreme Court case where Chief Justice Hugh Murray delivered the court's opinion that an 1850 state statute prohibiting Blacks, Mulattoes, and Indians from testifying in court against whites applied to the Chinese as well.

families.[59] Ed Liu describes Richmond specials as "three-level homes where it's two levels of apartments and at the ground level is the garage, where he [the owner] builds an in-law [quarters]." Against the backdrop of chronic housing scarcity in a city famously short on space, Chinese Americans with extended families were heavily represented among owners of Richmond specials and thus opposed the RCA, while neighborhood and historic preservation groups pushed for the law. According to Richard DeLeon, these latter groups, concerned that Richmond specials overshadowed neighboring homes and detracted from the architectural integrity of the neighborhood, opposed them "as if they were the plague, to the point of organizing neighborhood watch patrols to look for construction violations, screening building permit applications, and engaging in related surveillance activities."[60]

SFNA took the position that the RCA unfairly targeted Chinese immigrants, who were more likely to live in extended families. Ed Liu explains:

San Francisco housing is very, very, very difficult because number one, the lot sizes are small. And it is incongruent for many Chinese families, especially extended families, whether you're a Vietnamese Chinese or a Hong Kong Chinese or a Chinese like me from Southeast Asia, we have large, extended families. Many of us who buy our homes find that it is very, very difficult to live in San Francisco with the houses so tiny. Looks like little matchboxes. Just not adequate. So there is a huge movement to try to expand, increase the height. The big fight is in the perimeters. ... Chinatown cannot grow. So the Chinese are compelled to go to areas where the housing remains affordable. So we went to the Richmond district first, then to the Sunset district, and then to the outlying areas where the Blacks were clustered, Bayview, Excelsior. ... And so white folks in the city, eco-racist, the environmentalist, the green people, who want to make the city small. "We must control growth, we must limit density, this city must be green. It cannot exponentially grow with more population, more density. More density means the character of our city is gonna be dramatically altered, and that is totally unacceptable to us." So one of the propositions that was being [advanced] by the environmentalists, including the Sierra Club, including a lot of these green people, including many of these liberals, is that we must limit the size, the height, the density level of our neighborhoods. And they focused on a lot of these neighborhoods where the Chinese were clustered, especially in Richmond, in Sunset, in Excelsior. You know what they were proposing to do? Height. You can't build more than 30 feet or 32 feet. If I remember, it was 32 feet. You can't build more. That means, effectively, any Chinese family, parents, children, brothers and sisters, grandparents, you're gonna be effectively barred from adding another level. Density level in terms of open space area, in terms of the lot size, you must limit the available backyard. The lot size cannot build beyond a certain foot print in all of the city lots. And so the issue of zoning, planning, land use became a flash point. The San Francisco Neighbors Association was formed primarily on these issues.

For Liu, environmentalism shades easily into ecoracism, or racism that expresses itself in the guise of environmental values. He explicitly alludes to *Yick Wo v.*

Hopkins (1886), where the U.S. Supreme Court ruled that a law that is facially neutral with regard to race but applied in a racially discriminatory manner violates the Equal Protection Clause of the Fourteenth Amendment:[61]

From my point of view, when I researched the topic [of the RCA], it was *Yick Wo v. Hopkins*. Essentially it's race-neutral. From its outset, it looked racially neutral. You're only targeting woodsheds for laundry, you're not targeting brick buildings. But everybody knows it's only the Chinese who are operating woodshed laundries. Similarly, with respect to height restriction, although on its face it's neutral, on its face it says, "Okay, we're concerned about the density level of the city." So in a no-growth city in which we're talking about no growth, height limitation from the outset on a superficial level looks like it's very coherent. It's about sustainably living, about quality neighborhood, and in the Richmond and the Sunset, we need to restrict the heights of properties because it increases the density level. Number two, aesthetically, the concerns of many white people is that aesthetically it's ugly. It destroys the character of the neighborhood. "Neighborhood character" – that was the buzzword.

In Liu's view, the live animal market campaign and the state's ban on the sale of shark fin in 2011 (see Chapter 5) were examples of ecoracism as well. Are these instances of racism cloaking itself in facially neutral guises or instances where the charge of racism functions to shut down other kinds of important moral claims? Is the problem ecoracism or the imperialism of race?

SFNA founder Julie Lee got involved in the fight against the RCA because of her concern about housing:

I say, "Gee, I'm just a mother-homemaker and small business owner. I'm not for politics, you know. And I'm too straightforward." I will – I probably cannot please everybody, because, you know, when you're too principled, it's hard. But then when they formed these – I know housing is so important for Asians, particularly for the new immigrants. They came here, don't own anything, and we always – every one of us believe owning a home or a house is very important. So in the housing situation, I said, "Okay, I willing to help." Then I become the group's [SFNA's] treasurer, just watch their money. That was the beginning.

The SFNA organized a forum (broadcast in English and Cantonese) for mayoral candidates at Richmond Middle School, where they asked each candidate's position on the RCA in front of a mostly Chinese audience of more than 1,000 people. The candidates backed away from the law, which later failed to pass.

After prevailing on that fight, SFNA activists turned to the controversies over the Central Freeway and the live animal markets. Again, they focused on issues (transportation and food) affecting the quality of people's daily lives. Like the Embarcadero Freeway, the Central Freeway, a major artery connecting the Richmond and the Sunset to Chinatown and the downtown area, was damaged in the 1989 Loma Prieta earthquake. By all accounts, the adverse impact on Chinatown businesses was severe. Chinese American groups pushed for the Embarcadero to be rebuilt but Mayor Art Agnos acceded to business interests

---

[61] See Chapter 3, note 48.

who wanted to tear it down and build up the waterfront. Ed Liu explains that it was Rose Pak's "flip flop" on the Embarcadero that led to their personal falling out:

In the aftermath of the October 17th, 1989 earthquake, I formed the Chinatown Merchants Association, which is a separatist group from the Chinese Chamber of Commerce. That's where my rivalry with the Chinese Chamber and Rose Pak happened. Because Rose Pak and the Chinese Chamber, in the aftermath of the earthquake, was one of the propelling forces that pushed for the immediate retrofitting and fixing of … [the Embarcadero], because Chinatown depends on this lifeline to access. Our businesses are hurting. But lo and behold, less than two months after the earthquake, Rose Pak flipped. … Because Art Agnos, then mayor of San Francisco, was a Democrat, and Rose Pak was very closely aligned with Art Agnos. Rose Pak initially said, "Let's retrofit," and she organized the merchants to shut down for one day, rushed to City Hall, went to the Board of Supervisors, the city council, "retrofit, retrofit, retrofit." Merchants cooperated. Everybody shut down for one day. We went to City Hall all together, coalescing around the issue of getting Chinatown open again, getting the freeways done and quickly fixed as expeditiously as possible. But the forces in this city were against us. And guess what? Downtown, they saw the damaged freeway as an opening to open up the waterfront. So businesses like The Gap, which has its corporate headquarters in the waterfront with this ugly freeway blocking their ocean view, Bechtel Corporation, with its headquarters here, all these major downtown interests perceived the freeway as an aesthetic eyesore to the city. They wanted to free up the waterfront, open up the land, to create real estate possibilities for downtown interests. … [So] downtown and the business interests, and the so-called "Untie freeways," the green groups, the eco-racists, I call them, these are the environmentalists, these are the green people, these are the leftists, these are the liberals. … It becomes environmental issues clouded with racism. … So the momentum shifts. Art Agnos arm-twisted Rose Pak. Rose Pak said, "OK, let's tear it down." Merchants got livid. My client, one of the major merchants in Chinatown, who owns a slew of gift stores, came to see me. He said, "What's the matter with them? How did they decide to flip-flop without even consulting with the merchants and the rank and file? Was there a vote done by the Chinese Chamber when they flip-flopped and changed the decision in favor of tearing down the freeway?" We were livid. So a group of merchants decided, "Let's secede. We're gonna form Chinatown Merchants Association." … So we were David against Goliath. So we lost. Chinatown Merchants Association and Chinese Chamber of Commerce became two separate rival business chambers, and it continues to not talk to each other right now in Chinatown. Rose Pak organizes her Chinese New Year festival and Chinese New Year parade. Chinatown Merchants Association organizes and sponsors its annual Moon Festival and Street Fair that comes during September or October in commemoration and celebration of Moon Harvest Festival, which is a traditional annual harvest festival. Moon Festival versus Chinese New Year. Two separate, distinct festivities.

Hoping to achieve a different outcome the second time around, SFNA activists took up the fight to compel the city to rebuild the Central Freeway. The response among Chinese Americans was explosive, Julie Lee explains:

Without transportation, paralyzed. And we did that because San Francisco had torn down the [Embarcadero] freeway to Chinatown, [Route] 480. I don't know if you know that, and the freeway was not damaged at all. They torn down simply for the waterfront. Their people, the property value double and triple once they tore down the freeway. They supposed to put a subway like New York to help the transportation, but once they tore down, it's gone. And that make Chinatown never survived. It can never be as good as before. Now who cares? And we got out to do that, to defend Central Freeway. We say, "Hey, no more. Don't do this to us. Enough is enough." And that echoes through whole people like firecracker. Just go like that. It cost us lot of – oh, this office like war zone, you know? Day and night, volunteer. We try to reach out two, three hundred thousand voters. We don't have the money, so we mobilized the volunteer. We have a block captain, each street we have, Chinese live there, they become block captain for us. ... Every dollar for us. That's how we did it.

In July 1997, SFNA activists collected more than 30,000 signatures (almost three times the number required) to put Proposition H (compelling the city to rebuild the Central Freeway) on the November ballot.[62]

The SFNA got involved in the live animal market controversy, too, because it affected the daily lives of Chinese San Franciscans. Rose Tsai explains:

San Francisco Neighbors Association really revolves around ordinary people's livelihood. We talked about, in Chinese we say "clothing, food, housing, transportation." ... [W]e call it, those four things, what ordinary people's lives revolve around. So we talked about issues involving all those things. It was very emotional at that time, this particular issue. You know how Chinese love to eat, right? And having fresh food, it's extremely important to them, especially for the older generation. It was just – they had always taken it for granted. All of a sudden, this whole tradition and culture is being threatened. ... You're talking about their dinner and their lunch, what they put on the table for their family. And food is an extremely important element in the Chinese culture. ... Even for people like myself, who was never raised in Chinatown, never lived or worked in Chinatown, who doesn't even really patronize the market, we understood the issue, because it's such an integral part of our culture.

Ed Liu comments:

The feeling at the time was a feeling of being bullied. ... We are being bullied, and we feel the weight of persecution, that somehow we were ethnically mistreated, and we were mistreated because of the way they feel about certain things, whether or not it deals with housing, with food taste, with our cultural practices.

In response, SFNA activists used talk radio to mobilize Chinese listeners to join the fight. Rose Tsai recalls how effective radio was in getting people to turn out to CACW hearings:

[W]e talked about a lot of issues, but this got a lot of press, because it is considered, I guess, a very controversial issue. And I think it's one of the few times when the ethnic Chinese, the monolingual Chinese-speaking community really came out in force. I was kind of shocked, too. And we didn't expect over a thousand people to turn up when we talked about it. But it was an extremely emotional issue for a lot of people. ... So basically we talked about it, it's a call-in show. People talk about their opinions. And we give them the time and place when public hearings are being held and suggestions as to what they could do to try to change the minds of the legislators. I think it was the first time when a Chinese

[62] Proposition H passed but the fight over the Central Freeway continued.

organization had kind of laid it out for regular people who are usually not involved in politics or activism, to feel like they can be involved, they can make a difference. ... It's not like I called them out, like I was the organizer, no. We just talked about it. "This is what's happening." And people came from all over ... just regular people who like to buy fish to eat and grandmas and working people.

For Julie Lee, the live animal market issue was an opportunity to promote Chinese political empowerment more generally:

When people called into the show, did they agree with your perspective?

They angry.

About what?

They simply angry. To me, I use every opportunity to tell people go register to vote. You want to be voice to heard? Register to vote. That's the only way the politician will hear you.

What were they angry about?

They angry about why they tell us how to eat, why they want to close down the restaurant. See, special for Cantonese, southern Chinese, live fish is very important. Steamed fish is one of the most important dish in their life. How can you take that away from them? ...

So people were angry and then you'd say, "Go register to vote"?

If you want your voice to be heard, if you want to appoint Chinese to the different departments, different commissioner, if you want to have power, this is democratic country. The law is there to make fair to everybody. But if you don't get involved, you give up your rights. ... Later on we elect Willie Brown to the – I had dinner with him a couple nights ago. He's a great mayor. ... Yeah, he is very hard-working chief executive, very smart, good memory. He just – he put Asian into every department. He put Asian into every commission. No one ever did that before. And that makes me realize, it is important. If you didn't vote for him to be the mayor, this would never happen. We would never be the same level, lost down below. And it's also important, in my radio program, I always advise people, we are first generation. We have children. Children go to school and do very good. Try to influence them. It's very, very important to get them to be aware. It's not because they made it through, not because they made it to Berkeley, they should be happy. Get involved. Carry on this tradition. Get involved.

Which tradition?

To care for the community. We are not takers. We give things back to the society. Keep the good tradition. Be generous. Get involved. That's very important.

Julie Lee and Rose Tsai had some early meetings with the CCBA and invited CCBA leaders to come on their show to talk about the live animal market issue, but they mostly followed their own course, parallel with other Chinese American organizations.

Asian Week covered the SFNA's emergence with excitement, reading it as a sign of the Chinese American community's political ascendancy. In "Making Radio Waves" (January 17, 1997), columnist Samson Wong discusses how Julie Lee used her radio show to encourage Chinese listeners to naturalize, register, and vote in the 1997 elections, reminding them that a ban on live food might find its way onto the ballot. In another article, "What Are Neighbors For? A

New Asian American Community Group Challenges the Political Structure in San Francisco" (October 9, 1997), Bert Eljera describes Julie Lee and Rose Tsai as an "unlikely pair" that "is changing – perhaps forever – the political landscape of San Francisco" and "leading a grassroots movement [that is] fast becoming a vehicle for the political awakening of the huge Chinese American population in San Francisco."[63]

For its founders, the SFNA represented the promise of something new and important. Julie Lee saw it as an expression of a new orientation to civic engagement on the part of Chinese immigrants:

We don't vote. We don't register. We too busy taking care of children. We're too busy making a living. We're too busy saving money to buy a house. Also, we came from the country, the old tradition in Asia, there's no such thing as vote, register. We simply don't know. In China, you get involved in politics, you lose your head. So people, they're afraid. They just say, "Okay, working hard, raise your children, teach them, give them enough education, don't get involved or you lose your head." That's how we brought up. But we came here, hey, there's something else missing, you know?

For Ed Liu, the SFNA was a chance to do politics differently. As a nonpartisan organization, it could keep its focus on what was good for Chinese Americans rather than getting caught up in party politics:

I think one of the strategic mistakes about a lot of the Chinese American civil rights activists is that they reposed all their eggs into the Democratic Party. So the left-liberal agenda became the Chinese American activist agenda. And so the association and affectation of Democratic Party goals and imperatives becomes part and parcel of the activist agenda, which to me, when I started getting involved with the San Francisco Neighbors Association and the Chinatown Merchants Association, I began to realize that it's not a party thing. It's neither conservative nor liberal. It is culture. It is race, and race and white supremacy in my mind is neither the Republican or Democratic party. Because the race issue transcends the American partisan or the mainstream party issues.

As a grassroots organization, Liu explains, the SFNA meant going beyond the old Chinese pattern of giving donations to politicians and expecting nothing in return:

[M]y feeling about the old traditional family associations is that they never rock the boat hard enough. They were always doing these photo ops, face time, Howdy Doody. The way Julie and I and Rose looked at traditional Chinese politics with City Hall, when we started out with Rose, Julie, and I, we were looked at as outsiders. As much as we knew all this history, all of us felt – and I remember one of the radio talk shows we talked about was that, even though we didn't come up front about bring critical of specific family associations, we talked about Chinese politics with City Hall. I remember a show in which we said, "Look, the Chinese here in San Francisco, we are viewed mainly as the gas pumps. Every time there's an election, all these white politicians come here to San Francisco Chinatown and we are being used as the gas pump. … [T]hey come here and pump our gasoline and just

---

[63] Eljera also reports that SFNA claimed to have registered approximately 10,000 new Chinese American voters over the past two years.

walk away without paying." So implicitly there, we're basically challenging them, saying, "Why are you guys here in the traditional family associations leading all of these fund-raising campaign banquets?" … Every time there's a politician that wants to raise money from the Chinese, they come to these gatekeepers. And they would come here and use these brokers to raise money for them. What do we get out of it, other than a few photo ops?

In Liu's eyes, Rose Pak is "a nemesis that has made Chinatown stagnant, for the reason that the political style that she operates under is based on machine, on influence-peddling, on pay-to-play." The SFNA was intended as an antidote to the corruption of Chinatown politics – an alternative model of popular engagement and political accountability.

Chinese American activists responded to the live animal market campaign by asserting an optic of racism and cultural imperialism and situating it within the city's bitter history of anti-Chinese agitation. Combining gentle calls for multiculturalist affirmation of cultural difference with forceful accusations of racial persecution, they dismissed the question of cruelty to animals as culturally intolerant, hypocritical, trivial, or pretextual. Established Chinatown organizations vied for leadership on the issue, and a new Chinese organization outside of Chinatown stepped into the fray as well. With the help of the Chinese-language media, these organizations mobilized the Chinese community, promoted racial consciousness, and encouraged political participation at a time of rising Chinese political power in the city. When animal advocates took the fight to the California Fish and Game Commission in Sacramento – the subject of the next chapter – Chinese American activists organized to meet them on the new terrain.

5

The Optic of Ecological Harm

Protecting "Nature" in a Neoliberal Age

> There seems to be abundant evidence that these animals [imported turtles and frogs] are more ... than a threat. There seems to be no reason that we should allow these things into the state.
>
> – Fish and Game Commissioner Mike Sutton

When it became clear that the San Francisco Board of Supervisors would not enact the Commission on Animal Control and Welfare's proposed ban on the sale of live animals, animal advocates pursued their cause in the courts and in the California legislature, as discussed in Chapter 3. They also approached the California Fish and Game Commission (FGC), an advisory body to the California Department of Fish and Game, the entity charged with stewardship over the state's natural resources.[1] Setting aside the argument about cruelty, which was beyond the purview of the Fish and Game Commission, animal advocates advanced an optic of ecological harm, arguing that turtles and frogs imported for food sometimes get released or otherwise escape into the wild, where they act as invasive species who harm native species of frogs and turtles through predation, competition, and disease.

---

[1] Active since 1870, the Fish and Game Commission has five parttime Commissioners who are appointed by the governor and confirmed by the State Senate. The Commission holds monthly public meetings as well as special meetings as the need arises. "Probably the best known responsibility of the Commission is its general regulatory powers function, under which it decides seasons, bag limits and methods of take for game animals and sport fish" ("About the Fish and Game Commission," www.fgc.ca.gov/public/information/about.asp). The Commission is generally seen as an advisory body to and liaison to the public for the California Department of Fish and Game, which regulates hunting and fishing and manages conservation projects, although the exact nature of the relationship between the two bodies is indeterminate, as discussed in this chapter. Although the two bodies are distinct, they share a common discourse, so I refer to "Fish and Game discourse" throughout this chapter. The Department of Fish and Game was renamed the Department of Fish and Wildlife in 2012, but I use the original name because it was the name in use at the time of these events.

The Fish and Game Commission could fix the problem, according to animal advocates, by passing a ban on the importation of live turtles and frogs for food. When Chinese American activists once again invoked the optic of racism, the question became the degree to which this state body located in Sacramento would be insulated from the Chinese American political clout that had stymied local efforts against the markets. In the tradition of commissions, the Fish and Game Commission held public hearings, consulted scientific experts, and debated the matter on and off for thirteen years before finally recommending an importation ban in the spring of 2010. But in the end, Chinese Americans had enough political power to prevent the enactment of this ban as well.

In sporadic debates across these thirteen years, Fish and Game Commissioners, animal advocates, and Chinese representatives fiercely contested the meanings of race, species, nature, and culture. What constrained and shaped these debates was the official discourse of the FGC, whose contours testify to the impact that neoliberalism has had on environmental thought and language in the United States. The two central tropes of FGC discourse – nature as a "resource" and nature as a pristine (white) space – reflect, respectively, the instrumentalization of nature and anxiety about migration and borderlessness, two hallmarks of the neoliberal age. Together, the two tropes construct nature as a global commons that must be neutrally managed by scientific experts for the good of the whole, a notion that pointedly denies the *politics* of the matter – both the prevalence of conflicts over the use of nature and the systematic tendency of patterns of usage to privilege certain groups over others. The universalism of environmental discourse veils and promotes particular racial and class (and human) interests.

Neoliberalism's imprint on this story is indeed unmistakable. Just as "cruelty" is defined in U.S. law so as to protect "customary business practices" that reduce animals to commodities, so is "ecological harm" defined in state discourse so as to protect the "resources" threatened by "invasives." Maximizing the utility of the animal-instrument is the core logic in both instances, rather than moral concern for the animals themselves. Of course, it is unseemly to promote this logic too openly in an era of increasing public consciousness about animal and environmental issues. So the Fish and Game Commission presents itself as a neutral and scientifically minded "steward" of the environment and touts "ecological values" in a way that disguises the deep pervasion of its mission, discourse, and practices by economic values and priorities. For their part, animal advocates advanced an optic (of ecological harm) that went along with rather than challenge the reduction of animals to fungible "resources." This is the activists' dilemma here and in many places: in order to enter the public debate and be heard, one must accede to the discursive terms set by the powerful, but in doing so, one may end up compromising that which one is fighting for.

NEOLIBERAL IMAGININGS: NATURE AS A "RESOURCE"

Neoliberalism, ascendant in the global sphere since the 1970s, is characterized, according to Lisa Duggan (2003), by the implementation of certain types of policies – fiscal austerity, privatization, market liberalization, and governmental stabilization – designed to promote the operation of free markets and stymie any public efforts to impede or control them. Together, institutions such as the International Monetary Fund, the World Bank, and the World Trade Organization have advanced this policy agenda with the conviction that "open, competitive, and unregulated markets, liberated from all forms of state interference, represent the optimal mechanism for economic development."[2] One hallmark of the neoliberal age is what Jean Comaroff and John Comaroff (2001) call the "depoliticization of politics" whereby global capitalism presents itself as the only real alternative and "hides its ideological scaffolding in the dictates of economic efficiency and capital growth, in the fetishism of the free market, in the exigencies of science and technology" (242).

Ecocentric views of nature emerged momentarily in the U.S. public sphere in the 1980s, only to be driven underground by an instrumentalizing view of nature more consonant with neoliberal sensibilities. In his "Platform for Deep Ecology" (1988), Arne Naess condemns the "shallow ecology" of mainstream environmentalism for its anthropocentrism and proffers an alternative view that "the flourishing of human and non-human life on Earth has inherent value" and "[t]he value of non-human life-forms is independent of the usefulness of the non-human world for human purposes."[3] Deep ecology came under fire from both social ecologists (who challenged its depiction of humans as outside of and against nature, as well as its neglect of power differentials among human groups) and ecofeminists (who challenged its blindness to patriarchy), but it was ultimately its polar opposite that came to prevail in U.S. public life.[4] As De Paiva Duarte puts it, this neoliberal view of nature entails "managing, monitoring and planning the planet's resources, to ensure a continual supply of raw materials to meet the demands of industrial production."[5]

The instrumental view of nature embraced by neoliberals is not new, of course. Val Plumwood reminds us that the Western dualism of reason over nature – where nature is defined "as passive, as non-agent and non-subject, as the 'environment' or invisible background ... as a *terra nullius*, a resource empty of its own purposes or meanings" – traces back at least as far as Plato.[6] What is distinctive under neoliberalism is the aggressive pervasion of market values into many previously nonmarketized aspects of social and political life. Today, for example, we talk and think about social programs (and their beneficiaries),

[2] Brenner and Theodore (2002), 2.
[3] Naess (1988), 130.
[4] Bookchin (1987); Fox (1989).
[5] De Paiva Duarte (2001), 96.
[6] Plumwood (1993), 4.

educational institutions, and our relations to animals and nature in terms of market practices and values – and this development has become thoroughly *naturalized*. Language has been an important vehicle of this encroachment. As Donna Haraway writes: "Discourses are not only social products, they have fundamental social effects. They are modes of power."[7]

De Paiva Duarte (2001) shows that global environmental politics has become unapologetically neoliberal. Emerging from the United Nations Conference on the Human Environment in 1972, the Stockholm Declaration (Principle 10) declared: "The natural resources of the earth ... must be safeguarded for the benefit of present and future generations through careful planning or management." Similarly, the Rio Declaration (Principle 12) produced at the United Nations Conference on Environment and Development in 1992 encourages states to "cooperate to promote a supportive and open international economic system that would lead to economic growth and sustainable development in all countries, to better address the problems of environmental degradation."[8] That same year, the Convention on Biological Diversity, an international environmental treaty, stated its goals to be "the conservation of biological diversity, the sustainable use of its components and the fair and equitable sharing of the benefits arising out of the utilization of genetic resources" (Article I). Sarah Whatmore observes: "The logic here is to establish a universal exchange rate between the scientific value of animal (and plant) life, measured in units of biological rarity, and that most pervasive of human currencies – economic value."[9] As never before, the planet as resource is being "observed, scanned, measured, monitored and quantified"[10] by NASA, the United Nations Environmental Program's Global Environmental Monitoring System and Global Resource Information Database, and the United Nations' Earthwatch Global Observing Systems. Wolfgang Sachs writes, "Once, environmentalists called for new public virtues, now they call for better management strategies."[11]

Global environmentalism promotes a universalizing discourse that disguises the uneven distribution of economic benefits along national, racial, class, gender, and other lines (Di Chiro 2003). At the Stockholm Conference of 1972, as world leaders discussed how to save the planet from *and* for capitalism, they generated "rhetorics of universality, one-worldism, and common fate" and articulated "a discourse of commonality, communication, and cooperation across racial/ethnic, class, geographic, or national divisions."[12] Talk of the "global commons," of a universal stake in the husbanding of natural resources, gave a gloss of democratic legitimacy to an approach that "effectively amounted to a new enclosure policy or privatizing of nature ... to secure control over

---

[7] Haraway (1989), 289.
[8] Cited in De Paiva Duarte (2001), 97–8, 102.
[9] Whatmore (2001), 22.
[10] De Paiva Duarte (2001), 105.
[11] Sachs (1994), xv, cited in De Paiva Duarte (2001), 103.
[12] Di Chiro (2003), 205.

those components of the global environment – the atmosphere, the oceans, the genetic wealth of biodiversity – that are necessary" to economic production.[13]

Global environmental discourse trickles down in much the way the benefits of global capitalism are supposed to. The California Fish and Game Commission explicitly labels wildlife as "resources." The very name of this state entity, of course, reflects a reading of the wild animal through its utility for humans (as "game"). Acts passed by the California legislature between 1968 and 1981 direct the Department of Fish and Game to protect species and habitats with the understanding that "wildlife is a renewable resource that can provide for economic contributions which can accrue through regulated management."[14] What does it mean to call an animal a "resource"? Among other things, it means a moral devaluation of the animal as an individual and a species. According to *Merriam-Webster*, a "resource" is defined as:

a: a source of supply or support: an available means
b: a natural source of wealth or revenue
c: a natural feature or phenomenon that enhances the quality of human life.[15]

A resource is a means to an end and never an end in itself. In Kantian terms, a resource lacks moral autonomy and thus intrinsic worth. A resource cannot be the source of moral claims. Note that a conflict of interests between wildlife and people is rendered logically impossible by this language because "resources" cannot be said to be in conflict with people. Human proprietary interests in nature are paramount – they cannot be restricted in the name of wild animals, now reimagined as "resources," but only by the proprietary interests of other humans. The term "resource" appears technical, neutral, and apolitical, but applying it to wild animals is a profoundly political move that settles, at least provisionally, the moral status of the wild animal.

Fish and Game officials claim to use "the best available science." They declare: "All resource management decisions should be based on sound biological information. While other considerations affect decisions, they should be secondary to the needs of the resource."[16] Can a "resource" have needs? Here FGC officials are referring to the biological requirements for wildlife species survival, which in turn has economic and noneconomic value for humans. An article entitled "Current Issues – Improving Scientific Capacity," posted on the DFG Web site, states: "The Department of Fish and Game (DFG) is staffed by some of the foremost fish, wildlife and habitat scientists in the country. These experts are often consulted by natural resource conservation organizations around the globe."[17]

---

[13] Ibid., 210.
[14] *The Department of Fish and Game/The 1990's and Beyond/A Vision for the Future*, 17–18.
[15] http://www.merriam-webster.com/dictionary/resource.
[16] *The Department of Fish and Game/The 1990's and Beyond/A Vision for the Future*, 9.
[17] "Current Issues – Improving Scientific Capacity."

If science is the instrument, protecting the shared proprietary stakes in the global commons (or, in this case, the state commons) is the goal. The 1976 California Fish and Wildlife Protection and Conservation Act stated: "[F]ish and wildlife resources protection and conservation are of the utmost public interest. This is so because they are the property of the people, and provide a major contribution to the state's economy and a significant part of the people's food supply."[18] Striking the same note, in a revealing statement to the press, Department of Fish and Game warden Jerry Karnow commented, "A hunter is a person who engages in lawful activity, and a poacher is a criminal who steals your natural resources."[19] The person who shoots a deer with a hunting license is law-abiding and righteous; the person who shoots a deer without a license is stealing your property and your children's heritage.

The self-presentation of Fish and Game officials suggests several elisions and contradictions. To begin with, Fish and Game claims to protect wildlife even as it licenses its killing. The language of care, protection, and safeguarding sits uneasily with the violent actions involved in fishing and hunting. At a Fish and Game Commission meeting on February 2, 2006 in Sacramento, Commissioner Richard Rogers stated:

There's not a person in this room – you would not be in this room if you did not care about a resource, whether it's a sturgeon or a turtle or whatever. ... [I]t is in everyone's vested interest to have more wardens out there to keep the bad guys ... out of there. That way your resources are going to be protected, and those of us who enjoy fishing and hunting in this state and enjoy having something to fish and hunt in this state, will be able to continue to do that.

What are being cared for and protected are not wild animals per se but rather wildlife "resources" that fishermen and hunters wish to consume.

Consider, too, that Fish and Game officials claim that *everyone* benefits from hunting and fishing. Because hunters and fishermen pay licensing fees and taxes, they help to fund Fish and Game's protective activities, which include maintaining species and their habitats. This benefits not only hunters, who always have enough animals to shoot, but also nature lovers and wildlife enthusiasts, as well as all Californians who are said to benefit economically from the multiplier effects of hunting. The DFG Web site features a page called "The Economic Importance of Hunting," which states: "New studies now show that annual spending by America's 14 million hunters amounts to $22.1 billion. By comparison, and if hypothetically ranked as a "corporation," that revenue figure would put hunting in thirty-fifth place on the Fortune 500 list

---

[18] Cited in *The Department of Fish and Game/The 1990's and Beyond/A Vision for the Future*, 18.
[19] Carpenter (2007).

TABLE 5.1. *U.S. 1996 Hunting Economic Impacts*

	Deer	Migratory Birds	Upland Game Bird	All Hunting
Retail Sales	$10,324,904,373	$2,996,257,139	$1,895,704,348	$22,104,313,660
Multiplier Effect	$27,858,958,706	$8,154,525,482	$4,903,780,081	$60,998,344,806
Salaries/Wages	$7,200,082,463	$2,116,177,982	$1,201,073,493	$16,120,559,638
Jobs	331,904	95,748	55,546	704,601
State Sales Tax Revenues	$581,054,859	$178,480,197	$128,803,838	$1,068,110,791
State Income Tax Revenues	$148,594,333	$37,995,873	$22,524,049	$322,236,505
Fed. Income Tax	$763,392,226	$216,155,138	$125,587,037	$1,725,812,994

California Department of Fish and Wildlife webpage, "The Economic Importance of Hunting" http://www.dfg.ca.gov/wildlife/hunting/econ-hunting.html

of America's largest businesses, right between J.C. Penney and United Parcel Service" (Table 5.1).[20]

One can also access a PDF of a paper written by Eric Loft of the DFG's Wildlife Management Division, entitled "Economic Contribution of Deer, Pronghorn Antelope, and Sage Grouse Hunting to Northeastern California and Implications to the Overall 'Value' of Wildlife."[21] Loft's declared goal is the "development of minimum economic values of wildlife." He writes: "Wildlife advocates often talk about a somewhat vague 'intrinsic' value rather than a dollar value, but it's a valuation made stronger when substantiated dollar values are added."[22]

Even the fish and wildlife are said to benefit from fishing and hunting because their numbers are kept high and their habitats are protected. Of course, this argument depends on the assumption, frequently asserted in environmental discourse, that wild animals are fungible and that their individuality is of no import (Kheel 2009). Is it reasonable to view the individual black bear killed by a licensed hunter as a beneficiary of the Fish and Game regulatory regime? Once we consider the individuality of wild animals, the notion of a win-win-win scenario unravels, exposing a host of conflicting interests, needs, and claims.

Fish and Game's official discourse returns continually to the central tension between economic/instrumental and ecological values and "resolves" it by explicitly denying that the tension exists. The Department of Fish and Game's official mission statement reads:

The Mission of the Department of Fish and Game is to manage California's diverse fish, wildlife, and plant resources, and the habitats upon which they depend, *for their*

---

[20] "The Economic Importance of Hunting."
[21] Also published in *California Wildlife Conservation Bulletin*, No. 11, 1998.
[22] Loft (1998), 2.

ecological values and for their use and enjoyment by the public.... [The DFG] maintains native fish, wildlife, plant species and natural communities *for their intrinsic and ecological value and their benefits to people.* This includes habitat protection and maintenance in a sufficient amount and quality to ensure the survival of all species and natural communities. The department is also responsible for the diversified use of fish and wildlife including recreational, commercial, scientific and educational uses (italics added).[23]

The use of the conjunction "and" in the two highlighted sentences suggests that ecological values and instrumental values are fully consistent and thus do not even require balancing. Again, language glosses over potentially irreconcilable interests, needs, and claims. The ubiquity of this formulation – ecological *and* instrumental – in Fish and Game discourse suggests what an important ideological function it plays.

Sensitive to the charge that it is a willing arm of the hunting lobby, the FGC offers on its Web site:

This is another allegation rapidly refuted by reviewing the facts. Actually, the Commission spends more of its time dealing with matters of environmental quality, additional species protection, and rehabilitation of depleted populations and habitat than it does with matters of consumptive use. This by no means implies that the Commission is totally protectionist-orientated. It is fully aware that optimum use of our renewable wildlife resources must provide for a variety of consumptive and nonconsumptive needs. Wildlife, in contrast with inanimate objects, cannot be stored indefinitely for future use. Seasons and bag limits established on species with adequate reproductive potential reflect the best use of a biological surplus. In these cases, there always is prior provision for ample breeding stock and for a continuing population which can be enjoyed by naturalists, photographers and other nonconsumptive users.[24]

Here Fish and Game officials cannot seem to decide which charge is worse – that they are insufficiently protectionist or excessively protectionist. A declaration of commitment to species and habitat protection is followed, two sentences later, with a description of wildlife as something that must be used now because it cannot be stored for future use. Care and utilization, protection and killing.

In characterizing its instrumental stance toward wildlife as ecologically minded, the DFG is responding to both the decline of the hunter and the rise of the wildlife enthusiast in California. Since 1970, the number of people holding hunting licenses in the state has fallen 61 percent despite a doubling of the state's population. Environmental and animal protection groups, in the meantime, have made headway, banning mountain lion hunting, outlawing steel leghold traps, defeating plans to expand black bear hunting, and helping to establish "no fishing zones" off the coast.[25] *The Department of Fish and Game/The 1990's and Beyond/A Vision for the Future* (1993/2011) mentions "changing public attitudes," the emergence of "new constituencies who

---

[23] http://www.dfg.ca.gov/about/.
[24] http://www.fgc.ca.gov/public/information/.
[25] Rogers (2012).

promote natural area conservation and enjoy photography, birding, whale watching, animal rehabilitation," and the Department's shifting revenue base (from hunting/fishing licenses and taxes to environmental license plates and legislative funds).[26]

It is in the nature of contradictions, of course, that they cannot be perfectly concealed. Some years ago, a poll of the DFG's own employees indicated that they had profound doubts about the Department's mission. Conducted by California Public Employees for Environmental Responsibility in October/ November 1998 and released in the spring of 1999, the poll revealed that DFG employees believe that it is not science but politics – and ultimately the politics of greed – that drives the DFG's decisions. Eighty one percent of respondents strongly agree or agree that "Scientific evaluations at DFG are influenced by political considerations," while only 1 percent strongly agrees and 10 percent agrees that "The DFG uses the best scientific data to make permitting, policy and enforcement decisions."[27] Asked about the biggest challenges facing the Department, respondents wrote in replies:

- "Overcoming 15 years of political interference in the DFG's legislative mandates and public trust responsibilities."
- "Constant political pressure to accommodate development/strike deals, lack of institutional support to enforce endangered species violations."
- "The realization that public trust responsibilities should override recreation and commodity interests (i.e., that the state's biota are our primary constituents – not special interest groups)."
- "To reduce the intrusion of politics into resource management."
- "To make correct environmental decisions based on the biological sciences and not on the opinions of stakeholders who simply want to further their own economic interests."
- "[Resist] the insinuation of business and commercial interests in resource management issues."

Asked about the most important changes the Department should make, respondents wrote in:

- "Make decisions for the environment, not the pocketbooks of developers and big companies."
- "Abolish DFG and replace it with an organization NOT controlled by Ducks Unlimited and California Waterfowl Association."

What emerges from this poll is a picture of a Department whose own employees overwhelmingly believe that its claims about scientific priorities and environmental protection are a cover for its actual mission – the promotion of commercial interests.

---

[26] *The Department of Fish and Game/The 1990's and Beyond/A Vision for the Future*, 27.
[27] Stienstra (1999).

There are moments, too, when the violence of hunting becomes uncon-
cealed, even on the DFG's own Web site. One page on the Web site is entitled
"Attention Bear Hunters." The section "Mandatory Presentation of Bear Skull"
reminds hunters that they must deliver the specimen to the Department within
ten days of killing the bear because the premolar tooth is used for the purposes
of "bear management," or assessing the health and size of the bear population:
"IMPORTANT! Place a stick or other object in the bear's jaws so that the
mouth remains open. Do not present frozen skulls to have the premolar tooth
removed. Premolars break easily when the skull is frozen." Another capitalized
suggestion: "TO SAVE TIME, PLEASE CALL AHEAD BEFORE BRINGING
YOUR BEAR SKULL TO A DEPARTMENT OFFICE."[28] This matter-of-fact
attitude tempts us to forget the violence involved in killing the bear, cutting off
his or her head, propping open his or her jaws, and delivering his or her head
to the Department office. Through its scientific management regime, Fish and
Game treats animals as fungible, as units of "bearness," constituent elements
of the resource to be managed before they are "harvested." But the bear head
delivery protocol reminds us that it is the individual bear – not the species, not
the resource – who suffers and dies.

A recent flap involving Fish and Game Commission president Dan Richards
also laid bare the contradictions at the heart of Fish and Game's mission. In
February 2012, the story broke that Richards, a Republican commercial real
estate developer and National Rifle Association member, had successfully
hunted a mountain lion in Idaho. A picture of him gleefully hoisting the body
of his prey, originally posted on a hunting site by Richards himself, went viral.
Richards went out of state to accomplish this feat because mountain lion hunting is not legal in California. (Governor Ronald Reagan banned it in 1972
for five-year increments, and voters passed Proposition 117 in 1990 to make
the ban permanent.) Led by Assemblyman Ben Hueso (D-San Diego), forty
members of the California Assembly signed a letter to Richards challenging his
fitness as "primary public steward" of the state's wildlife resources and calling
for his resignation. Lieutenant Governor Gavin Newsom joined the call, as did
the Humane Society of the United States.

Critics averred that Richards had shown bad judgment and disrespect for his
constituents even if what he did was technically legal. One blogger wrote: "He
should lose his job. He has no regard for wildlife whatsoever. ... He is in the
wrong business altogether."[29] Defiant, Richards sent a letter to Assemblyman
Ben Hueso on February 28, 2012:

While I respect our Fish and Game rules and regulations, my 100 percent legal activity
outside of California, or anyone else's for that matter, is none of your business. ... Under
your standards all Californians who enjoy gaming in Nevada are somehow ethically challenged as true Californians and should be removed from any official position. My guess

---

[28] http://www.dfg.ca.gov/wildlife/hunting/bear/docs/TagValidation.pdf.
[29] Sherbert (2012).

is the Legislative chambers might look a little barren should that logic prevail. ... I will
continue to hunt and fish wherever I please, as I have always done, ethically, licensed and
proudly associating with true conservationists who daily fund, protect, enjoy and enhance
our bountiful resources while not trying to limit others [*sic*] enjoyment of same. There is
ZERO chance I would consider resigning my position.[30]

Richards commented in an interview: "This is about enviro-terrorists who are
trying to take over a state agency. They attack. They're attacking me. ... I find
most of them disgusting."[31] Hunters from all over the state vigorously defended
Richards in cyberspace and dozens showed up at the March 2012 Fish and
Game Commission public meeting to support him. Because Richards was a frequent swing vote on the five-person Commission, which is split between those
perceived to be relatively pro-environment and those perceived to be more
pro-business, there was a lot at stake in this controversy. On August 8, 2012,
the FGC voted 5–0 to remove Richards as president and replace him with Jim
Kellogg. Richards remained on the Commission and stepped down at the end
of his term in January 2013.

   In the wake of the Richards controversy, Assemblyman Jared Huffman
(D-San Rafael), chair of the Assembly's Water, Parks, and Wildlife Committee,
introduced a bill (AB 2402) to change the Department's name from "Fish
and Game" to "Fish and Wildlife," a symbolic measure meant to soften the
Department's image and suggest a more protectionist bent.[32] Huffman claimed
that the new name would more "accurately reflect the state agency's broader
mission," but a spokesman for the U.S. Sportsmen's Alliance (a hunting group)
said it augured "a shift toward butterflies, endangered species and other stuff
like that" (Llanos 2013). In addition, State Senator Ted Lieu (D-Torrance)
introduced SB 1221 to ban the use of hounds in bear and bobcat hunting in
California, calling Dan Richards's use of dogs to tree his prey "cruel." Both bills
were signed into law. A year before, then-Assemblyman Lieu, who is Chinese
American, had confronted Richards for supporting the proposed ban on the
importation of turtles and frogs for food during a Fish and Game Commission
hearing, leading to a memorable exchange about racism and ecological harm.
I discuss this exchange later in this chapter.

NATURE AS A PRISTINE (WHITE) SPACE

The optic of ecological harm advanced by animal advocates before the FGC
drew on the well-established invasive species/native species trope. The notion
that "invasive" or "alien" species enter spaces where they do not belong and

---

[30] http://www.scribd.com/doc/83209820/Daniel-Richards-Letter-to-Assemblymember-Ben
-Hueso.
[31] Schmidt (2012).
[32] The bill also proposed increasing nonhunters' access to state wildlife refuges and creating a ten-
member advisory board of biologists for the Department (Rogers 2012).

threaten "native" species – and that this is a matter of scientific and moral concern – has been a central postulate of various fields of science, including conservation biology and restoration ecology, for some time. Globalized human activity has been seen as a major culprit here because trade and migration dramatically increase the introduction (intended and unintended) of plant and animal species into new spaces – through packing crates, in the ballast water of ships, on the soles of people's shoes. Invasive aliens, the story goes, threaten not only native species and their local habitats but also global biodiversity and the myriad human economic interests interwoven with it. Thus, as Woods and Moriarty (2001) note, biologists, ecologists, and environmental scientists have largely concurred in recent decades that we can and should clearly identify certain invasive alien species as bad and seek to eliminate them. The matter is usually posed with some urgency, as when NASA officials stated: "Non-indigenous invasive species may pose the single most formidable threat of natural disaster of the 21st century."[33]

The "invasive species" problematic has been institutionalized on the international, national, and state levels during the past thirty years. In the mid-1980s, the Scientific Committee on Problems of the Environment, a product of the International Council of Scientific Unions, created a program of symposia to investigate the issue of introduced species (Simberloff 2003). In 1996, a United Nations Conference on Alien Species in Trondheim, Norway brought together scientists from eighty countries and launched the Global Invasive Species Programme, whose mission was "to conserve biodiversity and sustain livelihoods by minimising the spread and impact of invasive species."[34] In the United States, President Bill Clinton issued Executive Order 13112 (1999) mandating the formation of a National Invasive Species Council, which produced the first National Invasive Species Management Plan two years later.[35] More than twenty-four states have Invasive Species Councils as well. There is federal-state cooperation on the issue: the California Department of Fish and Game Invasive Species Program manager, for example, is both the liaison to the Invasive Species Council of California and the chair of the federal Organizational Collaboration Committee of the federal Invasive Species Advisory Committee.

---

[33] Cited in Burdick (2005), 36.
[34] https://www.ippc.int/index.php?id=gisp.
[35] Executive Order 13112 estimates the damage done by nonnative species in the United States to exceed $120 billion per year. It aims "to prevent the introduction of invasive species and provide for their control and to minimize the economic, ecological, and human health impacts that invasive species cause." http://www.gpo.gov/fdsys/pkg/FR-1999-02-08/pdf/99-3184.pdf. The National Invasive Species Council consists of the Secretaries and administrators of thirteen federal departments and agencies and is cochaired by the Secretaries of Commerce, Agriculture, and the Interior.

A product of the neoliberal age, the invasive/native species trope reflects anxieties specific to the global project of breaking down all political, spatial, and natural barriers to market expansion and flourishing. The first is the anxiety that nature will not remain the compliant substratum of raw materials that global capitalism needs it to be. At the heart of the invasive/native species trope is terror that nature will be noncompliant or recalcitrant – that it will reveal itself as agent rather than object – in a way that interferes with economic accumulation. Almost every invasive species horror story is at bottom a story about economic damage and threat. Native species and their habitats have become imaginative proxies for human business interests, and the language of environmental care and protection is carefully deployed to simultaneously veil and promote the instrumentalization of nature. Once again, ecological and economic interests are elided so that ecological language – in this case about "global biodiversity," "endangered species," and "habitat protection" – can provide legitimating cover for fundamentally economic concerns.

Consider the July/August 2004 issue of *Environment*, whose cover story is entitled "Alien 'Invasives': Ecosystems at Risk."[36] Jeffrey McNeely's article in this issue defines invasive aliens as "non-native species that become established in a new environment then proliferate and spread in ways that damage human interests" and argues they "are now recognized as one of the greatest biological threats to our planet's environmental and economic well-being."[37] McNeely includes a table showing a sampling of invasive aliens in different nations and the costs associated with containing or eradicating them (hundreds of millions or billions of dollars each). Similarly, in his keynote address on the Global Invasive Species Program at a meeting organized by the Secretariat of the Convention on Biological Diversity in Montreal in 2000, Harold Mooney plainly characterizes invasives as "Fire stimulators and cycle disruptors; Water depleters; Disease causers; Crop decimators; Forest destroyers; Fisheries disruptors; Impeders of navigation; Clogger of water works; Destroyer of homes and gardens; Grazing land destroyers; Species eliminators; Noise polluters and Modifiers of evolution."[38] The California Department of Fish and Game has a new newsletter, *Eye on "Invasives,"* and chose in its first issue to spotlight quagga and zebra mussels, who damage boats, hamper sport fishing, and even lead to the closing of waterways to recreational activities.[39]

The invasive/native species trope also expresses anxiety about the multiculturalism that neoliberalism inadvertently fosters. It is a metaphor for the feared displacement of whites by immigrants of color. As Jean Comaroff and John Comaroff argue, the trope voices neoliberal worries about the unprecedented movement of (human and animal) bodies, the insufficiency of

---

[36] Vol. 46, no. 6.
[37] McNeely (2004), 17.
[38] "Invasive Alien Species – The Nature of the Problem."
[39] Summer 2001.

borders, and the challenge of maintaining national identity in a maelstrom of change:

Could it be that anxious public discourse here over invasive plant species speaks to an existential problem presently making itself felt at the very heart of nation-states everywhere: in what does national integrity consist, what might nation-hood and belonging *mean*, what moral and material entitlements might it entail, at a time when global capitalism seems everywhere to be threatening sovereign borders, everywhere to be displacing politics as usual?[40]

As borders and identities are challenged, Comaroff and Comaroff continue, autochthony – "elevating to a first-principle the ineffable interests and connections, at once material and moral, that flow from 'native' rootedness, and special rights, in *a place of birth*"[41] – becomes more appealing, as does the idea of reasserting sovereignty and policing the borders. The invasive species trope reads the drama and affect of national, cultural, and racial politics into biological processes.

Indeed, the racialization of the invasive/native trope has become so pronounced that scholars have started to fret openly about their colleagues' "bioxenophobia" and "biological nativism." Sagoff notes: "Biologists sometimes attribute to immigrant species some of the same characteristics that nativists and xenophobes have ascribed to immigrant humans: sexual robustness, excessive breeding, low parental involvement with the young, a preference for degraded conditions."[42] We are reminded of the conjoined logics of race and species, but now it is *species that is a metric of raciality* rather than the other way around – that is, the construction of "invasives" as heedless, destructive, and hyper-fertile aliens draws from white imaginings about nonwhite immigrants, especially Latinos. Invasives take on color, and nature as the space that they threaten is raced, too, as white.

Nature has been white for well over a century, but it was very dark before that. As William Cronon recounts in his essay, "The Trouble with Wilderness" (1985), the modern idea of wilderness, which emerged in the late 1800s and early 1900s, grew out of the specific race and class relations of that period. In the 1600s, the "wild" of America was imagined as a dark place where savage Indians skulked among savage beasts. It was a space untouched by God, civilization, or progress – the antithesis of everything English.[43] By the late 1800s, in part because of the closing of the frontier, wealthy white businessmen took to reimagining the "wild" as a sanctuary, the temple of the natural, untainted by the corruption of civilization. The nature/culture dualism was preserved but inverted. Of course, Indians had to be removed, both literally

[40] Comaroff and Comaroff (2001), 236–7.
[41] Ibid., 240.
[42] Sagoff (2000). See also Subramanian (2001).
[43] In the 1700s, "wilderness" in the English language meant "deserted," "savage," "desolate," and "barren." Cronon (1995).

and imaginatively, for this notion of the "wild" to work. Once it was Indian-free, nature could function as a magnificent theater for affluent white men to demonstrate their mastery over nature and animals. Thus nature, Cronon argues, changed in concept and value – from a shadowy savage place to a "pristine sanctuary where the last remnant of an untouched, endangered, but still transcendent nature can for at least a little while longer be encountered without the contaminating taint of civilization."[44] As nature got whiter, civilization got darker.

American cities, receiving large numbers of racialized immigrants from Southern and Eastern Europe, were seen as filthy and polluted. Bruce Braun notes that in this historical context nature "served as a purification machine, a place where people became white, where the racial and hereditary habits of immigrants could be overcome." Thus "the journey *into* nature was just as much a journey *away* from something else, and that something else was race."[45]

As with immigrants, invasive species are imagined to pose a threat that is racial and economic and environmental at once. Consider how similarly immigration from Mexico and "invasive" zebra and quagga mussels are depicted graphically. The Web site for David Sadler, Republican candidate for Congress in the 12th Congressional District of Illinois, contains a striking image entitled "New Aztlan?"[46] It is a map of the United States showing the geographical distribution of Latinos. The Southwest is darkened blue and the stain seems to be seeping inward toward the center of the country. The image deliberately elides the fact that the concentration of Mexican Americans in this region is due in part to the fact it was once part of Mexico – and taken by force during the U.S.-Mexican War of 1846–8 – and not just to immigration, in order to construct a sense of a dynamic and growing threat.

Then consider a map entitled "Zebra and Quagga Mussel Sightings Distribution" from the U.S. Geological Survey Web site.[47] Against the somber hues of the U.S. topographical map, the bright red and green circles representing zebra and quagga mussels (densely concentrated in the Great Lakes area and spreading outward from there) have an alarming effect. Trespassing in the white space of the nation/nature, immigrants/invasives are a spreading blight, a stain that begins on the margins and seeps insidiously toward the heartland.

[44] Ibid.
[45] Braun (2003), 197.
[46] http://www.david-sadler.org/pages/news/immigrate/aztlan/aztlan.htm. Accessed December 30, 2013. The site claims to have taken the image from http://www.aztlan.net, a Web site that has no content as of this writing. The image is an almost exact replica of another image available online, entitled "Conquest of Aztlan," which has been displayed on some nativist Web sites. Aztlan is a place with significance in Chicano history and lore; it refers both to the mythical homeland of Aztec warriors in the distant past and the imagined homeland of Chicanos in the future.
[47] http://nas.er.usgs.gov/taxgroup/mollusks/zebramussel/maps/current_zm_quag_map.jpg. There is an animated version of the map available on the Web site as well.

Preying upon the national commons of the nation/nature, they devour resources to which they have no claim, threatening the political, economic, and biological integrity of these spaces. One is reminded of the *Wasp*'s nineteenth-century depictions of the Chinese as marauding wild pigs and swarming grasshoppers. The more economically threatening a species is perceived to be, the more deeply it is racialized.

During a Fish and Game Commission hearing in Ontario on March 3, 2010, Karen Benzel of In Defense of Animals gave a PowerPoint presentation that included the following:

[PowerPoint slide: Non-native. Never good.]

[PowerPoint slide: Who pays? Taxpayers. Native populations fighting non-natives for their survival.]

BENZEL: You have the power to say no more, no more excuses, no further delay.

[PowerPoint slide: You have the evidence. You have the responsibility. You have the power. Laws are being broken. Your own regulations ignored.]

BENZEL: Non-natives are not good. They are usually ecological disasters in almost every case. Someone is going to make money, like the pet trade, but it won't be you. You will end up cleaning up the mess, wasting time and resources that should have been spent protecting California's wildlife, not bringing more in. Make the decision, make it now, make non-natives illegal.

Benzel's presentation is technically colorblind: race is never mentioned. But her dramatic language about nonnatives harming the nation, costing taxpayers, breaking the laws, and threatening the survival of natives resonates unmistakably with conservative political rhetoric denouncing "illegal" Mexican immigration.[48]

Recent depictions of Asian carp in the waterways of the Midwest have raised the specter of the Yellow Peril once again. Introduced Asian carp reached the lower reaches of the Mississippi River in the 1970s and have been moving since then toward the Great Lakes. Because they eat plankton, they disrupt the food chain that nourishes trout and other native fish.

---

[48] Although many environmental organizations in the United States maintain a neutral stance on immigration, environmentalism and immigration have a somewhat troubled recent past. In the 1970s, environmentalists debated immigration with reference to issues of environmental degradation, natural resource depletion, and overpopulation. When John Tanton, who had chaired the Sierra Club's National Population Committee in the early 1970s, founded U.S. English in 1983 (which sought to make English the official language of the nation), and other environmentalists helped to create Federation for American Immigration Reform (which argued that immigration was the nation's leading environmental problem), observers started talking about the "greening of hate" (Coates 2007). These tensions came to a head in 1998, when an internally riven Sierra Club held a referendum on whether or not to take a policy stand on immigration. Sixty percent voted to maintain neutrality on immigration, but the process left some feeling that nativists were trying to infiltrate the organization and hijack the environmental agenda, and others feeling that charges of nativism and racism had prematurely closed off debate on an issue of vital environmental concern (Coates 2007).

In addition, they have a tendency to launch themselves several feet out of the water, where they sometimes collide with and injure recreational boaters. In both ways, they threaten the Great Lakes' multibillion dollar commercial and sport fishing industries (Rudolf 2010). One journalist wrote: "There are illegal immigrants on the loose in the Midwest. Originally hailing from Asia, they're about 3 ft. (90cm) long and weigh up to 100 lb. (45 kg), and are known to resist capture. Once they establish residency, they can eat you out of house and home" (Walsh 2010). In another article, "Asian-Carp Invasion of American Waters," the author depicts Asian carp as a threat not only to the Great Lakes region but to the nation itself – to "American Waters." He writes: "Not to get too sentimental about it, but the Mississippi River is us, and vice versa. It's our bloodstream. ... Possibly, these carp will change large parts of our national watersheds forever. We may be infected with a virus for which there is no cure" (Frazier 2010). The White House responded by appointing a "carp czar" or Coordinated Response Commander for Asian Carp and organizing an "Asian Carp Summit" (February 8, 2010), where it announced the commitment of $78.5 million to build new barriers to impede the Asian carp's movement.

This barely suppressed terror about the infection of the American "bloodstream" appears in much of the writing about invasive species. Myerson and Reaser, for example, write: "Bioterrorist acts are relatively unpredictable, rare, and thus far small-scale events. In contrast, biological invasions are occurring daily in the United States and have significant impacts on human health, agriculture, infrastructure, and the environment, yet they receive far less attention and fewer resources."[49] An author reviewing headlines from newspapers from around the world – including ones like "Giant Rats Invade Florida Keys" and "Ring-Necked Parrots Take over Germany and Southern England" – notes —sardonically, "I could have slipped in 'Attack of the Killer Tomatoes' among these without some readers noticing the fakery."[50] In this atmosphere of manufactured and racialized terror, George W. Bush's administration opted to merge part of the Animal and Plant Health Inspection Service (responsible for monitoring invasive species) into the newly created Department of Homeland Security, which also houses Immigration and Customs Enforcement (Larsen 2005).

The invasive/native species trope has not gone unchallenged. In 1994, Michael Pollan's *New York Times* article "Against Nativism" denounced those concerned with protective native plants for perpetuating the Nazi preoccupation with "purity" and advocated a cosmopolitan or "multihorticulturalist" view of the plant world as an alternative. Are invasives agents of

---

[49] Myerson and Reaser (2003), 307, cited in Gobster (2005), 265.
[50] Gobster (2005), 262.

multihorticultural diversity or agents of botanical imperialism? Is it racist to defend local distinctiveness? To promote ecological homogenization?[51]

Critics have also argued that the invasive/native species trope is bad science, riddled with faulty claims, arbitrary conceptualizations, and ideological presuppositions. Clinton's Executive Order 13112 defines "native" thus: "with respect to a particular ecosystem, a species that, other than as a result of an introduction, historically occurred or currently occurs in that ecosystem."[52] This suggests we can identify a pristine original state, classify the animals who were present then as "natives," and use this as a baseline for measuring all future ecological change. Most scientists see this as a fallacy, insisting that the record is one of continuous change, with some periods witnessing a greater rate of change than others (Peretti 1998). Nor does it help us to use the arrival of Columbus as a historical marker. Coates writes:

Despite its powerful popular and scientific orthodoxy, a distinction between native and nonnative based exclusively on this historic watershed – and on the absence of direct human intervention implicit in the phrase "naturally occurring" – is problematic. This is so partly because of our incomplete knowledge of the pre-Columbian complement of species. We also easily forget that Native Americans were themselves invaders. Who knows for sure what seeds accompanied those who migrated across the Bering land bridge from Siberia some 14,000 years ago at the tail end of the last great glaciation, whether carried deliberately or stuck to hair, clothes, or feet? Once settled in the Americas, the invaders' descendants undoubtedly shifted plants around both by design and unintentionally.[53]

Warren concludes that the invasive/native species trope is "historically arbitrary, geographically ambiguous, ecologically unsound, culturally insensitive, sociopolitically dubious and economically futile."[54]

The invasive/native species trope also trades upon an outdated notion that ecosystems are stable, balanced, and closed, and that "invasions" are abnormal and destructive. Since the 1970s, many scientists have argued that nature is rather "a chaotic, random, and structurally open system" where "frequent invasions are a natural, normal process."[55] In this view, there is no "balance of nature" to preserve, and invasions are ordinary, not exceptional. Globalization has accelerated biological change, but evolutionary and biogeographical history shows prior periods of comparable or greater change (Brown and Sax 2004). In an article from a *Discover* issue entitled "Are Invasive Species Really So Bad?" Alan Burdick writes: "Invasions

---

[51] For the latter term see Warren (2007). Scientists disagree about the impacts of "invasions" on global biodiversity as well as the meaning of those impacts (Brown and Sax 2004).
[52] http://www.gpo.gov/fdsys/pkg/FR-1999-02-08/pdf/99–3184.pdf.
[53] Coates (2007), 11.
[54] Warren (2007), 441.
[55] Peretti (1998), 187. See also Woods and Moriarty (2001).

don't weaken ecosystems – they simply transform them into different eco-systems, filled with different organisms of greater or lesser value to us … the point is that the only reliable measure for the value of native species is our desire."[56]

Relatedly, Stephen Jay Gould notes that the invasive/native species trope promotes the "evolutionary fallacy" of "equating native with best." Precisely because evolution "includes no concept of general progress or universal bet-terment," it is in fact much more apt to say that certain plants are "locally prevalent" but not "optimal." After all, why would native plants succumb to introduced species, as they sometimes do, if evolution had rendered them opti-mal inhabitants of a given ecosystem? Natives, then, are merely "first-comers," a revision that seems to dramatically undercut the moral significance of the term.[57]

In all of these instances, the trope's attribution of structure (a demarcation between a pristine state and a polluted state, the closed and stable ecosys-tem, the teleology of evolution) where there is none, or at least not the kind imputed, and its related denial of randomness, contingency, open-endedness, and continual flux, leads to an oversimplification and distortion of biological processes of change. Instead of imagining nature as a pure state that we must preserve from degradation – an inherently conservative vision that slips easily into political and biological nativism – we might do well to remember that all ecosystems are always already "hybridized palimpsests of human and non-human influences."[58] The changes wrought by introduced species are real (and sometimes alarming), but the invasive/native species trope closes down the very debate that needs to occur over how to determine when biological change is problematic, for whom, and what, if anything, should be done about it.

---

[56] Burdick (2005), 40. Burdick's point is that we judge nonnative species as good or bad depending on their economic impact – and not by alternative measures. Many nonnative species (which includes almost all crops) confer benefits that far outweigh costs. Even the zebra mussel, which is the poster animal for "invasive" damage because it has the costly habit of clogging intake and distribution pipes, cleans lakes and rivers by eating excess nutri-ents and algae produced by waste and agricultural runoff, which has enabled fourteen native aquatic plants to reestablish themselves and has boosted fish and duck numbers (Sagoff 2000). Meanwhile, nonnatives who do harm but are economically useful do not become objects of our concern. Cattle, for example, threaten more native plant species than do undo-mesticated nonnatives and almost as many native animal species as nonnative predators do (Burdick 2005).

[57] Gould (1997), 15, 17.

[58] Warren (2007), 439. See Sarah Whatmore for a notion of wildlife as "a relational achieve-ment spun between people and animals, plants and soils, documents and devices in heteroge-neous social networks which are performed in and through multiple places and fluid ecologies" (2001, 14).

THE FISH AND GAME HEARINGS: RACE, CULTURE, SCIENCE, AND ECOLOGICAL HARM

Fish and Game discourse firmly defined the parameters of what could be said during the Commission's monthly public hearings. Those who raised other kinds of issues (or used other kinds of language) were promptly reminded by Commissioners that their concerns were neither discussable nor actionable. Animal advocates adapted to these constraints by setting aside the optic of cruelty and advancing an optic of ecological harm. Eric Mills, who had started off as an environmental activist and continued to work on other invasive species issues (e.g., the presence of African clawed frogs in Golden Gate Park), knew how to speak the language of Fish and Game even if he did not like it:

Yeah, I was using that language [about wildlife as resources]. I don't like it either. But words are important. ... So to call these animals "resources," it's money in the bank. "Human resources" – we're treated the same way. We're just ciphers and corporations run the world now. They run everything.

Mobilizing around the invasive/native species trope, Mills and his colleagues found themselves with some strange bedfellows. Supporters of the ban came to include not only environmental and animal protection groups but also sportsmen's organizations such as United Anglers of California, California Trout, and Pacific Coast Federation of Fishermen's Associations.

Mills understood well that the power of environmental language lies in its universality. In a letter to the editor of *Capitol Weekly* (February 23, 2006), he wrote:

I hope you'll not refer to us as "animal rights activists." This is decidedly NOT an animal rights issue. It's a matter of species depletion, environmental degradation, public health and safety, diseased and parasitized animals, and horrendous animal cruelty. Surely these are concerns for all of us.

Virginia Handley made a similar argument at a Fish and Game Commission hearing on February 5, 1999:

Please do not make this a racial issue. Please don't fall for that, and please don't fall for the politics of this. That's one of the reasons why we brought this issue to you, and I must say, from the beginning we brought environmental concerns, not just humane, but we brought them to you because we thought maybe somewhere in the state there's gonna be an unbiased body that we can bring this issue to that won't bring politics into it.

Environmental discourse links to science, rationality, objectivity; race and politics, on the other hand, involve "special interests."

The optic of ecological harm introduced a radically different script with an entirely new cast of villains and victims. By the cruelty script, the villains are the merchants and the victims are the turtles and frogs (and other animals) they kill. In the new script, these same animals – the imported red-eared sliders (*Trachemys scripta elegans*) – and imported American bull-frogs (*Rana catesbeiana*) – are reimagined as villains, and the new victims are "native" wild species, particularly the Western pond turtle (*Clemmys marmorata*) and the California red-legged frog (*Rana draytonii*). Although the two scripts are logically compatible, they produce an affective disso-nance: Is the bullfrog in the market (who may get released into the wild via a Buddhist ceremony or some other means) a hapless victim, a ruthless pred-ator, or both? The common site in both scripts, of course, is the live animal market, the node of commerce where unbridled greed leads to cruelty and environmental damage.

There is a notable governmental, scientific, and journalistic consensus that the native species in question are in fact threatened by the invasive spe-cies in question. Both the Western pond turtle and the California red-legged frog are recognized as "threatened" under the federal Endangered Species Act and as "species of special concern" by the California Department of Fish and Game. Introduced species are widely recognized as one cause of their decline in numbers. The U.S. Fish and Wildlife's "Proposed Designation of Critical Habitat for the California Red-legged Frog" (April 13, 2004) stated: "Several researchers have attributed the decline and extirpation of California red-legged frogs to the introduction of bullfrogs (*Rana catesbeiana*) and predatory fishes … [through] both predation and competition."[59] California red-legged frogs, once found all across California, have lost 75 percent of their historic range and 90 percent of their population.[60] An article in *Outdoor California* (May–June 1998) notes: "Once a common site along most low elevation ponds and streams, the western pond turtle is quietly disappearing from the California landscape. … Where the turtles can still be found, many populations no longer produce offspring, the result of dis-turbed nesting grounds and the predation of young turtles by non-native bullfrogs and black bass."[61]

To make their case about ecological harm, animal advocates marshaled sci-entific data and the testimony of scientific experts. Todd Steiner, a biologist and director of the Sea Turtle Restoration Project, made a statement at a Fish and Game hearing on February 5, 1999:

Are illegal and potentially serious threats to our native pond ecosystems being posed by turtle species and their diseases that might be released into the wild and outcompete with our own seriously depleted turtle species, the Western pond turtle? Are Western pond

---

[59] P. 19622. http://ecos.fws.gov/docs/federal_register/fr4239.pdf.
[60] "Twain's Frog Gets Reduced Living Space." The problem is not limited to the California red-legged frog. Nearly one-third of amphibian species in the world are threatened, and California alone is home to sixteen of these species. Up to 200 amphibian species have disappeared in recent years worldwide. See testimony of Kerry Kriger, founder of Save the Frogs!, at the May 4, 2010 hearing of the Fish and Game Commission.
[61] Garrison (1998), 29.

turtles being collected locally and illegally being sold for food in San Francisco markets? … It may be necessary to ban the sale of live animals until such time as the situation can be controlled. The California red-legged frog was recently listed as threatened under the Endangered Species Act. … Bullfrogs outcompete and actually eat our own endangered red-legged frog. The continued importation of bullfrogs poses a potentially accelerated threat to California's frog species. The sale of live bullfrogs should be banned throughout California.[62]

The SFSPCA, in its "Statement on the Import of Live Turtles and Bullfrogs for Food" (January 23, 1998) submitted to the Fish and Game Commission, cites a 1996 scientific study showing that the introduced bullfrog is implicated in an "unambiguous pattern of decline" in native amphibian populations including the federally threatened California red-legged frog.[63]

A later SFSPCA report, "Import of Live, Non-Native Turtles and Frogs for Food; Supplemental Report #2" (January 15, 1999) cites "The Western Pond Turtle: Habitat and History" (August 1994), in which Oregon Department of Fish and Wildlife expert Dan Holland discusses the adverse impact of introduced bullfrogs and turtles on this threatened species.

Animal advocates also submitted a study entitled "The Distribution and Census of Freshwater Turtles in Golden Gate Park Lakes" by biologist Stacey Vonita Brey.[64] Noting that the Western pond turtle is recognized as threatened by both the federal government and the California Department of Fish and Game, Brey argues that bullfrogs and red-eared sliders are its main nemeses. She writes: "Introduced bullfrogs (*Rana catesbeiana*) prey on hatchling or juvenile turtles, and may be responsible for significant mortality rates because they occupy shallow-water habitats in which the youngest age groups of turtles are frequently observed," and the red-eared slider (*Trachemys scripta elegans*) "is the most successful invasive freshwater turtle species throughout the Western United States," competing for food and basking and nesting sites with the Western pond turtle, as well as threatening the latter with disease and parasites.[65] Brey concludes: "From these observations and comparisons it is clear that the native species is at a competitive disadvantage. *Clemmys marmorata* must compete with a species [*Trachemys scripta elegans*] with a fecundity rate potentially greater than six-fold the native's optimal ability. … From this study, it is apparent why domestic

---

[62] The statement was read into the record by his colleague Fran Strichter.
[63] Fisher and Shaffer (1996). The statement also points to the efforts of the Golden Gate National Parks Association and the U.S. Fish and Wildlife Service in 1997 to protect native aquatic wildlife like the California red-legged frog by eliminating nonnative bullfrogs through the draining of three artificial ponds in the Golden Gate National Recreational Area in San Francisco. Under the Endangered Species Act of 1973, federal agencies are responsible for enacting conservation programs to protect endangered and threatened species.
[64] Brey (2006).
[65] Ibid., 2, 3.

and international organizations seek to ban imports of this globally invasive species."[66]

Scientific data was also marshaled to show that invasives harm natives by spreading disease. Eric Mills commissioned Miles Young, a retired Department of Fish and Game warden, to put together an "Investigative Report on the Sale of Live Turtles and Frogs as Food Items in California Markets" (August 22, 2006) for submission to the Fish and Game Commission. Exhibit 9 of Young's report is a *National Geographic* article, "Farewell to Frogs? Deadly Fungus Attacks Amphibians" (January 2006), which examines the rapidly spreading chytrid fungus deadly to amphibians. Exhibit 10 is a scientific article by Rolando Mazzoni and colleagues, entitled "Emerging Pathogen of Wild Amphibians in Frogs (*Rana catesbeiana*) Farmed for International Trade." Young quotes Mazzoni and colleagues: "Chytridiomycosis is an emerging disease responsible for a series of global population declines and extinctions of amphibians. ... Our findings suggest that international trade may play a key role in the global dissemination of this and other emerging infectious diseases in wildlife."[67] Save the Frogs! founder Kerry Kriger, who testified at the May 4, 2010 Fish and Game Commission hearing that several million bullfrogs were farmed overseas and imported into California each year, cited a study showing that more than 60 percent of them are infected with the chytrid fungus.[68] Finally, an SFSPCA report (April 2, 1999) submitted to the Fish and Game Commission conveyed the results of a veterinarian's necropsies conducted on four bullfrogs and four turtles taken from Chinatown markets: all showed signs of "parasitic infestation, respiratory infection, bacterial hepatitis, septicemia, and other potentially devastating bacteria."[69] Two other veterinarians submitted necropsy reports indicating that market turtles carried parasites that could threaten "native" species.[70]

For their part, Chinese community leaders argued at the Fish and Game hearings that there was no definitive proof linking the problem of invasives to the Chinese markets. Chinese merchants obeyed the Fish and Game regulation requiring the dispatching of animals at the point of sale, they argued, so there was no reason to think that the markets were responsible for any invasives entering the wild. Blaming the markets for this environmental problem was, in their view, racially discriminatory and damaging to both the cultural integrity and the economic well-being of the Chinese community. According to Pius Lee, San Francisco alone had four companies managing turtle and frog

---

[66] Ibid., 11.
[67] Mazzoni et al. (2003).
[68] "California Upholds Ban on Importation of Nonnative Frogs and Turtles for Food."
[69] San Francisco Society for the Prevention of Cruelty to Animals (SFSPCA). "Statement of the SFSPCA Pursuant to Proposed Regulatory Action."
[70] Dr. Lexie Endo's February 27, 1998 letter to the Fish and Game Commission submitting results of two turtle necropsies; Dr. Kenneth Harkewicz's September 20, 1999 report on a turtle necropsy.

imports, with combined annual sales in the millions.[71] Then there was the impact on retailers and workers to consider. While animal advocates argued that the importation ban would promote the good of the whole, Chinese representatives emphasized the specific harms that the ban would impose on the Chinese community. Against the optic of ecological harm they invoked the optic of racism.

Pius Lee and the CCBA organized Chinese participation in the Fish and Game hearings.[72] Lee's "No Ban Coalition," composed of more than seventy-five Chinese live animal merchants and their advocates from both San Francisco and Los Angeles, circulated flyers, organized letter writing and phone calling, lobbied, and turned people out to Fish and Game hearings. One of their flyers, entitled "Oppose the Ban on Importation of Live Turtles and Bullfrogs," summarized the cultural and economic arguments against the ban:

Asian Pacific Americans have been consuming live turtles and frogs for decades in California. Our ancestors have consumed them for thousands of years. We believe they are an integral part of our diet. We believe they are healthy and nutritious for our bodies. We believe eating fresh food is good for our minds and souls. Wholesalers and restaurants in California purchase approximately 1 million pounds of live turtles and bullfrogs each year. They are sold at restaurants and markets in Asian Pacific American communities throughout California. We believed a ban will adversely affect these and related business in the State. Wholesalers, restaurants, food markets, herbal stores, importers, exporters and airlines stand to lose over 1 million dollars in business revenues annually. This does not include individual employees losing their jobs with these businesses.

The Chinatown Economic Development Group, of which Lee was cochairman, passed a resolution on February 27, 1998 declaring the proposed importation ban "an unprincipled attack on Asian culture and values" and promising to fight "any attempt by any special interests to trample on Chinatown's historical, cultural and economic importance."

Ordinary Chinese Americans spoke at the Fish and Game hearings to explain why the importation ban mattered to them personally. One older Chinese woman spoke with the help of an interpreter at the February 5, 1999 meeting:

WEI: [speaking in Chinese]

INTERPRETER: Her name is Jane Ho Wei. She is going to give two examples why the continuation of the turtle and frog is essential for food. Two reasons.

WEI: [speaking in Chinese]

INTERPRETER: After cleaning up the turtles and making boil the soup, turtle soup, it will increase the rapid recovery of sickness. People get sick, they will recovery much faster.

---

[71] Yu Ning, "Proposal to Ban the Importation of Live Turtles Will Affect California's Economy."
[72] The Chinese Chamber of Commerce did not get involved and the San Francisco Neighborhood Association only briefly.

WEI: [speaking in Chinese]

INTERPRETER: The turtle soup for the elders when they have arthritis, it will be much relieved and even cure the arthritis for the elders.

WEI: [speaking in Chinese]

INTERPRETER: This method of treating illness is traditionally for thousands of year in China. She suggests that actually put in test, put in hospital that the certain patient, we see this turtle soup, frog soup, and then see if they do recover faster.

WEI: [speaking in Chinese]

INTERPRETER: The fast recovery of sickness will decrease the medical cost and the government will benefit. She thank you.

Another Chinese woman, Rose Lee, explained that she had just stumbled upon the meeting but felt she had to speak up:

I happen to be here to attend my own meeting, and there I heard this hearing. Of course I read in Chinese newspaper many, many, many times, so I figured I need to come here to listen and observe. ... I've been listening to the speakers. Many of them claim this has nothing to do with culture. And I'm afraid I have to disagree. I came from China. I understand the Chinese habit. For some of them, you and I might not agree. For myself, I probably do want to eat frog. But that's besides the point. I think the group of people also Chinese Americans in California and also around the whole nation, they do have the right to carry their culture and to enjoy their life the way they used to. So just like I was impressed by your Christmas, people talk about the turkey, why the turkey? You agree that was fine. So actually, in America you're having turkey celebrating your holiday. Actually not much different than Chinese people, they like to eat turkey and other things. Turkey, too, but, but turtles and frogs. It's just something in our culture. For more than 5,000 years, no one actually got sick because they were eating that, either. I don't want to point that out. So I personally feel it is a culture question.

Chinese American animal advocate Michelle Tsai vehemently disagreed with this culture line. At the February 2, 2006 Fish and Game hearing, she stated: "Sorry, it's not our culture. We, the majority of the Chinese people, are kind, gentle, compassionate. We follow the Buddhist beliefs of nonviolence and kindness. We are ashamed of these live markets. We don't want them to continue to operate, especially with the killing of these poor turtles. ... It's not a cultural issue, it's a money issue. It's just a money issue. Don't tell me culture. It's just money."

Some Chinese elected officials publicly affirmed Chinese live food practices in an effort to forestall an importation ban. On March 23, 1998, Supervisor Mabel Teng introduced a resolution that stated (in part):

WHEREAS, State and local laws already exist to regulate environmental and health safety and to prohibit releasing of non-native species in the wild; and

WHEREAS, Many of San Francisco's live food markets sell fresh food, including live frogs and turtles; and

WHEREAS, Chinese Americans have a long tradition of eating fresh food; and

WHEREAS, The proposed ban will cause severe hardships to many of San Francisco's merchants, resulting in job loss.

The resolution, which was purely hortatory and had no binding power, concluded by urging the Fish and Game Commission not to pass the importation ban and urging the governor to oppose the ban. In a letter to the Fish and Game Commission later that month (March 31, 1998), Supervisor Leland Yee, too, registered his strong opposition to the proposed importation ban, describing it as "a not very subtle attack on a cultural practice that is important to many Chinese Americans in California."

The *World Journal*'s news reporting constructed a sense of threat around the proposed importation ban and urged community mobilization. The article "Proposal to Ban the Importation of Live Turtles Will Affect California's Economy" (February 25, 1998) quotes Pius Lee urging Southern California Chinese communities to attend the Fish and Game hearing in Long Beach to oppose the ban and predicting "inestimable statewide [economic] losses" if it should pass.[73] Another article featured the subtitle "Pius Lee Calls On All Chinatown Shopowners to be Self-Disciplined and United; If the Ban Is Passed, Fresh Food May Not Be Bought All over America" (January 28, 1999).[74] The article "Northern and Southern California Are United in Fight Against the Proposed Ban on the Importation of Live Turtles and Frogs" (April 1, 1998) celebrates the "unprecedented cooperation" between Northern and Southern "compatriots" over this issue.[75]

World Journal news articles also routinely conveyed mobilizing information to readers. One article conveyed Assemblyman Mike Honda's fax number and mailing address as well as his request that anti-ban readers contact him before the April 1 Fish and Game vote in Long Beach.[76] In another, Julie Lee invited those who could not speak English to express their views about the ban through the San Francisco Neighborhood Association. She also offered taxi rides to the next Fish and Game hearing in Sacramento and gave out the SFNA's phone number.[77] In another article, CCBA officials announced that they would charter a bus to the April 2, 1999 FGC meeting in Visalia and invited people to meet in front of CCBA headquarters in Chinatown at 7:30 AM for the trip.[78]

The intimate, mutually beneficial relationship between Chinese advocates and the *World Journal* is captured in the article "San Francisco Representatives Return Triumphant from the Public Hearing: 'Unity Is Power, Thanks to Our

[73] The author is Yu Ning.
[74] The author is Yu Ning.
[75] The author is Yu Ning.
[76] Yu Ning, "Proposal to Ban the Importation of Live Turtles Will Affect California's Economy."
[77] Yu Ning, "Frog and Turtle Case Will Be Discussed Again and a Public Hearing Will Be Held in Early February."
[78] Yu Ning, "Public Hearing Will Be Held on April 2."

Compatriots and the Media'" (April 2, 1998).[79] Pius Lee is quoted saying
that he took forty copies of the *World Journal* containing a report on how
"frogs stack up by nature" – commissioned and paid for by the *World Journal*
itself – to the Long Beach FGC hearing as proof that keeping frogs stacked
in crates in the markets is not cruel. Also quoted is Chinatown market owner
Zhang Kemei, who expresses gratitude for the newspaper's coverage of the
issue: "If it is not advocated for like this, nobody will pay attention to it and
compatriots and politicians will not stand up and speak out and voices cannot be heard, and the [ban] proposal cannot be defeated by only a few shop
owners."

The Fish and Game Commission considered the importation ban on and
off for thirteen years. Although the Commissioners were appointed by the
governor and not beholden to electoral constituencies, they were subjected
to intense lobbying from both animal advocates and Chinese community
activists. They managed these conflicting pressures by at once declaring their
respect for all cultures and reiterating their commitment to protecting the natural resources of the state. As Commissioner Boren stated at a Fish and Game
hearing on February 5, 1999, "[W]hat we're trying to do is to be sensitive
to the needs of different ethnic communities in our society, to allow them to
continue a way of life that they've enjoyed, but at the same time honor our
fiduciary duty of not allowing exotic imported animals into the wild to affect
the ecosystem."

In 1997, when animal advocates first brought the issue to them, the
Commissioners considered the ban but delayed action. A vote was scheduled
for April 1, 1998, and hundreds of people from the Bay Area traveled to that
meeting in Long Beach. At that meeting, the Commissioners learned about
the Joint Guidelines drawn up by the SFSPCA and the CCBA and once again
delayed action on the ban, opting instead to require merchants to post signs
in their stores saying that releasing animals into the wild was illegal and that
all animals had to be killed before leaving the stores. Months later, upon
receiving public testimony that the signs were being ignored by merchants
and customers alike, the Commission again considered and then delayed
action on the ban, citing the imminent passage and uncertain impact of AB
238 (the Honda bill). It was some time before animal advocates persuaded
the Commission to take up the issue again. Some Commissioners were clearly
more eager to enact the ban than others, but the overall impression was of an
official body that was reluctant to take action and was looking for reasons
not to.

When the Fish and Game Commissioners did move toward taking action,
they did so in the name of "honoring [their] duties as trustees of the resource."[80]
As public servants and stewards of the state's natural resources, it was their

---

[79] The author is Yu Ning.
[80] Commissioner Boren, Fish and Game Commission Hearing, February 5, 1999.

charge to think about the big picture and the long term, setting aside politics and the self-interested pleading of particular groups. Commissioner Mike Sutton stated at a Fish and Game hearing on September 3, 2009 that the science of the matter was clear:

There seems to be abundant evidence that these animals are more ... than a threat. These are active predators of our native wildlife. There seems to be no reason that we should allow these things into the state. Maybe we can just cut to the chase and get it done. ... I'm also of the opinion that the Commission is pretty united on this. It's been before us forever. We are constantly criticized by the legislature and others for dragging our feet on issues where the Commission could have been proactive. This seems like a perfect example of a situation where we could take action before the legislature compels it. We have lots of evidence that that's necessary and appropriate, that these exotic animals are threats to our native wildlife, and I for one would just like to do it, get it done, after all these years.

The following year, at the April 8, 2010 meeting in Monterey, the Fish and Game Commission voted 3–0 to enact an importation ban on turtles and frogs for food.[81] The statement read as follows:

> 1. The Fish and Game Commission and the Department of Fish and Game have been charged by the Legislature to protect and wisely manage the State's living natural resources and the habitats upon which they depend.
> 2. The importation of non-native turtles and frogs poses threats not only to the State's native turtles and frogs, but also to the native source populations of the imported turtles and frogs.
> 3. These threats include, but are not limited to: disease, hybridization, competition, and predation.
>
> Therefore, it is the policy of the Fish and Game Commission that the Department of Fish and Game shall cease issuing importation permits for any live non-native turtles or frogs pursuant to Section 236, Title 14, CCR.

Once enacted, the ban promised to halt the annual importation into California of 2 million bullfrogs raised commercially in Taiwan and more than 300,000 freshwater turtles taken from the wild in the Southeastern United States.

But the drama was not over. The issue of race, deliberately sidelined by the Commissioners, came back with a vengeance. On May 4, 2010, six Asian American elected officials from the Bay Area – Assemblywoman Fiona Ma, Senator Leland Yee, Assemblyman Ted Lieu, Assemblyman Warren Furutani, Assemblyman Mike Eng, and Assemblyman Paul Fong – wrote a letter to the

---

[81] Richard Rogers, Mike Sutton, and Dan Benninghoven voted yes. Dan Richards was absent and President Jim Kellogg recused himself, citing a possible conflict of interest.

Fish and Game Commission asking it to reconsider the ban.[82] The letter stated: "A disturbing part of your recent decision is that it appears to disproportionately target Asian American owned businesses." Most of the countermobilization against the live animal market campaign took place as a specifically Chinese phenomenon, but here is an instance where the broader Asian American experience and sensibility were invoked. At the next Fish and Game hearing on May 20, 2010, in a historically unprecedented development, several Asian American elected officials (as well as a large number of Chinese American folks) showed up in person to urge the Commission to rescind the ban.

The Commissioners argued that they had shown the utmost respect for the Chinese advocates' position all along – as Commissioner Boren put it, "With regard to the Chinese community, this Commission is going over backwards to try to preserve this way of life and this tradition."[83] Thirteen years of reflection without action indeed suggests that concern about being and appearing discriminatory, combined with other factors such as institutional inertia, had overdetermined the Commission's inaction. But when directly challenged as discriminatory, the Commissioners pushed back forcefully, arguing that they had put "sound enlightened resource management" before politics as usual. Commissioner Dan Richards had this exchange with Assemblyman Ted Lieu during the meeting:

COMMISSIONER DAN RICHARDS: The state's being permeated with invasive species across the board. ... [H]ow is it as a Commission that we're supposed to manage this problem statewide if we don't start putting some lines in the sand and saying, "We're just not going to tolerate this any more. We've got to stop it." You kindly and accurately did acknowledge we have a problem here with invasive species in the state. ... We have a bear parts issue around the state, we have a sturgeon issue, very similar populations feeling that it's important to their historical cultures, and yet it's causing great harm to the resources within the state. ... [C]andidly, this is just a pinprick. This is just getting started, and the Commission's finally addressing what is universally acknowledged in almost all communities, that we have a very serious, growing problem on these invasive species.

...

ASSEMBLYMAN TED LIEU: But your initial determination, I believe, has a disparate impact against the practices of a racial minority, particularly Chinese Americans. The decision is discriminatory. I have not seen that it is these operators that cause the invasive species problem. It is my understanding that you have yet to issue a violation to these operators, and the fact that you haven't banned turtles and frogs for pet stores shows me that this was a pretty discriminatory decision. And this is not a pinprick. This is a massive hammer to people who are going to be put out of business, and there's no evidence that they have caused this problem. I think you need far more study. You need to link it to

[82] Furutani is Japanese American; the others are Chinese American.
[83] Fish and Game Commission Hearing, February 5, 1999.

these folks, which you have not. I urge you to reverse your decision. It is discriminatory on its face.

...

COMMISSIONER DAN RICHARDS: Just for the record, and I want to make sure we're perfectly clear, I find that to be one of the most preposterous assertions I've ever heard in my life, that this is discriminatory. We have a major problem here –

ASSEMBLYMAN TED LIEU: You cannot show that they have caused this problem.

COMMISSIONER DAN RICHARDS: You're welcome to have your opinion –

ASSEMBLYMAN TED LIEU: And yet, why have you not issued a single violation, citation, to these operators?

COMMISSIONER DAN RICHARDS: That's a different issue than calling it discriminatory, and I find that ridiculous.

ASSEMBLYMAN TED LIEU: It's discriminatory because you have not shown any evidence that these operators cause this problem. That's why it's discriminatory. It's singling out Chinese Americans.

COMMISSIONER DAN RICHARDS: Oh, Jesus. [sighs] Thank you.

...

COMMISSIONER DAN RICHARDS: I must tell you, Assemblyman Lieu's comments on discrimination infuriated me, because that is exactly the politics that enter into these decisions that should never enter into it. It's got nothing to do with discrimination, and he knows that. I find that offensive to this Commission who works so hard to make the right decisions. But anyway, I see no need to change what we've already done, and candidly, it just puts on our radar screen that we need to now expand it and continue our – and I'm gonna call it a "war," for lack of a better word – on the invasive species that are decimating our native wildlife.

At the same meeting, Commissioner Richard Rogers defended the ban by reiterating the Fish and Game Commission's mandate:

I'm immensely sensitive to the needs of the ethnic communities of the state of California, their historical and cultural issues. But that is something that is outside of the purview of the Fish and Game Commission. The Fish and Game Commission needs to worry about the native resources of the state of California, and any threat to those resources is something that we have to address. We are required to do so, in all sensitivity to people's cultural needs and concerns. Here in the state of California, the primary responsibility of this Commission is not cultural interests but the needs of the native wildlife.

For Richards and Rogers, Lieu's invocation of race constituted special pleading, the inappropriate injection of politics or particular interests into the proceedings. Lieu, on the other hand, saw the Commissioners' universalist posture as a cover for reproducing white privilege – another set of particular interests. A year after this exchange, at the height of the Dan Richards mountain lion hunting scandal, Lieu introduced a bill to ban the use of hounds in bear and bobcat hunting, in a pointed rebuke to the Commissioner.

What happened next was an eerie recapitulation of the drama at the Commission on Animal Control and Welfare fourteen years earlier. There, as discussed in Chapter 3, the optic of cruelty prevailed and the CACW voted to recommend a ban on the sale of live animals in the city, only to find that the Board of Supervisors would not follow the recommendation. Here, the optic of ecological harm prevailed and the Fish and Game Commissioners voted for the importation ban, only to find that the Department of Fish and Game would not follow the recommendation. Political considerations undoubtedly shaped the Department's decision. At a Fish and Game Commission hearing on September 16, 2010, the Department's deputy director, Sonke Mastrup, indicated that the director of the Department was under "intense pressure" from the Chinese community not to enact the ban. Commissioner Dan Richards then pressed him to explain why the director had not followed the Commission's instructions:

DEPUTY DIRECTOR SONKE MASTRUP: The director works for the Governor.

COMMISSIONER DAN RICHARDS: He listens to us [the Fish and Game Commission], though. We're the ones that give him direction.

DEPUTY DIRECTOR SONKE MASTRUP: Actually, the Governor gives him direction.

COMMISSIONER DAN RICHARDS: Oh, I'm sure he gives him direction, but we have the authority to give him direction here.

DEPUTY DIRECTOR SONKE MASTRUP: I'm just telling you the predicament we're in.[84]

Frustrated and angry, the Commissioners lacked the authority to compel the Department to change course. At a Fish and Game Commission hearing on March 3, 2011, Commissioner Dan Richards spoke scornfully of the Department director's memo explaining his refusal to enact the ban:

The structure is woefully broken. The Department of Fish and Game is supervised, managed, and directed by the Fish and Game Commission, yet we don't supervise, manage, direct, or discipline the Director. He takes his direction from the Governor, and the Governor, or his department, his people, whoever, told him that they wanted the non-native frogs and turtles to be imported alive into the State of California. So he just took that approach, and is trying to back it up with a bunch of B.S. in this memo.

Both of these venues – the Commission on Animal Control and Welfare and the Fish and Game Commission – were putatively designed to give citizens a voice and make government more responsive to public opinion. In both, animal advocates "won" the argument but lacked the political power to actualize the changes they sought.

CODA: THE SHARK FIN BAN AND THE ELECTION OF ED LEE

The coda to this story involves two roughly coterminous events from 2011 – the state legislature's passage of a ban on the sale of shark fin (used in

---

[84] Fish and Game Commission Hearing, September 16, 2010.

traditional Chinese soup) and the election of the city's first Chinese American mayor. Together, these events raised a number of questions about the political status of the Chinese American community in San Francisco. If the inaction of the DFG on the turtle and frog importation ban reflected Chinese American clout, was the passage of the shark fin ban evidence that this clout was limited? Was the shark fin ban proof of continued Chinese racial and cultural marginalization or a sound environmental decision that had nothing to do with race and culture? Did the election of Ed Lee signify genuine community empowerment and a shift in the city's power structure, or was it simply more politics as usual – only this time with a Chinese face and name? Like the live animal market controversy, the fight over the shark fin ban was a site of intense contestation over the meanings of race, species, nature, and culture. This time, however, animal and environmental protectionists won a clear victory.

Assemblymen Paul Fong (D-Cupertino) and Jared Huffman (D-San Rafael), cosponsors of AB 376 (the shark fin ban), introduced the bill on February 14, 2011. According to the *San Francisco Chronicle*, the tradition of eating shark fin soup dates back 1,800 years to the Han dynasty. Today, it is an expensive delicacy – a bowl costs as much as $100 and a pound of dried shark fin costs several hundred dollars – typically served at Chinese weddings and other special occasions.[85] Shark fin is procured through a process known as "finning," which involves capturing the shark, cutting off its fin, and throwing the animal back in the water, where it sinks to the bottom and dies. Dozens of environmental groups, animal protection groups, fishermen's groups, and Asian American groups came together in support of the bill.[86] Assemblyman Paul Fong, the cosponsor of the bill, was one of the authors of the letter that Asian American legislators sent to the Fish and Game Commission in May 2010 asking for the importation ban on turtles and frogs to be rescinded. Fong had argued that the environmental science concerning the turtle and frog ban was unpersuasive and that the proposed action was racially discriminatory. With regard to the shark fin ban, however, Fong argued that the environmental science was irrefutable and that the bill was not racially discriminatory.

Armed with numerous scientific studies, the bill's advocates made their case at hearings of the Assembly Water, Parks, and Wildlife Committee in the spring of 2011. They argued that the global shark fin trade was decimating

[85] Cited in the bill analysis prepared by the Assembly's Water Parks and Wildlife Committee, March 14, 2011. http://www.leginfo.ca.gov/pub/11–12/bill/asm/ab_03510400/ab_376_cfa_20110408_095618_asm_floor.html.

[86] These included the California League of Conservation Voters, Defenders of Wildlife, Environmental Defense Fund, Monterey Bay Aquarium, Action for Animals, Coastside Fishing Club, United Anglers, The Sportfishing Conservancy, Asian Pacific American Ocean Harmony Alliance, Asian Pacific Islander California Action Network, and Asian Americans for Community Involvement.

shark populations, with ominous implications for the integrity of the oceans. According to the Monterey Bay Aquarium, more than a third of the roughly 400 shark species worldwide are threatened with extinction. Sharks are especially vulnerable to overfishing, according to the National Oceanic and Atmospheric Administration, because they take a long time to mature and have only a few offspring at a time. The demand for shark fin in China and throughout the Chinese diaspora, which results in the killing of 73 million sharks per year, has contributed to this grim scenario. From an environmental point of view, sharks are vitally important because as the top predators in the ocean, they maintain the overall balance and health of ocean life. So while the bill's advocates acknowledged that the Chinese tradition of eating shark fin soup dates back thousands of years, they nevertheless asserted that "the collapse of ocean ecosystems must take precedence over cultural culinary heritage."[87] They also mentioned the cruelty and wastefulness of finning. Finally, advocates noted that other states and territories – Hawai'i Oregon, Washington, Guam, and the Commonwealth of the Northern Mariana Islands – had already banned the shark fin trade.[88]

Opponents of AB 376 included Chinese American individuals and family associations as well as several Asian and Chinese American restaurant and food trade associations.[89] They challenged the science of the matter, arguing that most shark species were not threatened or endangered and pointing out that only three were formally listed by CITES (Convention on International Trade in Endangered Species). The bill would imperil thousands of jobs and cause a loss in tax revenue, they averred, and was unnecessary because of extant federal and international laws against finning. But the crux of their argument was that the bill discriminated against the Chinese culture. Because many people around the world kill sharks for meat but only the Chinese kill sharks for their fins, the legislature's targeting of shark fins revealed discriminatory intent, they argued. Once again, the optic of racism was advanced as a counterweight to the optic of ecological harm.[90]

When Mayor Ed Lee, who was appointed interim mayor in January 2011 to replace Gavin Newsom (who had been elected lieutenant governor), spoke

---

[87] Bill analysis prepared by the Assembly's Water Parks and Wildlife Committee, March 14, 2011. http://www.leginfo.ca.gov/pub/11–12/bill/asm/ab_03510400/ab_376_cfa_20110408_095618 _asm_floor.html.

[88] Bill analysis prepared by the Assembly's Water Parks and Wildlife Committee, May 19, 2011. http:// www.leginfo.ca.gov/pub/11–12/bill/asm/ab_0351-0400/ab_376_cfa_20110520_155812_asm _floor.html.

[89] Opponents of the shark fin ban included the Asian Food Trade Association, Asian Nutrition and Health Association, Chung Chou City, Inc., National Chinese Welfare Council of Los Angeles County, Oriental Food Association, Stockton Seafood Center (6 Groups), plus various individuals and Chinese family associations.

[90] Bill analysis prepared by the Senate's Committee on Natural Resources and Water, June 14, 2011. http://www.leginfo.ca.gov/pub/11–12/bill/asm/ab_0351–0400/ab_376_cfa_20110610_163334 _sen_comm.html.

out against AB 376, the public response was sharp. An online *City Insider* article, "Mayor Ed Lee Opposed to Shark Fin Soup Ban" (April 26, 2011), by Heather Knight, provoked hundreds of comments, the vast majority of which were pro-ban[91]:

- "News flash, Asians don't own the Pacific Ocean nor the life contained within it. We share the waters and the actions in the East affect the ecosystem of half the world's water."
- "I suppose we'll just have to file this under 'Hey, I'm Chinese, and I'll do whatever Chinese thing I damn well want to and to hell with the rest of the world.'"
- "Toxic toys, slave labor, child labor, spitting in public, killing baby girls … respect their culture?" [16 minutes later from the same person]: "Stealing copyrights, screaming in libraries, female infanticide, ignoring health codes, building codes, environmental laws. …"
- "There may be a cultural basis for the ritual of eating shark fin soup, but does that mean that members of the Chinese community cannot reassess the practice in light of current environmental realities? Is it not possible to assess the torture inflicted on the animal, and the waste of killing an entire creature just for the fin and throwing the rest away? Is it 'racist' to appeal to the Chinese community's higher consciousness and ask it to do the right thing?"
- "Even within the confines of China today there is far too much variation to have a single 'Chinese culture.' So, enough with the strawman, Mayor Lee."
- "I'm waiting for the usual … 'If you don't respect his culture, then you're a Chinese hater/racist.'"
- "'Attack on a culture'? Nonsense. Perhaps if a culture has elements that are backward or not acceptable on moral or environmental grounds that culture needs to adapt and change, not blindly defend and accuse others of racism or insensitivity."
- "Protecting animals and the environment is an American value. You do identify as Americans, don't you?"

Several of the live animal market controversy themes reemerged here, including the notion of nature as a global commons; the imagining of Chinese culture as cruel, selfish, and transgressive; the sense of Chinese Americans as un-American; and an impatience and fatigue with the optic of racism.

Despite Mayor Ed Lee's opposition to the bill, Assemblyman Fong succeeded in gaining the support of other important Chinese American politicians in San Francisco and the Bay Area. Indeed, the fight over the shark fin ban unfolded against the dramatic political backdrop of a mayoral contest in full swing. After promising not to run for mayor in the November 2011 election, interim mayor Ed Lee changed his mind and entered a field that

---

[91] Knight (April 26, 2011). As of May 1, 2011, there were 426 posts on this blog.

already included several Chinese American candidates. David Chiu and Phil Ting, both running for mayor against Lee, appeared at a news conference organized by the conservation group WildAid to express support for the shark fin ban, and U.S. Representative Judy Chu also declared her support.[92] Yao Ming, the former NBA star from China, strongly endorsed the bill. In addition to lobbying against the shark fin trade in China, he made a public service announcement that was shown in San Francisco, and he also appeared on city buses and billboards in ads that said in both Chinese and English, "Join me, say no to shark fin soup."[93] A poll released by the Monterey Bay Aquarium in May 2011 showed that 70 percent of Chinese American respondents favored the shark fin ban, although CAVEC director David Lee pointed out that the poll sampled only registered voters and thus probably overstated Chinese support.[94]

There was also significant Chinese opposition to AB 376, and the Chinese-language media provided a window onto this intra-community dissension. While the *World Journal* covered the press conference where Assemblymen Fong and Huffman introduced AB 376 with the slogan "Conserve Sharks, Conserve Oceans" in Chinese,[95] it also gave significant coverage to those mobilizing against the ban. Just a week after the bill's introduction, it reported that State Senator Leland Yee, also running for mayor, had called a press conference where he denounced AB 376 as "unfair" and "disrespectful to the Chinese community."[96] The *World Journal* article "Oriental Food Association Says No to Shark Fin Ban" (February 23, 2011) reported that the OFA, composed of Bay Area Asian food importers, opposed AB 376 in the name of consumers' rights rather than culture – because it "deprived consumers of their right to choose whether to eat shark fins or not."[97] Similarly, the *Sing Tao Daily*

---

[92] Hindery (2011).

[93] Kurtenbach (2011); Hindery (2011). The bill's sponsors understood the importance of garnering Asian American support. On April 8, 2011, I participated in a meeting of Asian American faculty and students at University of California, Irvine, organized by Damon Nagami of the National Resource Defense Council and UCI Law student Jean Su. The point of the meeting was to enlist support for the bill and to brainstorm about how to promote the bill in the Asian American community.

[94] Hindery (2011); Kwong (2011). A recent survey showed that 78 percent of Hong Kong residents think it is "acceptable" to leave shark fin soup off of the menu at ceremonial events like weddings, signaling a possible shift in attitudes there (Wassener 2011). In Beijing, Ding Liguo, a deputy of the National People's Congress, filed a proposal to ban the shark fin trade, and WildAid's executive director, Peter Knight, says that the Chinese government allowed them to run ad campaigns on the mainland with the aid of the state-run media.

[95] Li Xiulan, "Shark Fin Ban Proposed by Paul Fong and Jared Huffman."

[96] "Amended Shark Fin Ban Measure Proposed by Leland Yee." Yee initially took a strong stand against the shark fin ban and then seemed to back down from it, provoking charges of slipperiness. At the Alice B. Toklas LGBT Democratic Club Debate, Yee was asked if he favored the shark fin ban and "brought down the house" by holding up the sign to say yes then switching it to no then yes then no. The reporter notes: "The beautiful part is, he still never answered the question" (Nevius 2011).

[97] Li Xiulan, "Oriental Food Association Says No to Shark Fin Ban."

article "Bay Area Chinese Merchants Protest Against Shark Fin Ban" (April 5, 2011) recounted that businesspeople involved in the shark fin trade were holding meetings, collecting signatures, and planning protests. The article quotes one San Francisco Chinese community leader condemning AB 376 as "a proposal full of double standards, discrimination, criticism, ethnic division and prejudice" that is intent on "demonizing, criminalizing, discriminating against and convicting a specific culture."[98] That AB 376 had a Chinese American cosponsor with strong community bona fides as well as other Chinese/Asian American support helped to inoculate it against the racism charge and secure its passage.[99]

Just weeks after Governor Jerry Brown signed AB 376 into law, San Franciscans elected their first Chinese American mayor.[100] It was the first time that ranked-choice voting was used to select the mayor of a major U.S. city.[101] In this system, voters rank their top three candidates. If no one secures the majority of first-place votes, the last-place candidate is eliminated and second and third choices are also counted. This is repeated until one candidate has more than 50 percent.[102] With sixteen candidates in the field, it took eleven rounds of ranked-choice voting and the elimination of every other candidate except Supervisor John Avalos before Lee moved past the 50 percent mark. Ed Lee won with less than one-third of the first-place votes. Turnout was also low – around 40 percent, whereas the past ten mayoral contests in the city had had an average of 50 percent turnout.[103] Indeed, it was the lowest turnout in a competitive mayor's race in the city since 1975.[104] On the other hand, Lee won all but three of eleven supervisorial districts and defeated Avalos in his own district by an almost 2-1 margin.[105] And Chinese turnout, according to

[98] Han Qiuping, "Bay Area Chinese Merchants Protest Against Shark Fin Ban."
[99] In July 2009, Governor Schwarzenegger signed ACR 42, a bill proposed by Paul Fong that admits and officially apologizes for the past persecution of Chinese immigrants in California. Fong has been working with U.S. Representatives Mike Honda and Judy Chu to get the U.S. Congress to issue an apology for the Chinese Exclusion Act of 1882. Wang Jincheng, "Paul Fong Pushes Congress to Apologize for Chinese Exclusion Act."
[100] The law says it is "unlawful for any person to possess, sell, offer for sale, trade, or distribute a shark fin" and conveys several legislative findings/declarations about sharks' role in ocean ecosystems and how they are declining and how this relates to shark fin trade. For example, Section 1c of the law states: "Sharks occupy the top of the marine food chain. Their decline is an urgent problem that upsets the balance of species in ocean ecosystems and negatively affects other fisheries. It constitutes a serious threat to the ocean ecosystem and biodiversity."
[101] Progressives initially backed ranked-choice voting to avoid problems related to run-off elections (expense and undue influence of moneyed interests). San Francisco was the first major U.S. city to implement it. Supervisors there were elected using ranked-choice voting for the first time in 2004.
[102] Knight (November 10, 2011).
[103] Wildermuth (2011).
[104] Knight (November 13, 2011).
[105] Garcia (2011). "Most of Lee's support came from the so-called 'donut' of less liberal and more heavily Asian precincts on The City's perimeter. Second and third place finishers Avalos and

CAVEC executive director David Lee, was more than 50 percent, the highest on record.[106]

Given San Francisco's unique history as a center of anti-Chinese sentiment and practice in the 1800s, it was perhaps inevitable that observers chose to read Lee's election through a triumphalist frame. With rapid post-1965 population growth, the Chinese had made steady and significant progress in gaining seats on the Board of Supervisors and in both houses of the state legislature, but the mayor's office had proven elusive to that point.[107] Even Lee's original appointment as interim mayor to replace Gavin Newsom (who had been elected lieutenant governor), therefore, prompted an outpouring of celebratory, historically minded commentary. Scholar Ling-Chi Wang wrote:

> It is hard to imagine San Francisco, the city that gave birth to such well-known 19th century venomous slogans as "The Chinese must go!" and "Not a Chinaman's chance!" and initiated no fewer than 15 Chinese exclusion laws enacted by Congress between 1882 and 1943, is now headed by a Chinese American interim mayor, Edwin Lee. Even though he is merely a caretaker and has pledged not to run for the same office this year, his accession represents a significant, albeit snail-pace, step in the Chinese American uphill quest for racial justice and political empowerment in a city ironically known across the nation for its liberal outlook and progressive politics.[108]

Rachel Gordon's article "SF Asian Americans Ascending in Halls of Power" (*San Francisco Chronicle*, January 11, 2011) noted that Lee's appointment and David Chiu's selection as president of the Board of Supervisors heralded "the coming of age politically of a community."[109] Geron and Lai described Lee's appointment as the culmination of a long journey for the Chinese "from political outsiders to insiders."[110]

The triumphalist narrative about a unified Chinese community awakening to its own strength, overcoming barriers, and making history was haunted by two contradictions. First, the fact that Ed Lee's appointment as interim mayor resulted from backroom deals and power plays raises questions about whether he represented something new and different. It was widely reported that former mayor Willie Brown and Rose Pak of the Chinese Chamber of Commerce had arranged for Lee's ascension. In "Behind-the-Scenes Power Politics: The

---

Herrera did better in the 'hole,' also known as 'the creamy hipster center' that includes San Francisco's interior neighborhoods like Mission, Castro and Noe Valley" (Schreiber, November 11, 2011). Lee's strongholds of support included Chinatown, the Richmond, the Sunset, the Marina, Ingleside, Visitacion Valley, and Bayview-Hunters Point. Gordon (November 13, 2011).

[106] Knight (November 13, 2011).
[107] In 2008, David Chiu became the first Asian American Supervisor to be elected in District 3 (which includes Chinatown). As of 2012, there were four Asian American Supervisors – Eric Mar (District 1), David Chiu (District 3), Carmen Chu (District 4), and Jane Kim (District 6) (Geron and Lai 2011).
[108] Wang (2011).
[109] Gordon (January 11, 2011).
[110] Geron and Lai (2011), 1.

Making of Ed Lee" (*The Bay Citizen*, January 6, 2011), Gerry Shih reported that Brown called his longtime ally Pak because he didn't like the three progressive candidates most likely to replace Newsom. Pak then called Lee on his cell phone when he was in the airport on his way to Taiwan and persuaded him to serve as interim mayor. She and Brown spent the next forty-eight hours in an "extraordinary political power play," outflanking the Board's progressive wing and securing a majority of votes for Lee. David Chiu, ordinarily allied with the progressives on the Board, provided the decisive vote for Lee.[111] Supervisor John Avalos commented: "This was something incredibly orchestrated, and we got played. I'm still trying to figure out what happened. I don't know what the game was about, except that it was to muscle someone into office." Pak said to the reporter: "Now you know why they say I play politics like a blood sport."[112]

If Rose Pak handpicked Ed Lee and made his appointment happen, would she have too much influence in his administration? Even some Chinese American supporters of Lee, including Reverend Norman Fong and Gordon Chin, conceded that the process had been ugly and that it raised questions about whom Lee would be accountable to.[113] Supervisor Chris Daly, who opposed Lee's appointment, did not pull his punches:

> It seems as if according to her, Miss Pak and former Mayor Willie Brown were very involved in setting up this potential appointment of Ed Lee as successor mayor and I think that it was so well done that if nominations were reopened I would go ahead and nominate Rose Pak for the position of interim mayor and vote for her. Why not, why not cut out the middle man. If Rose Pak is putting, is the one who is putting this together. If Rose Pak is the one who has the talents and the ability to make this happen, the most important decision that I have seen on the Board of Supervisors in 10 years, then rightfully why not go ahead and make Rose Pak successor if she has that level of savvy and ability to put together in three short days the most important decision this board has made in 10 years.[114]

Asked if she wanted to be interim mayor, Pak responded: "Well, provided if Chris Daly will become my chief of staff."[115] In "Ed Lee – A Coup for S.F. Power Couple Brown, Pak," Phil Bronstein of the *San Francisco Chronicle* called Pak "San Francisco's new 'it' girl" and declared: "Rose and Willie are the power couple, the enduring San Francisco puppeteers. ... At least we know who's in charge."[116]

Ed Lee's decision to break his pledge and run for election when his term as interim mayor ended revealed a second contradiction – between the projected image of a unified Chinese American community and the reality of intense competition among Chinese American candidates. Despite tremendous excitement about the Chinese role in this election – from the "unprecedented impact"

[111] Jones (2011).
[112] Shih (2011).
[113] Jones (2011).
[114] Sabatini (January 7, 2011).
[115] Ibid.
[116] Bronstein (2011).

of Chinese-language newspapers[117] to the estimated percentage of Asian voters (20 percent)[118] to the presence of four serious Chinese candidates – the fact was that the Chinese candidates were competing for the same votes.[119] Rose Pak and other Lee supporters started a "Run, Ed, Run" campaign to make it look as though Lee was a reluctant candidate thinking only of the good of the city, but his opponents were not persuaded. In his article "David Chiu-Ed Lee Bromance Is So Over" (*City Insider*, August 12, 2011), John Coté reported that at a mayoral debate on August 11, 2011, Supervisor David Chiu, who had apparently cast his vote for Lee as interim mayor with the understanding that Lee would not run for mayor in November, said to Lee: "I have to say, Mr. Mayor, it felt a little like meeting an ex-girlfriend after a breakup."[120]

But the rivalry that emerged between State Senator Leland Yee and Mayor Ed Lee was a singular phenomenon. Part of the backdrop was that Yee's relationship with Rose Pak was one of long-standing animosity. Ed Liu comments:

In Chinatown right now, Leland, in terms of Rose Pak, they're enemies. … It's personal. It has to do with who's going to be the number one player. And the perception of Leland from Rose Pak is that Leland doesn't play, Leland doesn't defer to her. It's a matter of ego, of power, of leverage, of whether or not Leland is willing to defer to Rose Pak as the number one China person. … In my view, Rose Pak wants anybody but Leland [to be mayor].

In his article "Anyone But Yee for Mayor" (*San Francisco Examiner*, January 8, 2011), Ken Garcia quotes Rose Pak as saying, "Anybody but Leland Yee, I've said that from the start." Pressed to give a reason, Pak says it has something to do with "moral turpitude" but declines to elaborate.

Yee's base was outside of Chinatown – in the Sunset, the Richmond, and beyond the city limits. Despite his highly public attempts to act as a defender and spokesperson for the Chinese community – on the live animal market controversy, the shark fin ban, and other issues – he was for many Chinatown leaders a persona non grata because he had joined the Hilton Corporation in opposing the construction of a City College campus in Chinatown. Former CCBA president Raymond Mah explains:

Leland Yee, before, OK. After that Chinatown college, whole community against him. … At that time, they want to put a City College in [Chinatown]. And then he got against it. Leland Yee is against us. … Because he got the money from the Hilton lobby during his campaign, Hilton group. Right now the hotel, they are [near the proposed site]. … They don't want Chinatown, the college, built there. … Now Leland Yee want to come back Chinatown to run for mayor. … Because his term two more years all gone, the state [Senate seat] gone, he want to come back here. Now he get a third person to ask me, "You don't

[117] Tsai (2011).
[118] Sabatini (March 2011).
[119] Political consultant David Latterman said: "Asians are one of the most cohesive voting blocs around. Chinese voters are more likely to vote one, two, three for each other and they're more likely to have ethnic voting patterns rather than ideological ones." Schreiber (November 10, 2011).
[120] Coté (August 12, 2011).

support me, OK, but don't act against me." But I don't talk to him directly yet. ... But after the City College Chinatown thing, he already [lost] about 70 percent community. I'm the leader. I'm gonna lead the people against him on that time.

Who was authentically Chinese and truly spoke for the Chinese? The racial politics between Leland Yee and Ed Lee became quite intricate as the two campaigns strategized about what to say to Chinese and non-Chinese audiences. When Yee ran an attack ad on English-language television charging Lee with breaking his promise to not run and with being beholden to Rose Pak, Lee responded with an ad on Cantonese television. Lee's ad asks: "Why is Leland Yee using your tax dollars to smear San Francisco's first Chinese mayor?" and suggests that Yee is duplicitous and cowardly for attacking Lee in the English-language media but not the Chinese-language media. Yee's campaign responded that Lee was running his attack ad only in Chinese so as to perpetuate the broader public's mistaken notion that he was civil and polite.[121] Each suggested the other was two-faced and untrustworthy.

Tensions escalated as the election neared. In late October, an altercation broke out outside of Yee's campaign office. Yee was about to announce his allegation that Lee's supporters had violated the law by paying $150 in cash to more than thirty poor Bayview residents to post campaign signs and doorhangers and by offering them jobs and bonuses in the event of a Lee victory. Lee's campaign manager and spokesman showed up and there was yelling back and forth between staff from the two campaigns.[122] A few days later, the Chinese Chamber of Commerce (Rose Pak's group) and the vice president of the Lee Family Association (which claimed Ed Lee as a member) called upon Yee to end his Cantonese-language robo-calls warning voters not to hand their ballots to Lee campaign workers.[123] Then there was *The Real Ed Lee: The Untold, Untold Story*, a book produced by the Yee campaign to satirize the celebratory volume, *The Ed Lee Story: An Unexpected Mayor*. Yee's campaign staff left their book, which calls Ed Lee, Rose Pak, and Willie Brown "the Three Racketeers," on voters' doorsteps. The tone of the book is captured in this quote: "From 'Willie & Rose's No Longer Secret Make-a-Mayor Recipe': VERY IMPORTANT: Mix all contents together in back room; if any part of the mixture is exposed to sunshine, it will be ruined. ... Pour mixture into an empty vessel – any loyal bureaucrat will do."[124]

In the months leading up to the election, Ed Lee's campaign came under fire for numerous alleged improprieties, contributing to the sense that he represented corrupt machine politics rather than something progressive and new. Five of his rivals joined to call for an investigation into alleged campaign finance violations by Progress for All, the ad hoc group working with Rose Pak to organize the "Run, Ed, Run" campaign. The local Democratic Party chair Aaron Peskin asked the city's ethics commission to investigate the group's

---

[121] Coté (September 16, 2011).
[122] Schreiber (October 26, 2011).
[123] Schreiber (October 28, 2011).
[124] Crawford (October 31, 2011).

claims to be an independent expenditure committee (which can accept unlimited donations) as opposed to a candidate committee (which can only accept donations up to $500 per person).[125] Questions also arose over whether Rose Pak had inappropriately pressured workers at Recology, a company that had won the city's $112 million garbage-shipping contract, to help with the Lee campaign. Retired judge Quentin Kopp asked the city's district attorney and the U.S. Attorney's office to launch a criminal investigation into this matter.[126] In addition, the district attorney investigated whether the Lee campaign had engaged in voter fraud in October by setting up makeshift voting booths on Stockton Street in Chinatown, helping older voters fill out mail-in ballots, and then collecting those ballots in bags.[127] None of these investigations resulted in any findings of wrongdoing. Rose Pak emerged unscathed. Days after the election, the *New York Times* ran a front-page story on her entitled "Power Broker Savors a Victory in San Francisco."[128] Local reporters declared, "Rose Pak is back and bigger than ever," to which Pak responded: "People give me more power than I really have, and half the crap I'm not even remotely interested in. All I'm interested in is advancing my community."[129]

When animal advocates took the fight to the California Fish and Game Commission in Sacramento, they conformed to the strictures of the Commission's neoliberal discourse by emphasizing an optic of ecological harm rather than cruelty. The turtle and frog importation ban did pass – against the supposed universalism of ecological concerns, Chinese arguments about race-specific impacts were cast as selfish, particular, and narrow – but it was thwarted by Chinese American political clout exercised behind the scenes. The subsequent controversy over the statewide shark fin ban and the hotly contested San Francisco mayoral election of 2011, however, demonstrated that Chinese Americans, far from moving in lockstep, are as dynamic, complex, and fractious as any other group. The victory of Ed Lee raised lingering questions, too, about whether his ascension is a sign of meaningful Chinese American political empowerment or merely a simulacrum. In the next chapter, I look at how single-optic thinking led to a posture of mutual disavowal between animal advocates and Chinese American activists in the live animal market conflict and suggest that an ethics of mutual avowal might serve better if the aim is to disrupt the conjoined logics of race and species and destabilize the edifice of power they sustain.

[125] Coté (July 29, 2011).
[126] Coté (August 1, 2011).
[127] Schreiber (November 10, 2011).
[128] Eckholm (November 11, 2011), a1, 15.
[129] Matier and Ross (January 9, 2012).

6

Vision/Critique/Avowal

> We may disagree with some aspect of their [minority cultures'] moral, ethical, or evaluative practices without dismissing or holding in disrespect their life-worlds altogether. Most human encounters … occur in this in-between space of partial evaluations, translations, and contestations.
>
> – Seyla Benhabib

In the Chinatown live animal market conflict, the optics of *cruelty*, *racism*, and *ecological harm* highlight and challenge (or purport to challenge) different dimensions of power – human domination over animals, white domination over the Chinese, and human domination over nature, respectively. Each optic directs our focus to a specific issue in a particular way, even as it necessarily diverts our attention away from other concerns. Single-optic vision of this kind tends to lead in the course of political struggle to a posture of mutual disavowal, where each group elevates its own suffering and justice claims over the suffering and justice claims of the other group, either partly or wholly invalidating the latter as a matter of political and moral concern. Disavowal, an act of dis-association and rejection, can range from failing to recognize that one is causing harm to the other group to refusing to acknowledge that the other group suffers or has valid justice claims to actively and knowingly reproducing patterns of social injury to the other group.

The posture of mutual disavowal is unsurprising in one sense: politics as a struggle over scarce resources (material, symbolic, and other) is by its very nature oppositional – one is always mobilizing for and therefore against something, so disavowing an opponent's claims and perspective is par for the course. The rub arises when one is mobilizing not against an oppressive majority but rather against another subordinated group (or, in the case of animal advocates, those representing a subordinated group). If we believe that justice requires the mitigation or cessation of various forms of social domination, the possible implications of disavowal here should give us pause.

There are both ethical and strategic factors to consider. If one's own group claims rest upon the fundamental notion that domination is unjust – that is, if one embraces anti-subordination as a central political principle – then one's actions toward other subordinated groups, whose positionality relative to one's own is likely not ascertainable in any clear or definitive way, should be conditioned by an awareness of their experience of subordination. Pragmatically speaking, too, the logics of race and species, intimately conjoined over the course of centuries in the white imagination, do not look to be disentangled from each other easily or quickly. If race is in part a metric of animality, a set of categories constituted through species distinctions, then one cannot reproduce degraded meanings of animality and nature without inflaming notions of racial difference. It may be that there will be heathen Chinese and Negro beasts and Indian savages as long as there are "animals," and that the synergistic taxonomies of race and species will need to be dismantled together or not at all. In this light, the posture of mutual disavowal between animal advocates and race advocates is troubling.

If single-optic vision leads to mutual disavowal, where does multi-optic vision lead? I suggest in this chapter that multi-optic vision encourages an openness to other subordinated group experiences and thus potentially encourages an ethics of mutual avowal. This is not to say that multi-optic vision does or should disable critique. *Seeing* and recognizing another group's oppression does not require uncritically embracing all of that group's practices, especially the ones that enact another form of oppression. Avowal and critique, that is, are not mutually exclusive positions. We can and sometimes must critique a specific tradition practiced by another group while simultaneously avowing that group's overall justice claims.

In this chapter, I argue that animal advocates' claims about colorblindness and racial innocence in the Chinatown dispute constituted a disavowal of Chinese claims about racism. Chapter 3 showed that the campaign originated as a sweeping move against the city's live food establishments and not as an anti-Chinese project; here I want to explore with greater nuance the campaign's complicated and multifaceted relationship to race. I then examine Chinese American activists' disavowal of the animal question: almost all were energetically and unabashedly speciesist in their declarations, although they did face limited dissent from within their community. Finally, I suggest that multi-optic vision can point us toward an ethics of mutual avowal that takes seriously the imperative of challenging domination's multiple dimensions.

COLORBLIND ANIMAL ADVOCACY? DISAVOWING CLAIMS ABOUT RACISM

Frosty Wooldridge, an anti-immigration activist, writes in "Immigration's Third World Cruelty to Animals" (February 18, 2004):

Whether it is animal sacrifice in New York, horse tripping in immigrant enclaves in our Southwest, dog and cat fighting where newcomers band together – this cruelty crisis raises the question of "What is America becoming?" What about the human cruelty of "female genital mutilation clitorectomies" to baby girls of immigrants from Africa and the Middle East? Why are we inviting this depraved behavior into our country? Where is this massive invasion of incompatible cultures from the Third World taking us? Who is responsible for facilitating this invasion of 1.5 million legal and the estimated 1 million illegal aliens rushing across our borders annually? When will Congress own up to this outrage? Do we want our children meshed with such cultural barbarism? Can we educate enough immigrants fast enough to stop the uncivilized behaviors they bring to our country? Will we be able to withstand their numbers as they "demonstrate or vote" for their "rights" to maintain their barbaric cultural practices? At 2.3 million arriving annually, the answer is, "NO!" We need a ten-year moratorium on all immigration into America so we can catch our national breath and regain a semblance of what this country means to humanity.[1]

Wooldridge's article is a primer on how to essentialize and denounce cultures *in toto* on the basis of specific practices, how to deploy notions of civilization and barbarism to construct the racial/colonial other as moral reprobate, and how to glorify the United States as the last bastion of virtue and reason in the world. Because every other article on Wooldridge's Web site fulminates about overpopulation and the evils of immigration, and this is the only one that mentions animals, it is not unreasonable to surmise that Wooldridge is using animals as instruments to whip up nativist sentiment.

Eric Mills and his colleagues are not Frosty Wooldridges. The core activists in the Chinatown conflict have worked in the trenches as animal advocates for decades, targeting majority as well as minority practices. Their goal in this campaign was not to escalate border patrol enforcement or encourage nativist persecution but to mitigate the suffering caused by particular animal practices. This not to say that any activism that is less odious than Wooldridge's passes muster (that would be setting the bar abysmally low), but that the moral distinction between cynically using animals as a bludgeon against immigrant minorities and speaking up for animals even at the risk of antagonizing or harming the latter is an important one that is often denied in denunciations of the Chinatown campaign as racist.

The leaders of the Chinatown campaign did not sound or act like racists or cultural imperialists. They did not denigrate the Chinese as a racial group, belittle Chinese culture, make comparisons that valorized American culture over Chinese culture, call for the destruction of Chinese culture, or admonish the Chinese to assimilate. They did not suggest that live animal markets were central to Chinese culture and somehow revealing of its essential barbarity. Indeed, they made no claims about Chinese racial or cultural proclivities at all. Rather, they advanced an argument about the moral wrongness of causing pain and suffering to animals – everywhere and in the specific instance of the markets.

As recounted in Chapter 3, the live animal market campaign originated with multiple targets in mind, and the decision to let go of Fisherman's Wharf

---

[1] http://www.frostywooldridge.com/articles/art_2004feb18.html.

was made slowly and with great reluctance. Activists did not want to target Chinatown alone – and were aware of the negative ramifications of doing so – but they ended up doing just this in order to fashion a "doable" and "winnable" campaign. Clearly, this was not racial targeting in the conventional sense of persecuting a group out of racial animus, but it was, at least in part, the relative racial/linguistic/economic disadvantage of Chinatown vendors that made them appear to be a more feasible target than the vendors at Fisherman's Wharf. Whether we think this presumptively invalidates the campaign depends to a large degree on whether we believe that the suffering of the animals in the markets is morally important enough that it must be challenged, even at the risk of doing potential harm to a racialized immigrant minority.

Accused of racism, animal advocates insisted that the campaign was color-blind and had "nothing to do with race." Sometimes, they expressed fatigue and frustration with the charge of racism, which they read as an exercise in deflection. Eric Mills commented:

It [the campaign] was not an attack upon Asian culture or anything else, just let's help these animals, obey the law, do what's right. … And I can appreciate the history of the Chinese, their past history in this area, so of course they're on the defensive, understandably. … [T]hey think we're picking on them and their culture when we're going after the cruelty to animals itself. That's the issue. So to say anything otherwise, I think, is a bogus argument. Somebody said patriotism is the last refuge of the scoundrel. I hear a lot about racist charges, a lot of which I think is not true. I've been called a Nazi in a letter to the editor of *Asian Week* here a few years ago. … At least I'm an equal opportunity Nazi. I don't care if it's God or Mother Teresa who's abusing animals, I'm gonna be out on the picket line. It's irrelevant who it is.

Miles Young, a retired Fish and Game warden who authored a 2006 investigative report on turtles and frogs in the Chinese markets for Eric Mills and colleagues, also expressed impatience with the playing of the "race card":

I'll tell you this. If I was to testify in front of any committee right now, I'd say, first of all, this isn't a race issue. It's an environmental issue. It just so happens that the Germans, the French, the Scottish, the Russians aren't importing diseased frogs and turtles. Sorry. It just so happens that this particular ethnic group of people is. It's got nothing to do with that. It's a business practice that they're doing, and I'm getting tired, frankly, of everybody saying that this is a racial issue. Because the essence of it, the problem has nothing to do with race. … It's much easier to make a race issue out of it. It gets more press. And it diverts the attention from what the problem is. I get very uptight about that. This is not in my mind a race issue. Every time the race card is played, that's just a diversion, an excuse.

You think it's like throwing up smoke and mirrors?

Absolutely. You've brought it up a half a dozen times. … But if you make it bare bones, what are we talking about? We're talking about turtles and frogs from live markets that keep ending up out in the wild. Let's look at the chytrid fungus and all the diseases they're bringing. We can go right now, buy some critters, and I'll pay your bill here, they're all gonna come back diseased, with things that go into the wild. Why is that a racial issue?

As FGC president Dan Richards did when he was arguing with Assemblyman Ted Lieu, Miles Young casts his own environmental concerns as universalistic and just and Chinese charges of racism as the special pleading of a self-interested group.

However devoutly animal activists may wish to be able to carve out space where they can speak and act without racial implications, professions of colorblindness can never rise above the level of fantasy in a profoundly racialized society like this one. Race as a hierarchical classification system, as a taxonomy of power, permeates every aspect of society, so that *there is no race-free space*, no standpoint of racial innocence.[2] Race, like other systems of meaning, saturates our thinking, our discourse, our experience, and our actions. It resists bracketing. As many scholars have pointed out, claims of colorblindness actually tend to protect racism from challenge or, worse yet, reproduce it (Gotanda 1991; Bonilla-Silva 2009).

In any case, the response of some secondary activists and members of the public to the Chinatown controversy rudely disrupted the fantasy of racial innocence. While Eric Mills and his closest colleagues restricted themselves to de-raced arguments about cruelty and ecological harm, others did not hesitate to invoke the deeply embedded trope of Chinese cultural otherness, cruelty, and transgressiveness. Some of the thousand-plus letters sent to the Fish and Game Commission in favor of the importation ban expressed hostile and xenophobic views toward Chinese Americans. One letter from a Floridian (March 25, 1998) stated:

Banning the sale of live animals in markets is NOT, repeat NOT, anti-Asian; rather, it is anti-cruelty. This is America, and we have laws in this country. If any group does not want to abide by these laws and insists on perpetrating their brutal mores from the old country in America, they should be told, in no uncertain terms, that this is not acceptable and won't be tolerated. If they come to America and do not want to live the American way, well, planes and ships leave everyday for the Orient.

Another letter from a resident of Sacramento (March 31, 1998) declared:

It's time the Chinese abandoned their disingenuous red herring of "cultural insensitivity" to realize they have insulted the mores and practices of the host culture. ... Let the Chinese return to their homeland – or stay there – if they are unwilling to compromise in the necessary exercise of living in harmony with their new American brethren. ... Let the Chinese learn to compromise and practice assimilation.

Richard Avanzino recalls the nativist tone expressed by unidentified animal advocates at a CACW hearing held at the Chinese American Citizens Alliance in Chinatown in October 1996:

One night there were public hearings in a couple of different parts of Chinatown, and we went to one, and the emotions were pretty intense. ... Several incidents happened during that meeting. One was, when one of the speakers got up there who was an animal rights

---

[2] Omi and Winant (1994), Razack (1998), Bonilla-Silva (2009).

proponent, started talking about, "If you don't believe in American society, go back home," and then there was a chant that started in the front row, or up front, about "USA! USA! USA!" It got very intense, very emotional. Unwelcome hysteria, I'm going to say.

A similar incident occurred at the Fish and Game Commission meeting in Long Beach on April 1, 1998, where the Commission was preparing to vote on the importation ban. During the meeting, the following exchange unfolded among animal advocate Marshall Thompson, an unidentified white woman, and some unidentified Chinese Americans. Marshall Thompson and his spouse, Susan Tellem, both of American Tortoise Rescue, actively participated in the Chinatown conflict, although they were not part of the core leadership circle. The exchange begins with Thompson voicing outrage that Chinese Americans opposing the ban are being permitted to hold signs up during the meeting:

THOMPSON: [shouting] And this is special exclusive treatment for specific cultural groups, and I protest it as an American! [applause]

CHINESE VOICES: We are Americans, too! We are Americans!

THOMPSON: [shouting] I know you're all Americans, I know you are. But this is a special treatment for one group, and I protest it! [shouting, loud voices]

COMMISSIONER THIERIOT: Gentlemen, please! [pounding gavel]

CHINESE VOICE: Are you only American?

THOMPSON: No, you are, too, and so are they, so sit down and obey the law! And no demonstrations in this council chamber! [loud voices]

COMMISSIONER THIERIOT: Gentlemen, please sit down! [loud voices, "Get out!"]

THOMPSON: They said get out. Why am I being ejected?

COMMISSIONER THIERIOT: Gentlemen, sit down!

THOMPSON: No demonstrations! This is an illegal demonstration! I don't see any of us making this kind of a fuss.

FEMALE VOICE: How come you don't speak English?

CHINESE VOICE: You are racial!

FEMALE VOICE: Oh, no!

CHINESE VOICE: If you say that, you are racial!

FEMALE VOICE: You've been here many years, why don't you learn the language?

COMMISSIONER THIERIOT: Please, please, please!

In both of these incidents, white animal advocates suggest that Chinese Americans are unassimilable foreigners who can never be bona fide Americans.[3] Again, the language of "special treatment" delegitimates group-specific claims by holding them up against a backdrop of supposedly universalistic values (the environment, colorblindness, the law).

Asian American activists and animal activists wrestled in the aftermath of this Fish and Game Commission exchange. Stewart Kwoh and Betty Hung of

---

[3] Kim (1999), Gotanda (2001).

the Asian Pacific American Legal Center, a leading Asian American advocacy organization, wrote a letter to Eric Mills and Virginia Handley, asking them to apologize for their supporters' comments at the hearing. The letter, dated April 22, 1998, mentioned two speakers who had behaved "in an unacceptable manner":

[N]either of the individuals understood that comments with racial overtones such as these can cause great harm. When Asian Pacific Americans are seen as perpetual foreigners, not "real Americans," violence and harassment against Asian Pacific Americans has often followed. ... Given this pattern, it is disturbing that your supporters used such derogatory and disrespectful language. ... We would hope that you and your supporters would be cognizant of the need for reasoned, constructive discourse and advocacy; if the animal rights and environmental movements are to gain the support of the public in the United States and worldwide, it is crucial that you avoid engaging in divisive and ethnocentric politics now and in the future.

Animal activists exhibited a range of responses to this letter. None endorsed or defended Marshall Thompson and the unidentified white woman, but they manifested different degrees of openness to the concerns Kwoh and Hung expressed. In a June 12, 1998 response to Kwoh and Hung, Virginia Handley recalled numerous episodes when Chinese Americans had behaved poorly at public hearings – hissing, booing, yelling, drowning out speakers, and, on one occasion, knocking an animal advocate to the ground. She wrote: "I claim no responsibility for the actions of others at a public hearing any more than I hold you personally accountable for the actions listed above." Handley continued: "If our actions are motivated by racism, we would not also be working on rodeos, bear hunting, circuses, zoos, and trapping, all activities that are identified with 'American' culture." In a May 6, 1998 letter to Kwoh and Hung, Pat Briggs wrote that she "wholeheartedly agreed the woman made statements that shouldn't have been made, and I was equally as angry with her as were you," but also defended Marshall Thompson's point that the Chinese in attendance were violating the Commission rule against carrying signs within the hearing room. Briggs then suggested with Handley that Kwoh and Hung apologize for the poor behavior of Chinese Americans at prior hearings.

Attorney Baron Miller, on the other hand, responded to Kwoh and Hung's letter by apologizing for animal advocates' racially charged remarks. He did this, he explains, even though he had never met Marshall Thompson and was not at the hearing:

I felt a need because I was so offended by it. I was hurt for the people that he offended. I thought an apology is necessary. I'm in a position of authority on this issue by reason of taking on this case and speaking out and being an advocate, and it was at the level of this Asian Pacific Legal Center attorney, and I thought it was appropriate for me to formally respond to him. And I thought maybe he could pass the letter around, they could see that not everybody's like this Marshall guy. I wasn't representing Marshall. ... I didn't know who he was. I still don't know who he was. I'm still angry at him. ... [T]he animal rights movement is about respect, and racism is about disrespect. It's just racism violates the whole animal rights philosophy and animal rights concept and attitude.

Miller also wrote a letter directly to Marshall Thompson on May 11, 1998, in which he said that he was

very concerned about comments attacking the culture and sensitivities of Asians. It seems that a belief was expressed that Asian culture has some special responsibility for animal abuse. I would disagree strongly with this. ... I would point out that only in the West has animal exploitation been industrialized. ... American culture needs change at least as desperately as any other culture.

Richard Avanzino of the SFSPCA, less concerned than Miller about guilt by association, suggested that having questionable allies was an inevitable part of activism:

[W]hen you get into some of these causes, some of your friends are less than perfect beings. Sometimes your allies are people that might be using it as a way to try to demean another culture or something like that. But you're fighting your cause not for that. You can't basically worry about who your allies are, you've got to basically talk about what you think is the right thing to do, with the understanding that you're not all-powerful. ... It's basically trying to move the needle. Even if the needle doesn't move, the whole idea is, you get up there and fight for what you believe in.

Pushing back against charges of racism, Eric Mills reflected on the connections among different forms of domination:

We need to do better on this planet than we do. We don't treat each other much better many times. A big connection for me is, it's in the language. Think of all the anti-animal words which are applied to women. Pussy, beaver, dog, bitch, cow, you name it. ... We treat animals as if they were women. We treat gay people as if they were women. I'm gay myself, and I've made these connections over the years. ... All these things are interconnected. It's a domination trip, it's man over beast, man over nature, straight man over gay folk, non-whites generally. ... [W]e're a bizarre species.

As a practical matter, Mills set about reinforcing troop discipline. He sent copies of a newspaper article reporting on the Fish and Game exchange to his network of animal people, with a photocopied handwritten note saying, "NOT good, folks We can't do this! It only hurts the animals."[4]

In the end, animal activists disavowed Chinese claims about racism not by elevating animals over the Chinese or by denying the existence of anti-Chinese racism in society but by choosing, for the most part, to *not* recognize the potentially harmful racial implications of their own campaign and to *not* grapple with the ethical dilemmas thereby generated. "Race has nothing to do with this," the core activists said again and again. But race mattered in the rendering of Chinatown a feasible target, in the trope of Chinese unassimilability (unwittingly but perhaps inevitably) invoked by the campaign, in the expressions of anti-Chinese feeling on the part of some animal advocates and members of the public. The core animal advocates wished to have nothing to do with race, but race still had something to do with them.

---

[4] "Turtles in Trouble Have a Defender in Annie Lancaster."

CHINESE AMERICAN SPECIESISM? DISAVOWING CLAIMS ABOUT
CRUELTY TO ANIMALS

If animal activists were moved to disclaim the charge of racism, Chinese leaders felt no equivalent pressure to disclaim cruelty or mastery over animals
and nature. In every venue of conflict, they dismissively waved off the alleged
impact of Chinese merchants' commercial activities on animals and nature
and asserted racism to be the only moral concern at hand. Many essentialized the live animal market campaign as a racist project, situating it in the
historical trajectory of anti-Chinese thought and action in San Francisco.
Depicting animal advocates as part of an oppressive white power structure
helped them to consolidate a simplified David versus Goliath narrative even
if it strained credulity – both by disregarding the state's hostility toward
animal advocates and understating Chinese American political strength in
San Francisco. The specter of a racist and tyrannical majority mobilized the
Chinese American community even as it endlessly deflected the question
raised by animal advocates: Is the treatment of animals in Chinatown's markets morally problematic?

Chinese activists disavowed the claims of animal advocates directly by
unapologetically asserting the primacy of the human, the moral inconsiderabil-
ity of "food" animals, and the triviality of their suffering. For Julie Lee, killing
animals for food was a universal practice that did not require defense:

What do you think is the right relationship between humans and animals?
Okay, in Chinese culture, in China is old saying. "Anything four legs for human to eat."
You ever heard that? That's Chinese saying. "Anything with four legs, the back is faced to
the sky, it's good to eat." … [D]uring the demonstration, we have one sign saying "Human
rights versus animal rights." You know? Western hemisphere, also they say God created
these for us to eat, right?

Rose Pak also emphasized the normativity of the practice, saying of animal
activists' claims:

I think they're very ludicrous concerns. Why don't they worry about humans? They carry
it too far. These animals are for consumption. We've been doing this for thousands of
years. … How far do we go on this? The next thing we start, the vegetables are alive, too.[5]

Being concerned about "food animals" was so preposterous, in Pak's view, it
was one step shy of being concerned about the welfare of bok choy. Stella Kung,
owner of Ming Kee Birds, sounded a similar note: "How about the homeless
people? Why don't the animal people use their energy to care for those people?
They have no homes! They are hungry!"[6] Ed Liu, too, thought animal issues
were distractions from more important matters: "I told this to [Assemblyman]
Paul Fong down in the Peninsula. He's championing environmental issues like
[a ban on] shark fins and all of that. … Look, not that I'm against any of these

[5] Delgado (1996).
[6] Golden (1996).

issues. What I'm saying is, where are our priorities? Good grief, where are our priorities?"

The editors of the English-language periodical *Asian Week*, based in San Francisco's Chinatown, explicitly argued that killing animals for food is natural and right. In "Animal Rights Wrongs" (March 13, 1998), they wrote:

> [W]e are on the side of the Chinese merchants. Racism is not an idle charge. ... By singling out Chinatown merchants, the animal-rights activists have shown their bias and contempt for something they view as "foreign." We also acknowledge that there are well-meaning Asian Americans who are appalled – as everyone should be – by animal cruelty. But there is no "humane" way to kill. Dunking a live crab into boiling water is just as cruel as skinning a turtle alive. To differentiate one from another simply by the color of the skin of the person doing the killing is perhaps more repugnant. For as long as man is man, he'll kill animals for food.

The editors pay lip service to the concern about animal cruelty, only to dismiss it and focus on the more significant offense of racism. Killing animals for food involves cruelty, we are told, and that's the way it is.

Some Chinese advocates suggested that "pet animals" and "food animals" were two separate categories of being, with the former deserving some consideration and the latter none. At the April 1, 1998 Fish and Game Commission meeting in Long Beach, Pius Lee explained:

> And I want to say to some of the animal folk ... You want to treat the animal very well. I understand, but best animal for food consumption, for human consumption, and animal for pet, the standards would be different. They cannot mix them together. I think it's unfair to demand a high standard. I think for food consumption should be different, and the animal for pet having high standard.

Attorney Paul Wartelle echoed this distinction:

> [I]t does seem to me that there's a difference between the community that we have with animals that are companion animals and shellfish. It was like, at the first of the meetings I went to, there was a big sign from the Crustacean Liberation Front. I thought, "This is just silly. This is morally trivial." And they take the intensity of real moral challenge and pour it into this silly paper cup.

Indeed, supporters of the Chinese vendors characterized concern for "food animals" as either moral confusion or a pretext for racial persecution, which meant that animal advocates were either "crazies" who thought that "food animals" mattered morally or racists using animal and environmental claims to mask their true agenda. In his *San Francisco Examiner* column, "Crabs Have Feelings, Too" (May 8, 1997), William Wong presents two crabs, saying it is not fair that they are exempted from the CACW's proposed ban on the sale of live animals. One says to the other, "Our supposed friends, the animal rights activists, are violating the Crustacean Creed of treating every animal equally." Animal activists are absurd for caring about the crabs of Fisherman's Wharf in the first place, Wong suggests, as well as racist and hypocritical for abandoning them to focus on Chinatown.

Chinese activists thus challenged white supremacy while openly avowing human supremacy, charging animal advocates with racism while arguing that some animals are good to eat. They went beyond claiming innocence or attempting to bracket animal concerns to explicitly dismissing animal concerns as morally trivial. There were dissenting Chinese and Asian American voices, however. Things got very heated in the "Letters to the Editor" section of *Asian Week*. One reader wrote that he was indignant over "the xenophobic arrogance of some Americans ... how certain cultures get easily labeled as pathological, barbaric, or more 'primitive.'" He continued: "Make up your mind: are we a model minority or not? You can't have it both ways. Maybe you can because you want to remind us that this is not our country. It is, and we're here to stay."[7] Then there was a letter by Perry Yee on March 5, 1998, condemning "animal rights Nazis Emil Guillermo and director/monitor for the white supremacist thought police, Eric Mills":

The Imperialist West is the greatest criminal against humanity and nature that history will ever know. To deny their horror, they're forcing onto the world new standards of "humanity." ... Western humanity is a contradiction in terms. ... Do you know what an animal rights activist is? An animal rights activist is a Westerner who is a failure at being human.

The following week Janice Yee wrote a letter in response (March 12, 1998):

[C]ulture is not an excuse for cruelty. I am Chinese American, a vegetarian, and ... a member of PETA, and see no conflict between my belief in the humane treatment of animals (and my corresponding abhorrence of the sale of live animals in Chinatown) and my cultural integrity. ... I also want to thank Eric Mills for withstanding the assaults on his racial attitudes and continuing to focus on what is really pressing. The complaints that he is race bashing sound like knee-jerk reactions, based on little insight. Overt and covert anti-Asian racism is, unfortunately, extant, but not in this matter. I feel that Eric Mill's beliefs resonate with humaneness, not racism.

She signs her letter, "Mercifully no relation to Perry Yee of Richmond." Not to be outdone, Perry Yee responded on March 26, 1998: "I'm glad your weak line is not part of my heritage. If you have to clarify your non-relation, it only shows the kind of racist company you keep. The Yees that I come from stand against evil. We do not suffer from Helsinki syndrome, nor do we find value in worshipping neo-imperialist whites." His message was clear: real Chinese people stood up against the animal campaign; those who supported it were brainwashed by their white oppressors.

Janice Yee's desire to stake out space where one could be Chinese and concerned about animals, her desire to reclaim Chinese culture from the Perry Yees of the world, was echoed in this September 17, 1996 letter from Chin Chi (who would later sit on the Commission for Animal Control and Welfare) to the *San Francisco Independent*:

---

[7] Lee (1996).

We [a number of Chinese Americans] feel the issue is not one of race, and to label it as such only diminishes, even distorts, the significance of the struggle for equal rights for all. I know from personal experience that the animal-rights advocates are not racists. … [They] have fought bravely against such rich and powerful forces as the National Rifle Association, the factory farmers, the fur and cosmetic industries, etc. – organizations all controlled by wealthy white men. … People like us support humanitarian measures not because we are influenced by some "weird white-American notion" but because we honor Buddhism, one of China's prevalent religions, and Taoism, one of China's greatest philosophies, as well as the Christianity of St. Francis – they all teach respect and compassion for all life.

Chin Chi pushes back against the notion that caring about animals is some "weird white-American notion" by identifying indigenous Chinese sources of concern for nonhuman life.

In an October 8, 1996 letter to the *San Francisco Chronicle*, Vicky Lynn Ho, another Chinese American CACW Commissioner, responded to Supervisor Tom Hsieh's accusations that Eric Mills and his colleagues were racist:

When [Hsieh] calls an issue being racist against Chinese, he is representing all Chinese but a lot of intelligent Chinese people like me and others don't feel that way. He should not go around acting as if he represents all Chinese on this issue. He is a Supervisor and he is supposed to set a good example for people to follow, not to go around helping certain Chinese with special interests to get their support.

Ho is concerned here not only to puncture the myth of Chinese organic unity but also to highlight the venal motives of the merchants who deploy this myth for their own ends. As Uma Narayan points out, a practice achieves the status of a "cultural tradition" as an *effect* of the debate over its status, and exhortations to tradition are always "motivated by *present* economic and political agendas."[8]

Filipino American columnist Emil Guillermo wrote several pieces in *Asian Week* in which he dissented from the magazine's editorial stance, argued for the moral considerability of animals, and criticized the optic of racism. In "I Must Take Offense: Fresh Kill and the Race Card" (October 11, 1996), Guillermo wrote:

The race card is the person of color's all-purpose trump. It beats all moral hands. All suits. All face cards. You just can't beat the race card in terms of gaining the upper hand. That's why it's like having a nuclear warhead in your arsenal. Its use is not to be taken lightly. Use only in desperation. O.J. plays the race card. Farrakhan plays the race card. You don't play the race card to sell live animals in Chinatown. … And as far as being a cultural habit dating back to the 1800s, so was opium, and you don't see Tom Hsieh or the other politicians advocating bringing back the opium den. … The ban to end fresh kill is being proposed not because of race, but because of cruelty and inhumanity to animals.

After Judge Carlos Bea ruled against the animal advocates in the suit brought by Eric Mills and others, Guillermo wrote in "Species Bias Is in Poor Taste" (July 31, 1997):

[8] Narayan (1997), 21.

Bea's opinion was fundamentally biased. He couldn't see the application of humane and animal cruelty laws because he didn't see a real victim. The animals weren't harmed; they were killed and eaten. From the judge's perspective, that's the way it's supposed to be. ... Kill 'em, eat 'em, digest 'em. ... What Asian Americans should really be thinking about is the plight of the truly voiceless, the animals. ... [C]onsider this exercise. Think about the animals the next time you experience a pang of discrimination, or the next time someone – your boss, a colleague, a stranger – says something or does something to indicate that you hardly exist.

Asian Americans should use their personal experiences of racial subordination to empathize with animals and understand their plight. White supremacists and human supremacists, Guillermo suggests, are birds of a feather.

THE POSSIBILITY OF CRITIQUE

The methodology of multi-optic vision can help us pivot away from a posture of mutual disavowal and toward a different way of relating to other justice struggles. Rejecting the myopia of single-optic vision, it forcibly decenters the way we see. It illuminates (making us more deeply cognizant of other struggles and perspectives) even as it disorients (rendering what was solid ground suddenly shaky). But if it opens us to the experiences of others, multi-optic vision does not disable our critical faculties. Avowing another group's justice claims does not mean placing that group beyond the reach of moral criticism. Indeed, because multi-optic vision grows out of a broad normative vision of justice, it may well generate critique as an anti-subordination practice. Looking at the Chinatown dispute multi-optically, we may be moved to avow Chinese American claims about racism *and at the same time* endorse the critique of Chinese live animal market practices.

In this multiculturalist age, the critique of another culture is not to be undertaken lightly – especially if one is criticizing a Third World or minority culture from within a Western or dominant culture. No one has made this point more brilliantly and unforgettably than postcolonial feminist theorists responding to Western feminists' assertions of a global feminism. Susan Okin's *Is Multiculturalism Bad for Women?* (1999) made two famously controversial claims: that Western culture is demonstrably and measurably less sexist than minority cultures within the United States; and that therefore women in these minority cultures might be better off if their cultures went extinct. In a powerful response, Azizah Al-Hibri (1999) called Okin out for writing from the perspective of a dominant cultural Western "I" and for taking an orientalist, reductionist approach to Islam in particular. Similarly Inderpal Grewal and Caren Kaplan (1996) criticized Alice Walker and Pratibha Parmar's *Warrior Marks* (1993), a film expressing a global womanist critique of female genital mutilation in Africa, for "neo-colonial representational practice[s]" that resulted in "imperializing and racist forms of 'knowing' those constituted as 'others'" (6). Coming from outside and above, products of the imperial gaze, Western critiques of Third World/minority cultures are profoundly suspect.

But if cultural critique is terrain that must be entered thoughtfully, it is not terrain that we can or should avoid altogether. Critique is an intervention on behalf of the subordinated; in Okin's case, on behalf of the least visible and least powerful members of racially subordinated communities. We can only cordon off a racial/cultural group from criticism about its internal practices toward women or animals if we make an a priori determination that racial/cultural domination is so much more important than patriarchy or speciesism as a political and moral concern that it prevents us from speaking of the latter. Multi-optic vision discourages this kind of move, attuning us to worlds of suffering we might otherwise not see and thereby working to keep the question of ranking oppressions *open*, at least for a while. When we see multi-optically, subordinated groups become more visible to us *and* more transparent to us – that is, their location in various skeins of power, their simultaneous roles as oppressed and oppressor, become more apparent.

Commenting on the necessity and possibility of critique from outside/above, Uma Narayan persuasively argues that what we should strive for is not detachment or silence but honest, thoughtful moral engagement, however difficult:

[W]hat mainstream Westerners who seek to come to terms with a history of misrepresentation of Other cultures need to cultivate is not a "refusal to judge." Rather, they need to be willing to engage in the considerably more difficult tasks of trying to distinguish misrepresentation and "cultural imperialism" from normatively justifiable criticisms of Third-World institutions and practices. They need to be willing to take on the risks and effort of sharing their critical responses, and subjecting their views and evaluations to refinement and revision in the light of different (and often multiple) analyses of these institutions and practices by "Insiders."[9]

Narayan recognizes that this process is fraught with peril precisely because of the context of uneven power between Western critics and Third World communities, but reminds us there are significant risks involved in forswearing critique as well – such as coming to relate to Third World denizens as unassimilable others with whom moral dialogue and community is impossible:

"Refusing to judge" issues affecting Third-World communities … is often a facile and problematic attempt to compensate for a history of misjudgment. Such refusals can become simply one more "Western" gesture that confirms the moral inequality of Third-World cultures by shielding them from the moral and political evaluations that "Western" contexts and practices are subject to. … While there are "arrogant" forms of criticism of one's Others, not all such criticism is necessarily arrogant; and there is potential for serious arrogance in refusing to share one's critical responses.[10]

Bhikhu Parekh (2000), too, recognizes that intergroup arguments about cultural practices are always structured in dominance but believes this can be mitigated by making the arguments "bifocal," or focused on both majority and minority traditions. It is hard to imagine the alternative of cordoning off

9 Ibid., 151.
10 Ibid., 150.

specific communities from criticism and erecting moral-discursive boundaries around cultural groups. Every way one turns, there are risks.

Those who express suspicion toward criticism from outside/above often exhort us to support insider critics as those who have real standing to criticize a group's practices (Gaard 2001). As a practical matter, though, insider critics are by definition relatively powerless minorities. In many cases, they are not listened to respectfully by others in their communities but rather actively discredited as brainwashed tools of Western imperialists and traitors to their own people. Narayan writes: "When essentialist definitions of Third World cultures are cloaked in the virtuous mantle of resistance to Western cultural imperialism … [those] who contest prevailing norms and practices are discursively set up in the roles of 'cultural traitors' and 'stooges of Western imperialism.'"[11] Recall that Perry Yee stipulated in his letter to the editor in *Asian Week* that real Chinese people defend Chinese cultural traditions, while insider critics are at best inauthentically Chinese and at worst race traitors. This dynamic around insider critics played out forcefully in the Makah controversy as well, as we shall see in Chapter 7.

Nor is it self-evident that insiders can see more clearly or understand better by virtue of being insiders. That they have access to different kinds of knowledge than outsiders seems plausible. Someone who grew up in a Chinese family that for generations purchased live animals for food might well have an intimate material knowledge of this practice as well as a close appreciation of its cultural meaning. But this knowledge, like all knowledge, is partial and contingent. An insider who has a deep appreciation of live food practices *for that very reason* lacks the critical distance that is one component of ethical evaluation. An outsider who has never eaten freshly killed animals and does not associate the practice with his most beloved relatives or his community's survival is more likely to achieve this critical distance, even as he cannot fully grasp the practice's cultural or social meaning. Insiders bring something to the table with regard to ethical evaluation, then, but so, too, do outsiders. Because there is no standpoint of perfect knowledge and understanding, it is not clear why outsiders should be a priori disqualified from expressing moral criticism, particularly if they can be persuaded to do so in a way that avoids arrogance and ethnocentrism.

The issue of standing comes up again with the "double standard" objection to outside criticism. In *The Cultural Defense* (2004), Alison Renteln argues that it is hypocritical to criticize minority practices when the majority engages in practices that are comparably objectionable. How can activists complain about the treatment and killing of animals in Chinese markets, Renteln asks, and at the same time turn a blind eye to the treatment and killing of animals in the nation's farms and slaughterhouses? The implication here is that the majority should leave disadvantaged minorities alone until they clean up their own house. In other words, minorities' disadvantages earn them *a place at the end*

---

[11] Narayan (1998), 91.

of the reform queue, whatever the issue at hand. Depicting animal advocates as a vanguard of an imperialist majority is, I have already explained, taking some license with empirical reality. But the moral aspect of this argument is equally perplexing.

Why should disadvantage along one dimension (race/culture) translate into relative immunity along another (sex or species)? This only makes sense if one assumes without argument that the dimension of race/culture is so much more important than the others that we must refrain from critique about sex or species *for fear of* aggravating racial/cultural marginalization. If we see multi-optically, however, we understand that this argument has not been made conclusively (and perhaps cannot be), so that racially/culturally subordinated groups do not have, by virtue of that subordination, a "get out of jail free" card that licenses their participation in other forms of domination and exempts them from moral critique. Unjust disadvantage in one sphere does not earn unjust advantage in another. Having endured racism and colonialism, subjects deserve justice and reparations from their oppressors, but they do not therefore deserve to dominate women, animals, and nature. We need only consider what it would look like to take the "get out of jail free" logic to its extreme – only white, affluent, straight, able-bodied men would be fair game for criticism and everyone else would be free to engage in unlimited exploitative practices with impunity – to recognize that it is not morally tenable.

As Paula Casal (2004) asserts with the "principle of noncomparative desert," restricting a particular inhumane activity is worth doing in and of itself whether or not other equally or more inhumane activities are being challenged at the same moment. This ethical imperative to challenge cruel practices exists independently of questions of "comparative desert." Animals suffer under minority practices just as they do under majority practices, and while the first type of suffering is no more important, morally speaking, than the second, it is no less so either. To return to Alison Renteln's chicken once more, we have no reason to believe that it makes a difference to the chicken if the person killing her is a Santería priest or a slaughterhouse worker. Harm is harm, no matter who is inflicting it. It would be ironic if in the name of anti-subordination we licensed some groups to engage in unlimited degrees of domination with no fear of censure. It may be that Chinese Americans raised on live food and/or vegans have more credibility than white meat eaters in challenging Chinese market practices, but that does not mean that the latter have no standing. They can have imperfect knowledge and suffer from hypocrisy and still be right about the cruelty of the markets.

Of course, critique presumes that there is some choice being exercised by racialized minorities – that they have the option *to not* engage in the animal practice in question. There are instances of animal usage where choice is significantly more constricted. The Inupiat of Alaska have historically and continuously hunted bowhead whales for subsistence, for example, and their diet, culture, and way of life are intimately bound up with whaling.[12] For this reason, the United States continued to request bowhead quotas from the International Whaling Commission in the 1970s on behalf of the Inupiat, even when the bowhead whale was clearly endangered.[13] Do the Inupiat have a meaningful choice to not whale? The cases I examine in this book – live animal markets, whale hunting, and dogfighting – are more straightforward with regard to the issue of choice. Chinese Americans in San Francisco can do without animal flesh from live animal markets; the Makah can extend their seventy-year hiatus from whaling; and Michael Vick and his associates can find a pastime other than dogfighting.

CRITIQUE AND AVOWAL

So critique, yes, but how? Both Sherene Razack and Maneesha Deckha warn that criticism of racialized groups on behalf of other subordinated groups can produce significant racial harm. Razack argues that sexual violence against Aboriginal women in Canada and Third World refugees to Canada is problematized through discourses that reproduce racist beliefs: "[I] is through various orientalist and imperialist lenses that women's gender-based persecution becomes visible in the West."[14] Women's legal claims in both instances are most likely to succeed when they invite the state to step in in imperialist fashion and act "as [a] saviour of Third World peoples."[15] Razack calls out the danger of pursuing women's claims against Aboriginal or Third World men "while under the gaze of white society"[16] and urges women's advocates to consider First World (colonial) complicity in producing the sexual and racial persecution of Aboriginal and Third World women. A "politics of accountability," she argues, mandates that women's advocates be "guided by a search for the ways in which [they] are complicitous in the subordination of others."[17]

Similarly, addressing animal activism against the practices of racialized minorities, Maneesha Deckha articulates an "anti-imperialist concern" of "not wanting to further entrench majority/minority power differentials and colonial or otherwise hegemonic positions and narratives by opposing the important practices of such groups and/or using animals as an imperial register of cultural backwardness of civilization difference and inferiority."[18] To promote the issue of animal considerability ethically, Deckha proposes the development of a "post colonial posthumanist theory of cultural rights" that calls for: a) listening to other perspectives and being aware that colonialism taints Western ways

[12] See Wenzel (1991) for a discussion of the Inuit and anti-sealing activists.
[13] Harris (2003).
[14] Razack (1998), 93; Deckha (2007, 2013).
[15] Razack (1998), 89.
[16] Ibid., 63.
[17] Ibid., 159.
[18] Deckha (2007), 192–3.

of knowing; b) striving for consistency by criticizing mainstream practices, too, and "conscientiously and systematically avoiding the racialization of animal exploitation by selective critique";[19] and c) making judgments only after good faith consultation and collaboration.[20]

Without argument, then, both Razack and Deckha suggest that racism/imperialism is the original and most important sin in a discernible hierarchy of harms. Patriarchy and animal exploitation are acknowledged, respectively, but critique of these practices is constrained, in the last analysis, by the imperative of not producing racial harm. And this constraint works in one direction only – that is, neither scholar suggests that the critique of racism should be constrained by the imperative of not causing harm to women or animals.

Although I share Razack and Deckha's concerns and find their overall analyses powerful and generative, I question this notion of constraining critique for two reasons. First, as discussed in Chapter 1, I believe the question of ranking oppressions is at least provisionally irresolvable. I say "provisionally" to leave the question open because it is logically possible that a conclusive answer exists (and has been proffered) and that we will come up with a means of collectively recognizing it as such. Multi-optic vision helps to prevent the premature shutting down of the question by recognizing but also decentering multiple group experiences and perspectives. It works against both presumptive, automatic rankings of oppressions *and* a mindless pluralism that presumes fungibility. Rather than suggesting that all group claims are equally valid and that we cannot make moral or political judgments among them, multi-optic vision helps to ensure that whatever judgments we do choose to make are informed intellectually and affectively by the experiences of others. In this sense, it serves as a prelude to a conversation about oppressions, a condition of its possibility. In any case, we need not settle the question of hierarchy in order to posit that other justice struggles should be taken seriously and avowed. My gentle correction to Razack and Deckha, then, is that the consideration of impact should go both ways: feminist and animal activists, on the one hand, and race activists, on the other, need to reflect on and take seriously their impact on *each other's* struggles.

In addition, it might be useful to go beyond juridical notions such as "accountability" and "rights," which express a defensive, minimalist, do-no-harm posture, to the more expansive notion of mutual avowal, which names an active process of affirmation and relating to. This is easier to do once we step outside of the legal arena, where both Razack and Deckha focus their attention, and into the cultural and political arena. The first set of terms delineates hard boundaries among groups/struggles, reads boundary crossings through the lens of transgression, and ossifies group identities. The notion of mutual avowal, on the other hand, puts pressure on intergroup boundaries, plays with the

---

[19] Ibid., 223.
[20] Ibid., 220–3.

productive possibilities of boundary crossing, and shakes up group identities by emphasizing the intimate connections among domination's multiple forms.

Not that multi-optic vision calls upon us to avow all extant group viewpoints. To say that we are obliged to consider the Tea Party's laments about the parasitism of racialized minorities or the Minutemen Project's violence-laced diatribes about "illegals" would be comparable to arguing that white claims of "reverse racism" must be treated exactly the same as Black claims of racism because both involve deviations from the norm of colorblindness. Creating an equivalence between "reverse racism" and anti-Black racism deliberately (and destructively) abstracts from the material history of white supremacy and Black subordination (Gotanda 1991). Along the same lines, multi-optic vision is not a detachable tool for assessing from a "neutral" perspective any and all perspectives, regardless of whether they support or challenge historical patterns of oppression. Rather, it is a critical methodology dedicated to understanding and challenging racism, heteropatriarchy, speciesism, the exploitation of nature, and neoliberal capitalism.

Embracing an ethics of avowal would mean engaging politically without brackets, without the fantasy of innocence, with full cognizance of one's potential impact on and relation to other subordinated groups. Animal advocates operating from a framework of avowal might still, after serious deliberation and reflection, choose to engage in critique – to organize a campaign against Chinatown's live animal markets, for example. However, rather than proclaiming their colorblindness, they would engage the issue of racism in good faith – not as a particularistic concern that deflects from more universal concerns but as a serious matter of justice that is deeply connected to the question of the animal. They would turn toward the other struggle, exploring their connection with it *and at the same time understanding* the ways that their own racial situatedness (more precisely, their whiteness) complicates their intervention. They would educate themselves deeply about the history of anti-Chinese persecution and current patterns of cultural marginalization and civic ostracism, aggressively call out racism within their own leadership ranks and among supporters, and strive to unconceal and explain the ways racism is inextricably intertwined with the derogation and mistreatment of nonhuman animals. That is to say, animal advocates would address the Chinese market practices in a manner that respected rather than denied racial context. Rather than isolating the question of market practices and challenging the Chinese on this single issue, they would situate their critique of market practices within a larger framework of justice that confronts multiple, interconnected forms of domination at once.

For their part, Chinese American activists who embraced an ethics of avowal would continue to call out any racism they perceived, but they would also engage the issue of cruelty to animals (and perhaps speciesism more generally) in good faith. They would recognize the integrity of animal activism (rather than reducing it to racism), acknowledge the ethical and ecological quandaries that many San Franciscans believe are posed by the markets, and confront and explore the intimate connections between the domination of racial others and the domination of nonhuman animals. They would respond to the market campaign in a manner that recognized rather than denied the ambiguous positionality of Chinese merchants, relatively marginal figures in human society who nevertheless possess unlimited power over the animals they keep and kill. They might broaden the discussion to include the majority's farming and slaughtering practices – a different, more productive way of addressing the "double standard" objection – and engage the question of how to address the suffering of all animals raised for food. In short, both sides to the dispute would acknowledge the moral complexity of the situation and move beyond the kind of Manichean rhetoric that facilitates mobilization in the short run but does harm to the struggle for justice in the long run.

It may seem inconceivable that actors would make these moves in the heat of political struggle. But mutual disavowal is a strategy we can no longer afford, if we ever could. Is it reasonable to labor away in our separate silos and disavow one another while neoliberal capitalism and its associated "isms" are generating unheard of inequalities among human groups, unheard of suffering for animals, unheard of planetary damage? In the Chinatown story, and in the Makah and Michael Vick stories discussed in the next two chapters, the conjoined logics of race and species – two taxonomies that instrumentalize different bodies and convert them into disposable commodities – show us that the struggle against racism and the struggle against speciesism, while not the same struggle, are not entirely separable struggles either. They are fatefully linked. An ethics of avowal can grow out of such a recognition, helping us to deeply see and avow the suffering of others as important and as connected to our own.

Developing an ethics of avowal is the first step in a long process of transformation that lies ahead. Val Plumwood (1993, 2001) argues that we need to challenge the instrumentalizing stance of mastery that lies at the core of neoliberal capitalism, the logic of supremacist thinking and action itself. Partly this will require, at the level of discourse and imagination, disrupting the classificatory systems of race, species, sex, and sexuality, and, relatedly, reimagining the human, the animal, and nature outside of relations of mastery and domination. The group identities around which we build today's politics are likely to be radically refashioned as part of this dynamic. And the vision of mutual justice that emerges will go beyond justice for X (people of color, women, animals, or LGBT folks) to a broader, deeper notion of mutuality and connectedness.

In this chapter, I conclude the analysis of the Chinatown dispute by showing how animal advocates and Chinese American activists moved seamlessly from single-optic thinking to actively disavowing each other's claims in multiple ways. I then argue that multi-optic vision, by helping us to remain open to the suffering and struggles of others, can be a source of both intergroup critique and avowal of other groups' overall experiences of and struggles against oppression. An ethics of avowal among subordinated groups holds out the possibility of recognizing the connectedness of multiple forms of domination and acting against them in concert. The next chapter explores another impassioned dispute over race, species, nature, and culture: the controversy over the Makah nation's bid to resume whaling in the 1990s after a hiatus of seventy years.

PART III

OTHER DISPUTES

7

Makah Whaling and the (Non) Ecological Indian

Whales should not be slaughtered anytime or anywhere by any people.
 – Sea Shepherd Conservation Society

Them [protesters] being here is like bringing a blanket of smallpox.
 – Wayne Johnson, Makah Whaling Captain

Early in the morning of May 17, 1999, in the Pacific waters off of the northwest tip of Washington State, a three-year-old female gray whale swam up alongside a canoe of Makah hunters, expressing the curiosity that many gray whales show toward humans. Theron Parker, the harpooner, stood up, and launched the first of three harpoons into her back. The hunt was being filmed, and television viewers across the globe watched "as the wounded whale struggled, twisting and zig-zagging, pulling the Makah hunters a short distance, three harpoons lodged in her 30-foot body." As "bloodied waters swelled outward from the dying whale in crimson waves,"[1] the Makah hunters then shot her three times with a powerful rifle. The last bullet penetrated the gray whale's brain and killed her. The broadcasting of the hunt prompted both exultation on the part of many Makah and intense expressions of sorrow and outrage on the part of other Makah and non-Makah.[2] Alberta Thompson, a Makah elder who opposed the hunt, named the whale who had been killed "Yabis," which means "beloved" in the Makah language.[3]

It was the first time that the Makah had successfully hunted a whale in more than seventy years. Once legendary whale hunters of the Pacific Northwest Coast, the Makah ceased whaling in the 1920s, in part because of the depletion of whale populations brought about by European and American commercial whaling. Since that time, international and domestic practice and opinion had largely turned against whaling, so the tribe's announcement in the mid-1990s

---

[1] Peterson and Hogan (2002), 148.
[2] The hunt can be viewed at http://www.youtube.com/watch?v=cGmc1-fbs5U.
[3] Peterson and Hogan (2002), 152.

that it wished to resume whaling set off a global firestorm that raged from the Makah reservation in Neah Bay to the National Marine Fisheries Service in Washington, DC to International Whaling Commission meetings in Europe over what constitutes a subsistence hunting tradition, who owns the seas and living marine resources, the biological and moral status of the gray whale, the cultural rights of indigenous peoples, and the imperatives of environmental protection. The Makah whale hunt has been the site of intense political, legal, moral, spiritual, and physical struggle from the moment it was proposed in the mid-1990s until today, when, deterred from whaling by legal and bureaucratic obstacles, the Makah wait to hunt again.

In this conflict, as in the others examined in this book, race, species, nature, and culture are passionately contested in a discursive-political space defined in part by multiculturalist norms and the values and practices of neoliberal capitalism. Indianness continues to be constituted here in relation to species and nature; claims of tribal identity and culture are both accorded presumptive weight and seen as special pleading against the universalist claims of environmental and animal protection; environmental and animal protection claims, in turn, are cast as racist and imperialist; and the neoliberal instrumentalization of nature as a "resource" proceeds in the face of unspoken collective anxiety about the rightness of this course. But the Makah whaling story also contains many distinctive elements, from the imagining of the "ecological Indian" in U.S. culture; to the special status of the whale as an intelligent mammal and environmental icon; to the vexing tangle of treaty rights, federal law, and international conservation law that contours this dispute; to the highly charged global politics of whaling; to the utterly unique political and legal status of indigenous peoples as nations rather than minorities within the United States.

As in the Chinatown case, a racial trope of considerable vintage took center stage in the discourse about the conflict. As discussed in Chapter 2, as far back as the 1600s, whites imagined the North American Indian as a constituent part of nature and apart from civilization – and this idea proved remarkably tenacious over the centuries. In the 1970s, in the context of the modern environmental movement, the idea reemerged in the trope of the "ecological Indian," the Indian who is a natural conservationist, lives simply and virtuously, maintains a spiritual balance with nature, and thus serves as the perfect foil for the Western capitalist, whose greed and rapaciousness leave him severely out of joint with (not to mention a serious threat to) the natural world.[4] In this trope, the culture/nature divide is maintained and the Indian is still identified with nature, but now it is nature not culture that is valorized. The 1971 antipollution television commercial featuring Iron Eyes Cody as an Indian weeping over whites' despoliation of nature exemplified this trope. In the whaling conflict, this trope was evoked by members of the public (and occasionally by environmental and animal protectionists) to castigate the Makah for acting

---

[4] See Krech (1999) and Nadasdy (2007).

non-ecologically, or betraying their Indianness. That is, the "ecological Indian" trope functioned as a disciplinary tool, essentializing Native Americans (in the guise of lauding them) and erecting a behavioral ideal that was both restrictive and unattainable.

In many ways, the debate over the relationship between Indians and nature was at the heart of the Makah whaling conflict. Native American leaders and scholars regularly assert that "indigenous standpoints" (Tallbear 2011) have something distinctive and important to say about human relations with non-human animals and nature, and they argue that Native peoples were practicing "sustainability" long before this ethos surfaced as an eleventh-hour response to the excesses of neoliberal capitalism (Coté 2010). But they did not therefore embrace the "ecological Indian" trope, the dualistic premises of which are alien to Native American ontologies, which rest on different foundational under-standings about humans, animals, and nature than do Western ones (Deloria 2001; Tallbear 2011).

A few environmental and animal protectionists deployed the "ecological Indian" trope against the Makah, but most argued instead for moving beyond the dualisms of culture/nature and human/animal and rejecting the positioning of animals and nature as objects beneath us. For them, recognizing the whale's subjectivity, understanding human-whale continuities, and respecting the whale *logically entailed a prohibition on* hunting the whale. But Native American ontologies, which have always viewed humans, animals, and other beings in nature as all animate and all related (non-dualistically), *simultaneously* recog-nize the animal's kinship with the human and the rightness of killing animals for food (Nadasdy 2007). For Native Americans like the Makah, recognizing the whale's subjectivity, understanding human-whale continuities, and respect-ing the whale *logically allowed for* hunting the whale.[5]

Chinatown leaders enthusiastically espoused the instrumentalization and commodification of "food" animals, out-whiting whites in their dualistic per-ceptions of humans and animals. (Recall Rose Pak's acerbic observation that animal advocates would be worried about vegetables next.) Animal advocates responded by arguing the moral considerability of the animals sold by the markets. The debate in the Chinatown conflict, therefore, was between seeing these animals as morally considerable or not. But Makah leaders presented an *alternative* ontology that sees animals as respect-worthy and important but still edible. Environmental and animal protectionists did not acknowledge or grapple with this different moral and spiritual understanding of human-whale relations, but simply dismissed it. This attempt to erect a Western framework of understanding upon the elision of a Native one elicited the charge of colo-nial domination from the Makah.

---

[5] My thanks to Kim Tallbear for insight on these points. See Plumwood (2000) for a Western ecofeminist defense of the Native understanding of hunting and Eaton (2002) for a commentary on Plumwood's argument.

I begin with a historical account of the Makah tribe, gray whales, and the ·
International Whaling Commission and then tell the story of what happened
when the Makah sought to resume whaling in the mid-1990s. Next, I examine the optics of ecological and ethical harm articulated by environmental and
animal protectionists, as well as the optic of ecocolonialism articulated by the
Makah in response. I then show how animal and environmental activists and
Makah activists disavowed each other's claims and perspectives in the course
of political struggle. Here I pause to reflect first, on the historical relationship
of Makah whaling to slavery and sex inequalities within the tribe, and second,
on what it means to consider that gray whales might have their own perspective on the whaling issue. I conclude with a brief discussion of what an ethics
of mutual avowal might entail in this case.

HISTORIES: THE MAKAH, GRAY WHALES, THE INTERNATIONAL
WHALING COMMISSION

The Makah are a Native people who have lived on the tip of the Olympic
Peninsula for thousands of years (see Figure 7.1). Based on the neighboring
Clallam tribe's description, whites gave them the name "Makah," meaning
"generous with food." Their name for themselves is *kwih-dich-chuh-ahtX*,
meaning "people who live on the cape near the rocks and seagulls."[6] The
Makah are culturally and linguistically related to the Nuu-Chah-Nulth tribes
on western Vancouver Island (just across the Strait of Juan de Fuca), who are
First Nations in Canada. As a coastal people whose lands are largely inhospitable to agriculture, the Makah have traditionally lived off of the sea, developing
deep local knowledge of the ocean's shelves and currents and skills in fishing
and sea mammal hunting.[7]

Archaeological research at the Ozette site, discovered in the 1970s, indicates
that for more than 1,500 years, whaling was an integral aspect of Makah life.
Whales occupy a central status in Makah religious and spiritual practices, cultural ceremonies, and artwork. The practice of whaling reflected and in turn
reinforced social organization and stratification within the tribe. Whaling was
the preserve of chiefs or titleholders who owned not only the whaling equipment (canoes, buoys, harpoons) but also the songs and ceremonial rituals that
accompanied the hunt. The practice enabled chiefs to amass the resources
(including whale meat and whale oil) to hold potlatches – lavish ceremonial
feasts where chiefs encouraged the consumption of goods and distributed
goods in order to demonstrate and thereby shore up their power and authority.
The Makah put almost every part of the whale's body to use in some way, and
evidence from the Ozette site suggests that whale products made up more than
80 percent of the tribe's diet at one point.[8]

---

[6] Coté (2010), 18.
[7] Coté (2010).
[8] Coté (2010), 12.

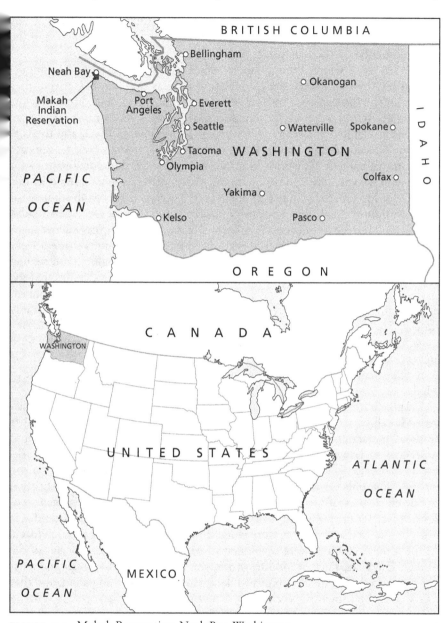

FIGURE 7.1. Makah Reservation, Neah Bay, Washington.

Whaling was also the key to the Makah's commercial success during the mid-1800s. Although the first contact with Europeans occurred in the late 1700s, it was not until the 1840s that American and European whalers became a significant presence in the waters of the Pacific Northwest. The Makah, who had already established a thriving commerce in whale oil and dogfish oil with neighboring tribes, commenced trading with the Hudson Bay Company as well, trading up to 30,000 gallons of whale oil a year and becoming one of the wealthiest tribes in the region.[9]

The arrival of whites brought short-term enrichment but long-term immiseration. By the mid-1800s, the colonization process that had begun centuries earlier on the Eastern Seaboard of the United States had reached the Pacific. The Indian Removal Act of 1830 had forced Native American tribes from the southeastern United States to move west of the Mississippi River, and the U.S. government was setting up a system of reservations upon which to relocate them. In this context, Governor Isaac Stevens of the Washington Territory sat down with Makah elders to negotiate the Treaty of Neah Bay in 1855. In this treaty, the Makah ceded most of their lands, accepted the establishment of a reservation at Neah Bay of approximately 27,000 acres, received sums of money, and agreed to various regulations banning slavery, the sale of alcohol, and other practices on the reservation.[10] Historical accounts make it clear that the Makah were intent on preserving their fishing, whaling, and sealing rights and that they received assurances from Governor Stevens's aides that the United States would support these.[11] Makah Chief Stecowilth stated memorably, "I want the sea. That is my country."[12] Article IV of the Treaty of Neah Bay states: "*The right of taking fish and of whaling or sealing at usual and accustomed grounds and stations is further secured to said Indians in common with all citizens of the United States.*" The Treaty of Neah Bay is the only Native American treaty with the U.S. government that explicitly secures the right to whale.

Despite its assurances, the U.S. government set out to radically restructure Makah society. The story is tragically reiterative of the histories of other Native American tribes. The plan was to forcibly assimilate the Makah into American society, which first required the strategic eradication of all markers of difference – that is, of Makah language, religion, and culture. Colson writes: "The policy was one of wholesale transformation, or the substitution of one entire way of life for an alien one."[13] To this end, U.S. government representatives set up a boarding school for Makah children in 1874. Attendance was compulsory, and parents were jailed if they resisted sending their children. At the school, children were forbidden to wear traditional dress or speak the Makah language. For ten months of the year, they were relentlessly indoctrinated into believing that all things Makah were backward and pagan, and that Christianity and English were the keys to salvation.[14]

---

[9] Miller (2005), 127. Also see Renker (2012).
[10] http://www.fws.gov/pacific/ea/tribal/treaties/MAKAH_1855.pdf.
[11] Coté (2010).
[12] Peterson and Hogan (2002), 121.
[13] Colson (1953), 12.
[14] Coté (2010).

U.S. government agents took other steps to dismantle Makah society and rebuild it in their own image. They instituted a system of elected tribal government. They encouraged the destruction of the wooden longhouses where Makah kin groups lived and the construction of single-family homes in their place. They tried to stamp out potlatches, which they viewed as heathen rituals hampering assimilation. Instead of providing fishing and hunting equipment as promised, they distributed agricultural equipment. Hunters and fishermen had to be turned into farmers because agriculture was the foundation of civilization (even if the topography of the area did not support agriculture). The barbaric savage would be made Christian and civilized whether he wished this or not.[15] By and large, he did not wish this. The Makah continued to speak to their children in the Makah language and to teach them about their history and culture. They engaged in potlatches under the creative cover of Christian rituals like Christmas or in physical sites (e.g., Tatoosh Island) free of government supervision.[16] They accepted the agricultural equipment and transformed it into whaling equipment.[17]

Despite these forms of resistance, Makah society experienced significant political, social, and cultural disruption. The imposition of elected government and policies of cultural suppression (including the suppression of the potlatch) weakened the authority of titleholders: "[T]he Indian agents' attempts to displace the authority, and consequently diminish the acquisition of wealth that accompanied chiefly positions, including that of the titled men who once carried out the whale hunt, took its toll on the community's recognition of traditional leadership."[18] Diseases introduced by whites – including smallpox, influenza, and tuberculosis – devastated the Makah population during the mid- to late 1800s, accelerating social change and disrupting the passing on of cultural knowledge and "proprietary rights regarding ownership of dances, songs, and other ceremonial and economic privileges."[19] By 1890, such diseases had reduced the Makah population by 75 percent.[20]

With lines of traditional authority and cultural transmission interrupted, whaling became more difficult, and many Makah turned to sealing. The rise of commercial pelagic sealing in the 1860s enabled many Makah to thrive selling furs, working as laborers on sealing vessels, and occasionally purchasing and operating such vessels themselves. By 1875, sealing was the tribe's principal source of income.[21] In sealing, commoners could make a living on their

[15] Miller (2005).
[16] Coté (2010). Colson (1953) mentions that the Makah reproduced the potlatch in the guise of Christmas.
[17] Coté (2010); Renker (2012).
[18] U.S. Department of Commerce, National Oceanic and Atmospheric Administration, National Marine Fisheries Service, Northwest Region, *Draft Environmental Impact Statement for Proposed Authorization of the Makah Whale Hunt* (May 2008) (hereafter DEIS), 3–236.
[19] Renker (2012), 41.
[20] Ibid., 40.
[21] DEIS, 3–235.

own, no longer dependent on a chief who controlled access to resources.[22] The changing Makah social structure, that is, made whaling more difficult and sealing more plausible. In the 1890s, the combination of faltering seal populations and new government regulations on sealing prompted the Makah to return to whaling and other forms of fishing, but the alteration in the social structure that whaling had depended on and reinforced, as well as the steady depletion of whale populations due to European and American commercial hunting, led the Makah to gradually cease whaling by the 1920s.

In 2010, the population of the Neah Bay reservation was 1,414, 75 percent of whom were Makah tribal members. Another 1,512 Makah tribal members lived off of the reservation.[23] The Makah Tribal Council is the governing body and consists of five members who are elected for staggered three-year terms.[24] Commercial fishing and timber are current mainstays of the tribe's economy, as well as tourism and sport fishing.[25] As a result of extensive litigation in the 1970s, the tribe co-manages various fisheries with the state and other entities and gets a direct allocation of various kinds of fish (including halibut and black cod/sablefish) every year.[26] The decline of the Pacific Northwest timber industry and salmon fisheries in the past few decades has impacted the tribe's economic welfare, however, and poverty, unemployment, drug abuse, and alcoholism are all notable problems on the reservation. Per capita income on the reservation in 2007 was $11,030, as compared with $21,587 for all Americans, and the unemployment rate was 51 percent (this figure climbs even higher in the winter season). Almost 40 percent of reservation households are below the federal poverty line.[27] Makah Tribal Council members say they are a people in crisis and claim that whaling will restore tribal unity and pride, promote social cohesion, and reinvigorate their culture.

Gray whales pass through the Makah usual and accustomed hunting grounds twice a year on their famed migrations along the Pacific coast between their birthing lagoons in Baja Mexico and their summer feeding grounds in the Bering and Chukchi Seas off of Alaska (see Figure 7.2). They are uniquely vulnerable to human activity because they inhabit and migrate through shallow coastal waters. Human-related threats to their survival include ship strikes, fishing nets, pollution, global warming and its impact on their prey, oil and gas exploration, military activities, and hunting. One-third of calves do not survive their first year and the momentous migration northward.[28] Our ability to narrate the history of gray whales – and "scientifically manage" their

[22] Coté (2010).
[23] Renker (2012).
[24] According to the constitution and bylaws adopted by the Makah tribe in 1936 following the passage of the Indian Reorganization Act.
[25] DEIS, 3–184.
[26] DEIS, 3–193.
[27] Renker (2012), 62, 64.
[28] Peterson and Hogan (2002), 27.

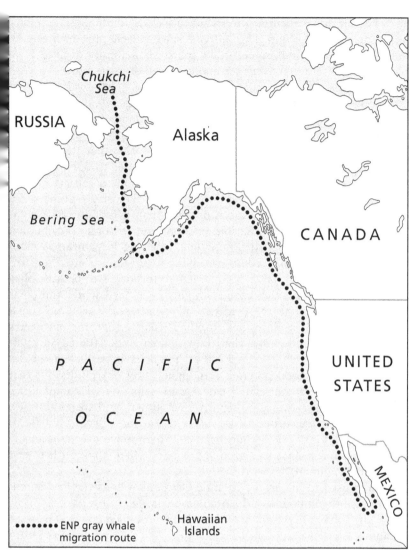

FIGURE 7.2. Gray Whale Migration Route, Mexico to Alaska.

populations – is compromised by the fact that scientific knowledge about them is provisional, incomplete, and vigorously contested.

Eschrichtius robustus is a species of baleen whale whose members grow to between thirty-six and fifty feet long, weigh between sixteen and forty-five tons, and may live as long as eighty years.[29] They feed in shallow coastal waters by scraping the mud bottom and using their baleen to filter out their prey, which

[29] http://www.nmfs.noaa.gov/pr/species/mammals/cetaceans/graywhale.htm.

consists of benthic and epibenthic invertebrates such as amphipods, decapods, mollusks, sponges, and shrimp. They also consume pelagic prey such as crab larvae and herring eggs and larvae.[30] Like other whales, grays evolved from land mammals who returned to the sea about 50 million years ago.[31]

Recent studies of closely related species, as well as behavioral studies of grays themselves, suggest that gray whales are intelligent mammals with cognitive abilities, emotional lives, and social relations. A 2006 study of other baleen whales (the humpback and finback) and toothed whales, conducted at the Mount Sinai School of Medicine, reported that these whales had, on a parallel track, evolved brain structures similar to our own, with specialized neurons called spindle cells that are linked to self-awareness, linguistic expression, compassion, and other traits. The study argued that these whales "exhibited complex social patterns that include intricate communication skills, coalition formation, cooperation, cultural transmission and tool usage."[32] Many scientists argue that cetaceans' large brains indeed "evolved to support complex cognitive abilities."[33] Odontocetes (toothed whales), in particular, have large brains relative to body size because they hunt for food in groups, which requires highly developed social and communication skills. Although the evidence of cognitive abilities and social relations is stronger for odontocetes (toothed whales) than for mysticetes (baleen whales), Simmonds notes that the latter are understudied and that recent studies on minke whales suggest that "the behavior of baleen whales may be more complex than previously thought."[34] Swartz points out that gray whales give care to unrelated calves and help injured companions, behaviors that suggest significant cognitive, emotional, and social abilities: "[O]n the Arctic feeding grounds, it was common for a second whale to remain with a harpooned one. In one instance, a harpooned pregnant female was supported at the surface by a second pregnant female that put her head and tail under the animal."[35]

Gray whales used to live in the Atlantic Ocean as well as the Pacific, but they were hunted to extinction in the Atlantic by the end of the 1600s.[36] They were very nearly driven to worldwide extinction by commercial whalers in the 1800s. Captain Charles Scammon's discovery in 1858 that gray whales return every year to birthing lagoons in Mexico led to the intensive slaughtering of whales there and sent the population numbers of gray whales plummeting. Scammon went after calves, knowing that gray whale mothers would come in close to try to protect their young. By the late 1930s, gray whale numbers were estimated at 1,500 worldwide, down from tens of thousands prior

[30] DEIS, 3–62.
[31] Peterson and Hogan (2002), 15.
[32] Siebert (2009), 35 citing a study published in *Anatomical Record* in November 2006.
[33] Marino et al. (2007).
[34] Simmonds (2006), 103.
[35] Swartz (1986), 222.
[36] DEIS, 3–58.

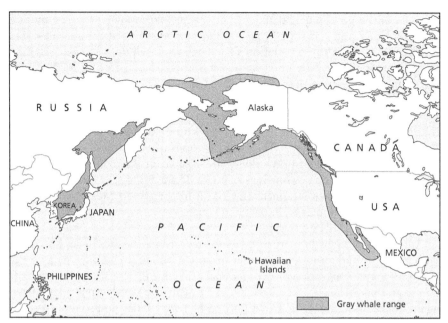

FIGURE 7.3. Ranges for Western North Pacific and Eastern North Pacific Gray Whales.

to the advent of commercial whaling.[37] In 1937, in recognition of the gray whale's dire situation, an international agreement on the regulation of whaling banned the commercial hunting of gray (and right) whales, with an exception for aboriginal hunting. Both the ban and the aboriginal exception were continued under the 1946 International Convention on the Regulation of Whaling (ICRW), the agreement that established the International Whaling Commission (IWC). In the 1970s, the United States extended the species additional protections by passing the Marine Mammal Protection Act of 1972, which prohibits the "taking" of marine mammals (with various exceptions), and listing the gray whale as an endangered species under the Endangered Species Act of 1973. Enacted in 1986, the IWC's moratorium on commercial whaling, again with an aboriginal exception, also protects gray whales.

Today, there are two surviving populations of gray whales: the Western North Pacific gray whale and the Eastern North Pacific gray whale (ENP). The Western gray lives along the coasts of Russia, Japan, Korea, and China, whereas the Eastern gray lives along the coasts of Mexico, the United States, and Canada (see Figure 7.3). The official stance of the U.S. National Marine Fisheries Service (NMFS) is that these are two genetically distinct populations with separate migratory routes and feeding and breeding grounds. When the NMFS advised the U.S. Fish and Wildlife Service to delist the gray whale

[37] DEIS, 3–71.

in 1994 – the governmental move that opened the door to the resumption of Makah whaling – it stated that the Eastern North Pacific gray whale had rebounded to a healthy population size of 20,000+, whereas the Western gray whale remained critically endangered at a population size of 100–200, and recommended delisting only the former. However, scientists have recently discovered that "at least some individuals from summer feeding grounds utilized by the endangered western stock migrate across the Pacific and into areas used by ENP gray whales," suggesting that the two populations may not be as distinct as previously thought.[38] The possible implications of these studies for the scientific management of gray whales are significant enough that the NMFS cited them in May 2012 as one reason it had decided to discard the 2008 Draft Environmental Impact Statement (DEIS) on the proposed Makah whale hunt and start the environmental impact assessment process over again. (It is ongoing at the time of this writing.)

Another reason given by the NMFS for discarding the DEIS also had to do with emergent data and scientific uncertainty. ENP gray whales engage in the longest biannual migration of any mammal, traveling up to 12,000 miles roundtrip from Baja Mexico to the Bering and Chukchi Seas in the spring, and back again in the fall. Each year, a small group of gray whales (approximately 200 individuals) does not travel all the way north to Alaska in the spring but instead chooses to spend the summer feeding in waters from Northern California to Northern British Columbia (an area that includes the Makah usual and accustomed fishing and hunting grounds). Scientists cannot explain why this subgroup of whales makes this decision, whether and to what extent these whales are distinguishable genetically or otherwise from whales who migrate all the way north to Alaska, or why the composition of this group varies to some degree but not wholly from year to year. What is certain is that the project of characterizing and understanding these whales has high political stakes. NMFS scientists call these whales the Pacific Coast Feeding Aggregation or Group (PCFA or PCFG) and emphasize that their composition varies somewhat annually, while whale advocates call them "resident" whales, speak of their "site fidelity," note that some have returned every year for twenty-five years, and emphasize their individual identities (to the extent these are known through photo identification and other techniques). Continuing uncertainty about these whales is cited by the NMFS as another reason why it began the environmental impact review process anew in 2012: "In 2010 and 2011, researchers studying the genetics of ENP and PCFG whales found evidence of population substructure indicating that PCFG whales may warrant consideration as a separate management unit."[39]

---

[38] U.S. Department of Commerce, National Oceanic and Atmospheric Administration, "Notice of Intent to Terminate the Existing Draft Environmental Impact Statement and Prepare a New Environmental Impact Statement," 29968.

[39] U.S. Department of Commerce, "Notice of Intent to Terminate the Existing Draft Environmental Impact Statement and Prepare a New Environmental Impact Statement," 29968.

Like the California Fish and Game Commission, the NMFS claims to base all of its decisions in gray whale management on the "best available" science, a phrase that hints at the provisional nature of this science even as it sanctifies it. In fact, the incompleteness and contingency of gray whale science is a pivotal part of the Makah whaling story. Scientists have been unable to explain, for instance, either the precipitous increase in gray whale deaths in 1999–2000, when strandings on the West Coast increased sevenfold, or the significant drop in calf production from 1999–2001.[40] The NMFS formed a special working group on the strandings, which it termed an "unusual mortality event," but the group could not provide a definitive explanation for the phenomenon, instead citing a number of possible factors such as starvation due to unavailability of prey brought about by global warming.[41] Although strandings have diminished and calf production has rebounded, opponents of Makah whaling have pointed to these issues as evidence of the fragility of the gray whale population and the insufficiency of the "best available" science on this species.

The NMFS held fast to its overall population estimates for the gray whale through the delisting process and the environmental assessment of the Makah hunt, claiming that gray whales' "historical abundance" or population before commercial hunting was between 15,000 and 24,000, and that its current population estimate of 20,000 plus indicates their full recovery, thereby justifying their delisting.[42] In 1991, the NMFS proposed delisting the ENP gray whale (but not the Western gray) "based on evidence that this [ENP] stock has recovered to near its estimated original population size and is neither in danger of extinction throughout all or a significant portion of its range, nor likely to again become endangered within the foreseeable future throughout all or a significant portion of its range."[43] The Fish and Wildlife Service approved delisting on June 16, 1994, accepting the NMFS's claims that the current population of ENP whales is close to historic abundance and that the ENP and Western grays are wholly separate stocks. Both of these claims are, in fact, based on uncertain and contested science. Recent research by Alter and colleagues (2007), based on genetic analysis of whale meat sold in Japanese markets, suggests that the historical abundance of gray whales may have been as high as 100,000, which casts the current population estimate of 20,000 plus and the delisting decision in an entirely new (and less favorable) light.[44] In their DEIS on the Makah hunt, the NMFS mentions the work of Alter and colleagues (2007) but

[40] Peterson and Hogan (2002), xvi.
[41] DEIS, 3–103, 3–107.
[42] DEIS, 3–70, 3–71, 3–108.
[43] U.S. Department of Commerce, National Oceanic and Atmospheric Administration, National Marine Fisheries Service, "Endangered Fish and Wildlife; Gray Whale," 58869.
[44] Alter et al. (2007). The impressive genetic diversity discovered suggests that the historic population of gray whales in the Pacific could have been up to three to five times higher than previously believed. See Alter et al. (August 2007).

dismisses it and stands by its original calculations of historical abundance.[45] Nevertheless, estimates of the historic population of gray whales remain highly contested among scientists.[46]

Biologists are not the only scientists perplexed by gray whales. For decades, this species has presented ethologists with a fascinating behavioral puzzle. In the birthing lagoons of Baja Mexico, locals have named gray whales "*Las Ballenas Amistosos,*" or "friendly whales." Friendlies, mothers who bring their calves right up to small whale-watching boats to be petted and adored by humans, often bear harpoon scars that indicate that they have encountered human hunters (probably Inupiat Eskimos). Why do whales who have had such experiences choose to approach humans and even encourage contact between their calves and humans? On a whale-watching excursion in Western Baja's Laguna San Ignacio, author Charles Siebert asked HSUS marine mammal biologist Toni Frohoff if the whales were possibly expressing forgiveness. Frohoff responds:

Those are the kinds of things that for the longest time a scientist wouldn't dare consider. But thank goodness we've gone through a kind of cognitive revolution when it comes to studying the intelligence and emotion of other species. In fact, I'd say now that it's my obligation as a scientist not to discount that possibility. We do have compelling evidence of the experience of grief in cetaceans; and of joy, anger, frustration and distress and self-awareness and tooluse; and of protecting not just their young but also their companions from humans and other predators. So these are reasons why something like forgiveness is a possibility. And even if it's not that exactly, I believe it's something ... I'd put my career on the line and challenge anybody to say that these whales are not actively soliciting and engaging in a form of communication with humans, both through eye contact and tactile interaction and perhaps acoustically in ways that we have not yet determined.[47]

The whale watchers in San Ignacio experience not only the whale's subjectivity – the sense, in ethologist Barbara Smuts's words, of looking in an animal's eyes and realizing there is "someone home" – but a moment of interspecies intersubjectivity. A moment of mutual beholding, when whale and human regard one another and say something to one another. Many remark upon the singular experience of being beheld as the whale turns on her side beside the boat and opens her eye to observe them.

The gray whale was pulled back from the brink of extinction in the mid-twentieth century by international conservation law. As mentioned earlier in this chapter, the International Convention for the Regulation of Whaling (1946) continued an earlier international agreement to protect grays from commercial

---

[45] DEIS, 3–71. Here the NMFS mentions Alter et al. (2007) and suggests that because the study's calculations of historic abundance included both western and eastern stocks and because carrying capacity may have declined over time, the study does not alter the NMFS's position on historic abundance and the advisability of delisting of the ENP.

[46] Pyenson and Lindberg (2011).

[47] Siebert (2009), 35.

hunting, with an aboriginal exception. The ICRW created the International Whaling Commission (IWC), whose original mission was not to protect whales per se but rather "to provide for the proper conservation of whale stocks and thus make possible the orderly development of the whaling industry."[48] The IWC wanted to conserve whales, in other words, so that there would be enough of them to hunt. There is little doubt that signatory nations viewed whales instrumentally, as means to human ends: until 1972, national whaling quotas were allocated in BWUs (blue whale units), with one BWU equaling two fin whales, two and a half humpback whales, or six sei whales. The whale was not an individual animal but a number of units of whale – a measurable commodity with a set exchange value. From the 1940s through the 1960s, the IWC set whaling quotas higher than its own Scientific Committee recommended, ignoring the latter's warnings that several whale species were headed toward extinction.[49]

Beginning in the 1970s, however, the body slowly but perceptibly adopted a more protectionist tone toward whales. To begin with, the United States turned decisively toward protectionism. Responding to domestic pressure from environmental and animal protection groups, the U.S. government placed several whale species on the newly created endangered species list and passed the Marine Mammal Protection Act (1972) prohibiting the "taking" of marine mammals domestically. Congress passed the Pelly (1971) and Packwood-Magnuson (1979) amendments to create more leverage for the United States to persuade noncompliant nations to abide by international conservation programs and ICRW regulations.[50] At the annual IWC meetings, the United States unsuccessfully proposed a global moratorium on commercial whaling in 1972, 1973, 1974, 1979, 1980, and 1981. Finally, in the early 1980s, a number of non-whaling nations joined the IWC, creating the three-fourths supermajority needed to approve the moratorium in 1982.[51] The international body that had been created to protect whales *for* the whaling industry was now protecting whales *from* the whaling industry.

---

[48] International Convention for the Regulation of Whaling, December 2, 1946, 161 United Nations Treaty Series 72. Today, the IWC maintains the Schedule, a program that regulates whaling through the maintenance of the commercial moratorium and the issuing of quotas for aboriginal subsistence whaling. The IWC also coordinates and funds conservation work and research. As of October 2012, it had eighty-nine member nations. See http://iwcoffice.org/history-and-purpose.

[49] Burns (1997).

[50] The Pelly Amendment (1971) gives the president authority to ban the importation of fish products from a nation contravening international fishery conservation programs. The Packwood-Magnuson Amendment (1979), passed because the Pelly sanctions process proved unwieldy, reduces a nation's fishing quota within U.S. waters by at least 50 percent if it is acting to diminish the effectiveness of the International Convention for the Regulation of Whaling. See Beck (1996) on why these amendments have been relatively ineffective.

[51] Beck (1996). The moratorium went into effect in 1986, with exceptions for scientific research and aboriginal subsistence whaling (ASW).

The implementation of the moratorium on commercial whaling in 1986 did not end the battle between pro- and anti-whaling nations in the IWC; it merely shifted the terrain. Several nations including Norway, Iceland, and Japan lodged objections to the moratorium, although Japan later withdrew its objection because of pressure from the U.S. government. Under IWC regulations, a member nation that lodges an objection to the body's decision can flout that decision with impunity, and Norway and Iceland have since resumed commercial whaling.[52] Pro-whaling nations have also sought to exploit the moratorium's two exceptions – for aboriginal subsistence whaling (ASW) and for "scientific research" – all the while shrugging off condemnation from the IWC and environmental and animal protection organizations worldwide. Japan has continued commercial whaling under the "scientific research" exception, claiming that it needs to kill whales to advance scientific knowledge. It has also argued continuously since the moratorium was enacted that what it calls STCW (small type coastal whaling), traditional hunting conducted with hand implements by coastal villagers, should be considered aboriginal subsistence whaling and thus permitted. Indeed, Japan has accused the United States and other anti-whaling nations of having a discriminatory "double standard" when it comes to the ASW exception.[53] In addition, pro-whaling nations have fought assiduously to overturn the moratorium within the IWC. The IWC has become a case study of an international organization struggling without enforcement powers to maintain compliance among member states to a global conservation regime. The moratorium is helping whale populations to recover, but it is a fragile and ongoing accomplishment, vulnerable to being overturned or rendered irrelevant by noncompliance. When the Makah signaled their eagerness to resume whaling in the mid-1990s, their story intersected explosively with this global political battle over whaling.

THE MAKAH WHALE AGAIN: SCIENTIFIC AND LEGAL UNCERTAINTIES

Interest in Makah culture and history was reinvigorated in the 1970s by the discovery of the Ozette site – a Makah village located thirty miles from Neah Bay that had been buried by a mudslide hundreds of years ago. The artifacts at Ozette, which turned out to be one of the most important archaeological finds in Pacific Northwest history, confirmed the historical centrality of whaling to Makah life and generated excitement within the tribe about this practice. The larger political environment in the region and the nation was also conducive to tribal revival. During the 1950s and 1960s, the Makah and other Northwest Coast tribes had been involved in extensive litigation to defend their treaty fishing rights, culminating in the favorable *Boldt* decision of 1974, which imposed a conservation necessity test on state regulation of tribal fishing

[52] Ibid.
[53] DEIS, 3–331.

and guaranteed tribes 50 percent of the harvestable fish in their usual and accustomed fishing grounds.[54] As part of this struggle, the Makah and other tribes had organized "fish ins," modeled on the sit-ins of the then-emergent civil rights movement. By the 1970s, movements were flowering within Black, Chicano, Puerto Rican, Asian American, and Native American communities across the nation. Liberation, self-determination, and sovereignty were the principles of the era. In this context, insistence on their right to whale came to be read by many Makah as an assertion of sovereignty and a rebuke to the failed designs of white colonialism.

Discussions about whaling percolated within the Makah tribe and in the 1980s, the Makah, along with other Northwest Coast tribes and fisheries, approached the NMFS about delisting the gray whale. Beck (1996), based on an interview with Makah Fisheries Director Dan Greene, writes that "from 1987 to 1993, [the Makah] were closely involved with NMFS's eventual 1993 recommendation to the U.S. Fish and Wildlife Service (FWS) for de-listing the gray whale from the Endangered Species list, approved by FWS in 1994."[55] This was the first step on a long journey through the intricacies of U.S. and international regulations relating to whaling, and the Makah brought to this process "political savvy gleaned from decades of experience with legal and political struggles through courts and directly with NMFS officials on issues involving fishing rights."[56]

This early Makah involvement in delisting the gray whale was behind the scenes and largely off the record, it seems; neither the Makah tribe nor the NMFS acknowledge it in the official documents they have produced concerning the delisting process and the subsequent tribal proposal to resume whaling. The official record of the NMFS indicates only that the agency received a 1991 petition for delisting from the Northwest Indian Fisheries (of which the Makah are a part) and that the NMFS disregarded the petition because the delisting process was already well under way.[57] The Makah tribe, for its part, implies

---

[54] *U.S. v. Washington*, 384 F. Supp. 312, 1974, U.S. Dist. Court. See also Coté (2010).

[55] Beck (1996), 377.

[56] Ibid., 376.

[57] U.S. Department of Commerce, National Oceanic and Atmospheric Association, National Marine Fisheries Service, "Endangered Fish and Wildlife; Petition and Finding to Remove the Eastern Pacific Gray Whale Stock From the List of Endangered and Threatened Wildlife," 64499. A few years later, the NMFS indicated that the Makah seeking to resume whaling was "unlikely," a strange claim if Dan Greene was accurate in saying that the Makah had been involved in the delisting process for years: "The question has arisen whether non-Alaskan natives would, in the near future, pursue traditional whaling and sealing activities. To date, only the Makah Tribe has expressed such an interest, but it is unclear at this time whether they would be interested in pursuing open-boat whaling or could satisfy subsistence and/or cultural needs by other means. For any Native American group to begin harvesting large whales, they would need to demonstrate a subsistence need and request (through the Bureau of Indian Affairs) the U.S. Commissioner to the IWC to petition that body for a portion of the subsistence quota for gray whales. Such a scenario is considered unlikely at this time." U.S. Department of Commerce, National Oceanic and Atmospheric Association, National Marine Fisheries Service, "Endangered Fish and Wildlife; Gray Whale," 3132.

that it was not involved in lobbying the NMFS for delisting and that it waited patiently until the NMFS acted of its own accord: "Once NOAA determined that the protections of the Endangered Species Act were no longer necessary, the Tribe notified NOAA that it wished to reinitiate a ceremonial and subsistence gray whale hunt."[58] Just as the NMFS wants to present its decision making as neutral and insulated from political pressure – based on the "best available science" – so, too, does the Makah tribe want to present its actions as environmentally sensitive. It would not enhance the tribe's image to be seen as pushing the NMFS to delist the gray whale for the sake of resuming the hunt.

Once the ENP grays were delisted, the Makah pressed the NMFS for permission to whale, and the U.S. government agreed to request a quota for the Makah under the ASW exception at the 1996 IWC meeting.[59] Although they came under immediate fire from whaling opponents at home and abroad, U.S. officials interpreted the government's historic trust responsibility toward the Makah as mandating this action. This trust responsibility toward Native American tribes was first articulated in *Cherokee Nation v. Georgia* (1831) and *Worcester v. Georgia* (1832), wherein Chief Justice John Marshall held that tribes were "domestic dependent nations," that their relationship to the state was that of ward to guardian, and that all three branches of the U.S. government had a fiduciary obligation to protect and support them.[60] In the modern era, the trust responsibility has been seen as an "explicit duty binding the U.S. to uphold Indian treaty obligations and act as trustee in promoting the economic and political development of the Indian tribes."[61] The Indian Tribal Justice Support Act (1993), the Department of Commerce's American Indian and Alaska Native Policy (March 30, 1995), and Executive Order 13175 (2000) all affirm the government's unique obligation to Native American tribes.[62]

Opposition to the Makah request emerged before the 1996 IWC meeting convened. More than 300 organizations worldwide signed an "Open Letter to the Makah Nation" asking them to reconsider their plan:

> The undersigned groups respectfully appeal to the Makah Nation to refrain from the resumption of whaling. People from many cultures worldwide hold whales to be sacred and consider each species a sovereign nation unto itself, worthy of respect and protection. Gray whales migrate vast distances each year and bring joy to many thousands of whale watchers. They only briefly pass through Makah waters. The resumption of the slaughter of these benign and trusting beings would bring to your nation swift and ongoing world-

---

[58] Makah Tribal Council, "Application for a Waiver," 10.

[59] Many Makah whaling advocates believe that their treaty right to whale is absolute and overrides both domestic law (the MMPA) and international law (the ICRW), but they have submitted to these legal-bureaucratic processes in order to demonstrate good faith and enhance the perceived legitimacy of the hunt. Some whaling opponents argue that the Treaty of Neah Bay was abrogated by the ICRW, the Whaling Convention Act of 1949 (which gives the U.S. Secretary of Commerce powers to enforce the ICRW domestically), and the MMPA.

[60] Coté (2010).

[61] Bradford (2000–1), 190. See also Miller (2005).

[62] DEIS, 1–12.

wide condemnation. We submit that important spiritual traditions must be observed in the context of a planet whose wildlife are being destroyed by habitat reduction, human over-population and exploitation, competition for food, and the proliferation of toxic chemi-cals. As global neighbors also committed to healing our spiritual connection to the natural world, we appeal to you to work with us to pursue creative alternatives to your planned whaling, avoiding a conflict that will have no winners.[63]

Predicting the intense conflict that would envelop the Makah whaling proposal, the letter highlights two counterweights to the Makah argument about cultural tradition: the fact that many other cultures believe that the whale deserves "respect and protection" and the idea that traditions should be flexible enough to take changing (ecological) circumstances into account.

During the 1996 IWC meeting, anti-whaling nations argued that the Makah request did not satisfy the terms of the ASW exception. A 1982 IWC report had clarified the following terms relating to the ASW exception:

Aboriginal subsistence whaling means whaling for purposes of local aboriginal consump-tion carried out by or on behalf of aboriginal, indigenous, or native peoples who share strong community, familial, social, and cultural ties related to a continuing traditional dependence on whaling and on the use of whales.

Local aboriginal consumption means the traditional uses of whale products by local aboriginal, indigenous, or native communities in meeting their nutritional, subsistence, and cultural requirements. The term includes trade in items which are by-products of subsis-tence catches.

Subsistence catches are catches of whales by aboriginal subsistence whaling operations.[64]

Critics argued that the Makah could demonstrate neither a "continuing tra-ditional dependence" on whaling nor a subsistence requirement for whale meat, and that they were therefore not eligible for the ASW exception. In addition, Alberta Thompson and other dissenting Makah elders arrived at the meeting to speak against their tribe's request. As Thompson puts it, "[We] were grandmoth-ers arriving at the IWC in wheelchairs."[65] The U.S. House of Representatives Committee on Resources seized the moment to unanimously pass a resolution expressing opposition to the Makah hunt.[66] U.S. officials decided to withdraw the request for a Makah quota.

At the next IWC meeting in 1997, the United States did an end run around the quota approval process by folding its gray whale quota request into that of the Chukotka (indigenous inhabitants of Russia) and trading part of the Alaskan Inupiat's bowhead whale quota in exchange for some of the Chukotka's gray whale quota. Member nations who opposed Makah whaling were left with lit-tle choice but to approve the Chukotka quota because this people clearly fit the

---

[63] http://www.earthisland.org/ei/immp/makah.htm, cited in Watters and Dugger (1997).
[64] *Report of the Aboriginal Subsistence Whaling Working Group*, 5.28.12, iwc/64/ASW5 Rev1, agenda item 5.1.
[65] Peterson and Hogan (2002), 125.
[66] Watters and Dugger (1997), 334.

ASW exception and received quotas every year from the IWC. They registered their protest by issuing a statement that the ASW exception applies only to those "whose traditional subsistence and cultural needs have been recognized by the IWC," but the United States succeeded in removing "by the IWC" from the statement, thus leaving the recognizing agent unspecified and the statement virtually meaningless.[67] Coming out of the 1997 IWC meeting, the NMFS and Makah claimed that the IWC had allocated the latter a gray whale quota, and whaling opponents (including anti-whaling nations such as Australia and New Zealand) claimed that the IWC never explicitly recognized the Makah under the ASW exception and that the Makah therefore had no legal right to whale.[68]

In April 1998, the NMFS announced that Makah subsistence and cultural needs had been recognized by both the United States and the IWC and issued the tribe a gray whale quota. The Makah hunted a gray whale in May 1999, as described at the opening of this chapter. Before the Makah could hunt again, a coalition of individuals and environmental and animal protection groups took the National Oceanic and Atmospheric Administration (NOAA) – of which the NMFS is a part – to court, arguing that it had shown bias (in favor of the hunt) and had rushed to judgment in its assessment of what kind of environmental impact Makah whaling was likely to have, thus violating the National Environmental Policy Act (NEPA) of 1970.[69] In *Metcalf v. Daley* (2000), the Ninth Circuit Court of Appeals ruled in favor of the plaintiffs, finding that the NOAA had indeed shown bias and violated NEPA by preparing an Environmental Assessment (EA) – which resulted in a FONSI or "finding of no significant impact" – of the proposed hunt after it had already committed itself in writing to supporting the Makah hunt.[70] The court wrote: "It is highly likely that because of the Federal Defendants' prior written commitment to the Makah and concrete efforts on their behalf, the EA was slanted in favor of finding that the Makah whaling proposal would not significantly affect the environment."[71] The court also affirmed that the U.S. Supreme Court "has clearly held that treaty rights such as those at stake in this case 'may be regulated … in the interest of conservation … provided the regulation … does not discriminate against the Indians.'"[72] The NOAA was ordered to set aside

---

[67] Hodges (2000).

[68] Peterson and Hogan (2002); Firestone and Lilley (2005).

[69] NEPA sets out procedures concerning proposed federal actions that might affect the environment, requiring an agency to collect information on the possible impact and disclose this information to the public.

[70] 214 F.3d 1135 (9th Cir., 2000). Plaintiffs-Appellants included Jack Metcalf, Australians for Animals, Beach Marine Protection, Alberta Thompson, the Fund for Animals, and others. Defendants-Appellees included William Daley, Secretary, U.S. Department of Commerce; James Baker, Administrator, NOAA; and Rolland Schmitten, Director, NMFS. Defendant-Intervener-Appellee was the Makah Indian Tribe.

[71] Section 35.

[72] Section 36.

the written agreement it had made with the Makah tribe, start the NEPA process again from scratch, and prepare a new EA.

After the NMFS issued a second EA in July 2001, again with a "finding of no significant impact" (FONSI), it found itself back in court. In *Anderson v. Evans* (2002), the Ninth Circuit Court of Appeals once again ruled in favor of the plaintiffs, finding that the NOAA had violated NEPA by preparing an EA rather than a more comprehensive Environmental Impact Statement (EIS).[73] The court argued that the impact of the Makah hunt on the small population of "local" or "resident" whales was "sufficiently uncertain and controversial to require the full EIS protocol."[74] The Court also remarked upon the IWC's ambiguous language about aboriginal and subsistence needs needing to be "recognized": "We cannot tell whether the IWC intended a quota specifically to benefit the Tribe. ... [T]he surrounding circumstances of the adoption of the Schedule cast doubt on the intent of the IWC to approve a quota for the Tribe. ... Whether recognition must formally come from the IWC or from the United States is not clear."[75] Noting the potential precedential impact of the scenario, the court remarks:

Prior to adoption of this language, the understanding among IWC members was that only the IWC could decide which groups met the subsistence exception. The 1997 IWC gray whale quota, as implemented domestically by the United States, could be used as a precedent for other countries to declare the subsistence need of their own aboriginal groups, thereby making it easier for such groups to gain approval for whaling.[76]

Environmental and animal protectionists expressed deep concern about the Makah hunt opening the door to the claims of other groups across the world. The Court's remarks recognized the legitimacy of those concerns.

The *Anderson* court also ruled that the Marine Mammal Protection Act (MMPA) of 1972 applies despite the Makah's treaty rights because the courts have recognized the government's right to regulate Native American fishing in the name of "conservation necessity."[77] The Makah were therefore required to

---

[73] 371 F.3d 475 (9th Cir., 2002). Plaintiffs-Appellants included Will Anderson, Fund for Animals, HSUS, Australians for Animals, Cetacean Society International, West Coast Anti-Whaling Society, and others. Defendants-Appellees were Donald Evans, Secretary, U.S. Department of Commerce; Conrad Lautenbacher, Administrator, NOAA; and William Hogarth, Assistant Administrator for Fisheries, NMFS. Defendant-Intervener-Appellee was the Makah Indian Tribe. Under NEPA, an Environmental Assessment (EA) either results in a FONSI (finding of no significant impact) or triggers the preparation of a full Environmental Impact Statement (EIS).

[74] Section 68.

[75] Section 95.

[76] Section 80–1.

[77] The MMPA prohibits (with exceptions) the "take" of marine mammals in U.S. waters, or by U.S. citizens on the high seas, as well as the importation of marine mammals and/or products into the United States. In 1994, the MMPA was amended to specify an exception for Alaskan Natives relying on marine mammals as a subsistence resource. http://www.nmfs.noaa.gov/pr /laws/mmpa. The court mentioned the three-part Fryberg test for conservation laws affecting Native treaty rights: The sovereign must have jurisdiction in the activity area; the statute must be nondiscriminatory; and the statute must be necessary to achieve the conservation purpose.

apply for a waiver from the MMPA in order to whale. Here the court argued
that Article IV of the Treaty of Neah Bay, which grants the Makah fishing,
whaling, and sealing rights "in common with all citizens of the United States,"
indicates a "cotenancy" relationship over these resources. According to the
court, the "in common with" language

> prevent[s] Indians from relying on treaty rights to deprive other citizens of a fair apportion-
> ment of that resource ... [which means] the Makah cannot, consistent with the plain terms
> of the treaty, hunt whales without regard to processes in place and designed to advance
> conservation values by preserving marine mammals or to engage in whalewatching, scien-
> tific study, and other non-consumptive uses. ... The MMPA will properly allow the taking
> of marine mammals only when it will not diminish the sustainability and optimum level of
> the resource for all citizens.[78]

In other words, gray whales are common property of U.S. citizens – *res
communis* – or part of the global (in this case, national) commons.[79] Thus the
Makah treaty right to whale, although valid, must be weighed against other
U.S. citizens' right to have (non-consumptive) access to this resource as well.
Unlike the environmental and animal protection groups who made various bio-
centric assertions in the "Open Letter to the Makah Nation," the court relied
on exclusively anthropocentric claims to make its case. Although the intent is
protectionist, the court's instrumentalizing language is eerily reminiscent of the
IWC's old unit of measurement, Blue Whale Units. Which type of argument has
more promise for protecting gray whales – a neoliberal one about resources
and property rights or an alternative one about ecological health and animal
well-being? Can they be deployed together or are they mutually exclusive?

In 2012, the NMFS abruptly announced that it was discarding the Draft
Environmental Impact Statement (DEIS) it had been working on and starting
the process from scratch, citing, as described earlier in this chapter, "several
substantive scientific issues [that] arose that required an extended period of
consideration."[80] With the NEPA process restarting, it will likely be several
more years until a new DEIS is produced, subjected to public comment, and
revised into a final EIS. Thus it will be several more years until the decision is
made to grant or not grant the Makah a waiver to the MMPA. The contingency of gray whale science surfaces and shakes things up, highlighting the
unstable foundation of scientific management efforts and the uncertain status
of the species. The scientific management of the commons in the public interest
turns out to be a fraught and deeply political project.

---

[78] Section 108.
[79] Burns (1997) asks if whales are *res nullius* resources (the property of no one, there for the taking) or *res communis* resources (common property of the world). He argues that international
agreements have tended to lean toward the latter definition. Burns does not consider a third
possibility: that whales are not resources or property at all.
[80] U.S. Department of Commerce, "Notice of Intent to Terminate the Existing Draft Environmental
Impact Statement and Prepare a New Environmental Impact Statement," 29968.

THE OPTICS OF ECOLOGICAL AND ETHICAL HARM

Environmental and animal protectionist organizations made two principal types of arguments against the Makah hunt.[81] These are analytically distinct optics that were often combined in practice. The first was that Makah whaling caused real and potential ecological harm by killing members of a species whose status is precarious and opening the door legally and morally to whaling by others around the world. The second was that Makah whaling caused ethical harm by taking the lives of animals who deserve significant moral consideration and, in the eyes of some, a "right to life." Thus many whale advocates went beyond admonitions about cruelty and the infliction of unnecessary suffering (arguments used in the Chinatown market case) to suggesting that whales, because of their special characteristics, deserve to be protected from hunting altogether.

Staff scientists from the environmental and animal protections groups challenged the NMFS's "best available science" at every turn – questioning specific studies and claims, requesting up-to-date and impartial research on all aspects of gray whale behavior, biology, and ecology, and emphasizing the indeterminacy of gray whale science. Reporting on the response of these organizations to the 2008 DEIS, the NMFS scoping report drily noted:

Ocean Defense International commented that the EIS needs to examine the methodology of population estimates over the last ten years ... because the assessments cannot be made on questionable or out of date data. Cetacean Society International commented that data must be sought from all legitimate sources (not just NMFS-funded), and asked for the EIS to discuss NFMS' funding priorities, or lack of, for assessments. The comment claimed that because NFMS has not funded and accomplished recent studies, the EIS cannot assert with objectivity that climate, population and habitat trends are suitable to allow whaling in a given future period, much less that the population will remain stable.[82]

In an August 10, 2012 letter to the NMFS, HSUS marine mammal scientist Dr. Naomi Rose urged NMFS officials preparing their new EIS to pay heed to the Alter and colleagues (2007) study on historical ENP population estimates so that they might develop a "proper environmental baseline" from which to analyze the environmental impact of the Makah hunt.

Whale advocates also warned insistently about the precedential dangers posed by Makah whaling. Some expressed strong concern that the Makah

[81] The coalition of groups included local groups (e.g., Peninsula Citizens for the Protection of Whales) as well as other whale and cetacean protection organizations (e.g., Cetacean Society International) and national and international environmental and animal protection organizations (e.g., HSUS, Sea Shepherd Conservation Society, Ocean Defense International, Animal Welfare Institute, Progressive Animal Welfare Society).
[82] U.S. Department of Commerce, NOAA, NMFS, "Scoping Report: Makah Whale Hunt Environmental Impact Statement," 12. While preparing the DEIS, the NMFS held four public scoping meetings in October 2005 (three in Washington State and one in Maryland) and solicited more than 300 written comments in 2005–6, the vast majority of which were sent by individuals.

would move from "cultural and subsistence" hunting to resuming full-scale commercial hunting. The fact that IWC regulations allowed the sale of handicrafts made from nonedible whale products seemed to blur the line between aboriginal and commercial whaling. In an October 24, 2005 letter to the NMFS, Cathy Liss, president of the Animal Welfare Institute, wrote: "AWI is concerned that the granting of an additional waiver to the MMPA [to the Makah] for the sale of handicrafts made from whale products within the United States might lead to commercialization of the whale as a resource."[83]

The Makah Tribal Council had assured the NMFS that they had no plans to resume commercial whaling, and the tribe's "Application for a Waiver of the Marine Mammal Protection Act Take Moratorium" (2005) clearly stated that the tribe wished to hunt only for local consumption and ceremonial purposes. Yet the Makah had openly discussed the resumption of commercial whaling early on in the approval process. Obtained through an FOIA request, an April 27, 1995 memo from an NMFS staffer to Michael Tillman, the deputy U.S. commissioner to the IWC, mentioned that the Makah planned "to operate a processing plant so as to sell [whale meat] to markets outside the U.S ... [and] have started discussions with Japan and Norway about selling their whale products to both countries."[84] John McCarty, executive director of the Makah Whaling Commission, remarked: "[S]elling the whale was a thought. And I'll be honest with you. Selling the whale could be very, very advantageous to the tribe."[85] In addition, in a May 5, 1995 letter to Will Martin of NOAA and David Colson of the Department of State, Makah Tribal Council member Hubert Markishtum states for the record that the Makah have the treaty right to hunt whales commercially and that they are not waiving that right by applying for an ASW exception.[86]

The precedential danger was magnified, whale protectionists argued, because of the U.S. government's demonstration of bias during the NEPA and IWC approval processes. The HSUS sent numerous scoping letters to the NMFS alleging the agency's bias and warning that Makah whaling would open the door to other groups and nations keen on expanding the definition of ASW. In a February 16, 2001 letter to the NMFS, HSUS marine mammal scientist Dr. Naomi Rose wrote that the just-released Draft Environmental Assessment (DEA), with its finding of no significant impact (FONSI), was misguided because it relied on the U.S. delegation's interpretation of what had occurred at the 1997 IWC meeting – an interpretation that was "entirely erroneous" and "self-serving": "The HSUS firmly believes that in order to avoid a lawsuit by the Makah Tribe regarding treaty rights, the US has wilfully misinterpreted the unambiguous statements and intentions of other IWC delegations." Rose points

[83] October 24, 2005 letter from Cathy Liss to Kassandra Brown of NMFS, Northwest Region.
[84] Russell (1999), 32. See also Schmidt (1998) and Firestone and Lilley (2005).
[85] Blow (1998).
[86] February 16, 2001 letter from Dr. Naomi Rose to Cathy Campbell of NOAA. See also "Native Americans and the Environment/The Makah Whaling Conflict: Arguments Against the Hunt."

to the verbatim record of the 1997 IWC plenary session, which indicates that a majority of the nations who voted for the Chukotka gray whale quota "specified that their votes were not to be perceived as support for the U.S. request for the Makah Tribe's ASW claims." In an October 24, 2005 letter to NMFS, Rose then highlights the IWC definition of "local aboriginal consumption" as including "nutritional, subsistence, and cultural requirements" and argues that transcripts of the 1996 and 1997 IWC meetings indicate dissensus on whether Makah nutritional needs had been adequately established. Finally, in an August 20, 2012 letter to the NMFS, Rose concludes that the Makah hunt does not "conform to international standards of subsistence whaling ... and threaten[s] to create (and has indeed *de facto* created) a new category of whaling – cultural whaling – that does not reflect a true subsistence need." The NMFS is responsible for this outcome as its actions "have consistently resulted in legal short cuts and questionable policy positions that have weakened domestic and international whale protection."

The ecological Indian trope was deployed as a disciplinary tool by some whaling opponents (both members of the public and a few advocates).[87] The suggestion here was that the Makah were betraying their Makahness by pursuing an activity that threatened environmental balance. In seeking to whale, they were being non-ecological or bad Indians. Consider this e-mail sent to the NMFS during the scoping period for the 2008 DEIS:

Whales are one of the wonders and treasures of the world, and their sacred being is for all mankind. It is very disheartening to see that the quest for their destruction for profit is still going on. I honor and respect our native peoples and have a reverence for their culture. Here in the San Francisco Bay Area, the history of the Oholone tribe has shown that they were one of the most peaceful, spiritual peoples that ever walked planet earth. ... I believe that any Makah who are willing to destroy one of the most magnificent creatures that the earth has provided are not true to their spirit. Surely, sharing and providing educational opportunities to view and be with these creatures would be a better income producing avenue for the Makah.[88]

A whale advocate made a similar point: "The Makahs are the cowboys here ... and we're the Indians. We're protecting nature with very few resources; the Makah are hunting with high-caliber weapons, and with the Coast Guard and the U.S. government behind them."[89] The force of this statement, of course, lies in its pointed reversal of the ecological Indian trope. It is the Makah who are the rapacious, powerful despoilers of nature, while their opponents struggle to

[87] There were aspects of Makah culture and history that made this mantle an awkward fit to begin with. The Makah's strong property orientation (they rendered property not just topographical features, marine resources, and physical material but also songs, dances, images, rites, and specific kinds of cultural knowledge), their history as commercial whalers and sealers, and their continued claim to the right to whale commercially – all of this disrupts the image of the Indian as an organic constituent element of nature.

[88] October 15, 2005 e-mail sent by a private individual to the NMFS during public comment on the DEIS.

[89] Martello (2004), 271, citing Schmidt (1999).

stymie their destructive advance. The Makah have become so non-ecological that they are like *cowboys*. Reprising a common theme among whaling opponents, one letter writer to the *Seattle Times* wrote:

Make your clothing on looms so you will look like your ancestors when you are hunting. Give up Gore-Tex and Thinsulate, wear moccasins instead of sneakers and hiking boots. Grow and hunt the rest of your food, stop going to grocery stores. Stop using electricity and all the appliances it supplies. ... If you really want to return to the "old days" of your culture, then turn around and go all the way back.[90]

The suggestion here was that the Makah tribe's embrace of things modern – including modern methods of hunting such as a high-powered rifle and a speed-boat – meant that the hunt was not authentic and that they were not acting like authentic Indians.[91] The tone of the quote is sarcastic and disparaging, implying that the Makah are using culture as an excuse to kill whales and that they want to have it both ways by claiming traditionalism while availing themselves of modern conveniences.

The second optic used by whale advocates focused on the ethical harm done by the Makah hunt to unique creatures who deserve human protection. Many of the e-mails sent by concerned individuals to the NMFS during the public comment period on the DEIS opposed the hunt on the grounds that gray whales were singularly "majestic," "ancient," and "intelligent," with large, complex brains and strong family bonds. Victor Sheffer, former chair of the U.S. Marine Mammal Commission, spoke for many when he stated: "I believe we ought to stop killing them [whales] unless for human survival only. ... I see no need to extend this protective ethic to rabbits, or chickens, or fish. Whales are different."[92] The uniqueness argument was an effective strategy for mobilizing public opposition to the Makah hunt, particularly because whales have been emblems of environmental consciousness in the United States since the "Save the Whales" campaign of the 1970s. That it straightforwardly asserted a species hierarchy and thus rendered other kinds of animals (rabbits, chickens, fish, and others) more killable, concerned some, including Gillespie, who recommends linking the critique of whaling to a broader discussion about the "the moral considerability of [all] animals."[93] Interestingly, the ontology explicated by Makah leaders accepts most if not all of these posited whale attributes – and still views whales as edible. Again, this was a wrinkle that environmental and animal advocates did not explore.

Several scholars have directly challenged the IWC's and NMFS's scientific management model for its reduction of whales to resources, calling instead for a reimagining of whales as morally considerable beings. Hawkins writes: "The central issue ... [is] not a matter of whether or not 'science' tells us that certain

---

[90] 1999 letter to the *Seattle Times*, cited in Erikson (1999), 575.
[91] Van Ginkel (2004).
[92] Cited in Gillespie (1997), 369.
[93] Ibid., 355.

whale populations can be 'harvested sustainably' given the industrial economic model; it is, rather, whether or not that model itself is an appropriate one for all, or any, of humanity to adopt and live by."[94] Addressing the question of Inuit whaling, D'Amato and Chopra challenge the anthropocentric view that the humans' (Inuits') are the only interests at stake: "[T]here is a second interest: that of the great whales in the survival of their species or – even short of claims of survival – in their right to live. The whales find their own sustenance in the oceans; by what right do the Inuit expropriate the bodies of the whales to serve as their food?"[95] The authors point to trends in international conservation law, evolving state practices, and a "broadening international cultural consciousness" as evidence that a "right to life" for whales is emerging as part of binding customary international law.[96] They argue that international institutions regulating whaling have gone through five incremental stages – free resource, regulation, conservation, protection, preservation – and are now entering the sixth stage of "entitlement."[97]

Of the broad coalition of groups opposing the Makah hunt, Sea Shepherd Conservation Society was the most visible. Unlike the local groups involved, SSCS operates globally and has an international reputation. Unlike broadstroke groups like the HSUS, SSCS maintains a specific focus on protecting marine life, especially whales. With its outspoken leader, Captain Paul Watson, SSCS has garnered attention as a direct-action group that seeks out dramatic encounters with whaling vessels on the high seas. SSCS holds that whaling by Norway, Japan, and others is illegal because it is done in defiance of (or by exploiting loopholes in) IWC regulations and casts itself in an international law enforcement role, per the UN statement authorizing citizens to undertake such action. The SSCS Web site lists "12 Primary Reasons for Opposing the Plan to Slaughter Whales by the Makah." Copied and pasted into many of the citizen e-mails sent to the NMFS, the list expresses the range of complementary arguments (paraphrased below, except for items 11 and 12, which are directly quoted) made against the hunt:

1. The Makah do not qualify for the IWC's ASW exception because they do not have an unbroken tradition of whaling and they do not have a subsistence dependence on whale meat.
2. The United States abrogated the Treaty of Neah Bay when it signed the IWC in 1946; it does not therefore have the right to grant a whale quota to the Makah.
3. The Makah will ask for quotas on other whales next.
4. Makah whaling will motivate tribes on Vancouver Island to resume whaling.

(continued)

---

[94] Hawkins (2001), 305.
[95] D'Amato and Chopra (1991), 59.
[96] Ibid., 49.
[97] Ibid., 23.

5. Allowing the Makah to whale will strengthen the position of Japan, Norway, and Iceland as they seek to expand their illegal whaling operations.
6. The original Makah plan was to whale commercially and sell the meat to Japan.
7. The IWC never granted a gray whale quota to the Makah.
8. Makah whaling will threaten resident whales.
9. Makah whaling will stress whales in the area, posing a danger to whale watchers.
10. Many Makah oppose whaling, which has been pushed through without full democratic tribal participation.
11. "Tradition and culture must not be the basis for slaughter. The ancestors of the Makah killed whales because they had to do so for survival. There is no survival necessity today to justify such killing. The treaty that the Makah cite as evidence of their right to whale specifically states that they have the right to whale 'in common with the people of the United States.' When the treaty was signed, all Americans had the right to kill whales. When whaling was outlawed for all Americans it included the Makah as the rights are 'in common' and not separate. There cannot be unequal rights granted in a system that promotes equality under the law. This is tantamount to extra special rights for a group of people based on race and/or culture and is contrary to the guarantee of equality under the law as guaranteed by the U.S. Constitution."
12. "Whales should not be slaughtered anytime or anywhere by any people. These are socially complex, intelligent mammals whose numbers worldwide have been diminished severely. Sea Shepherd is dedicated to the objective of ending the killing of all whales in the world's oceans forever. In this effort, we speak for the whales as citizens of the Earth whose right to live and survive on this planet must be defended."[98]

The eleventh item reads the "in common with" language from the Treaty of Neah Bay not as indicating "cotenancy" in whales as resources, as the *Anderson* court asserted, but rather as indicating that the Makah right to whale was abrogated along with other Americans' right to whale by the ICRW/WCA and the MMPA. The suggestion that the Makah are asking for "special rights" (point 11) reverberates loudly with the claims of opponents of Native American rights and minority rights more generally.

THE OPTIC OF ECOCOLONIALISM

The Makah Tribal Council (MTC) attributed the furor over its attempted resumption of whaling to ecocolonalism or ecoracism – that is, to the continuation of

[98] http://www.seashepherd.org/whales/makah-tribe.html.

historical colonialism in contemporary ecological garb. Reading environmental and animal activists' efforts through the lens of anticolonialism, they rejected their ontological and moral claims outright. In their view, whaling had been central to Makah culture for millennia and it had been secured in perpetuity by their far-thinking ancestors in the Treaty of Neah Bay. To resume whaling meant honoring and connecting with those ancestors, recovering a suppressed tradition, restoring a severed bond between the Makah and the whale, making real a treaty right, and reinvigorating tribal culture and identity. As time went by, it also meant resisting colonial domination and asserting sovereignty, as the firestorm grew and public denunciations of the Makah intensified.

Responding to charges that their culture was reconstructed, adulterated, and inauthentic, Makah tribal leaders emphasized the continuity of their cultural traditions, characterizing the seventy-year hiatus from whaling as a brief interruption and pointing out the clear persistence of whaling songs, dances, stories, and images in contemporary Makah culture. Their culture was living and evolving, they argued, and technological change was a continuous part of this process. Just as shifting from using harpoons made of mussel shells to harpoons made of steel had not made the whale hunt less authentic, neither did using a rifle and speedboat, particularly because these latter adaptations were made to make the kill more humane and to enhance the hunters' safety.[99] A Makah with a rifle was still a Makah and still an Indian, not a cowboy. Makah leaders read criticisms of their practices as thinly veiled expressions of ethnocentrism and hostility – that is, as reiterations of the colonial impulse. In an "Open Letter to the Public from the President of the Makah Whaling Commission," (August 6, 1998), Keith Johnson wrote: "We don't take well to Sea Shepherd or PAWS telling us we should rise to a 'higher' level of culture by not whaling. To us the implication that our culture is inferior if we believe in whaling is demeaning and racist."[100] On the Makah tribe's Web site, www .makah.com, Makah leaders charge their opponents with manufacturing an uproar in an attempt to suppress Makah culture:

Much of this opposition has been whipped up deliberately by organized groups who have put out a blizzard of propaganda attacking us. ... The anti-whaling community is very well organized and very well financed and puts out a steady stream of propaganda designed to denigrate our culture and play on human sympathy for animals. Perhaps what is lost in all of their rhetoric is an appreciation of the value of preserving the culture of an American Indian Tribe – a culture which has always had to struggle against the assumption by some non-Indians that their values are superior to ours. ... We can only hope that those whose

[99] The NMFS required the Makah to use a rifle after harpooning the whale on the grounds that it was more humane than the traditional method, which involved harpoons and lances alone. The Makah tribe worked with a veterinarian to develop a rifle that would be powerful enough to penetrate a whale's skull and kill it instantly. Motorboats were used in addition to the whaling canoe in order to enhance the safety of the hunters.
[100] Johnson is responding in part to a PAWS (Progressive Animal Welfare Society) brochure that mentions the tribe's modern amenities (lighted tennis courts, Fed Ex deliveries, etc.) as a way of raising questions about the authenticity of the tribe's culture today.

opposition is most vicious will be able to recognize their ethnocentrism – subordinating our culture to theirs.[101]

Makah leaders directly linked the firestorm over whaling to practices of colonial domination manifested centuries earlier. Wayne Johnson, the captain of the Makah whaling crew in the 1999 hunt, said of protesters: "[T]hem being here is like bringing a blanket of smallpox," referring to the notorious plans of British officers to use blankets to infect the Delawares with smallpox during the Siege of Fort Pitt in 1758 during the French and Indian War.[102] As one observer noted, "The more the [Makah] tribe discussed the topic of whaling in the media, the more the boundaries between past federal conflicts and modern environmental frictions blurred."[103]

Some of the public criticism of the Makah lent credence to the notion that a colonialist mindset was at play. While environmental and animal protectionists mostly refrained from making comments on race or indigeneity and steered away from language that was obviously racially fraught, some members of the public did not hesitate to denigrate the Makah as savage, barbaric, and backward. In public scoping comments e-mailed to the NMFS about the DEIS, one person wrote: "It is difficult for civilized countries to imagine such barbarity towards endangered species of whales. ... These are primitive and savage acts that reflect badly on the Makah tribe and United States' citizens" (May 18, 2008). Other e-mailed comments included "These tribes need to come to terms with evolving with the civilized world" (May 12, 2008) and "It is time for the Makah to come out of the Stone Age" (May 9, 2008).

Other public comments were aggressively threatening and contemptuous toward the Makah. Bumper stickers that read "Save a Whale, Harpoon a Makah" reversed the status of animal and Indian, suggesting that the former deserved moral consideration while the latter was merely animal. In his analysis of letters and calls to the *Seattle Times* right after the 1999 hunt, Tizon (1999) notes that public opinion ran 10 to 1 against the hunt and categorizes critics of the hunt into three groups: those who decried the killing, those who decried the methods used, and a third, smaller group that expressed racial hatred toward the Makah, including these statements:

- "Publish this article but don't use our last names. We wouldn't want to lose our scalps."
- "These idiots need to use what little brains they have to do something productive besides getting drunk and spending federal funds to live on."
- "I am anxious to know where I may apply for a license to kill Indians. My forefathers helped settle the west and it was their tradition to kill every

[101] Makah Tribal Council and Makah Whaling Commission, "The Makah Indian Tribe and Whaling: Questions and Answers."
[102] Gorman (2000), 63. On Fort Pitt, see Ranlet (2000).
[103] Barton (2000), 187.

Redskin in the way. 'The only good Indian is a dead Indian,' they believed. I also want to keep faith with my ancestors."

These constructions of Native Americans as irredeemably savage, like most racial fantasies, have proven remarkably enduring across spatial and temporal dimensions. The cunning, parasitical Asian, the violent Negro beast, and the savage Indian are stock characters in the American cultural imaginary. The savage Indian is but the flip side of the "ecological Indian," of course: it is the Indian's embeddedness in nature, his quasi-animality, that makes him both attuned to ecological considerations and prone to barbarity.

Makah leaders and supporters pointed to Representative Jack Metcalf (R-WA) and Senator Slade Gorton (R-WA), both of whom vigorously opposed Makah whaling, as quintessential ecocolonialists. Gorton had represented Washington State against the U.S. government and Native American tribes in the *Boldt* decision and was a longtime crusader against treaty fishing rights.[104] Metcalf was the founder of Steelhead and Salmon Protection Action in Washington State (later known as United Property Owners of Washington), a group that opposed tribal rights on behalf of white landowners.[105] According to the League of Conservation Voters, Metcalf had one of the worst environmental voting records in Congress.[106] Metcalf took a prominent role in the fight against Makah whaling, cosponsoring a unanimous resolution in 1996 by the U.S. House of Representatives Committee on Resources opposing the Makah hunt and joining other individuals and groups in bringing the *Metcalf v. Daley* lawsuit in 2000. Both Gorton and Metcalf were white Republicans who supported fishing and hunting, had deep connections to the fishing industry, and devoted a good portion of their public lives to fighting Native American treaty rights as "special rights."[107] Given their histories, their interest in protecting the gray whales from the Makah struck many as going after Indians under the guise of environmental protection – the very definition of ecocolonialism. Sea Shepherd Conservation Society worked with Metcalf in a highly visible way on the Makah whaling issue, praising his leadership and appearing with him in public. Those familiar with Metcalf's reputation as an Indian hater excoriated SSCS for this association and raised questions about the group's motives for opposing the Makah hunt.[108]

The resumption of whaling promised to be, according to Makah leaders, a salve for the wounds inflicted by historical colonialism. What colonialism had rent asunder, they suggested, only whaling could put back together. In the tribe's "Application for a Waiver of the Marine Mammal Protection Act Take Moratorium" (2005), numerous social problems (teenage pregnancy, elevated high school dropout rates, drug use, juvenile crime) and economic problems

[104] Coté (2010).
[105] "Metcalf's Indian History."
[106] Miller (1999).
[107] Westneat (1999).
[108] Coté (2010) and Miller (1999).

(unemployment, poverty, substandard housing) afflicting the Makah reservation are identified and attributed to the U.S. government's past assimilation policies. Whaling is then presented as the solution to these problems:

Whaling was the keystone of traditional Makah society. Makah society was mirrored in the structure of the whale hunt, including ceremonial preparation, the hunt itself, and the ultimate acts of butchering and distribution. … Ceremonies to prepare whalers and their families for the hunt provided the Makah with a social framework that contributed to governmental, social, and spiritual stability. … Given the centrality of whaling to the Tribe's culture, a revival of subsistence whaling is necessary for the Makah to complete this spiritual renaissance and repair the damage done to the Tribe's social structure during the years of forced assimilation.[109]

In "Whale Hunting and the Makah Tribe: A Needs Statement" (2012), prepared on behalf of the tribe and submitted by the United States to the IWC, Dr. Ann Renker writes: "Current data from Neah Bay High School verifies that, in the absence of active whale hunting and its related preparations, one in seven male high school students was using or experimenting with drugs and/or alcohol in 2010."[110] Renker's phrasing suggests that student drug and alcohol use is *a direct result of not whaling*. Renker then echoes the "Application for a Waiver" by arguing that the resumption of whaling is necessary for the spiritual, cultural, social, and nutritional health of a people still grappling with the effects of colonialism. Prohibiting it would mean "introduc[ing] a new shroud of oppression into the daily life of Makah people."[111]

Responding to the optics of ecological and ethical harm, Makah leaders emphasized that their whaling proposal reflected their continuing spiritual relationship with nature as Native people.[112] In his "Open Letter to the Public from the President of the Makah Whaling Commission" (August 6, 1998), Keith Johnson writes: "We have an understanding of the relationship between people and the mammals of the sea and land. We are a part of each other's life. We are all part of the natural world and predation is also part of life on this planet." Charlotte Coté (2010), writing sympathetically about the Makah as a member of a closely related Nuu-Chah-Nulth tribe, writes: "Our cultures thrived in a world of reciprocity between us and our environment. Our relationship with animals has always been one based on respect and gratitude and there is a sense of sacredness attached to the spirit of the animal for giving itself to us for sustenance."[113] Coté references the Makah understanding that the whale gives himself or herself to the hunters if they are worthy and have conducted proper spiritual preparations – an understanding that makes it consistent to revere the animal and also kill her.

---

[109] Makah Tribal Council, "Application for a Waiver," 6.
[110] Renker (2012), 56.
[111] Ibid., 7.
[112] See Renker (2012) and the Makah tribe's Web site, http://www.makah.com.
[113] Coté (2010), 164–5.

From the viewpoint of Makah leaders, animal and environmental advocates are attempting to erase the Makah's historically and spatially embedded understanding of nature and impose their own ahistorical and abstract understandings of nature upon the tribe. If whites tend to define themselves as apart from nature and animals, which they alternately approach as exploiter or protector, Native peoples such as the Makah see themselves as intimately connected to other living beings in the web of life and death. Hunting, for them, is a form of reciprocal exchange between humans and animals (Nadasdy 2007). Moreover, they understand these relationships to be place-specific (Tallbear 2011): the Makah know whales and other sea life – not in the abstract, as rights-bearing subjects or ecological bellwethers, but as particular kin with whom they have shared Neah Bay's swells, currents, and cliffs for millennia. The sea is their country. Did it make sense for whites, who had nearly driven the gray whale to extinction, to block the Makah's efforts to resume a tradition of whaling that had always been "sustainable" and respectful toward the animal?

The effort to resume whaling has become inextricably tied to the question of sovereignty. The question "Who decides what the Makah can and cannot do?" hangs over every aspect of the controversy. Resuming whaling has been a costly endeavor: the tribe spent well over a million dollars of its own funds between 2003 and 2012 alone, and at least $335,000 of NMFS funds between 1995 and 1998.[114] For a brief moment, Makah leaders contemplated accepting financial incentives to desist, and some Makah favored developing a lucrative whale-watching industry instead of whaling, but in the end, the decision to pursue whaling was closely tied to a sense of collective self-determination and pride.[115] This is likely what the young Makah man felt as he held up a sign saying "Kill the Whales" in front of protesters.[116] And this is likely what Makah Tribal Council member Marcy Parker meant when she emerged out of a meeting where a financial offer to desist had been discussed and rejected and stated, "You can't buy our treaty right, and you can't buy our pride."[117] As opposition intensified, so did the resolve of many Makah to keep fighting. One scholar notes:

[I]t was almost a badge of honor to be disparaged by non-natives for continuing their cultural traditions. The whale hunters felt a connection to their ancestors who had been arrested for engaging in potlatches, beaten for speaking Indian languages in government boarding schools, or vilified by Christian missionaries as culturally inferior savages. With protests and other attempts to block the tribe's efforts seen as an extension of ongoing

---

[114] From 1995–8, the U.S. government spent $335,000 helping the Makah in their pursuit of whaling (Blow 1998). From 2003–7, the tribe spent approx. $675,000 of its own funds on the pursuit of whaling; from 2007–12, it spent $404,000 (Renker 2012).

[115] An assistant of Seattle communications billionaire Craig McCaw, who spent $12 million to return the orca Keiko of *Free Willy* fame to the wild, visited the Makah reservation to try to negotiate with Makah leaders, who had hinted that they might suspend the hunt if the financial incentive was significant enough. The negotiations came to naught (Tizon and Broom 1998).

[116] Van Ginkel (2004), 70.

[117] Russell (1999), 32.

processes of colonization, whaling and the activities surrounding it became a form of resistance to a larger history of cultural oppression.[118]

Interestingly, of the 93 percent of Makah who said in a survey that the tribe should continue to whale, more cited treaty rights as a reason (46 percent) than either cultural tradition (36 percent) or moral/spiritual benefits (20 percent).[119] It was the desire to preserve and exercise sovereign power that led many Makah to engage the whaling issue so passionately. If Chinese Americans in San Francisco wanted greater multiculturalist tolerance for and recognition of their foodways, the Makah, struggling with poverty and dispossession on the Neah Bay reservation, wanted to wrest back the power of self-determination that colonialism had stripped away.

The spirit of angry resistance sparked the so-called rogue hunt of 2007, when Makah hunters impatient with legal uncertainties decided to kill a whale without federal authorization. The Makah "Application for a Waiver" (2005) painstakingly explicates the tribe's commitment to humane killing, minimizing harm to whales (especially the PCFA or "resident" whales), protecting the environment, and abiding by federal and international laws. The "rogue hunt" ruptured, at least momentarily, the tribe's self-consciously projected image of unity, spirituality, ecosensitivity, and respect for the law. On September 8, 2007, five Makah men paddled out in the Strait of Juan de Fuca, where they harpooned a gray whale at least four times and shot him at least sixteen times. One reporter narrated: "The big gun misfired and fell overboard, and the only other means of quick dispatch at hand were a shotgun and a rifle. These lacked the strength to pierce the whale's thick skull, though, and anyway the men shot at the wrong spot. Then they ran out of bullets."[120] The whale, who bled for twelve hours before dying and sinking to the bottom of the ocean, turned out to be a whale whom scientists had labeled CRC-175, a "resident" gray whale who frequented the area summer after summer.[121] These whalers were not random hunters but central players in the ongoing drama over whaling rights: two of the men were Wayne Johnson and Theron Parker, members of the crew in the 1999 hunt; a third, Andy Noel, was a member of the Makah Whaling Commission. Because the tribe's application for a waiver from the Marine Mammal Protection Act of 1972 had not yet been granted, the hunt violated this federal statute.

The Makah Tribal Council held a news conference where it officially condemned the hunt and promised to prosecute and punish the five men to the fullest extent under tribal law.[122] The tribe also sent representatives to Washington, D.C. to reassure concerned government officials. In U.S. District Court, three of the men pled guilty to violating the MMPA and were placed on probation and

[118] Sepez (2002), 155.
[119] Renker (2012).
[120] Wagner (2009).
[121] Gottlieb (2009).
[122] Mapes (2008).

assigned community service. Wayne Johnson and Andy Noel were convicted in a bench trial and sentenced to five and three months jail time, respectively.[123] A defiant Johnson stated: "I'm proud of what we did. Some people are calling what I did an act of civil disobedience. I don't know much about that, but if civil is what the government is, then call my part savage disobedience."[124] Is Johnson an Indian hero, proudly carrying the banner of sovereignty into battle with the U.S. government? Or is he a troubled man struggling with what Cynthia Enloe calls "masculinized memory, masculinized humiliation and masculinized hope," indifferent to the impact of his acts on others?[125] Although many Makah expressed concern that the rogue hunt would damage the tribe's reputation and its chances for a legal waiver from the MMPA, there was sympathy for the hunters, too, and an unwillingness to punish them. In the end, the tribal court could not put an impartial jury of Makah together and tribal judge Stanley Myers dropped all charges against the whalers on the promise of a year's good behavior.[126]

Some Makah rejected the optic of ecocolonialism and openly dissented from the tribe's pursuit of whaling. During the 1996 IWC meeting, seven Makah elders, including descendants of whaling chiefs and signatories to the Treaty of Neah Bay, signed and circulated the following petition:

> We are elders of the Makah Indian Nation (Ko-Ditch-ee-ot) which means People of the Cape.
> We oppose this Whale hunt our tribe is going to do.
> The opposition is directly against our leaders, the Makah Tribal Council, Tribal Staff, and the Bureau of Indian Affairs, which is an arm of the United States Government.
> The Makah Indian Nation has been functioning without a quorum; two Councilmen are off on sick leave for very serious reasons, cancer.
> How can any decision be legal when our by-laws state the Treasurer shall be present at every meeting. The Vice Chairman is the other man out.
> The Whale hunt issue has never been brought to the people to inform them and there is no spiritual training going on. We believe they, the Council, will just shoot the Whale, and we think the word "subsistence" is the wrong thing to say when our people haven't used or had Whale meat/blubber since the early 1900's.
> For these reasons we believe the hunt is only for the money. They can't say "Traditional, Spiritual and for Subsistence" in the same breath when no training is going on, just talk.
> Whale watching is an alternative we support.

---

[123] "Makah Tribal Members Sentenced for Violating Marine Mammal Protection Act."
[124] Wagner (2009).
[125] Enloe (1989), 44, cited in Gaard (2001). See Sullivan (2000) for a revealing close-up portrait of Wayne Johnson.
[126] Mapes (2008).

The signatories were Isabell Ides (age 96), Harry Claplanhoo (age 78), Margaret Irvin (age 80), Ruth Claplanhoo (age 94), Viola Johnson (age 83), Lena McGee (age 92), and Alberta Thompson (age 72).[127] The petition suggests that Makah leaders are driven by greed and willing to violate tribal laws to achieve their aims. Dottie Chamblin, another Makah elder, stated: "They [the tribal leaders] say they're traditional but they are not listening to or protecting the elders. Shooting a whale with a machine gun is not a spiritual way ... no one in this village has a direct relationship with the whale any longer."[128]

Dissenters recounted the harassment and persecution they experienced within the tribe. Dottie Chamblin commented:

There's something very wrong here. We created a stir just by seeking the truth and asking them to tell it. Because of this treatment, no one else will speak up for the rest of the people, and that's a sad state of affairs. They've ostracized us. They've victimized us. It's difficult to get health care. They treat me badly. It's not the Makah way. There is a young, educated faction that is in breach of tradition.[129]

According to Chamblin, the tribal council's threat to banish dissenters from the reservation discouraged others from supporting or joining the dissenters.[130] The most outspoken dissenting elder was Alberta Thompson, a descendant of three signatories of the Treaty of Neah Bay, granddaughter of a whaler, and survivor of the government-run boarding school for Makah children. Once she publicly opposed whaling, Thompson was fired from her job as a coordinator at the Makah Tribal Senior Center on the grounds that she had spoken with Sea Shepherd Conservation Society representatives while at her job.[131] Her grandson was bullied at school and her dog was taken from her home, killed, and left on the side of the road a mile from her house. The acting chief of police informed Thompson that if she spoke about whaling or even "made a face" she would be arrested. Indeed, the Makah Tribal Council passed a resolution that only tribal council members and their hired public relations advisors could speak to the media. Thompson asked: "What has this old lady done to aggravate them? What am I onto that they would think I'm so dangerous?"[132] In 1997, oceanographer Jean-Michel Cousteau invited Thompson on a whale-watching expedition at San Ignacio. She recounted her experience, her eyes filling with tears:

In Baja, I met what I was fighting for, face to face. A mother whale rose up out of those warm waters right under my hand. She looked me straight in the eye, mother to mother. Then I saw a harpoon scar on her side, probably from up north in Siberia where the native people still hunt the whales for sustenance. The mother brought her baby over to

[127] Anderson et al. (2012).
[128] Hogan (1996).
[129] Ibid.
[130] Peterson (1996).
[131] Russell (1999), 32.
[132] Hogan (1996).

our little boat. I talked to them and I petted them. I felt their spirit of trust was somehow being conveyed to me. I laughed and I cried all the way back to shore, and all that night. I've never been the same since. When times get hard, I think of those great big wonderful beings.[133]

Thompson died in 2012. Her pastor "wept as he told the mourners at the packed church about her persecution."[134]

While surveys indicated overwhelming support for whaling within the tribe, a closer look at the numbers suggests a significant minority opposed the resumption of whaling for a variety of reasons, but that this opposition was *sub rosa*. One survey indicated that 95 percent of Makah respondents said they thought the tribe had the right to whale, but only 75 percent thought they should exercise this right.[135] Barton writes that most of those who opposed whaling in the survey were critical of the manner in which it was being conducted – that the hunters were not spiritually ready, that the federal government was dictating all of the terms – but that they were not necessarily outspoken about their views. She concludes: "[T]he vast majority of intra-tribal opposition was less visible than the media had portrayed."[136]

Many Native American organizations and tribes viewed the whaling issue as a matter of sovereignty and strongly supported the Makah. The Northwest Indian Fisheries Commission and Affiliated Tribes of Northwest Indians voiced their support.[137] Members of the Nuu-Cha-Nulth tribes of Vancouver Island attended the Makah celebration after the 1999 hunt. On June 23, 2004, the National Congress of American Indians, the oldest and largest national organization of Native American and Alaskan Native tribal governments, passed a resolution supporting the Makah tribe's right to whale.[138] Native scholars, too, celebrated the Makah's resumption of whaling. For example, Robert Miller, an eastern Shawnee, wrote: "The tribe has exercised its sovereignty and its right of cultural self-determination and has taken on all comers and overcome all obstacles to do so."[139] Other Native Americans disagreed, arguing that killing whales was not the right way to remedy past wrongs or assert sovereignty today. The First Nations Environmental Network issued an online statement that read: "Not all indigenous people support Makah whaling. ... While we respect Treaty Rights, this is political reason being used for killing and not a true meaning of need when it comes to the taking of another being's life."[140]

---

[133] Russell (1999), 31.
[134] Anderson et al. (2012).
[135] Barton (2000), 247–8.
[136] Ibid., 248.
[137] DEIS, 3–215.
[138] October 24, 2005 letter from Jacqueline Johnson, executive director of the National Congress of American Indians, to Kassandra Brown of NMFS, Northwest Region.
[139] Miller (2005), 145–6.
[140] Peterson and Hogan (2002), 215–16.

MUTUAL DISAVOWAL IN THE MAKAH WHALING CONFLICT

In the heat of political struggle, the parties to the Makah whaling conflict disavowed the other sets of claims in play. There were partial exceptions to the rule, however. Cetacean Society International (CSI), for example, spoke out in favor of Makah sovereignty and treaty rights and tried to organize start-up funding for a Makah whale-watching business as an alternative to the whale hunt, and Earth Island Institute suggested that the U.S. government give the Makah "a much larger land base; economic development grants; better health care; overall greater funding"[141] instead of granting them the right to whale. Both organizations attempted to signal that they were both pro-whale *and* pro-Makah and sought a solution to the conflict that was not zero-sum.[142] But neither organization could escape the dilemma that in rejecting the Makah's proposed remedy for the damage inflicted by colonialism and proposing other remedies, they were seen as continuing the colonial practice of imposing an external (Western) set of understandings on the Makah. In the eyes of Makah leaders, friendly colonialism was still colonialism.

The most visible anti-whaling group, Sea Shepherd Conservation Society, did not recognize the Makah's rights or claims in any way and chose instead to adopt the defensive posture that its agenda and actions had "nothing to do with race." In its "Equality Statement," SSCS says that it "operates internationally without prejudice towards race, color, nationality, religious belief, or any other consideration except for an impartial adherence to upholding international conservation law to protect endangered marine species and ecosystems."[143] It then states: "Sea Shepherd operates outside the petty cultural chauvinism of the human species. Our clients are whales, dolphins, seals, turtles, sea-birds, and fish. We represent their interests. ... We are not anti-any nationality or culture. We are pro-Ocean and we work in the interests of all life on Earth." SSCS leaders scoff at tribal, racial, and national concerns as narrow matters among humans, as "special interests," as a trivial distraction from the axis of power that really matters – that of human supremacy over animals. As in the Fish and Game Commission hearings in the Chinatown conflict, the universalistic language of equality, ecological health, and animal considerability is invoked to provide protection for nature and nonhuman animals – but at the expense of a racialized minority whose claims are derogated as particularistic and selfish.

It is not that SSCS is using eco-speak as a pretext for persecuting the Makah, then, but rather that it is advancing animal and ecological concerns in a way that manifestly trivializes concerns about tribal or racial justice. The history of colonialism and forced assimilation, of white encroachment upon Native fishing

---

[141] October 24, 2005 letter from Will Anderson, Earth Island Institute, International Marine Mammal Project, to Kassandra Brown of NMFS, Northwest Region.

[142] October 24, 2005 letter from William Rossiter, President of Cetacean Society International, to Kassandra Brown of NMFS, Northwest Region.

[143] http://www.seashepherd.org/who-we-are/equality-statement.html.

and hunting rights, of persistent anti-Indian racism and Makah marginalization – all of this is denied or elided. Moreover, SSCS declines to acknowledge that its own actions might aggravate racial problems by bringing anti-Indian public sentiment to the surface or giving succor to politicians like Jack Metcalf. Instead it insists that its practices are colorblind and its hands are clean.

Both animal protectionists and the Makah claim to revere and love the whale. At issue between them is whether reverence and love are consistent with killing the whale for food. At issue is the meaning of the killing – is it an exercise of unjust and unnecessary violence against another sentient being or is it the grateful acceptance of a gift from a kindred being in the context of the cycle of life and death? In trying to prohibit the hunt, animal and environmental protectionists disavowed (to varying degrees) Makah claims about racism and colonialism *as well as* Makah leaders' ontological claims about humans, whales, and nature.

Makah leaders and supporters, for their part, delegitimated the anti-whaling position and reduced it to a hatred of Indians or a desire to control them. They, too, chose not to approach the conflict as a confrontation of two reasonable but incommensurate views of whaling, but instead essentialized whaling opposition as racist and imperialist – *as not really being about whales at all.* In his "Open Letter to the Public from the President of the Makah Whaling Commission" (August 6, 1998), Keith Johnson writes: "We feel that the whaling issue has been exploited by extremists who have taken liberties with the facts in order to advance their agenda." And Native scholar Charlotte Coté writes:

> The vegan lifestyle is one that some people throughout the world have chosen to embrace, but it is ultimately a personal choice. We Native people do not want people who choose to live that way imposing their dietary rules on us, as this is just another form of cultural imperialism and food hegemony.[144]

Most whaling opponents said nothing about veganism so it may be that Coté raises the issue both because it powerfully evokes an image of Western privilege and because it allows her to depoliticize opposition to whaling as a "lifestyle" choice. Neither Johnson nor Coté acknowledges or attempts to reckon with an alternative ontology whereby respect entails protection and whereby the slaughtering of whales, who are seen as sentient beings and/or rights-bearing subjects, is an unjustifiable exercise of domination. This ontology, by virtue of being of Western origins, is dismissed as a product of and vehicle for colonialism.

The American public has in fact expressed growing concern about whales over the past several decades. In 1979, the U.S. Congress declared that "whales are a unique marine resource of great aesthetic and scientific interest to mankind" and that "the protection and conservation of whales are of particular

---

[144] Coté (2010), 163.

interest to citizens of the United States."[145] In 1993, Representative Gerry Studds introduced a House resolution (which passed unanimously) opposing the resumption of commercial whaling, stating: "[N]o other group of animals has so captured the imagination of the American people."[146] A poll conducted by International Fund for Animal Welfare in 1997 showed that 80 percent of Americans oppose whale hunting.[147] The increasing popularity of whale watching, the success of the *Free Willy* movie franchise, television programs like *Whale Wars*, and public interest in real life rescue stories involving gray whales all confirm that Americans believe that whales are due some significant measure of moral consideration and protection.[148] There has been, therefore, a notable cultural shift in American attitudes toward whales in recent decades.

In Coté's (2010) discussion of a "conservation burden," she asks: "Why should our culture and traditions be sacrificed upon the altar of the non-Indian conscience to pay for the environmental sins of the dominant culture?"[149] Because it was not the Makah who brought various whale species to the point of extinction, why should they be asked to bear the conservation burden of not whaling now?[150] Viewed anthropocentrically, this question makes a good deal of sense – it goes straight to the question of justice among human communities. But viewed ecocentrically or biocentrically, this question make less sense – if killing whales is a bad idea, for ecological or ethical reasons, it is no less a bad idea when the Makah do it. Gillespie writes: "[T]he fact that earlier colonial cultures ruthlessly exploited Nature does not give cultures with a traditional interest in the exploitation of Nature the right to finish off the job."[151] Indeed, one could equally ask "Why should whales be sacrificed on the altar of Makah sovereignty and anticolonialism?" Coté writes: "The antiwhaling groups saw the death of the whale through a Western cultural lens and thus ignored the spiritual and sacred elements attached to the Makah and Nuu-chah-nulth whaling tradition."[152] One could also say the Makah whalers (and Coté) saw the death of the whale through a Makah cultural lens and thus ignored the perspective(s) of environmentalists, animal protectionists, and the broader public.

What about the perspective(s) of the grays themselves? The question of what gray whales themselves want is a vexed one, of course, because all human interpretations of whale interests and desires are culturally mediated and

[145] 16 USC 916 note, Public Law 96–60, August 15, 1979, cited in DEIS, 3–198.
[146] H.R. Con.Res. 34, 103d Cong. (1993). See Gillespie (1997).
[147] Jenkins and Romanzo (1998), 111.
[148] See Wagner (2004–5). For stories of the rescue of J. J. in California and the grays of Point Barrows, Alaska, see Peterson and Hogan (2002).
[149] Coté (2010), 192.
[150] The same type of question comes up in international discussions about the environment, with China and India asking why they should bear the conservation burden now when U.S. industrial development has long had a disproportionately adverse effect on the environment.
[151] Gillespie (1997), 375.
[152] Coté (2010), 164–5.

inescapably so. We do not know what it is like to be a gray whale, as Thomas Nagel would remind us. In the Chinatown case, Chinese American advocates did not argue that market animals exercised volitional self-sacrifice; the only issue was whether or not the animals' suffering mattered morally speaking. But in the Makah whaling case, contradictory ontological claims about gray whales emerged, raising the question of whale phenomenology. Do whales, as sentient and intelligent creatures with life stories and familial and social worlds of their own, prefer being alive to being chased, harpooned, shot, and killed? In part, this is a matter of observing their behavior. Gray whales either try to flee when they are first harpooned – buoys are attached to the harpoons to keep the whales from diving and escaping – or in some cases fight back by thrashing and overturning the canoe. In the days before motorboats and guns, gray whales would sometimes flee for days, harpoons and buoys attached, lanced and bleeding from various parts of their bodies, before collapsing from exhaustion. Grays in particular used to be known as "devilfish" among hunters because they resisted slaughter.

Paul Nadasdy (2007) rightly cautions against the Western habit of dismissing Native understandings as "beliefs" (that is, superstitions) constructed to rationalize the violence of hunting and urges us to take seriously the possibility that Native understandings might be right. But fully assessing (as opposed to simply endorsing) Makah understandings requires us to consider that they function to cleanse the taint of domination from the act of killing. They function to reconcile reverence for the animal with killing him/her. The whale is not chased down and violently slaughtered; the hunters entreat and perhaps cajole her into giving herself in a spiritual and reciprocal exchange between human and animal. Environmental and animal protectionists doubtless have a stake in their own ontology as well, but there is no compelling reason to declare that the Makah are exempt from the human proclivity for self-rationalization. Westerners should be open to the possibility that the Makah are right. Should the Makah be open to the possibility that they are wrong?

Both Western and Makah ontologies are all too human. Makah ontological understandings about humans, whales, and nature are no more "constructed" or provisional than Western ones, but no less so either. They, too, are products of the human power to describe and attribute meaning to phenomena within the theater of power. We are back to Renteln's chicken once again, or the irreducibility of the animals' own phenomenal world(s). Does it matter to the chicken if she is killed in a Santería ritual or by the slaughterhouse worker? Does it matter to the gray whale if she is killed by a Norwegian commercial whaling boat or a canoe of ritual-observant Makah hunters uttering prayers? It may be that a fully developed "ecology of selves," in Eduardo Kohn's (2007) words, will reveal the phenomenal world(s) of the gray whales to us. Until then, it may be prudent to err on the side of caution and act as though gray whales wish to live. Otherwise, we humans, Native and non-Native, run the risk of imposing our own systems of meaning on those who lack the power to contradict us.

WHALING AND SOCIAL DOMINATION

Renker (2012) and others speaking for the Makah argue that the resumption of whaling is the essential antidote to colonial domination. What whaling proponents are conspicuously silent about is that Makah whaling historically depended on various patterns of *internal* domination relating to class/status and sex as well as species. Historically, Makah society was organized by descent group and ranked strata. Kin groups lived together in longhouses and were divided into chiefs or titleholders and commoners. Slaves acquired through trade, warfare, or purchase from neighboring tribes comprised the third, lowest stratum.[153] Whaling was the exclusive practice of chiefs, who inherited and owned both the physical equipment and ceremonial rituals and songs associated with the practice, and it was a crucial mechanism for shoring up their power and authority. Swan writes: "[I]t was considered degrading for a chief, or the owner of slaves to perform any labor except hunting, fishing, or killing whales."[154] By killing whales, chiefs demonstrated that they were gifted and worthy of the favor of the spirits. "Killing a whale," Coté writes, "was considered the highest glory: the more whales a chief caught, the more prestige, respect, and physical wealth he received, thus serving to elevate his status and position inside and outside his village or social group."[155] The butchering of the whale and distribution of meat followed strict guidelines that reflected the social hierarchy within the tribe. Whale meat and whale oil were also used for consumption and distribution at potlatches, ceremonies that expressed and enhanced a chief's power over rivals, commoners, and slaves.

According to Donald (1997), slavery played a vital role in Northwest Coast tribal cultures and economies, including the Makah's:

> Titleholders were able to undertake prestige-producing activities because they could control and manage resources and labor to produce the food and other goods and free the time needed for such activities. ... [S]lavery was essential ... because only slaves made it possible for titleholders – the exemplars of Northwest Coast culture – to live and act as titleholders.[156]

The labor of slaves, in other words, helped to underwrite the whaling exploits of chiefs. Slave status in Makah society was hereditary and slaves had no rights or privileges because they did not have membership in any kin groups. They were the property of their owners – exploited for their labor, traded for other goods, given as gifts, destroyed to demonstrate wealth and power. Slaves were sometimes killed during the funerals of Makah chiefs "both to accompany the deceased as servants in the next world and to show the power of the heir."[157] Among the many rituals whalers practiced, one involved draping a corpse

[153] Swan (1869).
[154] Ibid., 10–11.
[155] Coté (2010), 23.
[156] Donald (1997), 311.
[157] Ibid., 34. See also Swan (1869), 10.

across one's body as a charm to gain spirit power.[158] Parts of a deceased whaler's body were especially favored, but sometimes, according to Curtis, a small child was killed for this purpose, presumably a slave.[159]

The link between social hierarchy and whaling was sufficiently strong that when assimilation policies, disease, and other factors disrupted social structure, whaling became increasingly infeasible. The (selectively) egalitarian ideology of U.S. government agents also played a role: "For example, the American philosophy of social equality made it difficult for Makahs to select crew members and organize whaling canoes, and therefore households, according to the ancestral patterns."[160] In 1855, the U.S. government inserted into the Treaty of Neah Bay an article prohibiting slavery on the Makah reservation. Article XII states: "The said tribe agrees to free all slaves now held by its people, and not to purchase or acquire others hereafter." Subsequently, as Colson relates, "[T]he social status of the former slaves was ignored by [U.S. government] agents who attempted to treat all Makah as though they were on the same social level" and forbade "discrimination along the lines of status institutionalized in Makah society."[161] Although slavery did not end completely for several decades, these actions initiated its decline. "The presence of white men has exerted a salutary influence in this respect," Swan writes, "and the fear of being held responsible renders [the Makah] more gentle in their deportment to their slaves."[162] Ironically, then, slavery and social inequality were mitigated within Makah society through the imposition of colonial power on the part of a federal government that was itself a slave state (until the mid-1860s). While the requisite social structure for whaling was being dismantled, the "more egalitarian pursuit of sealing"[163] was open to all regardless of family or inherited privileges and displaced whaling among the Makah by the late 1800s.

As Gaard (2001) indicates, Makah whaling also reinforced traditional sex relations within the tribe. Women could not be chiefs and therefore could not whale. If a whaler's wife was menstruating at the time of the hunt, she was not allowed to touch the gear or come near him.[164] During the hunt, she was required to lie silent and motionless and to go without food or water so that the whale would stay calm and not swim out to sea:

[D]uring the hunt, the whaler's wife would act as if she had become the whale. Her movements would determine the behavior of the whale – if she moved about too much, the whale her husband was hunting would be equally active and difficult to spear; if she lay quietly, the whale would give itself to her husband. Towing chants often reflected this

---

[158] Gunther (1942).
[159] Curtis (1916), 39.
[160] Renker (2012), 40.
[161] Colson (1953), 15.
[162] Swan (1869), 54.
[163] Renker (2012), 39.
[164] Gunther (1942).

association, and the whalers addressed the dead carcass using a term that refers to a chief's wife.[165]

The woman was animalized, the animal feminized. The chief demonstrated his greatness by exercising mastery over whale, woman, and nature. In this scenario, women sometimes bore the blame for the failure of the hunt. One whaler's wife recalled what happened after she ate and drank a bit during a hunt: "When my husband came back he walked up to me and said, 'You drank something when you got up; we got a whale but he is not fat.' This frightened me very much and after that I never drank anything again.'[166]

Makah tribal leaders argue that whaling will restore social order and unity. Do they mean to suggest that it will reinvigorate the stabilizing social hierarchies of the past? Might the resumption of whaling reinforce old status distinctions among Makah families and sharpen inequalities between men and women in the tribe? In a gesture of democratic intent, the tribe invited all Makah families to participate in the Makah Whaling Commission in the 1990s, but this did not prevent concerns about family prerogatives and status from emerging in force. Dougherty (2001) reports that power struggles emerged over the composition of the 1999 whaling crew and that some members of the chosen crew "despised each other." Van Ginkel adds: "There was even greater animosity as to who was to be the captain of the whaling team. ... [Harpooner Theron Parker] and [Wayne] Johnson could not get along with each other, to put it mildly, but they finally worked out some kind of modus vivendi although the crew remained 'bitterly divided.'"[167] Parker and Johnson argued over whose family sacred whaling song would be sung when the whale was beached. Johnson recalled: "I told Theron there was going to be no family songs and dances. ... I didn't want just one family to take the glory. So when we got on the beach, he down-feathered it, claimed it with eagle feathers, sang his songs. ... I didn't want that to happen."[168] When Parker then took the first cut of whale meat, Johnson bristled again: "That was my job to do that. Not his job. It's not his whale. It's my whale."[169]

There are also signs that the gendered aspects of whaling would persist. Makah women were excluded from the whaling crew in the 1999 hunt. Denise Dailey, a Makah Fisheries biologist, was appointed to be executive director for the hunt, but "[b]ecause she was a woman, the [Makah whaling] commission insisted that she not speak for the crew, so Keith Johnson, the president of the whaling commission, was dubbed the spokesman for the hunt." Dailey remarked: "I'll never hunt a whale because I'm a woman and I'm okay with that."[170] Prior to the hunt, women were instructed about the historic rituals of

[165] DEIS, 3–228.
[166] Gunther (1942), 68.
[167] Van Ginkel (2004), 66.
[168] Dougherty (2001).
[169] Ibid.
[170] Sullivan (2000), 89.

ying silent and motionless and the "wives, partners, and mothers of the crew" chose to do this.[171] Also, "a group of young girls from the Neah Bay school went to their teacher and asked if they could take ten minutes to lie still and be quiet and pray while the hunt was taking place, because they had been told that that was historically what young women in the community did."[172] In one of Renker's surveys, of the few who opposed the hunt, some cited "the inequality of women's involvement in the hunt" as a reason.[173] Gaard (2001) suggests a connection between the masculinist, elitist aspects of whaling and "the tribe's current practices of silencing the dissenting voices of women elders who oppose the renewed hunt."[174] As Dottie Chamblin said, "It's grandmothers fighting this fight against them."[175] The argument over Makah whaling has been structured publicly as an argument between those concerned about colonial domination over the Makah and those concerned about human domination over animals. Perhaps the intimate connection of Makah whaling to other forms of social domination and inequality should figure in this debate as well.

CRITIQUE AND AVOWAL

The dilemma facing Cetacean Society International and Earth Island Institute, I mentioned earlier, was that their opposition to Makah whaling was taken as de facto evidence of colonial intent, regardless of their public stance calling for the federal government to redress the injuries inflicted on the tribe by colonialism. The member of the public who sent this e-mail to the NMFS during the October 2005 scoping period was also trying to be both pro-whale *and* pro-Makah:

I strongly believe that the United States Government has broken most of the treaties it has negotiated with Native Americans and many administrations in the 1800s were guilty of ethnic cleansing and genocide. I am generally in favor of giving Native American tribes the benefit of the doubt in most of their claims against state and federal governments. However, when it comes to whale hunting I believe that their traditions and treaties cannot take precedence over the lives of intelligent, self-aware animals such as whales.[176]

Is it possible to critique a specific Makah practice (and the understandings associated with it) in the name of anti-subordination and still meaningfully support Makah claims to sovereignty and redress? Can one argue against whaling and still be anticolonialist? One might respond that the Makah's ontology is central to their way of life so that a rejection of its implications for whaling is, in effect, a rejection of the entire Makah way of being. But, as discussed later in

[171] Renker (2012), 33. See also Bowechop (2004).
[172] Coté (2010), 141.
[173] DEIS, 3–242 citing Renker (2012).
[174] Gaard (2001), 16.
[175] Peterson (1996).
[176] August 27, 2005 e-mail from a private individual to the NOAA during the period of public scoping for the DEIS.

this chapter, other Pacific Northwest tribes with similar ontologies have elected to observe a continued moratorium on whaling and have not found their ways of life significantly compromised. For if Native American/Canadian ontologies hold whaling to be morally and spiritually permissible, they do not deem it morally or spiritually *compulsory*.

In the Makah whaling conflict, multi-optic analysis helps us to perceive clearly the varied perspectives, claims, and stakes involved. Once again, this does not have to lead to political or moral paralysis, but it should contour political action in particular ways. Thus seeing multi-optically would not necessarily stop someone from opposing Makah whaling (on anti-subordination grounds), but it would influence them to do so in a way that respected rather than denied the colonial context. Thoughtful critique of a racially marginalized group can be joined, then, to a posture of avowal toward that group's moral and political claims toward the larger society.

In this scenario, animal and environmental activists who chose to fight the resumption of Makah whaling would begin by recognizing their own racial situatedness and its implications for this story. They would learn about and respectfully engage Makah ontological claims about humans and whales, even if they ultimately disagreed with these claims and their implications. They would educate themselves deeply on the history of U.S. colonialism toward the Makah; think through the ongoing economic, social, and psychological effects of past and present governmental policies on the tribe; repudiate (rather than allying themselves with) the organized white political and economic interests who continuously seek to encroach on tribal fishing and hunting rights; actively condemn anti-Indian sentiments expressed by the public; and promote the Makah struggle for sovereignty and redress. They would *connect* the historical practices of colonialism with the violence against whales they are trying to curtail, while thinking through the impact of their activism on *both*. Rather than treating the question of whaling as an isolated issue that can be detached from the context of U.S.-Makah relations, they would situate the critique of whaling within a larger framework of justice that challenges multiple, interconnected forms of domination (including colonial domination) at once.

In this scenario, Makah leaders would not presumptively reduce all alternative perspectives to colonialism. They would take seriously and engage environmental and animal advocates' understandings and claims about both the ecological status of whales and what whales deserve and want, as well as learning about the long history of global activism to protect whales and the American public's growing concern about their protection. They would reflect upon the connections between colonialism and the mastery of nature and animals and question whether their own cultural understandings, too, might bear traces of domination (and self-rationalization). Rather than focusing exclusively on Coté's argument about the unfair "conservation burden" placed on the Makah, they would be open to assessing the possibly destructive implications of whaling, in particular the precedential dangers of stretching the ASW exemption in international conservation law.[177] Precisely because their culture is dynamic and living and evolving, they would consider and debate whether the fight for Makah sovereignty might be productively uncoupled from the issue of whaling, as Alberta Thompson and the other dissenting elders suggested. They would not need to repudiate their ontology or cultural understandings or tribal sovereignty to consider whether whaling is, all told, a practice worth resuming.

There are precedents for deciding that it is not. Down the coast of Washington from Neah Bay, the Quileute Tribal Council in La Push passed a resolution to not whale in 1988. Fred Woodruff, a member of the Quileute, hopes to build a whale-watching business using traditional whaling canoes. He comments:

Our tribe fully supports our Makah neighbors in their treaty rights. But our Quileute elders have made a different decision. Even though we and other tribes along the coast have the same treaty rights to hunt, our elders have chosen to support the gray whale. For thousands of years, this whale has been valuable under subsistence, but now the value is in its life. The gray whale is more valuable to the Quileutes living than hunted. We must begin the healing here in our village and hope it can help others, as well. We Quileutes would like to offer a new vision and a different model for other tribes, as well as peoples.[178]

Fred's brother, tribal chairman Russell Woodruff, adds: "We see the damage of what's taking place in Makah. Our neighbors do not own the story of the gray whales. ... The Quileute tribe would like to declare a Welcoming the Whale spring ceremony and invite all peoples to come celebrate the gray whales."[179]

In 2006, five groups of Nuu-Chah-Nulth on Vancouver Island (peoples who are closely related culturally and linguistically to the Makah) came together under the name Maa-Nulth and signed a historic treaty with the Canadian and British Columbia governments. The Maa-Nulth receive more than 24,000 hectares of land, $90 million in cash, up to $45 million for potential revenue-sharing projects, and $150 million for program financing.[180] In a side agreement, they promise not to hunt gray or sei whales for twenty-five years. The Maa-Nulth thus pursued reparations and redress while also protecting their right to whale – and they have chosen not to exercise this right, at least for the time being.

In this chapter, I analyze the Makah whaling controversy, tracing the history of the dispute and explicating the optics of ethical harm, ecological harm, and ecocolonialism. I discuss how the parties to the conflict advanced incommensurate ontologies about humans, whales, and nature, and how they disavowed one another's claims in the course of political struggle. I then suggest that

[177] In response to the Makah's attempt to resume whaling, the Nuu-chah-nulth tribe created the World Council of Whalers, an aboriginal lobbying group that receives funding from whaling nations like Japan and Norway and seeks to loosen IWC restrictions. Jenkins and Romanzo (1998), 76, n. 11.
[178] Peterson and Hogan (2002), 190–1.
[179] Ibid., 199.
[180] "Maa-nulth First Nations Sign Historic B.C. Treaty."

animal and environmental activists can critique Makah whaling mindfully, that is, in a way that engages and takes seriously the Makah's ontology and tribal justice claims. I also argue that the Makah, for their part, can move toward opening themselves to animal and environmental protectionist claims, building upon the example of some other Native American tribes and Canadian First Nations. The next chapter explores a second comparative case, the Michael Vick dogfighting scandal.

8

Michael Vick, Dogfighting, and the Parable of Black Recalcitrance

Vick beat dogs to death. He watched dogs drown in his swimming pool, he shot them, he electrocuted them, he buried them alive, he savagely abused them, he took great enjoyment in it, and he found it funny to watch family pets being torn apart.

        – Nathan Winograd

[What happened to Vick was] an electronic lynching.

        – Kwame Abernathy

On April 25, 2007, the Sheriff's Department in Surry County, Virginia executed a search warrant at 1915 Moonlight Road, a fifteen-acre property owned by NFL superstar and Atlanta Falcons quarterback Michael Vick. The search warrant was triggered by the arrest of Vick's cousin on marijuana possession charges, but investigators had heard rumors of Vick's involvement in dogfighting for years, so they asked Animal Control Officer Kathy Strouse to accompany them. At Vick's property, they found more than fifty dogs (many of them scarred or wounded), kennels, a fighting pit, and the standard paraphernalia of dogfighting, including breeding stand, treadmill, breakstick, and injectable steroids. Over the following months, investigators ascertained that Vick, who lived in Atlanta, had selected, purchased, built, and maintained the entire property for six years for the express purpose of housing his dogfighting operation, known as Bad Newz Kennels. Vick financed the operation, maintained several of his friends on the property to manage the breeding, training, and fighting of dogs, and visited every Tuesday (his day off from the Falcons) to supervise. Vick hosted fights involving dogs from many other states and took his dogs to fights in other states as well.

Thus began Michael Vick's precipitous fall from grace. Years earlier, Vick had vaulted from humble beginnings in a Virginia public housing project to NFL superstardom. Recognized as a prodigious talent, he was the first African American to be selected first in the NFL draft (in 2001 by the Atlanta Falcons) and became the highest paid player in NFL history. In 2004, he signed a

$130 million, ten-year contract with the Falcons, and he had endorsement con-
tracts with Nike, Coca Cola, Reebok, EA Sports, Kraft Foods, and many other
major corporations.[1] When prosecutors charged Vick and three of his friends
with several federal felony counts relating to the operation of an interstate dogfighting and gambling ring, Vick denied the charges and for months claimed
that he had had no involvement in or knowledge of his friends' criminal activities at 1915 Moonlight Road. But the evidence against him slowly mounted. As
it came to light, Vick was suspended from the NFL, lost his lucrative endorsement contracts, and filed for bankruptcy. When all three codefendants turned
state's evidence, Vick pled guilty and was sentenced to twenty-three months in
prison.

The Vick saga, like the Chinatown and Makah conflicts, is another contemporary U.S. site where race, species, and nature have been passionately
produced, contested, and reproduced. In this case, however, what was at issue
was not a historically embedded minority group practice valorized as a cultural tradition but rather a practice that has been long criminalized as felo-
nious activity and is undertaken surreptitiously by individuals across racial,
class, and geographic lines.[2] The matter was already clearly settled, at least in
public discourse, as to whether dogfighting should be allowed (not one person
who spoke out during the controversy argued that it should be), which shifted
the controversy to two questions: how much Michael Vick should pay for his
misdeeds and whether or not race was a "factor" in his prosecution and public
excoriation.

Animal advocates advanced an optic of cruelty to highlight Vick's cul-
pability, while Vick's defenders advanced an optic of racism, arguing that
critics were targeting Vick because of his color and invoking larger societal
debates about the U.S. state's turn toward mass incarceration policies as a
way of dealing with racial and social inequalities. When Vick's defenders
took this opportunity to weigh in about the racially oppressive aspects of the
criminal justice system, Vick's critics complained that they were "injecting"
race into the situation, "playing the race card," or even engaging in reverse
racism. The Vick saga, in other words, intersected forcefully with the ongoing passion play over whether or not the United States is now a postracial
society.

I argue in this chapter that rather than seeing race as "a factor" in the
story – as a discrete variable that can be disaggregated from other relevant
"factors" – we should instead understand race as constituting the very cultural
frame through which the story came to be read. What was at play was not only
"racism" in the sense of anti-Black animus but "race" in the sense of a taxonomy of bodies and a set of enduring, structured meanings about these bodies.

---

[1] Laucella (2010), 39 estimates that Vick lost a total of $142 million in salary, bonuses, and
endorsements.
[2] When the Vick story broke, dogfighting was a federal felony and a felony in forty-eight states.
Now, in part because of the Vick case, it is a felony in all fifty states.

The Vick saga was crafted as a *parable of Black recalcitrance about doing the right thing and succeeding*, and inasmuch as this parable drew upon the constraining, deforming tropes with which we think and do race – specifically, tropes about Black masculinity, criminality, brutality, and animality – we could not help but read the story this way. The parable presented Michael Vick as choosing between good and evil, sports and the gang life, the NFL and the ghetto, human and beast, and reaping the consequences of that choice. Vick made the right choice at first but then *slipped back*, losing the American Dream because of his own recalcitrance. This parable echoes across the centuries with Southern plantation owners' antebellum arguments that freed slaves would revert to (bestial) type as soon as the civilizing, disciplining influence of slavery was lifted. The Negro brute would never be more than a Negro brute. As an interpretive frame, the parable can be thought of, following Cole and King (1998), as a mode of displacement whereby the dramatic narrative of individual choice and responsibility elides the pervasive patterns of institutionalized violence against Blacks and institutionalized violence against dogs that subtend this story. The broader public, complicit in and privileged by these patterns, finds itself absolved as it turns its gaze upon the recalcitrant Vick.

The Vick controversy was explosive in part because its central players were, in the American cultural imaginary, the most animal of humans (the Black man) and the most human of animals (the dog). The human-animal boundary is continually crisscrossed here, race and species intersect often and urgently, and the distinctively tangled relationship between Black masculinity and animality runs like a bright thread throughout the narrative. Animal advocates talked about Vick's dogs in human terms – as having been executed, as experiencing redemption (Glick 2013) – even as other critics called for Vick to be caged, neutered, or placed in a fighting pit. Bruce Braun (2003) argues that Black men are not legible as wilderness adventurers because they are imagined as still inside of nature and thus unable to transcend it. Perhaps the same logic extends to the illegibility of Black men as dogmen (men who fight dogs). If the message to Chinese merchants and Makah whalers was that they needed to get with the American program, culturally speaking, the message to Vick was that he needed to discipline the bestial aspect of himself or it would be done for him, violently. The threat of Blackness is uniquely biological, uniquely incorrigible.

In this chapter, I examine the optic of cruelty advanced by animal advocates and offer a brief glimpse into the history and contours of dogfighting in the United States. I then turn to the optic of racism advanced by Vick's defenders and the overall framing of the story as a parable of Black recalcitrance. I also briefly discuss how the pit bull has been raced as Black over the past few decades and how this has dramatically altered the life chances of dogs of this breed. Finally, I show that Vick's critics and defenders adopted a posture of disavowal toward each other and reflect on how the two sides might move toward an ethics of avowal that considers both the institutionalized violence against Blacks and the institutionalized violence against dogs in contemporary society.

DOGFIGHTING AND THE OPTIC OF CRUELTY

Cruelty, like all valuations of ethical and political acceptability, has a history. Fighting dogs against other animals dates back in Europe to the fifth century BC and became widespread by the Middle Ages in England, where the baiting of bulls, bears, badgers, and rats was enjoyed by all classes in urban and rural areas alike (Kalof and Taylor 2007). It was only upon the withdrawal of upper-class patronage that these sports began to be seen a moral problem and that a political opportunity arose to curtail them. A simple reduction of early nineteenth-century British and American animal activism to class domination is too facile, however. If it is true that animal advocacy in Britain and the United States emerged in tandem with a project of race, class, and civilizational uplift at home and abroad (Davis 2013; Deckha 2013), it is also true that it was joined from the start to the ongoing abolitionist struggle in both locales, and that animal advocates strongly opposed the oppression of racialized others, women, children, prisoners, and workers, as well as nonhuman animals (Beers 2006).

Dogfighting was exported from Britain to the United States as early as the 1750s and increased in popularity over the next century so that, by the 1860s, professional pits in places like New York City and Boston were drawing large, raucous crowds, often composed of police officers and firemen.[3] From 1800 to 1860, the *Police Gazette* published dogfighting rules in the same tabloid that listed the latest crime and police news.[4] The rise of organized animal advocacy in Britain and the United States in the early 1800s eventually led to the prohibition of baiting sports, including dogfighting. Ironically, Britain's anti-baiting legislation of 1835 sparked an increase in dogfighting because it was easier to conduct surreptitiously than bull baiting or bear baiting. Massachusetts was the first state to ban dogfighting in 1835 (Strouse 2009), and most states followed suit over the next several decades. In 1867, at the behest of Henry Bergh, founder of the American Society for the Prevention of Cruelty to Animals (modeled on Britain's Royal Society for the Prevention of Cruelty to Animals), New York revised its anticruelty law to render all forms of animal fighting illegal for the first time. Precisely because so many police were avid dogmen, Bergh pressed successfully for ASPCA Humane Law Enforcement Agents to have the power to make arrests themselves in New York.[5] The United Kennel Club withdrew its official endorsement of dogfighting in the 1930s, and by 1976, the practice was illegal (that is, driven underground) in all fifty states.

I argue in Chapter 3 that the United States has seen in recent times, simultaneously and contradictorily, an intensification in the instrumental usage of animals, driven by consumer demand and enabled by technological innovation and neoliberal sensibilities about nature, *as well as* a widening and

[3] "Top Ten Dogfighting Questions"; Evans and Forsyth (1997).
[4] "A Brief History of Dogfighting."
[5] "Dogfighting FAQ."

deepening discussion over whether animals have the intrinsic right to be protected from such usage. For animals, it is the best of times and the worst of times. Dogfighting is embedded in this ambiguous picture. Public sentiment and the law have turned decisively against it; what was once the sport of English aristocrats is now a felony in all fifty states.[6] In 2007, with strong bipartisan support, Congress passed the Animal Fighting Prohibition Enforcement Act, which increases penalties for violations of the federal anti-animal fighting law.[7] The Vick case in fact furthered the criminalization of dogfighting by stiffening penalties and helping to make the practice a felony in Wyoming and Idaho, where it had been a misdemeanor.

At the same time, there are indications that dogfighting is on the rise in the United States and spreading out geographically. It is growing in popularity in its traditional stronghold – among white working-class men in Southern rural areas – and it has also been growing in poor urban Black neighborhoods since the 1990s (Burke n.d.; Mann 2007). Mark Kumpf, investigator with the National Illegal Animal Fighting Task Force, remarks: "It's definitely on the upswing. Communication on the Internet has made dogfighting accessible without the inherent risks of arrest that used to go along with it" (Simpson 2004). Numerous Web sites offer dogfighting equipment and pit bull puppies for sale, and trade journals such as *Your Friend and Mine*, *Game Dog Times*, *The American Warrior*, *The Pit Bull Chronicle*, and *Sporting Dog Journal* chronicle actual dogfights (under the guise of fictionality), binding together an underground community of fervent dogmen (Gibson 2005). An estimated 40,000 adults and 100,000 kids and teenagers in the United States fight dogs (Peters 2008), although the actual number is almost certainly higher. Consider that in 2003 alone, the city of Chicago responded to 1,093 animal fighting complaints.[8] In the early 1990s, pit bulls made up only 2 to 3 percent of the dogs coming into shelters; by 2007, they made up 30 to 60 percent, with a good number showing scars from fighting. With bets ranging from pocket change to tens of thousands of dollars, dogfighting is now a half-billion-dollar industry in the United States (Gibson 2005).

The life of the fighting dog is nasty, brutish, and short – and almost always ends in a violent death. Indeed, the cruelty of the practice, animal advocates say, lies as much in the way the dog is made to live as in the way he or she is made to die. To begin with, dogs are genetically manipulated to alter normal canine behavior (such as growling before attacking and ceasing to fight when injured or when the other dog submits), to be more dog aggressive, to have a more powerful bite, to be willing to fight through pain and to the death (Strouse 2009). Female dogs who resist breeding are placed in breeding stands

---

[6] Ibid.

[7] The Animal Fighting Prohibition Enforcement Act of 2007 was signed into law on May 3, 2007. The law upgrades current penalties by creating felony-level jail time (up to 3 years) for violations of the federal animal fighting law.

[8] Gibson (2005), 5.

or "rape racks" that immobilize them so that the male dog can penetrate them at will. Spending his entire life outside, chained to a buried car axle, with only a barrel or small kennel for protection from the elements, the fighting dog is kept just close enough to other dogs to keep him riled up but never close enough to have contact and become socialized. Dogmen routinely taunt, starve, and drug dogs to heighten their aggression, and they use cats, small dogs, and rabbits (some of whom are stolen family pets) as "bait" to create an appetite for killing and for blood. They put each dog through a grueling exercise regimen involving running with heavy chains around his neck and running on a treadmill and/or a jenny (where live bait is dangled in front of the dog to make him run; he is rewarded with the bait at the end of the session). Even after being bred and raised this way, some dogs still fail the viciousness test, showing little or no inclination to fight. These dogs are promptly killed. The fighting dog is a commodity, a product of intensive human forethought, artifice, and labor.

In a fight, dogs are placed in a dirt pit ranging from eight to sixteen square feet and surrounded by a three-foot-high fence and set upon each other for a fight to the death. Fights often last for hours and end with the death of one dog or when one dog cannot or will not continue. Semencic writes that a dogman capitalizes on his dog's desire to please him, changing position around the edge of the pit "in order to be in sight of his dog at all times."[9] The dog's love for his master, his desire to please, is the force that drives him to his own destruction. Dogs who do not die fighting will often die hours or days later from broken bones, puncture wounds, blood loss, shock, dehydration, or infection. Veteran criminal investigators describe finding pits full of blood, corpses of dogs, dogs with dozens of open wounds and half of their jaws missing, dogs with most of their bodies covered in scar tissue.

Consider this description of a fight:[10]

His face is a mass of deep cuts, as are his shoulders and neck. Both of his front legs have been broken, but Billy Bear isn't ready to quit. At the referee's signal, his master releases him, and unable to support himself on his front legs, he slides on his chest across the blood and urine stained carpet, propelled by his good hind legs, toward the opponent who rushes to meet him. Driven by instinct, intensive training and love for the owner who has brought him to this moment, Billy Bear drives himself painfully into the other dog's charge. ... Less than 20 minutes later, rendered useless by the other dog, Billy Bear lies spent beside his master, his stomach constricted with pain. He turns his head back toward the ring, his eyes glazed searching for a last look at the other dog as [sic] receives a bullet in his brain.

And this one:

Snow and Black lunge at each other. Snow rears up and overpowers Black, but Black manages to come back with a quick locking of the jaws on Snow's neck. The crowd is cheering wildly and yelling out bets. ... It looks like Black is hung up so Norman motions for the handlers to separate the dogs. ... [Next] Snow races toward Black and is not going to let

[9] Semencic (1992), 67–8.
[10] Gibson (2005), 7–8 quoting C. M. Brown, "Pit," *Atlanta Magazine*, 1982, 66.

Black get the best of her. Snow goes straight for the throat and grabs hold with her razor sharp teeth. Almost immediately, blood flows from Black's throat. Despite a severe injury to the throat, Black manages to continue fighting back ... this fighting continues for an hour. ... [Black] is severely wounded. Black manages to crawl across the pit to meet her opponent. Snow attacks Black and she is too weak to fight back. L.G. realizes that this is it for Black and calls the fight. Snow is declared the winner. Rick collects his money. L.G. then lifts Black from the pit and carries her out back. Her back legs are broken and blood is gushing from her throat. A shot rings out barely heard over the noise in the barn. (Evans and Forsyth 1997, 64–5)

Why must the losing dog be killed? Rhonda Evans, DeAnn Gauthier, and Craig Forsyth write, "In the sport of dogfighting, the actual combatants serve as *symbols* of their respective owners, and therefore any character attributed to the dogs is also attributed to the men they represent."[11] Dogmen attest to this: "I only expect a dog to be as good as the man behind him, not any more, not any less"; "I expect the same thing out of my dog as I expect out of myself. A dog is only as good as his master."[12] "Gameness" or the willingness to fight to the death, is the most prized quality, while the most despised dog is the so-called cur, one who turns away from the attacking opponent. Alan Dundes's description of cockfighting as a "thinly disguised symbolic homoerotic masturbatory phallic duel, with the winner emasculating the loser through castration or feminization" is an apt description of dogfighting, too.[13] Killing curs quickly and brutally helps to alleviate the owner's humiliation and restore his injured masculinity. Dogs who fight hard but lose may be killed or simply left to die. A dogfight, then, distributes honor, status, and manhood, not just prize money.

Dogmen deny charges of cruelty and insist that their dogs choose to fight, that they love doing it, that it's their nature (Forsyth and Evans 1998).[14] While they do not present an alternative ontology as Makah whalers do, they, too, interpret the human-animal interaction in a way that emphasizes reciprocity and elides any suggestion of coercion, domination, or violence. Likening themselves to coaches and their dogs to prizefighters, dogmen claim that they are in fact helping their dogs by enabling them to reach their full potential or fulfill their nature. It might be more accurate, though, to call dogmen artificers of dog natures rather than actualizers of dog natures. "Nature" has been carefully *made* in this case through centuries of selective breeding, myriad training techniques, and, ultimately, the elimination of dogs who do not want to fight. (Are these dogs betrayers of dog nature?) In dogfighting, as in rodeos and bullfighting, humans deliberately contour an animal genetically and biologically and manipulate the animal's physical and mental state of being – and then present the animal's behavior as a reflection of its pure "nature." It is only by

---

[11] Evans et al. (1998), 832.
[12] Ibid., 831.
[13] Cited in Kalof and Taylor (2007), 321; Dundes (1994), 251.
[14] This discussion of dogmen's claims is based on the scholarship cited, which looks at white Southern rural male subjects. Michael Vick has said very little publicly about his views on dogfighting, but the comments he has made are consistent with the perspective of these men.

concealing the hand of human artifice that the spectacle succeeds as a ritualized demonstration of the masculine conquest over (or within) nature.

What does it mean to say a dog chooses to fight? He certainly exercises agency in turning to face and attack the opponent, and in responding to the urgings of his owner/handler throughout the fight. But when human artifice is this heavily involved in the production of the fighting dog, ascertaining the dog's "choices" is not a straightforward matter. Dog phenomenal world(s) are closely imbricated with human phenomenal world(s) because of thousands of years of domestication, cooperation, and training (Haraway 2007). We have an intimate, daily knowledge of them that gives us confidence in declaring what they want or need, but it is their very intimacy with us – their acute responsiveness to our manipulations – that should shake this confidence. If dogs were not bred for aggression, were socialized with other dogs, were not subjected to training regimens and narcotics intended to heighten aggression, and were not urged on by their owners and handlers, would they choose to fight? If it is their nature to fight, why is all of this human labor necessary? If a human fought for his or her life under these circumstances, rather than submit to an attacking opponent, would we consider the word "choice" appropriate?

The analogy between the prizefighter and the fighting dog breaks down precisely because humans can meaningfully choose to fight – and part of what makes that choice meaningful is that they have other plausible options and can choose *not to fight*. They are authors of their own destinies in ways that dogs are not. The lethal brutality toward so-called curs is not consistent, in any case, with a framework emphasizing the dog's free will. It is consistent, rather, with a framework where the fighting dog is the symbol of his owner's aggression and strength. The proper fate for a disobedient symbol is elimination.

"Love" is the dogman's other answer to the charge of cruelty. Michael Vick said in a recent press conference that he has a "different kind of loving dogs" (Winograd 2011). Dogmen have powerful affective investments in their dogs and dogfighting, in many cases deriving their sense of self from this practice. They put in time and effort, enjoy a secretive social world stitched together by blood and illegality, and savor their dogs' victories as validation of their expertise, knowledge, and manhood. But the instrumentalization and commodification of the fighting dog, almost always ending in his or her violent destruction, is not a process that sits easily with a standard notion of love as an other-regarding disposition.

Michael Vick was not caught in the act of fighting dogs or killing dogs. The evidence against him, both testimonial and forensic, was slowly pieced together to suggest what he had done. In this sense, there was a spectral element to the story, with the dead dogs coming back to be heard through their bones and blood.[15] Animal control officer Kathy Strouse recalls that night at 1915

[15] On spectral dogs, see Carla Freccero (2010, 2011).

Moonlight Road when she climbed a ladder and came upon the room where Vick and his associates had fought dogs:

I climbed towards the opening that gave way to the second level, where I came face to face with a large drip of what appeared to be dried blood. Continuing upward, I finally stood and surveyed the room … the entire room was painted black. Despite the black paint, we could see spatters and smears of more blood on the walls. In the center of the floor was a clean rectangular pattern. It appeared that this was where the carpet had been laid to provide traction for the fighting dogs and to absorb the blood. Around the edges of this clean pattern were more blood spatters, stains and smears. Next to a folding chair on the right of the access opening, was a plastic bucket and lid. On top of this was a tooth. It looked like a canine tooth from a dog. There was a boom box on the floor and a blood streaked sweatshirt jacket hung from the air conditioner. None of us spoke.[16]

The dogs who bled and died there haunt the room, their physical traces evoking images of agony and death in those still living. Vick's friends testified to the methods they all used to kill dogs who did not seem interested in fighting:

- Hanging by a nylon cord thrown over a two by four nailed between two trees
- Drowning by holding the dogs' heads submerged in a five-gallon bucket of water
- Shooting in the head
- Electrocuting by attaching jumper cables to the dogs' ears and throwing them in the swimming pool
- Slamming against the ground repeatedly

Again, the dogs buried at 1915 Moonlight Road spoke from the grave. The forensic report indicated facial fractures, broken necks from hanging, broken legs and vertebrae, and severe bone bruising. Most of the dogs had skull fractures, possibly from a hammer. Jim Gorant (2010) writes of one dog who was still alive after being hung:

There was one last body that stood out from the rest. It had signs of bruising on all four ankles and all along one side. Its skull was fractured in two places and it had four broken vertebrae. … [A]s that dog lay on the ground fighting for air, Quanis Phillips grabbed its front legs and Michael Vick grabbed its hind legs. They swung the dog over their head like a jump rope and slammed it to the ground. The first impact didn't kill it. So Phillips and Vick slammed it again. The two men kept at it, alternating back and forth, pounding the creature against the ground, until at last, the little red dog was dead.[17]

Is haunting a form of justice, where the ungrievable dogs return to indict their killer? Vick's own body bore the signs of this haunting. After months of denying that he had personally killed dogs, he failed an FBI polygraph on the issue (October 12, 2007) and blurted out, "Yeah fine, I killed the dogs. I hung them. I slammed them. I killed all of them. I lost fucking millions, all over some fucking dogs" before his attorney Billy Martin ushered him out of the building.[18]

[16] Strouse (2009), 25.
[17] Gorant (2010), 93.
[18] Strouse (2009), 135.

Animal advocates, too, have been haunted by Vick's dogs. Donna Reynolds of BAD RAP (Bay Area Doglovers Responsible About Pitbulls), who helped to rehabilitate some of Vick's dogs, says she cannot get out of her head the details of dogs who were connected by cable to car battery terminals and then thrown in Vick's swimming pool:

I can't shake my minds-eye image of a little black dog splashing frantically in the bloody water ... screaming in pain and terror ... brown eyes saucer wide and tiny black white-toed feet clawing at anything, desperate to get a hold. This death did not come quickly. The rescuer in me keeps trying to think of a way to go back in time and somehow stop this torture and pull the little dog to safety. I think I'll be looking for ways to pull that dog out for the rest of my life.[19]

It is their ardent desire to make these dead dogs grievable, even if *retroactively*, that drives some animal advocates to refuse the notion that Vick has repented and is now redeemed. As long as Vick struggles, as long as the metaphorical jury on him is still out, there is a fragile portal open through which the spectral dogs can be heard.

This goes some way to explaining why Wayne Pacelle, president of the Humane Society of the United States, came under serious friendly fire when he signed Vick on as an anti-dogfighting spokesperson after his release from prison. Pacelle had in mind appropriating Vick's Blackness, fame, and urban authenticity for the anti-dogfighting cause, just as Vick set out to trade on the good reputation of the HSUS as part of his public rehabilitation campaign. It was a move that infuriated PETA and other animal advocates who wanted to maintain a chorus of condemnation against Vick indefinitely (Winograd 2011; Cooper 2012). Although it bolstered Vick's public relations project, Pacelle's intervention also had the important effect of shifting the issue from a purely characterological one (just how pathological is Michael Vick) to one that was still characterological but with social/political overtones (how do we persuade young Black and Latino men in blighted urban areas that dogfighting is a dead end?).

Some leading animal advocates pointedly shifted attention from Vick's specific deeds to the cruel animal practices of the broader society. Peter Singer, author of *Animal Liberation*, sometimes called the "bible" of the modern animal rights movement, observed: "[T]he people who are very quick to jump on Michael Vick maybe could spend some time thinking about how they participate in the cruelty to animals just by walking into the supermarket."[20] Similarly, in an article entitled "We Are All Michael Vick" (2009), legal scholar Gary Francione said the reaction to Vick revealed "our 'moral schizophrenia' about animals" in that the treatment of animals in modern industrial farming is just as cruel and no more justifiable than the treatment of fighting dogs.

[19] Keith (2009).
[20] "Are Animal Advocates Giving Michael Vick a Pass?"

Francione continues: "How removed from the screaming crowd around the dog pit is the laughing group around the summer steak barbeque?" Most of us presume that dogs are more important than cows and pigs and chickens; we presume, too, that we are innocent of cruelty while we shake our heads at Vick. Singer and Francione aim to disrupt our complacency and direct our attention to the institutionalized exploitation and violence toward animals that happens on a massive scale every day in this country *and is normalized*. However, it is not clear whether this rhetorical strategy makes us see animal suffering more broadly and more clearly or whether it makes us simply throw up our hands at its pervasiveness. Does the wrong of cruelty, once generalized, disappear from view? If everybody is cruel, is anybody cruel?

THE OPTIC OF RACISM AND THE PARABLE OF BLACK RECALCITRANCE

Blogger Kym Platt (2007), who is Black, wrote: "[M]any in the black community believe that because of his [Vick's] stature and fame and his blackness, he is being made an example of and is suffering from overly harsh public censures." In the blogosphere, on radio and television, and in print, Vick's defenders alluded to the criminal justice system as a historic instrument of racial oppression and terror and argued that whites took special delight in bringing down famous Black men such as Mike Tyson, O. J. Simpson, Kobe Bryant, Barry Bonds – and now Michael Vick.[21] For some Black civil rights and community leaders, this called for closing ranks around Vick as one of their own. Reverend Joseph Lowery, a veteran of the Montgomery Bus Boycott and other civil rights movement actions, said from the pulpit: "Michael Vick is my son. I've never met him. But he is my son." Southern Christian Leadership Conference president Charles Steele, too, stated: "We need to support him no matter what the evidence reveals." Kwame Abernathy's characterization of events as an "electronic lynching" was echoed by the head of the Atlanta chapter of the NAACP, Reverend R. L. White,[22] although the NAACP national office took no position on the matter and interim president Dennis Hayes commented: "[Vick] was in control of his actions at all times and should be held accountable for what he did" (Johnson 2007).

Polls suggested that Blacks were more likely than whites to think the media had covered Vick unfairly, to believe that Vick's punishment was too harsh, and to support his reinstatement to the NFL after his release from prison, although Blacks were far from unanimous on these issues. A Pew survey on August 28, 2007 showed that 51 percent of Blacks felt the press treatment of Vick had

[21] According to *Animal People* (June 2007, September 2007), Black NFL running back Todd McNair was twice convicted in the 1990s of animal neglect charges related to dogfighting and given fines and probation; NFL player LeShon Johnson and NBA player Qyntel Woods were also given fines and probation after being convicted of or pleading guilty to such charges.
[22] Thompson n.d.

been unfair, while 38 percent believed it had been fair. For whites, the figures were 12 percent and 60 percent, respectively.[23] Thirty-one percent of nonwhites and 9 percent of whites thought Vick's punishment was too harsh; 70.1 percent of nonwhites and 53 percent of whites agreed with Vick's reinstatement to the NFL.[24] A racial gap is evident in these numbers, but so, too, is the diversity of Black opinion.

When NFL players were polled by ESPN, 57.1 percent said they believed race "mattered" in the public's perception of Vick, and one specifically mentioned the imperative of putting a Black quarterback in his place.[25] Did Vick's anomalous position as a Black NFL quarterback make him an irresistible target? Scrupulously catalogued and scrupulously denied, "stacking" or positional segregation is a well-known secret in American professional sports (Schneider and Eitzen 1984; Coakley 1998; Buffington 2005).[26] Based on the notion that Black players are only bodies not minds, stacking involves placing white players in positions thought to require leadership, intelligence, and decision making (such as quarterback in football, point guard in basketball, and pitcher and catcher in baseball) while confining Black players to positions thought to require strength, speed, and agility (Primm, DuBois, and Regoli 2007). Both media commentators and football scouts continuously reproduce the racial tropes underlying this practice by describing Black athletes in physical terms and white athletes in mental ones (Woodward 2004; Mercurio and Filak 2010).[27] Standard descriptions of white quarterbacks ("An intelligent 4-year starter. Very productive." / "Heady quarterback who sees the field and reads defenses well." / "Natural leader with good size.") can be productively juxtaposed with standard descriptions of Black quarterbacks ("A *freakish* athlete who is more dangerous as a runner than a thrower." / "A Big, strong kid who can run.").[28] Despite the fact that nearly 70 percent of NFL players today are Black, the Black quarterback remained, until very recently, a relative rarity.[29]

[23] "Michael Vick Case Draws Large Audience."
[24] Piquero et al. (2011), 544. Unfortunately, the nonwhite category is not broken down here.
[25] Clemmons et al. (2011).
[26] My thanks to John Cline for raising this issue with me.
[27] The same goes for honorary white players. In Kim (2012), I note that Chinese American NBA player Jeremy Lin was heavily praised for his intelligence, diligence, organization, and preparation (all model minority traits) as a player.
[28] Bigler and Jeffries (2008), 134, 138.
[29] For decades, Black quarterbacks coming out of high school or college were persuaded to change positions in order to get hired by an NFL team. Some, like Warren Moon, opted to play in the Canadian Football League, which did not pursue stacking with the same zeal as its southern counterpart. From 1983 to 1998, Blacks were only 9 percent of quarterbacks in the NFL although they were more than 66 percent of overall players. In the early 1980s, there were only two consistently starting Black quarterbacks, Warren Moon and Doug Williams. In April 1999, three Black quarterbacks were chosen in the first round of the NFL draft, while up to that point only four Black quarterbacks had been first round picks in the entire history of the draft. By 1999, 21 percent of all quarterbacks were Black. See Lapchick (2001). The 2013 NFL season featured a record nine Black starting quarterbacks.

Vick's dramatic success on the field made him an intruder on hallowed (white) ground. Brock Cohen writes: "NFL quarterback is one of the last islands in the nation's collective cultural imagination that remains the exclusive province of white males. Which means the image of a black quarterback calling the shots on a last-minute, game-winning TD drive is ... alarming to a significant segment of the American populace."[30] Add to this the fact that Vick's style – in particular his penchant for running the ball – seemed so Black:

When Michael Vick plays, I see ... street basketball. Vick's style reminds me of Allen Iverson – the speed, the court sense, the sharp cuts, the dekes, the swag. ... Vick seems to have a deeply African-American approach to the game. I'm not saying that a black QB who stands in the pocket ain't playing black. I'm saying Vick's style is so badass, so artistic, so fluid, so flamboyant, so relentless – so representative of black athletic style.[31]

This commentator is celebrating what he sees as Vick's Black style, but many others in the media and NFL saw this style as something to be policed and contained. The anxiety about Black quarterbacks defying the rules and changing the game can be seen in descriptions of them as a "new breed," "running quarterbacks," or even "runningbacks at the quarterback position" (Buffington 2005).

A couple of dust-ups over the past decade indicate that Black incursions into this particular territory of whiteness continue to meet stiff resistance. On September 28, 2003, Rush Limbaugh remarked on Philadelphia Eagles quarterback Donovan McNabb on ESPN's *NFL Countdown*: "Sorry to say this. I don't think he's been that good from the get-go. ... What we have here is a little social concern in the NFL. The media has been very desirous that a Black quarterback can do well. ... There's a little hope invested in McNabb, and he got credit for the performance of his team that he didn't deserve."[32] Reiterating an insistent conservative political theme, Limbaugh not only denies the persistence of racism in the NFL but suggests that the real problem is one of preferential treatment for Blacks.

Years later, Hall of Fame Black quarterback Warren Moon asserted that Black quarterback prospects continue to be evaluated unfairly, pointing to a *Pro Football* weekly scouting report by Nolan Nowrocki on West Virginia's star quarterback Geno Smith. Nowrocki, who had famously trashed Black quarterbacks Cam Newton and Robert Griffin III in previous years, had this to say about Geno Smith: "Not committed or focused – marginal work ethic. Interviewed poorly at the Combine and did not show an understanding of concepts on the white board. ... Will be overdrafted and struggle to produce against NFL defensive complexities."[33] The Black athlete as body not mind. Moon's

---

[30] Cohen (2011).
[31] Toure (2011).
[32] Hartmann (2007), 46.
[33] Florio (2013). Geno Smith fared less well in the draft than expected. He was picked in the second round, thirty-ninth overall by the New York Jets. He is now their starting quarterback.

comments about Nowrocki provoked online responses that were scathing and revealing: "I maintain that Warren Moon is a racist" / "Warren Moon … The Al Sharpton and Jesse Jackson of the NFL" / "Every player, coach and owner could be black and this idiot would still be crying."[34]

That Vick was already seen at some level as representing transgressive, incorrigible Blackness in a white space made him a perfect subject of a racial parable. In 2010, Black Entertainment Television aired *The Michael Vick Project*, a ten-part series that described Vick's rise, fall, and attempted comeback. Partly a chronicle of penitence, mostly a hagiography, the series was a centerpiece, along with *Finally Free: An Autobiography by Michael Vick* (2012), in Vick's strategic effort, aided by "at least seven public relations advisors" (Leitch 2011), to rehabilitate his public image. BET's series is organized around a basic duality reflected in its cover graphic, a headshot of Vick with one set of words to his left (Crime/Tragedy/Shame/Fear/Failure/Consequences) and another to his right (Punishment/Triumph/Honor/Courage/Redemption/Truth). At the bottom of the image, a summarizing statement: "A Life in Progress." This is not just a film project about or by Vick, *Vick is the project*.

I suggested earlier that there was no way for us to read the Vick story other than as a parable of Black recalcitrance. That is to say, ubiquitous and tenacious tropes about Black masculinity as violent, criminal, hypersexual, and animal overdetermined the narrow terms in which Vick's story could become culturally legible to us. Vick came from the ghetto, he was sued by a woman for allegedly giving her genital herpes and sought treatment for herpes under the pseudonym "Ron Mexico," he was stopped in the airport for concealing marijuana in a water bottle, he gave booing fans the finger – all of the elements were in place. And the key element: that he overcame his origins and biology and achieved the American Dream, *only to slip back and lose it all*. It is this slipping back that makes it a story of recalcitrance, of his character's resistance to improvement. In the early 1800s, proponents of slavery argued that the institution improved and civilized the Negro, but only provisionally, and that his brute-like nature would reassert itself the moment his chains were removed (Fredrickson 1971). Lewis Gordon writes about the current life of this expectation:

They are waiting. For they know I have to be on the alert. I have to be on call – no respite, no letting my guard down. Somewhere out there, until the day I die, there is the weight of predestined failure. To be black is to *be*, as Du Bois observed, a "problem." I have seen many black men struggle, struggle hard, and then just when they are about to achieve their goal, they go to pieces. They slip into a horrid absurdity. "What's up with that?" a friend once asked. Yeah, what's up with that? But he knew. He knew what it was to be the exemplification of sin. To be, that is, guilty in advance. It waits. Guilty of what? Time will tell.[35]

[34] Smith (2013). Warren Moon was pressured to change positions, was passed over in the 1978 NFL draft, and spent six years in the Canadian Football League before becoming a successful NFL quarterback and the first Black quarterback in the NFL Hall of Fame.
[35] Gordon (1997), 22.

Michael Vick had it all but then predictably reverted to type. Rendered as commodified spectacle, the parable promotes the marketing of both dangerous Black masculinity in the global marketplace and national mythologies about merit, individual freedom, and opportunity (Kellner 2001; Leonard and King 2011). Structural barriers to the American Dream are refigured as character-ological or biological ones, and the drama of racial oppression is refigured as a drama of individual weakness.

Culture figured in the parable obliquely and ambiguously. Because dog-fighting is practiced by only a small segment of the Black community (and by Southern rural whites as well), culture entered the conversation not as grounds for marking and valorizing a group tradition but rather as an explanation for Vick's decisions – as an exculpatory device meant to problematize the matter of choice and thus responsibility. So, on September 4, 2007, actress Whoopi Goldberg said on ABC's *The View*: "He's [Vick's] from the South, from the Deep South. ... This is part of his cultural upbringing. For a lot of people, dogs are sport. Instead of just saying [Vick] is a beast and he's a monster, this is a kid who comes from a culture where this is not questioned." Months later, actor Jamie Foxx observed: "It's a cultural thing, I think. Most brothers didn't know that, you know. I used to see dogs fighting in the neighborhood all the time. I didn't know that was Fed time. So, Mike probably just didn't read his hand-book on what not to do as a black star."[36] Vick himself made a similar point in a *GQ* interview: "You got the family dog and the white picket fence, and you just think that's all there is. Some of us had to grow up in poverty-stricken urban neighborhoods, and we just had to adapt to our environment" (Leitch 2011). Ironically, it was left to HSUS president Wayne Pacelle, who is white, to say that dogfighting is not an accepted element of Black culture (Gorman 2007).

The parable of Vick's recalcitrance works off of a particular mode of imag-ining Black men in professional sports. In the NFL and NBA, the Black male athlete, unlike the white male athlete, is figured *ambivalently* as admirable and frightening, heroic and abject, "commodified and criminalized"(Leonard and King 2011), a site of both desire and terror (Griffin 2012). John Hoberman writes of "the white psyche's anxious oscillation between idealized and demon-ized images of blacks, who are always denied normal human status."[37] Even Michael Jordan's supposed transcendence of race was, as Ferber (2007) argues, less than a genuine transcendence than a displacement of the image of the violent Black criminal onto other players such as Charles Barkley, or later, Latrell Sprewell and Ron Artest.[38] This ambivalent figuration produces a suspenseful tension where the Black athlete is seen as always unpredictable – always about to be out of control, always about to revert to type, always a prisoner of his biology – and where his misdeeds are greeted with both condemnation and a

[36] http://www.starpulse.com/news/index.php/2007/08/24/jamie_foxx_defends_michael_vick.
[37] Hoberman (1997), xxxi.
[38] See also Hughes (2004) and Collins (2005).

pointed lack of surprise. This tension is, of course, precisely what the commodification of the Black male athlete under neoliberal capitalism requires. It is the
dangerous edge of Blackness that lures the white consumer, even as he insists
that Blackness be made safe for consumption. Thomas Oates notes that while
the NBA and NFL have for some time allowed white men "to both discipline
and imaginatively inhabit the bodies of powerful Black men," new media have
deepened the commodification process by allowing the "vicarious management"
of Black bodies through fantasy football and video games like *Madden NFL*.[39]

The NBA's shifting strategies for managing this tension around Blackness
have been remarkably transparent (Guerrero 2011). In 1984, with players widely
known for drug use and partying, teams losing money, and corporate sponsors
withdrawing, NBA commissioner David Stern said the league was "perceived as
a bunch of high-salaried, drug-sniffing black guys" and set about counteracting
this image.[40] But in the 1990s, in an effort to globalize the NBA's market appeal,
the league self-consciously attached itself to hip-hop in order to gain "urban, hip
authenticity."[41] Hip-hop stars were hired to create theme songs, some became
part owners of NBA teams, and extra baggy shorts became the norm for players. Perhaps inevitably, when the infamous "Palace Brawl" occurred in 2004
between the Detroit Pistons and Indiana Pacers, involving players going after
white spectators who had taunted them and thrown things at them, the media
laid the blame squarely on the excesses of the NBA's hip-hop culture (Leonard
2006). A league ban on hip-hop attire and other changes ensued.

David Leonard writes: "Black bodies, even those living the 'American
Dream,' functioning as million-dollar commodities, are contained and imagined as dangerous, menacing, abject, and criminal."[42] I would add: *as animal*.
Animal tropes pervade discussions of Black male athletes, to the point where
they have become normalized, working synergistically with tropes about Black
male violence, brutality, and dangerousness. Black football players, all body
not mind, are called "amazing specimen[s]" by draft experts (Bigler and Jeffries
2008). Thomas Oates writes about the assertion of the white "erotic gaze" at
the pre-NFL draft event known as the Senior Bowl, held in Mobile, Alabama
each January to showcase the best college senior players. Scouts, managers,
coaches, and the media assemble in a hotel ballroom to watch as young players, most of them Black, are stripped to their shorts, lined up, weighed, and
measured in various ways. Players say it makes them feel like a "prize bull" in
a "meat market." One team manager commented: "It's a livestock show, and
it's dehumanizing, but it's necessary ... If we're going to buy 'em, we ought to
see what we're buying."[43] The allusion to slavery, inadvertent or not, is hard
to miss. This routine, unremarkable NFL tradition functions as a ceremony of

[39] Oates (2009), 44.
[40] Guerrero (2011), 101.
[41] Ibid., 133.
[42] Leonard (2010), 259.
[43] Oates (2007), 77.

white racial power where young Black players, as object of the "erotic gaze," are raced, feminized, sexualized, and animalized all at once.

The media's treatment of Black male athletes, too, reminds us of the way that race and species continuously invigorate each other. The 2003 Nike television ad "The Battle" memorably juxtaposes gritty urban scenes of one on one basketball with a pit bull facing off against a Rottweiler in a fight. After the "Palace Brawl" of 2004, "the black bodies of the players climbing into the stands were represented as 'violent beasts.'"[44] Alluding to the fact that a white fan began the brawl by throwing a drink at Pacers players, Charles Barkley commented acerbically, "We're not animals in the zoo ... you can't throw things at us."[45] In April 2008, LeBron James was featured with supermodel Gisele Bundchen on the cover of *Vogue* magazine, and his hulking presentation, coupled with his evocative grasp on Bundchen, immediately raised questions about whether *Vogue* meant to depict him as King Kong. ESPN, in anticipation of the 2013 NBA Finals, showcased Spurs shooting guard Kawhi Leonard in a "science" segment where they measured his abnormally large "wingspan" and abnormally large "paws."[46]

Many of the cartoonists who satirized Michael Vick traded avidly in animal and racial tropes. The most salient idea was one of reversal between Vick and his dogs, between Black man and animal. One cartoon, for example, pictures Vick next to a fighting dog and the caption reads: "Pop Quiz: Find the True Animal." Dogs are frequently granted the agency of revenge, while Vick must suffer helplessly. (That Vick deserved to experience the same suffering he inflicted on his dogs was a recurrent theme in the blogosphere.) In one cartoon, a dog sitting curbside gives Vick the finger as Vick is driven away in a van labeled "Animal Control." In another, evocative of lynching, Vick is chased up a tree by a pack of braying dogs. Perhaps the most startling one shows Vick sitting in an electric chair placed in a tub of water, while a dog holding electrical wires approaches (see Figure 8.1). This powerful image not only suggests that Vick deserves a taste of his own medicine, it legitimates the U.S. criminal justice system as a tool of racial terror. The Black man must be contained or else killed, as journalist Tucker Carlson suggested when he opined on Fox News that Vick should be executed for what he had done to dogs.[47]

In these cartoons, state power champions the just cause of the dogs (the animal control van, the official tolerance of lynching, the infliction of capital punishment) and the recalcitrant Vick, victim of his own bad choices, is dealt with in a mode that can only be described as murderously carceral. The state's complicity in institutionalized violence against Blacks and dogs – in, among other things, the blight inflicted upon poor Black neighborhoods like Vick's by neoliberal capitalism, the injustice of mass incarceration and capital punishment

---

[44] Griffin and Calafell (2011), cited in Griffin (2012), 168.
[45] Griffin (2012), 169.
[46] June 5, 2013.
[47] "Tucker Carlson: Michael Vick 'Should Have Been Executed.'"

FIGURE 8.1. "If It's Good Enough for Dogs …". Cartoon courtesy of Mike Lester.

policies, and the "euthanasia" of millions of dogs a year in U.S. shelters – is, in the meantime, quietly and effectively concealed.

The parable of Black recalcitrance temporalizes the image of the ambivalently figured Black athlete, dramatizing his state of being as a movement or journey – "a life in progress." Ladies and gentlemen, what will the Black male athlete choose? Will he successfully transcend biology or will he revert to type? How many mistakes will he make and how many chances will he be given? Vick's attempted comeback since his release from prison fits squarely in this narrative. Maharaj (1997) notes that Black athletes are depicted as having to choose between the "nightmare/street" and the "dream/NBA"; Cole and King (1998) see the choice depicted as one between "gangs" and "sports." I suggest that another dyad overlaid upon these is that of "beast" and "human," so that the choice before Vick was one between ghetto, nightmare, criminality, evil, and bestiality, on the one hand, and riches, dream, sport, goodness, civilization, and humanity on the other. Vick chose well initially but then slipped back. He frequently blamed his involvement in dogfighting on his unsavory acquaintances: "A lot of my poor decisions and subsequent mistakes can be attributed mostly to two things: my weak resolve in telling people no, and the people I chose to be associated with. I had an entourage of pretty questionable characters."[48] Might it be that Vick, as a Black man, can only ever have a "life in progress" – one that perennially stops short of a fully human life?

[48] Vick (2012), 86.

The parable of recalcitrance has paused with a post-prison Michael Vick who is chastened, submissive, domesticated. There is now no sign of the attitude and swagger of old. Vick is no longer resisting the good and is eloquent about what his past resistance cost him. In *Finally Free* (a title that suggests he is both out of prison and rid of his inner demons), Vick sums up his story: He worked hard until he had it all. Then he lost his way, hit rock bottom, found God, and realized the error of his ways. Now he is climbing his way back to the top. The tripartite organization of the book – The Rise, The Fall, The Redemption – is a classical structure reminiscent of ancient Greek dramas and Christian morality tales. Indeed, the book is part American Dream, part *Autobiography of Malcolm X*, with a measure of Greek mythology thrown in (Vick compares himself to Icarus, whose hubris caused him to fly too high and too close to the sun). Vick's spectacle of penitence – his quiet apologies, subdued demeanor, and assumption of a new role as an anti-dogfighting spokesperson for the Humane Society of the United States – achieved its purpose. Vick was reinstated by the NFL, signed by the Philadelphia Eagles in 2009, and re-signed by Nike. He was nominated by his teammates for the Ed Block Award for courage and sportsmanship, and he also received the Associated Press NFL Comeback Player of the Year Award. In 2011, Vick signed an $80 million, five-year deal with the Eagles. The continuing cyberspace chatter about "what is really in Michael Vick's heart," however, suggests that for many observers, the conclusion to the parable is still uncertain.

HOW PIT BULLS BECAME BLACK

To Americans at the start of the new millennium, the dog is the most human of animals – not in terms of appearance or cognitive ability or percentage of shared DNA, but in terms of intimacy, familiarity, and identification. More so than with any other animal (including turtles, frogs, and whales), we feel for dogs and explore the frontiers of interspecies communication and love with them (Hearne 2007; Haraway 2007; Kohn 2007; Weaver 2013). We readily speak on their behalf and recruit them to causes, as when people dressed their dogs in t-shirts that read "My Dog Hates Michael Vick."

Of course, this intimacy is structured in dominance. Our concern for dogs is contingent and, from the dog's point of view, sadly unreliable. We use dogs as instruments for our own ends – companionship, security, vanity, to track missing children, to herd sheep, to rescue us in the Alps, to help us when we are disabled, to sniff out drugs in the airport, to cheer up sick children in the hospital. We are taken with dogs, but we dispose of them at will. We embrace them as family members, but we turn them into the local shelter to be killed when they pee on the rug one too many times. We countenance their maltreatment in research, breeding, entertainment, and sport. We seek out "pure breeds" from breeders and pet stores as millions of other dogs are slaughtered in shelters every year across the country. How we are with dogs is a reminder that benevolent dominance is still dominance (Tuan 2004).

Pit bulls in particular experience malevolent forms of human domination.[49] The breed's image and fortunes have declined precipitously in the past thirty years. In the 1800s, pit bulls were frontier farm dogs cherished as family companions because of their mild temperament and loyalty. In the early 1900s, they were the "all-American family pet": Helen Keller and Teddy Roosevelt owned pit bulls, and Petey in *The Little Rascals* was a pit bull, as was the dog in the beloved Buster Brown shoe commercials. Stubby the pit bull served in World War I, received both a Purple Heart and a Gold Medal of Valor, and was honored at a White House ceremony (Medlin 2007, Twining, Arluke and Patronek 2001). The decisive shift occurred when young Black men in blighted urban areas took up dogfighting in the 1980s and began using pit bulls "as extensions of social status, as symbols of masculine power, as tools to intimidate others, and as weapons for the protection of property and illicit drug activities."[50] A "pit bull panic" (Cohen and Richardson 2002) ensued, with the media widely sensationalizing pit bull attacks and demonizing the breed. By 1987, *U.S. News & World Report* dubbed the pit bull "the most dangerous dog in America."[51] Now the hypervisible image of the pit bull is one of a hired (and all too willing) assassin. Separately, the young Black man and the pit bull make people cross to the other side of the street; together, they are a picture of unmitigated threat.

The pit bull is now raced Black in the American imagination. As we saw in Chapter 5 with invasive species, animals are often raced in the national imaginary to register the sense of threat they pose. That is to say, race, which borrows from species, gives back to it; race is part of the lexicon by which species is made just as species is part of the lexicon by which race is made. Like Blacks, pit bulls have been constructed as a group of beings whose behavior is biologically determined as violent, ruthless, and dangerous. Like Blacks, pit bulls are often victims of a "shoot first and ask questions later" policy by police. Like Blacks, they are objects of public loathing and fear whose very presence provokes a strongly disciplinary (if not murderous) response. Subject to human cruelty but also putatively inclined to do great harm, the pit bull is both victim and aggressor, at best an ambiguously figured object of public sympathy in dogfighting cases.

Multiple practices further the process of dog racialization. Law enforcement has deepened the association of Black urban criminality and pit bulls with its

[49] Harlan Weaver writes about the loose definition of the pit bull breed: "Keeping in mind that contemporary dog breeds are regulated and determined by kennel clubs, not biologists, one can see that this confusion is partly due to the shifting history of breed politics: the American Kennel Club (AKC), in an effort to distance its registries from dogs with reputations as fighters, began to recognize the American Staffordshire Terrier (AmStaf) in the 1930s, while the United Kennel Club (UKC) continued to register the American Pit Bull Terrier (APBT) throughout the 20th century. Add to this the fact that the American Dog Breeder's Association (ADBA) also has a registry for APBTs, and the confusion as to what exactly pit bull stands for is easy to see" (2013, 691). See also Ortiz (2009).
[50] Kalof and Taylor (2007), 328.
[51] April 20, 1987.

recent development of state-level joint task forces aimed at tackling together a number of associated gang activities such as dogfighting, gambling, drug dealing, and illegal weapons sales (Malanga 2007; Siebert 2010).[52]

Although race is not openly mentioned in these efforts, the indelible impression here is pit bull = gang = Black. Hip-hop, too, cements this association. Resting on the commodification of Black urban authenticity, it treats dogfighting as an unquestioned aspect of this phenomenon. One of DMX's CDs, *Grand Champ*, features a pit bull on the cover; the liner notes explain that a grand champ is a three-time winner. Jay-Z's video *99 Problems* shows him handling a fighting dog in the pit, and 50 Cent and Snoop Dog have also referenced dogfighting in their music videos. Nor is it just in the music: DMX was convicted of animal cruelty charges in relation to dogfighting in 2009 (Medlin 2007).

Pit bulls are dying for being Black. Hundreds of U.S. cities and counties have responded to "pit bull panic" by passing breed-specific legislation (BSL) that bans or otherwise regulates the ownership of pit bulls. In places with strict bans, the state confiscates pit bulls from their owners and promptly kills them. Opponents of BSL call it BDL, or breed-discriminatory legislation, evoking the analogy to racial discrimination to awaken sympathy for the pit bull (but also unavoidably reproducing the association with Blackness).[53] Harlan Weaver writes: "BSL names and labels as innate (and often, unpredictable) the qualities of danger and viciousness in the bodies of specific kinds of dogs. ... [This is] pit bull profiling. Simply put, BSL produces pit bulls and pit bull-type dogs as criminalized beings." Weaver notes that pit bull advocates develop "pit bull underground railroad[s]" to evade BSL and that they speak of fighting "canine racism."[54] Attorney Ledy Van Kavage, who works for Best Friends Animal Society, deploys this analogy when she denounces BSL as "canine profiling" (Campbell 2009).

[52] A study of dogfighters in Chicago over a three-year period showed that 86 percent had two previous arrests, 70 percent had previously committed felonies, and 59 percent were in street gangs (Ortiz 2009, 57). Law enforcement is now going after dogfighting more seriously than before because they perceive it to be linked to myriad other illegal activities involving drugs, gambling, and weapons. As a result, they are developing policies intended to address all of these illicit practices together. See Randour and Hardiman (2007).

[53] The overall case against BSL or BDL is strong (Medlin 2007). Studies show that pit bull bans lead to an increase in other breed bites (See "Position Statement on Breed-Specific Legislation," American Society for the Prevention of Cruelty to Animals). Dog advocates instead favor breed-neutral dangerous dog laws that target owner behavior (spay/neuter, chaining, neglect) not dog breeds; these have been shown to reduce bites overall, whereas no studies show the effectiveness of BSL. A task force formed in Prince Georges County, Maryland in 2003 to examine the impact of the pit bull ban there concluded that the county spent more than $250,000 per year to round up and destroy banned dogs and that public safety had not been improved by the ban. In the hundreds of municipalities that have BSL, lawsuits have been filed arguing that the laws violate substantive due process and equal protection, and that they are unacceptably vague (Campbell 2009). Marmer (1984) argues that BSL is unconstitutional because it infringes on due process (because of the difficulty in identifying "pit bulls") and equal protection (because the laws are underinclusive).

[54] Weaver (2013), 693–4.

Pit bulls now make up an estimated 30–60 percent of the dogs at U.S. shelters and are the most frequently euthanized type of dog in the nation (Muhammad 2012). They are killed by dogmen when they resist fighting, they are killed by other dogs in fights, they are killed by shelter workers because they are discarded in large numbers and then passed over for adoption or not put up for adoption in the first place. About 75 percent of municipal shelters euthanize pit bulls *immediately* upon intake, without them ever having any chance at adoption.[55] An estimated 3 million pit bulls are killed in shelters annually in the United States.[56] In the Los Angeles area alone, 200 are put to sleep per day. A study by *Animal People* reports a 93 percent euthanasia rate for abandoned pit bulls and estimates that only 1 in 600 will find a forever home.[57]

All of this is based on racialized hysteria, not fact. Sensationalistic media accounts notwithstanding, there are no reliable findings on the relative dangerousness of pit bulls to other breeds (i.e., bite rates) because of inadequate data on how many pit bulls exist within the United States (Sacks et al. 2000). For this reason, the Center for Disease Control strongly recommends against BSL on the grounds that the data used by lawmakers is fraught with error.[58] The American Kennel Club, HSUS, ASPCA, American Veterinary Medical Association, and National Animal Control Association, too, among other organizations, oppose such legislation. Pit bulls have been bred to be aggressive toward other dogs but friendly to people so that they could be handled easily in the pit (Cohen and Richardson 2002). Indeed, the American pit bull terrier, Staffordshire bull terrier, and American Staffordshire terrier (all breeds that get placed under the imprecise rubric of "pit bull")[59] all earn an above-average and passing score on the American Temperament Test – near or above the Golden Retriever's score (Medlin 2007).

When the Vick story broke, animal advocates asked the public to move from seeing pit bulls as a raced threat that must be exterminated to subjects who deserve sympathy and care. The re-figuration of the pit bull as victim of human cruelty was precariously achieved and regularly contradicted, as when the HSUS pursued its policy of recommending that all dogs seized in fighting raids be killed. Because of the intervention of other animal welfare groups, the court appointed animal law professor Rebecca Huss as a special master to oversee temperament evaluations on Vick's dogs. In the end, only one of the more than fifty dogs was killed because of temperament problems. The rest were adopted into families or went to live in sanctuaries, such as Best Friends in Kanab, Utah, which took in twenty-two of the "Vicktory dogs" and created a blog about their rehabilitation.[60] Some became therapy dogs tasked with

---

[55] "Pit Bulls and Euthanasia Rates."
[56] *Off the Chain: A Shocking Exposé on America's Foresaken Breed.*
[57] "Pit Bulls and Euthanasia Rates."
[58] "Position Statement on Breed-Specific Legislation."
[59] See note 49.
[60] http://bestfriends.org/The-Sanctuary/Explore-the-Sanctuary/Dogtown/Vicktory-Dogs/.

FIGURE 8.2. Lucas.
Source: Photo courtesy of Best Friends Animal Sanctuary, Kanab, Utah.

comforting ailing human patients. Lucas (Figure 8.2), who died recently, was one of the Vicktory dogs. The animal advocates involved in these rescue and rehabilitation efforts saw the Vick case as a once in a lifetime opportunity to speak out for this maligned breed, to counteract the myths of biological determinism and demonstrate that pit bulls, if handled with love and care, are loyal, smart, affectionate, gentle, wonderful dogs. Above all, it was a chance to get the public to see these dogs as individual beings with life stories that mattered to them.

FROM DISAVOWAL TO AVOWAL (AND CRITIQUE)

During the Vick controversy, animal advocates and race advocates adopted a posture of disavowal toward each other's claims. Most animal advocates did not use explicitly anti-Black rhetoric about Vick, but their criticisms of him as cruel, brutal, and pathological resonated with persistent tropes of incorrigible Black male criminality and violence. In addition, they claimed that the Vick case had "nothing to do with race." One caller on NPR's *Talk of the Nation* said: "I don't care if Michael Vick was black, white, green, purple. To me, this is not a story about color."[61] PETA's blog on the Vick case stated emphatically,

---

[61] "Race Played Factor in Vick Coverage, Critics Say."

"This is not a race issue. We don't care if he's [Vick's] orange. This is not a race issue. White people who fight dogs need to fry. This is not a race issue."[62]

In the PETA post, the white animal advocates, who see race as a smoke bomb meant to distract from the issue of cruelty, evince race fatigue. But in their frustration they engage in the very thing they charge race advocates with – zero-sum, either/or thinking. Consider this white blogger discussing Black support for Vick:

> Aren't such racial stances racist in themselves? I don't see how you can support someone just because of the color of their skin while calling for racial equality, in spite of how damning and disturbing the evidence is to the crime. It's almost as if those groups are suggesting that Michael Vick should be let off because he's black. Despite whatever one's cultural views are, dog fighting is cruel and inhumane, bringing life into being only to torture and kill. And regardless of one's views, it's a crime. Race has no place in this issue.[63]

What this advocate seeks to do is bracket out race and assert a universalist narrative about cruelty that is free of racial implications. But there is no standpoint of racial innocence from which to make these or any other claims. There is no race-free space. Vick's critics said they didn't care if he was green, purple, or orange, but they are missing the point: no one in this country has ever been enslaved, auctioned off, or lynched for being green, purple, or orange. By asserting the colorblindness of their project, animal advocates deny their own racial situatedness and the ways that race mattered in this story, in addition to furthering a conservative discourse that proclaims racism to be over and done with and labels any effort to call attention to it reverse discrimination. Sherene Razack writes: "As long as we see ourselves as not implicated in relations of power, as innocent, we cannot begin to walk the path of social justice and to thread our way through the complexities of power relations."[64]

At the same time, many of Vick's defenders trivialized concerns about the dogs' suffering. They briefly acknowledged Vick's misdeeds but argued that his public excoriation was excessive: dogs are, after all, only animals. They pushed back at the raising of the animal question, which they saw as a deliberate deflection of the race question. Discussing the Vick case on *Real Time With Bill Maher* in August 2007, NPR host Michel Martin, whose husband Billy Martin was Vick's attorney, asked why people were up in arms about Vick but silent about the recent shooting deaths of Black people in Newark, New Jersey. And consider this exchange between host Allison Keyes and scholar Michael Eric Dyson, both of whom are Black, in a segment entitled "The Michael Vick Case: Is 'Supporting Our Own' Ok?":

DYSON: Lassie stayed on the air for 15 years, Nat King Cole couldn't stay on his show for six months. Dogs and animals have been treated – relatively speaking – with greater respect and regard ... than African American people. When you look at Hurricane

[62] PETA Files, "Vick at the Office, Part 2."
[63] "Michael Vick: Race, Reality and Society."
[64] Razack (1998), 22.

Katrina, they have a famous picture of a bus full of dogs and animals being treated to first-class citizenship rights in America while black people were drowning. ... [T]his is not to disrespect the needs of other sentient animals who would coexist with us on the human space called earth.

KEYES: So what disturbs me is that an African American man who came from that legacy [of slavery] could do the same thing to dogs that white people did to us during the civil rights movement.

DYSON: True. There's no question about that. But you know what? We're not dogs. We're not animals. We are African American human beings. ... [W]hat he [Vick] did was reprehensible ... but to put dogs and animals parallel to black people is the extension of the legacy of slavery, not its contradiction.

Keyes points out the ironic link between the brutality of racism and Vick's brutality toward dogs, but Dyson brushes aside her comments and re-centers race as the only subject at hand. In the same NPR segment, Mark Gray, host of the radio show *The Sports Groove* (WOL-am in Washington, DC) commented:

[I]n the African American community, I think there would be more of an anti-Vick sentiment if we were dealing with the killing of people as opposed to animals. ... [I]f the guy had raped someone, if the guy had killed somebody, a human being, they [Black people] would be more anti-Michael Vick. But the thing that it's animals is one of those things that have a lot of people on edge and a lot of people uncomfortable with the treatment of Vick.[65]

Antiracism does not logically require reinscribing the subordination of animals, but here Vick's defenders vigorously affirm both that Blacks are human and therefore more important than animals, and that animals do not merit much moral consideration.[66] From there they move to the conclusion that animal advocates' profound concern for Vick's dogs is perverse and morally out of joint – perhaps even a pretext for engaging in the persecution of a famous Black man. The focus on race subsumes, deflects, and ultimately denies the other set of moral claims being raised. When Kwame Abernathy called what happened to Vick an "electronic lynching," he echoed the words of Clarence Thomas, whose strategic decision to denounce the Senate Judiciary Committee hearings of 1991 as a "high-tech lynching" secured him a seat on the U.S. Supreme Court. Is the lynching metaphor being used once again to deflect our attention from another form of injustice – not male domination this time but human domination?

Michael Eric Dyson suggests that Blacks have the most at stake in shoring up the impassable line between humans and animals and erasing the human-animal borderlands into which Black people are continuously placed. But if white supremacy, heteropatriarchy, human supremacy, and mastery over

---

[65] "'Supporting Our Own': Blacks Split on Michael Vick."

[66] Sandra Kobin (2007) wrote of the Vick case: "The message is clear. Beat a woman? Play on. Beat a dog? You're gone." Rather than talking about how notions of masculinity lead to the abuse of both women and dogs, Kobin implies that things are topsy-turvy because dogs are being valued more than women, who clearly have more worth than dogs. See Siebert (2010) on the connection between animal cruelty and violence against women and children.

nature are all cut from the same ideological cloth and all reinforce one another
Black people have a very significant stake in redefining a borderlands wherein
humans and animals are reimagined and human-animal continuities (cognitive
social, emotional, moral) are avowed in ways that diminish neither humans nor
animals. Race has been so closely sutured with species in Western thought for
centuries – shoring up one and attacking the other puts one at cross-purposes
with one's self.

Once again, moving from a posture of disavowal to avowal does not mean
forswearing critique. But it does mean doing critique differently. An ethics of
avowal is about maintaining openness to the suffering of others and actively
acknowledging a connection to their experiences. So, animal advocates might
choose to condemn dogfighting and call for Vick's censure, but instead of
claiming racial innocence, they would advance their critique in a manner that
not only acknowledged but actively challenged the context of anti-Black racism. They would begin by understanding their own racial situatedness – that
white people clamoring for a Black man's (violent) punishment *can never, ever
be a race-neutral narrative.* They would educate themselves deeply about the
very issues displaced by the parable of Black recalcitrance: the economic, political, and ideological forces that produce blighted and segregated urban Black
neighborhoods, substandard and segregated education for Black children, pervasive job discrimination, and high levels of Black unemployment; the myriad
institutional causes of Black people's "differentiated vulnerability to premature
death," from inferior health care, to residential and occupational exposure to
environmental toxins, to vigilante violence, to the routinized violence of law
enforcement practices; and the criminalization of social problems and conscious deflection of public energies and funds away from social programs and
education and toward mass incarceration policies and the "War on Drugs."
They would connect these forms of institutionalized violence against Black
people to the many forms of institutionalized violence against dogs (and nonhuman animals generally), grasping that these phenomena are connected all
the way down.

Race advocates who embraced an ethics of avowal would still hasten to point
out the racialized aspects of the Vick controversy, but they would resist the
reflexive moves of asserting human superiority and reducing animal advocacy
to anti-Black racism. Rather than dismissing animal suffering, they would seek
to understand the exploitation and instrumentalization of dogs and explore the
connection between these phenomena and the exploitation and instrumentalization of Black people. They would take a hard look at the harms inflicted in
dogfighting; at the exploitation of dogs in the name of research, entertainment,
service, the military, and national security; at the unmerciful "mercy" killing
of millions of discarded dogs every year in U.S. shelters; and at the connection
between dogfighting and other forms of exploitative animal usage, including
modern industrial farming. They would explore how the conjoined logics of
race and species work together to decide who lives, who dies, who is used as
an experimental subject without consent, who is imprisoned, who is asked to

bear the cost of war, who is set upon each other for the entertainment of others, who is rendered a commodity, whose labor is exploited, who is fully grievable, and who is not.

This chapter examines the Michael Vick dogfighting story, exploring the optics of cruelty and racism in turn. The parable-ization of Michael Vick's life is analyzed as a mode of simultaneously reproducing negative tropes about Black masculinity and displacing collective attention from naturalized patterns of institutionalized violence against Blacks and dogs in the contemporary United States. I briefly discuss how animal advocates and race advocates disavow each other's claims in the course of conflict and suggest what it might look like if they instead embraced an ethics of avowal toward each other – an ethics predicated, at least in part, on the understanding that the taxonomies of race and species crucially energize and sustain one another. The next chapter offers some concluding thoughts on the themes of the book.

PART IV

CONCLUSION

9

We Are All Animals/We Are Not Animals

Impassioned disputes over the animal practices of racialized others open a window onto the synergistic workings of the taxonomies of race and species in the contemporary United States. Historically conjoined, the two logics continue to sustain and energize one another in the joint project of producing the human and the subhuman, not-human, less than human – with all of the entailments of moral considerability, physical vulnerability, and grievability that follow. The live animal market, whaling, and dogfighting conflicts discussed here appear at first glance to be zero-sum games, compelling us to choose between the interests and needs of racialized humans and the interests and needs of nonhuman animals. But this is a false choice, I have argued. In fact, the ultimate fates of these two groups of beings are irretrievably caught up together in the skein of power that traverses and binds the taxonomies of race and species.

In 2005, People for the Ethical Treatment of Animals (PETA) launched a traveling exhibit entitled *Animal Liberation Project: We Are All Animals*. Following on the heels of an earlier PETA exhibit that had likened modern industrial farming to the Holocaust, this one featured oversized panels juxtaposing images of the violence done to animals in industrial farming, scientific research, and the circus with the violence done to marginalized human others (slaves, lynching victims, subjects of the Tuskegee syphilis experiments, displaced Native Americans, force-fed suffragettes, and more) throughout U.S. history. Reactions were quick and fierce across the board, with Black civil rights leaders and the mainstream media alike excoriating the exhibit as racist, offensive, and outrageous (Kim 2011). In an official apology, PETA's president Ingrid Newkirk argued that the exhibit did not use the association of animals and nonwhites to denigrate the latter, but rather to uplift animals. The point of the exhibit, she claimed, was to expose the "might makes right" thinking underlying both types of oppression and to show how both groups have been seen as "deficient and thus disposable" (Newkirk 2005). As criticism persisted, Newkirk shut down the traveling exhibit but placed a virtual version of it on the organization's Web site, where it has gone through various iterations in the years since.[1]

That same year, Hurricane Katrina powerfully revived an animal-related trope in Black commentary on American racism. Images of animal welfare organizations rescuing dogs and cats from storm-devastated New Orleans went viral, provoking Black commentators to note, with anguish and anger, that poor Black residents were dying in large numbers as these pets were whisked to safety (Harris-Perry 2010). What these images suggested, echoing the Michael Vick controversy, was that the American cultural imaginary located Black people not just between whites and animals, but *below* animals – that whites cared more about "pets" than they did about Black people. This theme reemerged around the acquittal of George Zimmerman in the killing of Trayvon Martin in July 2013, as suggested by an article entitled "If Zimmerman Walks and Vick Didn't, Does that Mean that a Dog's Life Is Worth More than a Black Man?"[2] The perceived devalorization of Blacks relative to nonhuman animals suggested an extremity of degradation that can only be met with Michael Eric Dyson's assertion, "We're not animals."

As these two scenarios suggest, questions about synergistic taxonomies and the ethics of political struggle pertain well beyond the specific practice-based disputes examined in this book. They go to the issue of how movements see themselves in relation to other movements. In this sense, they go to the heart of American left politics today. In a field of power structured complexly around multiple dimensions, how should adherents of one progressive struggle imagine, speak to and about, and engage adherents of other progressive struggles? In the remainder of this conclusion, I want to use the notion of ethical avowal to think through the PETA and Katrina/Zimmerman scenarios, disturbing the claims about race, humanity, and animality being made in these conflicts and gesturing toward an alternative path of embracing the struggles of others.

Those who dismissed the PETA exhibit as an offensive stunt typical of the organization failed to grasp that analogizing to racial oppression, and specifically the Black experience, has been a central strategy of the animal liberation movement for some time. And not just the animal liberation movement. Slavery, along with the Holocaust, has become a political archetype of human suffering, and there is hardly a contemporary left cause in the United States that has not analogized to one or both, from AIDS activism to gay marriage advocacy to the struggle for Native American sovereignty to feminism.[3] In any case, the central frame of animal liberationists (as opposed to their more moderate counterparts, the welfarists/reformists) is indeed that of "abolition" (Francione

---

[1] www.peta2.com/alp/. Since 2005, a panel that juxtaposed the lynching of a Black man with the slaughter of a cow has been eliminated. New panels have been added on the Cambodian genocide, female genital mutilation, and political prisoners, presumably to "diversify" the human referents, make a point about the universality of oppression, and reduce the appearance of targeting Black people.
[2] "If Zimmerman Walks."
[3] Conservative movements (e.g., the prolife movement) sometimes use these analogies, too.

1996). Scholars and activists of this persuasion make continual comparisons to the institution of African slavery and postulate a moral extensionist reading of history whereby the circle of moral concern broadens over time to include, *in seriatim*, previously excluded beings – Blacks, women, and, soon, animals (Best and Nocella 2004).

Analogizers claim, as Ingrid Newkirk did, that they are highlighting the connections among forms of oppression and modeling their struggle upon another, archetypal one. Emulation is the sincerest form of flattery. Clearly, their cause stands to gain visibility, legitimacy, and an aura of inevitability through this association with the Black struggle. When gay marriage stopped being seen as a private matter of sexuality and love and was successfully reframed as a civil right similar to that of sitting in any seat on the bus, the issue picked up enormous momentum that shows no signs of slowing. But analogizees are rarely as sanguine about these comparisons, which they see as denying the uniqueness of their experience, appropriating and instrumentalizing their suffering, and diminishing their social capital or standing (Kim 2011). For some, analogizing reprises the original wounds of anti-Black racism – especially when one is being compared to nonhuman animals.

Indeed there are aspects of analogizing that should give us pause. Analogizers claim to be connecting and avowing, but in many cases they seem to be instrumentalizing the other cause in question or treating it as a means to an end. The analogizer does not connect x and y in the sense of exploring them as independently significant and conjoined logics. Rather, concerned to validate x, which is her true focus, the analogizer seizes upon y, which already enjoys some measure of social validation, and posits x = y. This exercise seeks to transfer the legitimacy and social importance of y to x. Nor does she consider the impact of this exercise on y. PETA's exhibit, *We Are All Animals*, resurrects fraught Black-animal associations without providing a historically informed, critical analysis of these associations. It also suggests that the Black story is a triumphalist one of overcoming racism, thus bolstering damaging white fantasies of colorblindness and postraciality. It succinctly repackages and falsely truncates the story of anti-Blackness to serve the present purposes of animal liberation. The Black struggle is not the subject (or even one of the subjects) of PETA's exhibit; it is symbol, tool, and prop.

A few years ago, I argued that PETA's claim "We are all animals" helps us to confront the arbitrariness of the human-animal divide and its denial of the many emotional, physiological, psychological, social, cognitive, and genetic continuities between humans and nonhuman animals (Kim 2011). I affirmed the moral stance of the exhibit while expressing concern that it would alienate potential political allies. I have since come to believe that the exhibit attempts to ground the argument for the moral considerability and grievability of animals upon the elision of race, and that this move makes the exhibit morally untenable. *We Are All Animals* makes a universalizing move that posits connection, affinity, and avowal between humans (as a general category of beings) and animals (as a general category of beings) but in doing so aggravates the specific

fault line of race by instrumentalizing Black suffering, denying the continuing
derogation of Blacks as subhumans, and concealing the unfinished status of the
Black struggle (as well as the reasons why it will always remain unfinished).[4]
    The Hurricane Katrina story is one of gross racial injustices layered on top
of one another all the way down – from the segregation and poverty that made
Blacks more vulnerable to the storm geographically and less able to evacuate,
to the failure of the state and federal governments to deliver food, water, and
medicine to thousands of devastated residents; to the law and order posture of
the police whereby they viewed Black residents as criminals to be controlled
rather than as citizens to be assisted; to the rebuilding of the city afterward in
ways that further marginalized the poor Black victims of the storm. The Katrina
story is, all told, a spectacular technicolor retort to white delusions about
postraciality. Several years later, in February 2012, the killing of seventeen-
year-old Trayvon Martin by George Zimmerman made the same point, more
intimately but no less painfully, about Black vulnerability and ungrievability.
    In the wake of Hurricane Katrina, the Black lament "We are not animals"
was a bid for the recognition of Black humanity. But defending Black humanity
does not logically require reinscribing the subordination of nonhuman animals.
The problem was not that the HSUS animal rescue team performed skillfully
or that the American public loves a good animal rescue story. The problem
was that race overdetermined the tragic and deadly outcomes of Katrina for
Black residents of New Orleans. Black people were seen and treated as less
than human, and this injury would not have been mitigated if all dogs and cats,
too, had been abandoned. Nor is it true that "pets" are generally valued and
cherished in this society. This nation is transfixed over the story of a Bichon
Frisé being thrown into traffic because of road rage but it also countenances
the slaughter of millions of healthy dogs and cats in shelters every year. To say
that animal rescue efforts after Katrina show that whites love "pets" is comparable to saying that the election of Barack Obama to the U.S. presidency shows
that racism is no longer a problem. It confuses the exception with the rule, the
photo-op for the deeper truth. It disavows the reality of how the taxonomy
of species authorizes the infliction of unremitting and profound suffering on
animals. Furthermore, to say that animal rescue efforts show that whites love
"pets" more than they do Black people reduces nonhuman animals to instruments for measuring degrees of anti-Blackness.
    "We are not animals," like "We are all animals," rests upon an untenable
elision – here the elision of species and the denial of profound and meaningful continuities between human and nonhuman animals. In the end, the effort
to gain full humanity by distancing from nonhuman animals, like the effort
to achieve moral considerability for animals through racially fraught, racism-
denying analogies, is a misbegotten project: it has not succeeded and cannot
succeed because race cannot be unsutured from species and dismantled while
species categories motor on in force. Rather, these two taxonomies, intimately

---

[4] My thanks to Jared Sexton for insight on this point.

bound with one another, must be disassembled together in our efforts to meaningfully and radically rethink the category of the human.

Pursuing an ethics of avowal leads us into uncharted territory. But a change of terrain could be just what is needed in this war. Structured by the post–civil rights regime, the American left is thoroughly segmented. Each cause has its cluster of advocacy organizations and corresponding academic field(s). Each engages the enemy from a separate bunker. Each resists coercive universalisms and coalitional possibilities, except momentarily. In the meantime, the forces of neoliberal capitalism face few obstacles as they transform racialized others, nonhuman animals, and the earth into "resources" in the game of perpetual capital accumulation.

Rethinking the human begins with the recognition that the human has always been a thoroughly exclusionary concept in race and species terms – that it has only ever made sense as a way of marking who does *not* belong in the inner circle. It means clarifying that the project before us is not an *extensionist one* (expanding the definition of the human to allow a few racialized groups or preferred ape species in) but rather a *reconstructive one* (reimagining humans, animals, and nature outside of systems of domination). In ecological terms, time is indeed short. But there is still a chance to open ourselves to each other, to see each other. There is still time to become and act together.

References

Court Cases and Government Documents

[Chinatown Case]

California Fish and Game Commission (now the California Fish and Wildlife Commission). [Minutes and transcripts from selected monthly meetings, 1997–2012.]

California State Assembly Committee on Water, Parks, and Wildlife. Chair Michael Machado. Hearing on "Importation of Bullfrogs and Turtles." Sacramento, California. April 13, 1999.

California State Assembly Committee on Water, Parks, and Wildlife. Chair Michael Machado. Hearing on "Live Animal Markets." Sacramento, California. July 20, 1999.

California State Senate Natural Resources and Wildlife Committee. Chair Tom Hayden. Hearing on AB 238. Sacramento, California. March 14, 2000.

California State Senate Natural Resources and Wildlife Committee. Chair Tom Hayden. Hearing on AB 238. Sacramento, California. June 27, 2000.

Coalition for Healthy and Humane Business Practices v. Never Ending Quails et al. (Super. Ct. S.F. City and County, 1998, No. CGC97986059).

The National Invasive Species Council. *National Invasive Species Management Plan, 2008–2012.* August 2008.

San Francisco Board of Supervisors. [Minutes and transcripts of selected monthly meetings, 1997–2000.]

San Francisco Commission of Animal Control and Welfare. [Minutes and transcripts from selected monthly meetings, 1995–2012.]

San Francisco Planning Department. *San Francisco Neighborhoods: Socio-Economic Profiles, American Community Survey 2005–2009.* May 2011.

Subcommittee on Crime, Terrorism, and Homeland Security, Committee on the Judiciary, House of Representatives, 109th Congress, Second Session on H.R. 4239. Hearing on "The Animal Enterprise Terrorism Act." May 23, 2006.

[Makah Case]

Anderson v. Evans, 314 F. 3d 1006 (9th Cir. 2002).
Metcalf v. Daley, 214 F. 3d 1135 (9th Cir. 2000).

"Scoping Report Makah Whale Hunt Environmental Impact Statement." Preparec by Parametrix for National Marine Fisheries Service. Bellevue, Washington January 2007.

U.S. Department of Commerce, National Oceanic and Atmospheric Administration. "Notice of Intent to Terminate the Existing Draft Environmental Impact Statemen and Prepare a New Environmental Impact Statement." *Federal Register*/Vol. 77 No. 98/Monday, May 21, 2012/Notices.

U.S. Department of Commerce, National Oceanic and Atmospheric Administration National Marine Fisheries Service. "Endangered Fish and Wildlife; Gray Whale." *Federal Register*/Vol. 56, No. 226/Friday, November 22, 1991/Notices.

U.S. Department of Commerce, National Oceanic and Atmospheric Administration National Marine Fisheries Service. "Endangered Fish and Wildlife; Petition and Finding to Remove the Eastern Pacific Gray Whale Stock From the List of Endangered and Threatened Wildlife." *Federal Register*/Vol. 56, No. 237/Tuesday, December 10, 1991/Notices.

U.S. Department of Commerce, National Oceanic and Atmospheric Administration. National Marine Fisheries Service. "Scoping Report: Makah Whale Hunt Environmental Impact Statement." January 2007.

U.S. Department of Commerce, National Oceanic and Atmospheric Administration. National Marine Fisheries Service, Northwest Region. "Draft Environmental Impact Statement for Proposed Authorization of the Makah Whale Hunt." May 2008.

U.S. Department of Commerce, National Oceanic and Atmospheric Administration. National Marine Fisheries Service, Northwest Region. "Makah Whale Hunt Environmental Impact Statement." May 2008.

U.S. Department of Commerce, National Oceanic and Atmospheric Administration. National Marine Fisheries Service, Northwest Region. "Public Comment on Notice of Intent to Terminate the Existing Draft Environmental Impact Statement and Prepare a New Environmental Impact Statement Relating to the Makah Tribe's Request to Continue to Exercise Its Treaty Right to Hunt Gray Whales." August 2012.

[Michael Vick Case]

"Bad Newz Kennels, Smithfield Virginia." Report of Investigation. Special Agent-in-Charge for Investigations Brian Haaser. USDA Office of Inspector General — Investigations. Northeast Region, Beltsville, Maryland. August 28, 2008.

United States of America v. Michael Vick. No. 3:07CR00274-00 (E.D. Va. Dec. 10, 2007).

United States of America v. Michael Vick. "Summary of the Facts." August 24, 2007. U.S. District Court for the Eastern District of Virginia, Richmond Division. Criminal No. 3:07CR274.

Chinese-Language Newspaper Articles

"Amended Shark Fin Ban Measure Proposed by Yu Yinliang [Leland Yee]." *World Journal.* February 22, 2011.

"Animal Protection Activists Admit 'The Ban Is Only Against Chinatown.'" *World Journal.* Editorial. March 9, 1998.

"Animal Protection Groups Think Chinatown Businessmen Still Mistreat Food Animals." *World Journal*. Editorial. July 3, 1998.

"California State Fish & Game Commission Permits Importation of Live Turtles and Frogs." *World Journal*. February 4, 2011.

Chen Tien-Shen. "Chinatown Merchants Counterattack Animal Rights Activists over Issue of Selling Live Animals for Food." *Sing Tao Daily*. October 8, 1996.

"Chinatown Economic Development Group Supports Selling Live Animals." *World Journal*. April 23, 1997.

Han Qiuping. "Bay Area Chinese Merchants Protest Against Shark Fin Ban." *Sing Tao Daily*. April 5, 2011.

Huang Yongjian. "At the Public Hearing, One Hundred and Fifty People Protest Strongly Against the Ban on Importation of Live Turtles and Frogs." *World Journal*. April 2, 1998.

"Chinese Communities in Southern California Are Mobilized to Fight Against the Ban on Importation of Live Frogs and Turtles." *World Journal*. March 26, 1998.

"Is the Day of a Total Ban on Live Poultry and Seafood Coming Soon? *World Journal*. January 27, 1998.

Li Xiulan. "Oriental Food Association Says No to Shark Fin Ban." *World Journal*. February 23, 2011.

"Shark Fin Ban Proposed by Fang Wenzhong [Paul Fong] and Jared Huffman." *World Journal*. February 15, 2011.

Liu Kaiping. "CCBA, CGCC and Animal Protection Association Publish an Open Letter." *World Journal*. July 10, 1998.

Lu Shiwei. "Anti-Chinese Wind Blows Heavily and the Chinese Need to Fight for Our Benefits." *World Journal*. April 19, 1997.

"San Francisco Shop Owners Are Sued for Selling Live Animals, Which Disappoints Chinese Councilors." *World Journal*. April 16, 1997.

"Mabel Teng: Anti-Asian Wind Blows for over Fifty Years." *World Journal*. November 19, 1996.

"Thomas Hsieh Condemns San Francisco Commission on Animal Control and Welfare for Banning Chinatown Live Animal Killing." *World Journal*. November 16, 1996.

Wang Jincheng. "Paul Fong Pushes Congress to Apologize for Chinese Exclusion Act." *World Journal*. February 22, 2011.

Xu Minzi. "Facing a Lawsuit by Animal Protection Activists, CCBA Calls for All Chinese Americans' Support." *World Journal*. April 27, 1997.

Yu Ning. "Public Hearing Will be Held on April 2." *World Journal*, April 1, 1999.

"Frog and Turtle Case Will Be Discussed Again and a Public Hearing Will Be Held in Early February: Pius Lee Calls On All Chinatown Shopowners To Be Self-Disciplined and United; If the Ban Is Passed, Fresh Food May Not Be Bought All over America." *World Journal*. January 28, 1999.

"Chinatown Shops Post the Regulations of Frog and Turtle Sales." *World Journal*. May 23, 1998.

"CCBA Will Not Harm the Interests of Chinatown Businessmen." *World Journal*. May 2, 1998.

"San Francisco Representatives Return Triumphant from the Public Hearing: 'Unity Is Power, Thanks to Our Compatriots and the Media.'" *World Journal*. April 2, 1998.

"Northern and Southern California are United in Fight Against the Proposed Ban on the Importation of Live Turtles and Frogs." *World Journal*. April 1, 1998.

"Food Animals and Pets Cannot Be Compared." *World Journal*. March 12, 1998.

"Proposal To Ban The Importation Of Live Turtles Will Affect California's Economy." *World Journal*. February 25, 1998.

"Chinese Americans Show Great Concern over the Ban on the Importation of Live Turtles and Frogs and Will Delay the Vote on This Proposal." *World Journal*. February 7, 1998.

"Nearly 1000 Chinese Were Crowded at the Venue and Launched a War of Words, Even Curse Words Were Spoken." *World Journal*. October 18, 1996.

"The Public Hearing on Chinatown Killing Live Animals was Heated and all Chinese-Americans Left." *World Journal*. October 18, 1996.

"Killing Live Animals in Chinatown Leads to Another Anti-Chinese Action." *World Journal*. October 8, 1996.

"Xie Guoxiang [Tom Hsieh] Swore to Fight for Chinatown Shop Owners to the End." *World Journal*. October 3, 1996.

"Strictly Ban the Sale of Live Animals and Implement Health Regulations." *World Journal*. August 9, 1996.

General References

"3rd Year in a Row a PFW Scout Calls Black QB Lazy, Is He Racist? No, He's Smart." n.d. http://www.yardbarker.com/nfl/articles/3rd_year_in_a_row_a_pfw_scout_calls _black_qb_lazy_is_he_racist_no_hes_smart/13289092.

"A Brief History of Dogfighting." Anti-Dogfighting Campaign. n.d. http://anti -dogfightingcampaign.blogspot.com/p/history.html.

"A Conversation with David Lee, Exec. Director of the CAVEC." *SPUR Newsletter*. January 2000. http://www.spur.org/publications/library/interview/davidlee01012000.

"Aboriginal Subsistence Whaling." International Whaling Commission. n.d. http://iwcoffice.org/aboriginal.

Adams, Carol. *The Sexual Politics of Meat: A Feminist-Vegetarian Critical Theory*, 20th anniversary edition. New York: Bloomsbury Academic, 2010.

"An Animal Manifesto: Gender, Identity, and Vegan-Feminism in the Twenty-First Century, an Interview with Carol J. Adams." *Parallax* 12, 1, 2006, 120–8.

Neither Man Nor Beast: Feminism and the Defense of Animals. New York: Continuum, 1995.

Adams Carol and Josephine Donovan, eds. *Animals and Women: Feminist Theoretical Explorations*. Durham, NC: Duke University Press, 1995.

Adams, Jill. "Genetically Engineered Animals and the FDA." *The Los Angeles Times*. January 26, 2009. http://articles.latimes.com/print/2009/jan/26/health/he-closer26.

Al-Hibri, Azizah. "Is Western Patriarchal Feminism Good for Third World/Minority Women?" in *Is Multiculturalism Bad for Women?* by Susan Okin with Respondents, eds. Joshua Cohen, Matthew Howard, and Martha Nussbaum. Princeton, NJ: Princeton University Press, 1999, 41–6.

Almaguer, Tomás. *Racial Fault Lines: The Historical Origins of White Supremacy in California*. Berkeley: University of California Press, 1994.

Alter, S. E. et al. "DNA Evidence for Historic Population Size and Past Ecosystem Impacts of Gray Whales." *Proceedings of the National Academy of Sciences, USA* 104, 2007, 15162–7.

Alter, S. E. et al. "Have Gray Whales Recovered From Whaling?" *Lenfest Ocean Program Research Series*, August 2007. http://www.stanford.edu/group/Palumbi/PNAS/LenfestRS.pdf.

Alter, S. E. and S. R. Palumbi. "Could Genetic Diversity in Eastern North Pacific Gray Whale Reflect Global Historic Abundance?" *PNAS* 104, 52, December 26, 2007, E3–E4. http://www.pnas.org/cgi/doi/10.1073/pnas.0710472105.

Anderson, Kay. "The Idea of Chinatown: The Power of Place and Institutional Practice in the Making of a Racial Category." *Annals of the Association of American Geographers* 77, 4, 1987, 580–98.

Anderson, Virginia. *Creatures of Empire: How Domestic Animals Transformed Early America*. Oxford: Oxford University Press, 2006.

Anderson, Will et al. "Alberta Nora 'Binki' Thompson, Defender of Whales." *Animal Welfare Institute Quarterly*. Summer 2012. http://awionline.org/awi-quarterly/2012-summer/alberta-nora-"binki"-thompson-defender-whales.

Andrews, David, ed. *Michael Jordan, Inc.: Corporate Sport, Media Culture, and Late Modern America*. Albany: State University of New York Press, 2001.

Andrews, David. "The Fact(s) of Michael Jordan's Blackness: Excavating a Floating Racial Signifier" in *Michael Jordan, Inc.: Corporate Sport, Media Culture, and Late Modern America*, ed. David Andrews. Albany: State University of New York Press, 2001, 107–52.

Andrews, David, Ronald Mower, and Michael Silk. "Ghettocentrism and the Essentialized Black Male Athlete" in *Commodified and Criminalized: New Racism and African Americans in Contemporary Sports*, eds. David Leonard and C. Richard King. Lanham, MD: Rowman & Littlefield, 2011, 69–93.

Ang, Audra. "Chinese Economic Concerns Trump Safety." *Associated Press Online*. August 15, 2003.

Anthias, Floya. "Beyond Feminism and Multiculturalism: Locating Difference and the Politics of Location." *Women's Studies International Forum* 25, 3, 2002, 275–86.

"Anti-Indian Movement." *Encyclopedia of Race and Racism*, ed. John Moore. Volume 1. Detroit, MI: Macmillan Reference, 2008, 102–5.

Anzaldúa, Gloria. *Borderlands/La Frontera: The New Mestiza*, 4th edition. San Francisco, CA: Aunt Lute Books, 2012.

"Are Animal Advocates Giving Michael Vick a Pass?" August 17, 2009. http://strikingattheroots.wordpress.com/2009/08/17/are-animal-advocates-giving-michael-vick-a-pass/.

Arluke, Arnold. "Our Animals, Ourselves." *Contexts* 9, 3, Summer 2010, 34–9.

Armistead, W. S. *The Negro Is a Man: A Reply to Charles Carroll's Book "The Negro Is a Beast or In the Image of God."* Tifton, GA: Armistead & Vickers, 1903. Reprint, Miami, FL: Mnemosyne Publishing, 1969. Page references are to the 1969 edition.

Arnold, Sue. "Petition to Designate the Eastern North Pacific Gray Whale (*Eschrichtius robustus*) as a Depleted Population Under the Marine Mammal Protection Act." October 11, 2010. Prepared on behalf of the California Gray Whale Coalition.

Ashley, Bob et al. *Food and Cultural Studies*. New York: Routledge, 2004.

Assessment and Management of Alien Species that Threaten Ecosystems, Habitats and Species. 2000. Secretariat of the Convention on Biological Diversity. CBD Technical Series no. 1.

Axtell, James. "The Scholastic Philosophy of the Wilderness." *William and Mary Quarterly* 29, 3, July 1972, 335–66.

Baker, Lee. *From Savage to Negro: Anthropology and the Construction of Race, 1896-1954.* Berkeley: University of California Press, 1998.

Barnsley, Paul. "Eco-Colonialism or Environmentalism: Makah Tribe Whaling Watch." *Windspeaker* 16, 7, November 1, 1998, 2.

Barry, Brian. *Culture & Equality: An Egalitarian Critique of Multiculturalism* Cambridge, MA: Harvard University Press, 2001.

Barton, Karen. "'Red Waters': Contesting Marine Space as Indian Place in the U.S Pacific Northwest." Dissertation in Department of Geography and Regiona Development. The University of Arizona. 2000.

Bataille, Gretchen. "Introduction" in *Native American Representations: First Encounters, Distorted Images, and Literary Appropriations,* ed. Gretchen Bataille. Lincoln University of Nebraska Press, 2001, 1–7.

Bataille, Gretchen, ed. *Native American Representations: First Encounters, Distorted Images, and Literary Appropriations.* Lincoln: University of Nebraska Press, 2001.

"B.C. First Nations Yield on Whale Hunt." *CBC News.* December 12, 2006. http://www .cbc.ca/news/canada/british-columbia/story/2006/12/12/bc-whaling.html.

Beck, Alma Soongi. "The Makah's Decision to Reinstate Whaling: When Conservationists Clash With Native Americans over an Ancient Hunting Tradition." *Journal of Environmental Law and Litigation* 11, 1996, 359–412.

Beech, Hannah. "Noxious Nosh: In China, People Are Hungry for a Taste of the Wild." *Time/Asia Magazine.* June 9, 2003.

Beers, Diane. *For the Prevention of Cruelty: The History and Legacy of Animal Rights Activism in the U.S.* Athens, OH: Swallow Books, 2006.

Bell, Jarrett. "Geno Smith the Latest to Pay the Black Tax." *USA TODAY Sports.* April 22, 2013. http://www.usatoday.com/story/sports/nfl/2013/04/21/bell-geno-smith -racial-bias/2101977/.

Beneke, Chris. "Andrew Luck, Robert Griffin III and the Most Racially Divisive Position in Sports." *Huffingtonpost.com.* April 26, 2012. http://www.huffingtonpost.com /chris-beneke/2012-nfl-draft_b_1456545.html.

Benhabib, Seyla. *The Claims of Culture: Equality and Diversity in the Global Era.* Princeton, NJ: Princeton University Press, 2002.

Bentham, Jeremy. *An Introduction to the Principles of Morals and Legislation.* New York: Hafner/Macmillan, 1948.

Berkhofer, Robert. *The White Man's Indian: Images of the American Indian from Columbus to the Present.* New York: Vintage Books, 1979.

Berry, Bonnie and Earl Smith. "Race, Sport, and Crime: The Misrepresentation of African Americans in Team Sports and Crime." *Sociology of Sport Journal* 17, 2000, 171–97.

Best, Steven and Anthony Nocella, eds. *Terrorists or Freedom Fighters? Reflections on the Liberation of Animals.* New York: Lantern Books, 2004.

Beston, Henry. *The Outermost House: A Year of Life on the Great Beach of Cape Cod.* New York: Holt Paperbacks, 2003.

Bieder, Robert. *Science Encounters the Indian, 1820–1880: The Early Years of American Ethnology.* Norman: University of Oklahoma Press, 1986.

Bigler, Matthew and Judson Jeffries. "'An Amazing Specimen': NFL Draft Experts' Evaluations of Black Quarterbacks." *Journal of African American Studies* 12, 2, June 2008, 120–41.

Bird, S. Elizabeth. "Gendered Construction of the America Indian in Popular Media." *Journal of Communication.* Summer 1999, 61–83.

Bird, S. Elizabeth, ed. *Dressing in Feathers: The Construction of the Indian in American Popular Culture.* Boulder, CO: Westview, 1996.

Bird, S. Elizabeth. "Introduction: Constructing the Indian, 1830s–1990s" in *Dressing in Feathers: The Construction of the Indian in American Popular Culture*, ed. S. Elizabeth Bird. Boulder, CO: Westview, 1996, 1–12.

Bishop, Katherine. "San Francisco's Chinatown Seeks to Save Its Soul." *The New York Times.* December 17, 1990.

Blow, Richard. "The Great American Whale Hunt." *Mother Jones.* September/October 1998.

Bogle, Donald. *Toms, Coons, Mulattoes, Mammies, and Bucks: An Interpretive History of Blacks in American Films*, 4th edition. New York: Continuum, 2001.

Bonilla-Silva, Eduardo. *Racism without Racists: Color-Blind Racism and the Persistence of Racial Inequality in America*, 3rd edition. Lanham, MD: Rowman & Littlefield, 2009.

Bookchin, Murray. "Social Ecology Versus Deep Ecology: A Challenge for the Ecology Movement." June 25, 1987. http://libcom.org/library/social-versus-deep-ecology -bookchin.

Borenstein, Seth. "Study Finds that Return of Pacific Gray Whale May Be Based on Miscalculation." *Associated Press.* September 10, 1997.

Bowechop, Janine. "Contemporary Makah Whaling" in *Coming to Shore: Northwest Coast Ethnology, Traditions, and Visions*, eds. Marie Mauzé et al. Lincoln: University of Nebraska Press, 2004, 407–19.

Brackenridge, Hugh Henry. "The Animals, Vulgarly Called Indians" in *The Indian and the White Man*, ed. Wilcomb Washburn (Document #30). Garden City, NJ: Anchor Books, 1964.

Bradford, William. "'Save the Whales' v. Save the Makah: Finding Negotiated Solutions to Ethnodevelopmental Disputes in the New International Economic Order." *St. Thomas Law Review* 13, 2000–1, 155–220.

Braun, Bruce. "'On the Raggedy Edge of Risk': Articulations of Race and Nature after Biology" in *Race, Nature, and the Politics of Difference*, eds. Donald Moore, Jake Kosek, and Anand Pandian. Durham, NC: Duke University Press, 2003, 175–203.

Brechin, Gray. "The Wasp: Stinging Editorials and Political Cartoons" n.d. http:// bancroft.berkeley.edu/events/bancroftiana/121/wasp.html.

Brenner, Neil and Nik Theodore. "Cities and the Geographies of 'Actually Existing Neoliberalism'" in *Spaces of Neoliberalism: Urban Restructuring in North America and Western Europe*, eds. Neil Brenner and Nik Theodore. Malden, MA: Blackwell, 2002, 2–32.

Brey, Stacey Vonita. "The Distribution and Census of Freshwater Turtles in Golden Gate Park Lakes." Masters in Science Thesis in Biology. San Francisco State University. May 2006.

Bright, Christopher. "Invasive Species: Pathogens of Globalization." *Foreign Policy* 1999, 50–64.

Bronstein, Phil. "Ed Lee – A Coup for S.F. Power Couple Brown, Pak." *San Francisco Chronicle.* January 24, 2011. http://www.sfgate.com/cgi-bin/article.cgi?f=/c/a /2011/01/24/EDE81HCJSD.DTL.

Brown, J. H. and D. F. Sax. "An Essay on Some Topics Concerning Invasive Species." *Austral Ecology* 29, 2004, 530–6.

Brumfield, Geoff. "NIH Takes Another Step Toward Retirement of Research Chimps." NPR.org. June 26, 2013. http://www.npr.org/blogs/health/2013/06/26/195926114 /nih-takes-another-step-toward-retirement-of-research-chimps.

Buffington, Daniel. "Contesting Race on Sundays: Making Meaning out of the Rise in the Number of Black Quarterbacks." *Sociology of Sport Journal* 21, 2005, 19–37.

Bulman, Erica. "Lust for Tiger Parts Whittles Away Species." *San Francisco Examiner* June 1, 1997, A7.

Burdick, Alan. "The Truth About Invasive Species: How to Stop Worrying and Learn to Love Ecological Intruders." *Discover*. May 2005.

Burke, Bill. "Once Limited to the Rural South, Dogfighting Sees a Cultural Shift." n.d. http://hamptonroads.com/print/283641.

Burns, William. "The International Whaling Commission and the Future of Cetaceans: Problems and Prospects." *Colorado Journal of International Environmental Law & Policy* 8, 1997, 31–88.

Butler, Judith. *Frames of War: When Is Life Grievable?* London: Verso Press, 2010.

Precarious Life: The Powers of Mourning and Violence. London: Verso Press, 2004.

"California Upholds Ban on Importation of Nonnative Frogs and Turtles for Food." June 10, 2010. http://www.reptilechannel.com/reptile-news/2010/06/10/california -ban-on-nonnative-frogs-turtles.aspx.

Campbell, Dana. "Pit Bull Bans: The State of Breed-Specific Legislation." *GPSOLO*. July/August 2009. http://www.americanbar.org/content/newsletter/publications /gp_solo_magazine_home/gp_solo_magazine_index/pitbull.html.

Cantzler, Julia Miller. "Environmental Justice and Social Power Rhetoric in the Moral Battle over Whaling." *Sociological Inquiry* 77, 3, August 2007, 483–512.

Carpenter, Mary. "Decline in Game Wardens Puts Wildlife at Risk." January 31, 2007. http://www.plumasnews.com.

Carroll, Charles. "*The Negro a Beast*" ... or ... "*In the Image of God*." St. Louis, MO: American Book and Bible House, 1900.

Carson, Rachel. *Silent Spring*, anniversary edition. New York: Houghton Mifflin, 2002.

Casal, Paula. "Justice across Cultures: Animals and Accommodation" in *Social Justice*, eds. Matthew Clayton and Andrew Williams. Malden, MA: Well, 2004, 241–63.

"Celizic: Dogfighting Is All About 'Keeping It Real.'" Posted by Paulsen, August 21, 2007. http://www.sportsmediawatch.com/2007/08/celizic-dogfighting-is-all-about/.

Champlin, Dell and Eric Hake. "Immigration as Industrial Strategy in American Meatpacking." *Review of Political Economy* 18, 1, 2006, 49–69.

Chan, James. "'Rough on Rats': Racism and Advertising in the Latter Half of the Nineteenth Century." n.d. http://www.chsa.org/2005/03/05/daniel-k-e-ching -collection-conference-excerpt/.

Chavez, Ken. "Rallying Chinese Americans on the Radio." *Sacramento Bee*. May 6, 1997, A11.

Chen, Yong. *Chinese San Francisco, 1850–1943: A Trans-Pacific Community*. Stanford, CA: Stanford University Press, 2002.

Cheng, Cindy. "Out of Chinatown and into the Suburbs: Chinese Americans and the Politics of Cultural Citizenship in Early Cold War America." *American Quarterly* 58, 4, December 2006, 1067–90.

Childs, Erica. "Images of the Black Athlete: Intersection of Race, Sexuality, and Sports." *Journal of African American Men* 4, 2, Fall 1999, 19–38.

Chinatown. VHS. Directed by Eric Lin. Forbidden City Films, 1999.

Chinatown Declared a Nuisance! Workingmen's Committee of California. March 1880. http://www.sfmuseum.org/hist2/nuisance.html.

Chinese American Voters Education Committee. "Chinese Newspaper Readers Poll."
Public Research Institute. San Francisco State University. 1999.

"Chinese Communities Shifting to Mandarin." December 29, 2003. http://www
.chinadaily.com.cn/en/doc/2003-12/29/content_294186.htm.

Clemmons, Anna Katherine et al. "Vick Confidential: Fans Are Split about Michael
Vick. But What Do His Peers Think?" ESPN the Magazine. September 5, 2011.
http://espn.go.com/nfl/story/_/id/6885697/nfl-michael-vick-nfl-peers-support
-anonymous-poll-44-players-reveals-espn-magazine.

Clifton, Merrit. "Virginia Dogfighting Case Embarrasses Pro Football." Animal People
18, 5, June 2007, 1, 17.

Coakley, J. Sport in Society, 6th edition. New York: McGraw-Hill, 1998.

Coates, Peter. American Perceptions of Immigrant and Invasive Species: Strangers on the
Land. Berkeley: University of California Press, 2007.

Cohen, Brock. "Too Black for Quarterback." Huffingtonpost.com. August 30, 2011.
http://www.huffingtonpost.com/brock-cohen/too-black-for-quarterback
_b_937080.html.

Cohen, Judy and John Richardson. "Pit Bull Panic." Journal of Popular Culture 36, 2,
November 2002, 285–317.

Cole, Cheryl and Samantha King. "Representing Black Masculinity and Urban
Possibilities: Racism, Realism, and Hoop Dreams" in Sport and Postmodern Times,
ed. Geneviève Rail. Albany: State University of New York Press, 1998, 49–86.

Collins, Patricia Hill. Black Sexual Politics: African Americans, Gender, and the New
Racism. New York: Routledge, 2005.

Colson, Elizabeth. The Makah Indians: A Study of an Indian Tribe in Modern American
Society. Minneapolis: University of Minnesota Press, 1953.

Comaroff, Jean and John Comaroff. "Naturing the Nation: Aliens, Apocalypse, and the
Postcolonial State." Social Identities 7, 2, 2001, 233–65.

Coogan, Dan. "Race and Crime in Sports Media: Content Analysis on the Michael Vick
and Ben Roethlisberger Cases." Journal of Sports Media 7, 2, Fall 2012, 129–50.

Cooper, Douglas Anthony. "Michael Vick Just Adopted a WHAT?" Huffingtonpost.
com. October 19, 2012. http://www.huffingtonpost.com/douglas-anthony-cooper
/michael-vick-and-the-huma_b_1976502.html.

Costello, Kimberly and Gordon Hodson. "Exploring the Roots of Dehumanization:
The Role of Animal-Human Similarity in Promoting Immigrant Humanization."
Group Processes & Intergroup Relations 13, 1, 2009, 3–22.

Coté, Charlotte. Spirits of Our Whaling Ancestors: Revitalizing Makah & Nuu-chah-
nulth Traditions. Seattle: University of Washington Press, 2010.

Coté, John. "S.F. Mayor Counters Yee's Attack Ad in Cantonese." SFGate.com.
September 16, 2011. http://www.sfgate.com/cgi-bin/article.cgi?f=/c/a/2011/09/16
/BAQ11L58LF.DTL.

"David Chiu-Ed Lee Bromance Is So over." City Insider. August 12, 2011.
http://www.sfgate.com/cgi-bin/blogs/cityinsider/detail?entry_id=95252.

"Kopp Wants Investigation of Mayor Lee's Friend, Rose Pak." City Insider. August 1,
2011. http://www.sfgate.com/cgi-bin/blogs/cityinsider/detail?entry_id=94462.

"SF Mayor Ed Lee's Rivals Seek Probe of His Backers." SFGate.com. July 29, 2011.
http://www.sfgate.com/cgi-bin/article.cgi?f=/c/a/2011/07/29/MNOV1KGCS9
.DTL.

Craddock, Susan. "Embodying Place: Pathologizing Chinese and Chinatown in
Nineteenth-Century San Francisco." Antipode 31, 4, 1999, 351–71.

"Sewers and Scapegoats: Spatial Metaphors of Smallpox in Nineteenth-Century Sar Francisco." *Social Science Medicine* 41, 7, 1995, 957–68.

Craven, James Michael. "Chronicles of Ecoimperialism: Real Whales, Real People." n.d http://www.chgs.unm.edu/histories/victims/nativeAmerican/ecoimperialism.html.

Crawford, Amy. "Leland Yee Parody Book Claims to Know 'the Real Ed Lee.'" *SFExaminer.com.* October 31, 2011. http://www.sfexaminer.com/local/2011/1c /leland-yee-campaign-book-parodies-ed-lee-bio.

Crenshaw, Kimberlé. "Mapping the Margins: Intersectionality, Identity Politics, anc Violence against Women of Color" in *The Public Nature of Private Violence*, ed Martha Fineman. New York: Routledge, 1994, 93–118.

"Demarginalizing the Intersection of Race and Sex: A Feminist Critique o Antidiscrimination Doctrine, Feminist Theory and Antiracist Politics." *University of Chicago Legal Forum* 1989, 139–67.

Cronon, William. "The Trouble with Wilderness; Or, Getting Back to the Wrong Nature" in *Uncommon Ground: Rethinking the Human Place in Nature*, ed William Cronon. New York: W. W. Norton & Co., 1995, 69–90.

"Current Issues – Improving Scientific Capacity." California Department of Fish and Game (now Department of Fish and Wildlife). http://www.fgc.ca.gov/public /reports/DFGissues/Improving%20Scientific%20Capacity.pdf.

Curtis, Edward S. "The Nootka. The Haida" in *The North American Indian: Being a Series of Volumes Picturing and Describing the Indians of the United States, and Alaska*, ed. Frederick Webb Hodge. Vol. 11, 1916. [Seattle]: [Cambridge, USA: E. S. Curtis, The University Press], 1907–30.

Dark, Alx. "The Makah Whaling Conflict: Arguments against the Hunt." *Native Americans and the Environment.* 2000. http://cnie.org/NAE/cases/makah /m5.html.

"The Makah Whaling Conflict: 'Eco-Colonialism.'" *Native Americans and the Environment.* 2000. http://cnie.org/NAE/cases/makah/m6.html.

"The Makah Whaling Conflict: Whaling Opponents." *Native Americans and the Environment.* 2000. http://cnie.org/NAE/cases/makah/m3.html.

"The Makah Whaling Conflict: Whaling Protests." *Native Americans and the Environment.* 2000. http://cnie.org/NAE/cases/makah/m4.html.

D'Amato, Anthony and Sudhir Chopra. "Whales: Their Emerging Right to Life." *The American Journal of International Law* 85, 1991, 21–62.

Davey, Gareth. "Chinese University Students' Attitudes toward the Ethical Treatment and Welfare of Animals." *Journal of Applied Animal Welfare Science* 9, 4, 2006, 289–97.

Davidson, Arnold. "The Horror of Monsters" in *The Boundaries of Humanity: Humans, Animals, Machines*, eds. James Sheehan and Morton Sosna. Berkeley: University of California Press, 1991, 36–64.

Davis, Janet. "Cockfight Nationalism: Blood Sport and the Moral Politics of American Empire and Nation Building." *American Quarterly.* Special issue "Species/Race/ Sex," eds. Claire Jean Kim and Carla Freccero. 65, 3, September 2013, 549–74.

Dawson, Michael. *Behind the Mule: Race and Class in African-American Politics.* Princeton, NJ: Princeton University Press, 1995.

D'Costa, Russell. "Reparations as a Basis for the Makah's Right to Whale." *Animal Law* 12, 2005–6, 71–97.

Death on a Factory Farm. DVD. Directed by Tom Simon and Sarah Teale. New York, New York: Teale-Edwards Productions, 2009.

Deckha, Maneesha. "Welfarist *and* Imperial: The Contributions of Anti-Cruelty Laws to Civilizational Discourse." *American Quarterly*. Special issue "Species/Race/Sex," eds. Claire Jean Kim and Carla Freccero. 65, 3, September 2013, 515–48.

"Animal Justice, Cultural Justice: A Posthumanist Response to Cultural Rights in Animals." *Journal of Animal Law & Ethics* 2, May 2007, 189–229.

"The Salience of Species Difference for Feminist Theory." *Hastings Women's Law Journal* 17, Winter 2006, 1–38.

DeLeon, Richard. "Only in San Francisco? The City's Political Culture in Comparative Perspective." *SPUR Newsletter*. November/December 2002, 1. http://www.spur.org/.

Left Coast City: Progressive Politics in San Francisco, 1975–1991. Lawrence: University Press of Kansas, 1992.

DeLeon, Richard and Katherine Naff. "Identity Politics and Local Political Culture: Some Comparative Results from the Social Capital Benchmark Survey." *Urban Affairs Review*, 39, 6, July 2004, 689–719.

Delgado, Ray. "Riotous Debate on Animal Sales." *San Francisco Examiner*. October 18, 1996, A11.

"S.F. Food Fight: Tradition, Animal Rights Clash in Chinatown." *San Francisco Examiner*. July 16, 1996, A1.

Deloria, Vine, Jr. "American Indian Metaphysics" in *Power and Place: Indian Education in America*, eds. Vine Deloria and D. R. Wildcat. Golden, CO: Fulcrum, 2001, 1–6.

De Paiva Duarte, Fernanda. "'Save the Earth' or 'Manage the Earth'? The Politics of Environmental Globality in High Modernity." *Current Sociology* 49, 1, 2001, 91–111.

Di Chiro, Giovanna. "Beyond Ecoliberal 'Common Futures': Environmental Justice, Toxic Touring, and a Transcommunal Politics of Place" in *Race, Nature, and the Politics of Difference*, eds. Donald Moore, Jake Kosek, and Anand Pandian. Durham, NC: Duke University Press, 2003, 204–32.

"Dogfighting a Booming Business, Experts Say." *CNN.com*. July 18, 2007. http://articles/cnn.com/2007-07-18/us/dog.fighting_1_illegal-blood-sport-underground-dogfighting-magazines-animal-shelters?_s=PM:US.

"Dogfighting FAQ." American Society for the Prevention of Cruelty to Animals. http://www.aspca.org/fight-animal-cruelty/dog-fighting/dog-fighting-faq.aspx.

"Dog-Fighting and the Neutering of Black Moral Outrage." Posted by BronxBoy, July 20, 2007. http://www.democraticunderground.com/discuss/duboard.php?az=view_all&address=389x1388619#1388619.

Donald, Leland. *Aboriginal Slavery on the Northwest Coast of North America*. Berkeley: University of California Press, 1997.

Donaldson, Sue and Will Kymlicka. *Zoopolis: A Political Theory of Animal Rights*. Oxford: Oxford University Press, 2011.

Dormon, James. "Shaping the Popular Image of Post-Reconstruction American Blacks: The 'Coon Song' Phenomenon of the Gilded Age." *American Quarterly* 40, 4, December 1988, 450–71.

Dougherty, John. "After a 70-year Hiatus and a Confrontation with the World, the Makah Tribe Resumes Its Communion with the Gray Whale." *San Francisco Resurrection*. July 11, 2001. http://www.sfweekly.com/content/printVersion/312202/.

Drexler, Peggy. "Michael Vick Should Work, but Never Again in the NFL." *Huffingtonpost.com*. July 29, 2009. http://www.huffingtonpost.com/peggy-drexler/michael-vick-should-work_b_247462.html.

Duggan, Lisa. *The Twilight of Equality? Neoliberalism, Cultural Politics, and the Attack On Democracy.* Boston, MA: Beacon Press, 2003.

Dunayer, Joan. *Animal Equality: Language and Liberation.* Derwood, MD: Ryce, 2001.

Dundes, Alan. "Gallus as Phallus: A Psychoanalytic Cross-Cultural Consideration of the Cockfight as Fowl Play" in *The Cockfight: A Casebook*, ed. Alan Dundes. Madison: University of Wisconsin Press, 1994, 241–82.

Duran, Bonnie. "Indigenous Versus Colonial Discourse: Alcohol and American Indian Identity" in *Dressing in Feathers: The Construction of the Indian in American Popular Culture*, ed. S. Elizabeth Bird. Boulder, CO: Westview, 1996, 111–28.

Eaton, David. "Incorporating the Other: Val Plumwood's Integration of Ethical Frameworks." *Ethics & the Environment* 7, 2, 2002, 153–80.

Ebanda de B'béri, Boulou and Peter Hogarth. "White America's Construction of Black Bodies: The Case of Ron Artest as a Model of Covert Racial Ideology in the NBA's Discourse." *Journal of International and Intercultural Communication* 2, 2, May 2009, 89–106.

Eckholm, Erik. "Power Broker Savors a Victory in San Francisco." *New York Times.* November 11, 2011, a1.

Ehrenreich, Nancy. "Subordination and Symbiosis: Mechanisms of Mutual Support Between Subordinating Systems." *University of Missouri Kansas City Law Review* 71, 2002, 251–324.

Eisnitz, Gail. *Slaughterhouse: The Shocking Story of Greed, Neglect, and Inhumane Treatment Inside the U.S. Meat Industry.* New York: Prometheus, 2007.

Elder, Glen, Jennifer Wolch, and Jody Emel, "*Le Pratique Sauvage*: Race, Place, and the Human-Animal Divide" in *Animal Geographies: Place, Politics, and Identity in the Nature-Culture Borderlands*, eds. Jennifer Wolch and Jody Emel. London: Verso, 1998, 72–90.

Eljera, Bert. "The Sum of Its Parts." *Asian Week.* February 12, 1998, 38.

"What Are Neighbors For? A New Asian American Community Group Challenges the Political Structure in San Francisco." *Asian Week.* October 9–15, 1997. http://www.asianweek.com/100997/feature.html.

"Cultural Divide: Tensions Rise over 'Fresh Kill' Controversy." *Asian Week.* October 25, 1996, 5.

Emel, Jody. "Are You Man Enough, Big and Bad Enough? Wolf Eradication in the US" in *Animal Geographies: Place, Politics, and Identity in the Nature-Culture Borderlands*, eds. Jennifer Wolch and Jody Emel. London: Verso Press, 1998, 91–116.

Enloe, Cynthia. *Bananas, Beaches, and Bases: Making Feminist Sense of International Politics.* Berkeley: University of California Press, 1989.

"Equality Statement." Sea Shepherd Conservation Society. n.d. http://www.seashepherd.org/who-we-are/equality-statement.html.

Erikson, Patricia. "A-Whaling We Will Go: Encounters of Knowledge and Memory at the Makah Cultural and Research Center." *Cultural Anthropology* 14, 4, 1999, 556–83.

Eskridge, Anna and Derek Alderman. "Alien Invaders, Plant Thugs, and the Southern Curse/Framing Kudzu as Environmental Other through Discourses of Fear." *Southeastern Geographer* 50, 1, Spring 2010, 110–29.

Evans, Rhonda and Craig Forsyth. "The Social Milieu of Dogmen and Dogfights." *Deviant Behavior: An Interdisciplinary Journal* 19, 1, 1998, 51–71.

"Entertainment to Outrage: A Social Historical View of Dogfighting." *International Review of Modern Sociology* 27, 2, Autumn 1997, 59–71.

Evans, Rhonda, DeAnn Gauthier, and Craig Forsyth. "Dogfighting: Symbolic Expression and Validation of Masculinity." *Sex Roles* 39, 11/12, 1998, 825–38.

Fagan, Kevin. "Census Shows Big Gains by Asian Americans, Latinos." *San Francisco Chronicle*. March 9, 2011. http://articles.sfgate.com/2011-03-09/bay -area/28670698_1_asian-numbers-asian-american-population-latino-population.

Fantz, Ashley. "Dogfighters Get Creative as Spotlight on Vick Case Fades." *CNN.com*. August 17, 2009. http://www.cnn.com/2009/CRIME/08/17/us.dog.fighting/index .html?iref=mp.storyview.

Farrar, Doug. "Vick on Dogfighting in GQ: 'People Act Like It's Some Crazy Thing They Never Heard Of.'" August 17, 2011. http://sports.yahoo.com/nfl/blog /shutdown_corner/post/vick-on-dogfig…like-its-some-crazy-thing-they-never -heard-of?urn=nfl,wp5294&print=1.

Feagin, Joe. *Racist America: Roots, Current Realities, and Future Reparations*. New York: Routledge, 2001.

Ferber, Abby. "The Construction of Black Masculinity: White Supremacy Now and Then." *Journal of Sport & Social Issues* 31, 1, February 2007, 11–24.

Fields, R. Douglas. "Are Whales Smarter Than We Are?" *Scientific American*. January 15, 2008. http://www.scientificamerican.com/blog/post.cfm?id-are-whales-smarter -than-we-are.

Firestone, Jeremy and Jonathan Lilley. "Aboriginal Subsistence Whaling and the Right to Practice and Revitalize Cultural Traditions and Customs." *Journal of International Wildlife Law & Policy* 8, 2–3, 2005, 177–219.

Fisher, Robert and H. Bradley Shaffer. "The Decline of Amphibians in California's Great Central Valley." *Conservation Biology* 10, 1996, 1387–97.

Fleming, David. "The Dog in the Room. A Lot of People Will Never Forgive Michael Vick. A Lot of People Wonder Why, Too." *ESPN The Magazine*. September 5, 2011. http:// espn.go.com/espn/commentary/story/_/id/6889579/espn-magazine-examining- michael-vick-where-dogfighting-falls-continuum-cruelty.

"There Is No Middle Ground." *ESPN The Magazine*. September 5, 2011. http://espn .go.com/espn/print?id=6885774&type=story.

Florio, Mike. "Nawrocki Provides Scathing Assessment of Geno Smith." April 1, 2013. http://profootballtalk.nbcsports.com/2013/04/01/nawrock-provides-scathing -assessment-of-geno-smith/.

Foer, Jonathan. *Eating Animals*, reprinted edition. New York: Back Bay Books, 2010.

Food & Water Watch. *Factory Farm Nation: How America Turned Its Livestock Farms Into Factories*. November 2010. http://www.foodandwaterwatch.org/reports /factory-farm-nation/.

"Food-Disparagement Laws: State Civil & Criminal Statutes." FoodSpeak, Coalition for Free Speech. http://cspinet.org/foodspeak/laws/existlaw.htm.

Forsyth, Craig and Rhonda Evans. "Dogmen: The Rationalization of Deviance." *Society & Animals* 6, 3, 1998, 203–18.

Fouts, Roger and Stephen Tukel Mills. *Next of Kin: My Conversations With Chimpanzees*. New York: William Morrow Publishing, 1998.

Fox, Warwick. "The Deep Ecology-Ecofeminism Debate and Its Parallels." *Environmental Ethics* 11, 1, Spring 1989, 5–25.

Francione, Gary. "We're all Michael Vick." August 14, 2009. http://www.philly.com /dailynews/opinion/20070822_Were_all_Michael_Vick.html.

Rain without Thunder: The Ideology of the Animal Rights Movement. Philadelphia, PA: Temple University Press, 1996.

Frazier, Ian. "Fish Out of Water: The Asian-Carp Invasion." *The New Yorker.* October 25, 2010. http://www.newyorker.com/reporting/2010/10/25/101025fa_fact_frazier ?currentPage=all.

Freccero, Carla. "Carnivorous Virility, or Becoming-Dog." *Social Text.* Special Issue "Interspecies," eds. Julie Livingston and Jasbir Puar. 106, 29, 1, 2011, 177–95.

"Figural Historiography: Dogs, Humans, and Cynanthropic Becomings" in *Comparatively Queer,* eds. Jarrod Hayes, Margaret Higonnet, and William J Spurlin. Basingstoke: Palgrave, 2010, 45–67.

Fredrickson, George. *The Black Image in the White Mind: The Debate on Afro-American Character and Destiny, 1817–1914.* Middletown, CT: Wesleyan University Press, 1971.

Fudge, Erica. *Perceiving Animals: Humans and Beasts in Early Modern English Culture.* Champagne: University of Illinois Press, 2000.

Gaard, Greta. "Tools for a Cross-Cultural Feminist Ethics: Exploring Ethical Contexts and Contents in the Makah Whale Hunt." *Hypatia* 16, 1, Winter 2001, 1–26.

Gaard, Greta, ed. *Ecofeminism: Women, Animals, Nature.* Philadelphia, PA: Temple University Press, 1993.

Garcia, Ken. "Election Results Strip Bare any Myths about San Francisco." *SFExaminer. com.* November 13, 2011. http://www.sfexaminer.com/local/2011/11/election -results-srip-bare-any-myths-about-san-francisco.

García, María Elena. "The Taste of Conquest: Colonialism, Cosmopolitics, and the Dark Side of Peru's Gastronomic Boom." *Journal of Latin American and Caribbean Anthropology,* 18, 3, November 2013, 505–24.

García, María Elena and José Antonio Lucero. "Exceptional Others: Politicians, Rottweilers, and Alterity in the 2006 Peruvian Elections." *Latin American and Caribbean Ethnic Studies* 3, 3, November 2008, 253–70.

Garrison, Bob. "Watchable Wildlife: Western Pond Turtle." *Outdoor California* May/ June 1998, 29.

Gee, Sherman. "Housing Profile of Chinatown." *Urban Action* 2007, 33–7. http://www .bss.sfsu.edu/urbanaction.

Geron, Kim and James Lai. "Race, Space, and the New Political Configurations of San Francisco Politics." August 18, 2011. Conference paper presented at the American Political Science Association Annual Meeting.

Gibson, Hanna. "Dog Fighting Detailed Discussion." Animal Legal and Historical Center. Michigan State University College of Law. 2005. http://www.animallaw .info/articles/ddusdogfighting.htm.

Gillespie, Alexander. "The Ethical Question in the Whaling Debate." *The Georgetown International Environmental Law Review* 9, 1997, 355–87.

Gilmore, Ruth. *Golden Gulag: Prisons, Surplus, Crisis, and Opposition in Globalizing California.* Berkeley: University of California Press, 2007.

Girgen, Jen. *Constructing Animal Rights Activism as a Social Threat: Claims-Making in the New York Times and in Congressional Hearings.* Dissertation in College of Criminology and Social Justice. Florida State University. 2008.

Glazer, Nathan. *We Are All Multiculturalists Now.* Cambridge, MA: Harvard University Press, 1998.

Glick, Megan. "Animal Instincts: Race, Criminality, and the Reversal of the 'Human.'" *American Quarterly.* Special issue "Species/Race/Sex," eds. Claire Jean Kim and Carla Freccero. 65, 3, September 2013, 639–59.

Gobster, Paul. "Invasive Species as Ecological Threat: Is Restoration an Alternative to Fear-Based Resource Management?" *Ecological Restoration* 23, 4, December 2005, 261–70.

Goff, Phillip et al. "Not Yet Human: Implicit Knowledge, Historical Dehumanization, and Contemporary Consequences." *Journal of Personality and Social Psychology* 94, 2, 2008, 292–306.

Golden, Tim. "Animal Activists Deplore Police: S.F. Groups Seek Change in Treatment of Fish, Turtles, Frogs in Chinatown Markets." *Daily News*. September 1, 1996.

Gompers, Samuel and Herman Gutstadt. *MEAT vs. RICE: American Manhood against Asiatic Coolieism, WHICH SHALL SURVIVE?* San Francisco, CA: Asiatic Exclusion League, 1908.

Gorant, Jim. *The Lost Dogs: Michael Vick's Dogs and Their Tale of Rescue and Redemption*. New York: Gotham Books, 2010.

Gordon, Lewis. *Her Majesty's Other Children: Sketches of Racism from a Neocolonial Age*. Lanham, MD: Rowman & Littlefield, 1997.

Gordon, Rachel. "How San Francisco's Neighborhoods Voted for Mayor." *SFGate.com*. November 13, 2011. http://www.sfgate.com/cgi-bin/article.cgi?f=/c/a/2011/11/13/MNBN1LTRRD.DTL.

"SF Asian Americans Ascending in Halls of Power." *San Francisco Chronicle*. January 11, 2011. http://www.sfgate.com/cgi-bin/article.cgi?f=/c/a/2011/01/11/MN8J1H6TKD.DTL.

Gorman, Richard William, Jr. "Whales, Guns, and Money? How Commercial and Ideological Considerations Influenced *The Seattle Times* Portrayal of the Makah Whale Hunt." Masters Thesis in American Indian Studies. University of Arizona. 2000.

Gorman, Steve. "Whoopi Goldberg Defends Vick's Dog-fighting Role." *Reuters*. September 4, 2007.

Gotanda, Neil. "Citizenship Nullification: The Impossibility of Asian American Politics" in *Asian Americans and Politics: Perspectives, Experiences, Prospects*, ed. Gordon Chang. Washington, DC: Woodrow Wilson Press, 2001, 79–101.

"A Critique of 'Our Constitution Is Color-Blind.'" *Stanford Law Review* 44, 1, November 1991, 1–68.

Gottlieb, Paul. "U.S. Halts Makah Whaling Study after Seven Years over 'New Scientific Information' (with link to video of 1999 whale hunt)." *Peninsula Daily News*. May 23, 2012. http://www.peninsuladailynews.com/article/20120523/NEWS/305239987/us-halts-makah-whaling-study-after-seven-years-over-new-scientific.

"Ten Years Today after Historic Hunt, Makah Wait to Whale Again." *Peninsula Daily News*. May 17, 2009. http://www.peninsuladailynews.com/article/20090517/news/305179997.

Gould. Stephen Jay. "An Evolutionary Perspective on Strengths, Fallacies, and Confusions in the Concept of Native Plants" in *Nature and Ideology: Natural Garden Design in the Twentieth Century*, ed. Joachim Wolschke-Bulmahn. Washington, DC: Dumbarton Oaks Research Library and Collection, 1997, 11–19.

Gould, Stephen Jay. *The Mismeasure of Man*. Revised and expanded edition. New York: W. W. Norton & Company, 1996.

"Gray Whale (*Eschrichtius robustus*)." National Oceanic and Atmospheric Administration Fisheries, Office of Protected Resources. n.d. http://www.nmfs.noaa.gov/pr/species/mammals/cetaceans/graywhale.htm.

Grewal, Inderpal and Caren Kaplan. "*Warrior Marks*: Global Womanism's Neo-Colonial Discourse in a Multicultural Context." *Camera Obscura* 39, 12, September 1996, 5–33.

Griffin, Rachel. "The Disgrace of Commodification and Shameful Convenience: A Critical Race Critique of the NBA." *Journal of Black Studies* 43, 2, 2012, 161–85.

Griffin, Rachel and Bernadette Marie Calafell. "Control, Discipline, and Punish: Black Masculinity and (In)visible Whiteness in the NBA" in *Critical Rhetorics of Race*, eds. Michael Lacy and Kent Ono. New York: New York University Press, 1997, 117–36.

Griffith, Marcie, Jennifer Wolch, and Unna Lassiter. "Animal Practices and the Racialization of Filipinas in Los Angeles." *Society & Animals* 10, 3, 2002, 221–48.

Groning, Gert and Joachim Wolschke-Bulmahn. "The Native Plant Enthusiasm: Ecological Panacea or Xenophobia?" *Landscape Research* 28 1, 2003, 75–88.

Gruen, Lori. *Ethics and Animals*. New York: Cambridge University Press, 2011.

Gruen, Lori. "Facing Death and Practicing Grief" in *Ecofeminism: Feminist Intersections with Other Animals & the Earth*, eds. Carol Adams and Lori Gruen. New York: Bloomsbury, 2014, 127–41.

Guerrero, Lisa. "One Nation under a Hoop: Race, Meritocracy, and Messiahs in the NBA" in *Commodified and Criminalized: New Racism and African Americans in Contemporary Sports*, eds. David Leonard and C. Richard King. Lanham, MD: Rowman & Littlefield, 2011, 121–46.

Gunther, Erna. "Reminiscences of a Whaler's Wife." *The Pacific Northwest Quarterly* 33, 1, January 1942, 65–9.

Gupta, Akhil and James Ferguson, "Culture, Power, Place: Ethnography at the End of an Era" in *Culture, Power, Place: Explorations in Critical Anthropology*, eds. Akhil Gupta and James Ferguson. Durham, NC: Duke University Press, 1997, 3–29.

Haraway, Donna. *When Species Meet*. Minneapolis: University of Minnesota Press, 2007.

The Companion Species Manifesto: Dogs, People, and Significant Otherness. Chicago, IL: Prickly Paradigm Press, 2003.

Primate Visions: Gender, Race, and Nature in the World of Modern Science. New York: Routledge, 1989.

Harris, A. W. "Making the Case for Collective Rights: Indigenous Claims to Stocks of Marine Living Resources." *Georgetown International Environmental Law Review* 15, 3, 2003, 379–428.

Harris-Perry, Melissa. "Michael Vick, Racial History and Animal Rights." *The Nation*. December 30, 2010. http://www.thenation.com/blog/157372/michael-vick-racial-history-and-animal-rights#axzz2eRL4U4Xx.

Hartmann, Douglas. "Rush Limbaugh, Donovan McNabb, and 'A Little Social Concern': Reflections on the Problems of Whiteness in Contemporary American Sport." *Journal of Sport & Social Issues* 31, 1, February 2007, 45–60.

"Rethinking the Relationships between Sport and Race in American Culture: Golden Ghettos and Contested Terrain." *Sociology of Sport Journal* 17, 2000, 229–53.

Hatton, Barry. "Whaling Talks Stalled: Situation Is 'Fragile'." *Huffingtonpost.com*. June 22, 2009. http://www.huffingtonpost.com/2009/06/22/whaling-talks-stalled_n_218987.html.

Hawkins, Ronnie. "Cultural Whaling, Commodification, and Culture Change." *Environmental Ethics* 23, Fall 2001, 287–306.

Hearne, Vicki. *Adam's Task: Calling Animals By Name*. Reprinted edition. New York: Skyhorse Publishing, 2007.

Hendrix, Anastasia. "S.F.'S Chinatown/ Almost All Residents Foreign-Born." *San Francisco Chronicle*. August 27, 2002. http://articles.sfgate.com/2002-08-27/news/17558683_1_chinese-immigrants-chinatown-elderly-immigrants.

Hindery, Robin. "Proposed Shark Fin Ban Makes Waves in San Francisco." *Associated Press*. May 6, 2011. http://www.sfgate.com/cgibin/article.cgi?f=/n/a/2011/05/06/state/n161729D19.DTL&feed=rss.news_politics.

"History and Purpose." International Whaling Commission. n.d. http://iwcoffice.org/history-and-purpose.

"The History of Sea Shepherd." Sea Shepherd Conservation Society. n.d. http://www.seashepherd.org/who-we-are/our-history.html.

Hoberman, John. *Darwin's Athletes: How Sport Has Damaged Black America and Preserved the Myth of Race*. Boston, MA: Houghton Mifflin, 1997.

Hodges, Brian Trevor. "The Cracking Façade of the International Whaling Commission as an Institution of International Law: Norwegian Small-Type Whaling and the Aboriginal Subsistence Exemption." *Journal of Environmental Law & Litigation* 15, 2000, 295–328.

Hogan, Linda. "Silencing Tribal Grandmothers – Traditions, Old Values at Heart of Makah's Clash over Whaling." *Seattle Times*. December 15, 1996. http://community.seattletimes.nwsource.com/archive/?date=19961215&slug=2365045.

Holcomb, Rodney et al. "Market Research Study: Organic, Free-Range and Pasture Poultry." Robert Kerr Food and Agricultural Products Center. n.d. http://www.fapc.biz.

Hopwood, Nick. "Pictures of Evolution and Charges of Fraud: Ernst Haeckel's Embryological Illustrations." *Isis* 97, 2, June 2006. http://www.jstor.org/stable/10.1086/504734.

Hsu, Hua. "Imagining Chinatown: Local Filmmaker Takes Ambitious Look at Contested Traditions." *Asian Week* 21, 36, 2000. http://asianweek.com/2000_05_04/ae_chinatownfilm.html.

Hua, Vanessa. "Chinatown: Housing Riddled with Violations/Neighborhood Shows Rampant Problems in Single-Room Occupancy Units." *San Francisco Chronicle*. September 23, 2005, F1.

"Newspaper War in the Bay Area/Ming Pao Becomes 6th Chinese-Language Daily." *SFGate.com*. August 3, 2004. http://www.c3.ucla.edu/newsstand/media/newspaper-war-in-the-bay-area-ming-pao-becomes-6th-chinese-language-daily/.

Hughes, Glyn. "Managing Black Guys: Representation, Corporate Culture, and the NBA." *Sociology of Sport Journal* 21, 2004, 163–84.

Huhndorf, Shari. *Going Native: Indians in the American Cultural Imagination*. Ithaca, NY: Cornell University Press, 2001.

"Humane Society Blames DMX, Jay-Z and Hip-Hop for Promoting Dog Fighting." July 20, 2007. http://www.xxlmag.com/xxl-magazine/2007/07/humane-society-blames-dmx-jay-z-and-hip-hop-for-promoting-dog-fighting/.

Humane Society of the United States. *Factory Farming in America: The True Cost of Animal Agribusiness for Rural Communities, Public Health, Families, Farmers, the Environment, and Animals*. n.d. http://www.humanesociety.org/assets/pdfs/farm/hsus-factory-farming-in-america-the-true-cost-of-animal-agribusiness.pdf.

Hutchinson, Darren. "Identity Crisis: 'Intersectionality,' 'Multidimensionality,' and the Development of an Adequate Theory of Subordination." *Michigan Journal of Race and Law* 6, 2001, 285–317.

"If Zimmerman Walks and Vick Didn't, Does that Mean that a Dog's Life I Worth More than a Black Man? *YourBlackWorld.net.* July 2013. http://www .yourblackworld.net/2013/07/black-news/if-zimmerman-walks-and-vick-didn -does-that-mean-that-a-dogs-life-is-worth-more-than-a-black-man/.

"International Laws and Charters." Sea Shepherd Conservation Society. n.d http://www.seashepherd.org/who-we-are/laws-and-charters.html.

"Invasive Alien Species – The Nature of the Problem." *Assessment and Managemen of Alien Species That Threaten Ecosystems, Habitats and Species.* Secretariat o the Convention on Biological Diversity. CBD Technical Series No. 1. Montreal Canada. 2000.

Jacoby, Karl. "Slaves by Nature? Domestic Animals and Human Slaves." *Slavery anc Abolition* 15, 1, April 1994, 89–99.

"Jamie Foxx Defends Michael Vick." *Starpulse News Blog.* August 24, 2007. http://www .starpulse.com/news/index.php/2007/08/24/jamie_foxx_defends_michael_vick.

Jeffries, Shavar. "Vick, Proportionality, and Race." August 27, 2007. http://www .blackprof.com/archives/2007/08/vick_proportionality_and_race.html.

Jefferson, Thomas. *Notes on the State of Virginia.* Philadelphia, PA: Printed for Mathew Carey, no. 118, Market Street, November 12, 1794.

Jenkins, Leesteffy and Cara Romanzo. "Makah Whaling: Aboriginal Subsistence or a Stepping Stone to Undermining the Commercial Whaling Moratorium?" *Colorado Journal of International Environmental Law and Policy* 9, 1998, 71–114.

Johanna. "Anti-Whaling Advocates and the Far Right." July 12, 2009. http:// vegansofcolor.wordpress.com/2009/07/12/anti-whaling-advocates-and-the-far-right/.

"John Chinaman." Anonymous. *The California Songster.* San Francisco, CA: Appleton, 1855. http://www.columbia.edu/itc/history/baker/w3630/edit/chinpoem.html.

Johnson, Alex. "Vick Case Divides African-American Leaders." *MSNBC.com.* August 23, 2007. http://www.msnbc.msn.com/id/20411561/page/2/print/1/displaymode/1098/.

Johnson, Keith. "An Open Letter to the Public from the President of the Makah Whaling Commission." August 6, 1998. *Native Americans and the Environment.* http://cnie .org/NAE/docs/makaheditorial.html.

Jones, Steven. "Power and Pragmatism." *San Francisco Bay Guardian.* January 11, 2011. http://www.sfbg.com/2011/01/11/power-and-pragmatism.

Jordan, Winthrop. *White Over Black: American Attitudes toward the Negro, 1550– 1812.* Chapel Hill: University of North Carolina Press, 1968.

Kalof, Linda and Maria Andromachi Iliopoulou. "Abusing the Human-Animal Bond: On the Making of Fighting Dogs" in *The Psychology of the Human-Animal Bond: A Resource for Clinicians and Researchers,* eds. Christopher Blazina et al. New York: Springer, 2011, 321–32.

Kalof, Linda and Carl Taylor. "The Discourse of Dog Fighting." *Humanity & Society* 31, November 2007, 319–33.

Kappeler, Susanne. "Speciesism, Racism, Nationalism … or the Power of Scientific Subjectivity" in *Animals and Women: Feminist Theoretical Explorations,* eds. Carol Adams and Josephine Donovan. Durham, NC: Duke University Press, 1995, 320–52.

Kaste, Martin. "Tribe Views Whale Hunters as Heroes, Nuisances." *NPR.org.* March 12, 2008. http://www.npr.org/templates/story/story.php?storyId=88159568.

Keith, Christie. "Michael Vick's Unpaid Dues: Why Dog Advocates Aren't Moving On." *SFGate.com.* November 3, 2009. http://www.sfgate.com/cgi-bin/article.cgi ?file=/g/a/2009/11/03/petscol110309.DTL.

Kellner, Douglas. "The Sports Spectacle, Michael Jordan, and Nike: Unholy Alliance?" in *Michael Jordan, Inc.: Corporate Sport, Media Culture, and Late Modern America*, ed. David Andrews. Albany: State University of New York Press, 2001, 37–63.

Kheel, Marti. *Nature Ethics: An Ecofeminist Perspective*. Lanham, MD: Rowman & Littlefield, 2007.

"License to Kill: An Ecofeminist Critique of Hunters' Discourse" in *Animals & Women: Feminist Theoretical Explorations*, eds. Carol Adams and Josephine Donovan. Durham, NC: Duke University Press, 1995, 85–125.

Kim, Claire Jean. "The Great Yellow Hope." *WBEZ.org*. March 8, 2012. http://www.wbez.org/blog/alison-cuddy/2012-03-08/jeremy-lin-great-yellow-hope-97098.

"Moral Extensionism or Racist Exploitation?: The Use of Holocaust and Slavery Analogies in the Animal Liberation Movement." *New Political Science* 33, 3, Fall 2011, 311–33.

"President Obama and the Polymorphous 'Other' in U.S. Racial Discourse." *Asian American Law Journal*, 18, Fall 2011, 165–75.

"Slaying the Beast: Reflections on Race, Culture, and Species." *Kalfou*. Inaugural Issue, Spring 2010, 57–74.

"Multiculturalism Goes Imperial: Immigrants, Animals, & the Suppression of Moral Dialogue." *Du Bois Review* 4, 1, Spring 2007, 233–49.

Bitter Fruit: The Politics of Black-Korean Conflict in New York City. New Haven. CT: Yale University Press, 2000.

"The Racial Triangulation of Asian Americans." *Politics & Society* 27, 1, March 1999, 105–38.

Kim, Claire Jean and Carla Freccero. "Introduction: A Dialogue." *American Quarterly*. Special issue "Species/Race/Sex," eds. Claire Jean Kim and Carla Freccero. 65, 3, September 2013, 461–79.

Kirksey, S. Eben and Stefan Helmreich. "The Emergence of Multispecies Ethnography." *Cultural Anthropology* 25, 4, 2010, 545–76.

Knight, Heather. "Low Voter Turnout Overall, but not Chinese Americans." *SFGate.com*. November 13, 2011. http://www.sfgate.com/cgi-bin/article.cgi?f=/c/a/2011/11/13/BAHP1LSSG9.DTL.

"Mayor Ed Lee Opposed to Shark Fin Soup Ban." *City Insider*. April 26, 2011. http://www.sfgate.com/cgi-bin/blogs/cityinsider/detail?entry_id=87736.

Knight, Heather and John Coté. "S.F. Ranked-choice Voting Hurts Progressive Backers." *SFGate.com*. November 10, 2011. http://www.sfgate.com/cgi-bin/article.cgi?f=/c/a/2011/11/10/MNIP1LSOF4.DTL.

Kobin, Sandra. "Beat a Woman? Play On; Beat a Dog? You're Gone." *Womensenews.org*. August 21, 2007. http://www.womensenews.org/article.cfm?aid=3285.

Kohn, Eduardo. "How Dogs Dream: Amazonian Natures and the Politics of Transpecies Engagement." *American Ethnologist* 34, 1, 2007, 3–24.

Krech, Shepard. *The Ecological Indian: Myth and History*. New York: W. W. Norton & Company, 1999.

Kurtenbach, Elaine. "Yao Ming, Branson Join to Fight Shark Fin Trade." *Associated Press*. September 22, 2011. http://www.sfgate.com/cgi-bin/article.cgi?f=/n/a/2011/09/21/international/i215838D27.DTL&type.

Kwan, Peter. "Complicity and Complexity: Cosynthesis and Praxis." *De Paul Law Review* 49, 2000, 673–90.

Kwok Hung Lee, Larry. "Letter to the Editor: Show Some Respect." *Asian Week*. November 22, 1996.

Kwong, Jessica. "More Voters, Chinese-Americans Included, May Favor Shark Fin Ban than You Think." *City Insider*. May 6, 2011.

Kwong, Peter. *Forbidden Workers: Illegal Chinese Immigrants and American Labor*. New York: New Press, 1997.

The New Chinatown. New York: Noonday Press, 1987.

Kymlicka, Will. *Multicultural Citizenship: A Liberal Theory of Minority Rights*. Oxford: Oxford University Press, 1995.

La Charreada: Rodeo a la Mexicana. Dir. Olga Nájera-Ramírez. Prod. Olga Nájera-Ramírez. 1996.

Laguerre, Michel. "The Globalization of a Panethnopolis: Richmond District as the New Chinatown." *Geojournal* 64, 1, September 2005, 41–9.

The Global Ethnopolis: Chinatown, Japantown and Manilatown in American Society. Houndmills, England: Macmillan Press, 2000.

Lai, Him Mark. "China and the Chinese American Community: The Political Dimension." *Chinese America: History and Perspectives* 1, 1999.

Lapchick, R. L. with K. J. Matthews. "The 2001 Racial and Gender Report Card." Northeastern University's Center for the Study of Sport in Society, 2001.

Larson, Brendon. "The War of the Roses: Demilitarizing Invasion Biology." *Frontiers in Ecology and the Environment* 3, 9, 2005, 495–500.

Laucella, Pamela. "Michael Vick: An Analysis of Press Coverage on Federal Dogfighting Charges." *Journal of Sports Media* 5, 2, Fall 2010, 35–76.

Lavoie, Judith. "Band Chief Criticizes Secrecy around Maa-Nulth Treaty Talks." *Victoria Times-Colonist*. May 31, 2003. http://groups.yahoo.com/group/protecting_knowledge/message/5491.

Lee, Henry. "S.F. Panel Debates Live-animal Sales." *SFGate.com*. August 9, 1996. http://sfgate.com/cgi-bin/article.cgi?f=/c/a/1996/08/09/MN56039.DTL.

Leitch, Will. "The Impossible, Inevitable Redemption of Michael Vick." *GQ.com*. September 2011. http://www.gq.com/sports/profiles/201109/michael-vick-gq-september-2011interview?printable=true.

Leonard, David. "Jumping the Gun: Sporting Cultures and the Criminalization of Black Masculinity." *Journal of Sport & Social Issues* 34, 2, 2010, 252–62.

"The Real Color of Money: Controlling Black Bodies in the NBA." *Journal of Sport & Social Issues* 30, 2, May 2006, 158–79.

Leonard, David and C. Richard King. "Celebrities, Commodities, and Criminals: African American Athletes and the Racial Politics of Culture" in *Commodified and Criminalized: New Racism and African Americans in Contemporary Sports*. Lanham, MD: Rowman & Littlefield, 2011, 1–22.

Leonard, David and C. Richard King, eds. *Commodified and Criminalized: New Racism and African Americans in Contemporary Sports*. Lanham, MD: Rowman & Littlefield, 2011.

Li, Peter. "The Evolving Animal Rights and Welfare Debate in China: Political and Social Impact Analysis" in *Animals, Ethics and Trade: The Challenge of Animal Sentience*, eds. Jacky Turner and Joyce D'Silva. London: Earthscan, 2006, 111–28.

"Animals in China: From the 'Four Pests' to Two Signs of Hope." *Animalpeoplenews. org*. October 2003. http://www.animalpeoplenews.org/03/10/animalsChina10.03.html.

Li, Wei. "Beyond Chinatown, Beyond Enclave: Reconceptualizing Contemporary Chinese Settlements in the United States." *Geojournal* 64, 1, September 2005, 31–40.

Lien, Marianne and Aidan Davison. "Roots, Rupture and Remembrance: The Tasmanian Lives of the Monterey Pine." *Journal of Material Culture* 15, 2, 2010, 233–53.

Lien, Pei-te. "Behind the Numbers: Talking Politics with Foreign-Born Chinese Americans." *International Migration* 42, 2, 2004, 87–112.

Lindemann, Jeffrey. "The Dilemma of the International Whaling Commission: The Loophold Provisions of the Commission vs. the World Conscience." *Journal of International Law and Practice* 7, 3, Fall 1998, 491–500.

Littlefair, Paul. "Why China Is Waking Up to Animal Welfare" in *Animals, Ethics and Trade: The Challenge of Animal Sentience*, eds. Jacky Turner and Joyce D'Silva. London: Earthscan, 2006, 225–37.

Llanos, Miguel. "California's Department of Fish and Game Gets a Name Change – and Controversy." *NBCNews.com*. October 5, 2013. http://usnews.nbcnews .com/_news/2012/10/03/14200590-californias-department-of-fish-and-game-gets -a-name-change-and-controversy.

Loft, Eric. "Economic Contribution of Deer, Pronghorn Antelope, and Sage Grouse Hunting to Northeastern California and Implications to the Overall 'Value' of Wildlife." *California Wildlife Conservation Bulletin*, No. 11, 1998 [also published on the California Fish and Wildlife Commission Web site].

Loo, Chalsa. *Chinatown: Most Time, Hard Time*. New York: Praeger, 1992.

Loo, Chalsa and Don Mar. "Desired Residential Mobility in a Low Income Ethnic Community: A Case Study of Chinatown." *Journal of Social Issues* 38, 3, 1982, 95–106.

Lovejoy, Arthur. *The Great Chain of Being: A Study of the History of an Idea*. Cambridge, MA: Harvard University Press, 2009.

Lubbers, Klaus. *Born for the Shade: Stereotypes of the Native American in United States Literature and the Visual Arts, 1776–1894*. Amsterdam: Rodopi, 1994.

Lupton, Deborah. *Food, the Body, and the Self*. London: Sage, 1996.

"Maa-nulth First Nations Sign Historic B.C. Treaty." *CBC News*. December 9, 2006. http://www.cbc.ca/news/canada/story/2006/12/09/bc-treaty.html.

Mackey, Robert. "FBI Calls Animal Rights Activist 'Terrorist.'" *The New York Times*. April 23, 2009. http://thelede.blogs.nytimes.com/2009/04/23/fbi-calls-animal -rights-activist-terrorist/.

Magubane, Zine. "Simians, Savages, Skulls, and Sex: Science and Colonial Militarism in Nineteenth-Century South Africa" in *Race, Nature, and the Politics of Difference*, eds. Donald Moore, Jake Kosek, and Anand Pandian. Durham, NC: Duke University Press, 2003, 99–121.

Maharah, Gitanjali. "Talking Trash: Late Capitalism, Black (Re)Productivity, and Professional Basketball." *Social Text* 50, 15, 1, Spring 1997, 97–110.

Makah Tribal Council. "Application for a Waiver of the Marine Mammal Protection Act Take Moratorium to Exercise Gray Whale Hunting Rights Secured in the Treaty of Neah Bay." February 11, 2005.

Makah Tribal Council and Makah Whaling Commission. "The Makah Indian Tribe and Whaling: Questions and Answers." www.makah.com. January 2005. http://www.makah.com/pdfs/makahwhalingqa.pdf.

"Makah Tribal Members Sentenced for Violating Marine Mammal Protection Act: Two Who Took Most Active Role, Leading Hunt, Sentenced to Jail Time." News Release of the United States Attorney's Office, Western District of Washington. June 30, 2008. http://www.justice.gov/usao/waw/press/2008/jul/whalesentencing .html.

"Makah Tribe – Fighting to Kill More Whales." Sea Shepherd Conservation Society. n.d. http://www.seashepherd.org/whales/makah-tribe.html.

Malanga, Steven. "The Sick Hipness of Dog Fighting." *Chicago Sun-Times.* June 17, 2007. http://www.manhattan-institute.org/html/miarticle.htm?id=3153#.US-5bY7A7a0.

"Mandate." Sea Shepherd Conservation Society. n.d. http://www.seashepherd.org /who-we-are/mandate.html.

Mann, Brian. "Illegal Dogfighting Rings Thrive in U.S. Cities." *National Public Radio.* July 20, 2007. http://www.npr.org/templates/story/story.php?storyId=12104472.

Mapes, Lynda. "2 Makahs Get Jail Time for Killing Whale." *Seattle Times.* June 30, 2008. http://seattletimes.com/html/localnews/2008026348_webmakah30m.html.

"Marine Mammal Protection Act (MMPA)." National Marine Fisheries Service. n.d. http://www.nmfs.noaa.gov/pr/laws/mmpa/.

Marino, Lori et al. "Cetaceans Have Complex Brains for Complex Cognition." *PloS Biology* 5, 5, May 15, 2007. http://www.plosbiology.org/article /info%3Adoi%2F10.1371%2Fjournal.pbio.0050139.

Marker, Michael. "After the Makah Whale Hunt: Indigenous Knowledge and Limits to Multicultural Discourse." *Urban Education* 41, 5, September 2006, 482–505.

Marmer, Lynn. "The New Breed of Municipal Dog Control Laws: Are They Constitutional?" *University of Cincinnati Law Review* 53, 1984, 1067–81.

Martello, Marybeth. "Negotiating Global Nature and Local Culture: The Case of Makah Whaling" in *Earthly Politics: Local and Global in Environmental Governance,* eds. Sheila Jasanoff and Marybeth Long Martello. Cambridge, MA: MIT Press, 2004. 263–84.

"Martin Luther King's Dream Partly Met, Still Unfulfilled – Obama." *ABC7.com.* August 28, 2013. http://abclocal.go.com/kabc/story?section=news/national _world&id=9221781.

Matier, Philip and Andrew Ross. "Rose Pak's Power Surges." *SFGate.com.* January 9, 2012. http://www.sfgate.com/cgi-bin/article.cgi?f=/c/a/2012/01/09 /BA851MM1CN.DTL.

Mazzoni, Rolando et al. "Emerging Pathogen of Wild Amphibians in Frogs (*Rana cates-beiana*) Farmed for International Trade." *Emerging Infectious Diseases* 9, 8, August 2003. http://www.cdc.gov/ncidod/EID/vol9no8/03-0030.htm.

McClintock, Anne. *Imperial Leather: Race, Gender and Sexuality in the Colonial Context.* New York: Routledge, 1995.

McNeely, Jeffrey. "The Problem of Invasive Species." *Environment* 46, 6, July/August 2004.

Medlin, Jamey. "Pit Bull Bans and the Human Factors Affecting Canine Behavior." *DePaul Law Review* 56, 4, Summer 2007, 1285–319.

Mercurio, Eugenio and Vincent Filak. "Roughing the Passer: The Framing of Black and White Quarterbacks Prior to the NFL Draft." *Howard Journal of Communications* 21, 1, 2010, 56–71.

"Metcalf's Indian History." *Indianz.com.* June 9, 2000. http://64.38.12.138/News /show.asp?ID=tc/692000-4.

"Michael Vick Case Blows Whistle on Dogfighting." *Animal People* 17, 6, September 2007, 1, 14, 15.

"Michael Vick: Race, Reality and Society." *American Whistle Blower.* August 27, 2007. http://americanwhistleblower.blogspot.com/2007/08/michael-vick-race-reality -and-society.html.

"Michael Vick's '60 Minutes' Interview." Video/Transcript. August 10, 2009. http://www.todaysdrumcom/7547/transcript-michael-vicks-60-minutes-interview/.

Miller, Arthur. "Anti-Racist Emergency Action Network Statement on Sea Shepherd and Jack Metcalf." June 6, 1999. http://www.mail-archive.com/nativenews@mlists.net /msg02969.html.

Miller, Robert. "Tribal Cultural Self-Determination and the Makah Whaling Culture" in *Sovereignty Matters: Locations of Contestation and Possibility in Indigenous Struggles for Self-Determination*, ed. Joanne Barker. Lincoln: University of Nebraska Press, 2005, 123–51.

Mills, Eric. "Culturally Sensitive Cruelty: Politically Correct Animal Suffering." *Country Connections*. January/February 1999.

Mirpuri, Anoop. "Why Can't Kobe Pass (the Ball)? Race and the NBA in an Age of Neoliberalism" in *Commodified and Criminalized: New Racism and African Americans in Contemporary Sports*, eds. David Leonard and C. Richard King. Lanham, MD: Rowman & Littlefield, 2011. 95–120.

Mitchell, Donald. "Predatory Warfare, Social Status, and the North Pacific Slave Trade." *Ethnology* 23, 1, January 1984, 39–48.

Moon, Krystyn. *Yellowface: Creating the Chinese in American Popular Music and Performance, 1850s–1920s*. Newark, NJ: Rutgers University Press, 2004.

Moore, David. "Return of the Buffalo: Cultural Representation as Cultural Property" in *Native American Representations: First Encounters, Distorted Images, and Literary Appropriations*, ed. Gretchen Bataille. Lincoln: University of Nebraska Press, 2001, 52–78.

Moore, Donald, Jake Kosek, and Anand Pandian, eds. *Race, Nature, and the Politics of Difference*. Durham, NC: Duke University Press, 2003.

Moore, Evan. "Why Most African-Americans Could Care Less about Animal Rights." *Chicagonow.com*. September 2, 2011. http://www.chicagonow.com/fanning -flames-since-1978/2011/09/why-most-african-americans-could-care-less-about -animal-rights/.

Morgan, Edmund. *American Slavery, American Freedom*. New York: W. W. Norton & Company, 1975.

Moss, Cynthia. *Elephant Memories: Thirteen Years in the Life of an Elephant Family*. Chicago, IL: University of Chicago Press, 2000.

Mossop, Joanna. "Domestic Implementation of Aboriginal Subsistence Whaling Quota: The Makah Saga Continues." OceanLaw On-Line Paper No. 19. n.d. http://www .intfish.net/ops.

Muhammad, Latifah. "Police Raid Rapper Young Calicoe's Home over Suspected Dog-Fighting." *Hiphopwired.com*. July 11, 2012. http://hiphopwired.com/2012/07/11 /police-raid-rapper-young-calicoes-home-over-suspected-dog-fighting-video/.

Municipal Reports of San Francisco 1869–70. Published by the Board of Supervisors. Printed by the Cosmopolitan Printing Company. 1870.

Myers, Micaela. "12 Reasons to Oppose Breed-Discriminatory Legislation." *Stubbydog. org*. July 12, 2012. http://stubbydog.org/2012/07/12-reasons-to-oppose-breed -discriminatory-legislation/.

Myerson, Laura and Jamie Reaser. "Bioinvasions, Bioterrorism, and Biosecurity." *Frontiers in Ecology and the Environment* 1, 6, 2003, 307–14.

"NAACP Official: Vick Shouldn't Be Banned from NFL." *CNN.com*. August 22, 2007. http://www.cnn.com/2007/US/law/08/22/vick.

Nadasdy, Paul. "The Gift in the Animal: The Ontology of Hunting and Human-Animal Sociality." *American Ethnologist* 34, 1, February 2007, 25–43.

"Transcending the Debate over the Ecologically Noble Indian: Indigenous Peoples and Environmentalism." *Ethnohistory* 52, 2, Spring 2005, 291–331.

Naess, Arne. "Deep Ecology and Ultimate Premises." *The Ecologist* 18, 4/5, 1988, 128–31.

Nájera-Ramírez, Olga. "The Racialization of a Debate: The *Charreada* as Tradition or Torture." *American Anthropologist* 98, 3, September 1996, 505–11.

"Engendering Nationalism: Identity, Discourse, and the Mexican *Charro*." *Anthropological Quarterly* 67, 1, January 1994, 1–14.

"*Haciendo Patria: La Charreada* and the Formation of a Mexican Transnational Identity." n.d. http://www.anthro.ucsc.edu/olga_pdf/hacpatri.pdf.

Narayan, Uma. "Essence of Culture and a Sense of History: A Feminist Critique of Cultural Essentialism." *Hypatia* 13, 2, Spring 1998, 86–106.

Dislocating Cultures: Identities, Traditions, and Third-World Feminism. New York: Routledge, 1997.

Nast, Heidi. "Critical Pet Studies?" *Antipode* 38, 5, 2006, 894–906.

"National NAACP Speaks about Vick and Dog Fighting; Vick to Face 'Tough but Fair' Judge" *Itchmo: News for Dogs & Cats.* August 24, 2007. http://www.itchmo.com/national-naacp-speaks-about-vick-and-dog-fighting-vick-to-face-tough-but-fair-judge-2455.

"Native Americans and the Environment/The Makah Whaling Conflict: Arguments against the Hunt." *Native Americans and the Environment.* n.d. http://cnie.org/NAE/cases/makah/m5.html.

Nee, Brian. "Michael Vick: Race, Reality and Society." *American Whistle Blower.* August 27, 2007. http://americanwhistleblower.blogspot.com/2007/08/michael-vick-race-reality-and-society.html.

Nevius, C. W. "S.F. Mayor's Race Is Finally Getting Colorful." *SFGate.com.* August 16, 2011. http://www.sfgate.com/cgi-bin/article.cgi?f=/c/a/2011/08/16/BAPK1KNIMU.DTL.

Newkirk, Ingrid. "PETA Apologizes for Holocaust Comparisons." *Jewish News Weekly of Northern California.* May 13, 2005. http://www.jewishsf.com/content/2-0-/module/displaystory/story_id/25858/format/html.

Niven, David. "Race, Quarterbacks, and the Media: Testing the Rush Limbaugh Hypothesis." *Journal of Black Studies* 35, 5, May 2005, 684–94.

Noske, Barbara. *Beyond Boundaries: Humans and Animals.* Montreal: Rose Books, 1997.

Nott, Josiah and George R. Gliddon. *Types of Mankind: Or, Ethnological Researches: Based Upon the Ancient Monuments, Paintings, Sculptures, and Crania of Races, and Upon Their Natural, Geographical, Philological and Biblical History, Illustrated by Selections from the Inedited Papers of Samuel George Morton and by Additional Contributions from L. Agassiz, W. Usher, and H.S. Patterson.* London: Trübner & Co., 1855.

Nussbaum, Martha. *Frontiers of Justice: Disability, Nationality, Species Membership.* Cambridge, MA: Harvard University Press, 2007.

Oates, Thomas Patrick. "New Media and the Repackaging of NFL Fandom." *Sociology of Sport Journal* 26, 2009, 31–49.

"The Erotic Gaze in the NFL Draft." *Communication and Critical/Cultural Studies* 4, 1, March 2007, 74–90.

O'Brien, William. "Exotic Invasions, Nativism, and Ecological Restoration: On the Persistence of a Contentious Debate." *Ethics, Place & Environment* 9, 1, 2006, 63–77.

Off the Chain: A Shocking Exposé on America's Forsaken Breed. Dir. Bobby J. Brown. Prod. David Roma, Richard Velazquez, and Troy Garity. Off the Chain Productions. 2005.

Okin, Susan. *Is Multiculturalism Bad for Women?* Princeton, NJ: Princeton University Press, 1999.

Omi, Michael and Howard Winant. *Racial Formation in the United States: From the 1960s to the 1990s*, 2nd edition. New York: Routledge, 1994.

Ortiz, Francesca. "Making the Dogman Heel: Recommendations for Improving the Effectiveness of Dogfighting Laws." 2009. http://works.bepress.com/cgi/viewcontent.cgi?article=1000&context=francesca_ortiz.

Osherenko, Gail. "Environmental Justice and the International Whaling Commission: *Moby-Dick* Revisited." *Journal of International Wildlife Law & Policy* 8, 2–3, 2005, 221–39.

"Our History." www.makah.com. n.d. http://www.makah.com/history.html.

Pacelle, Wayne. "Street Cred and Cruelty." *Blog "A Humane Nation."* June 25, 2007. http://hsus.typepad/com/wayne/2007/06/pop-culture-of-.html.

Pachirat, Timothy. *Every Twelve Seconds: Industrialized Slaughter and the Politics of Sight.* New Haven, CT: Yale University Press, 2011.

Parekh, Bhikhu. *Rethinking Multiculturalism: Cultural Diversity and Political Theory.* Cambridge, MA: Harvard University Press, 2000.

Patterson, Charles. *Eternal Treblinka: Our Treatment of Animals and the Holocaust.* New York: Lantern, 2002.

Peretti, Jonah. "Nativism and Nature: Rethinking Biological Invasion." *Environmental Values* 7, 1998, 183–92.

PETA Files. Vick at the Office, Part 2. 2007. http://blog.peta.org/archives/2007/10/vick_at_the_off.php.

Peters, Sharon. "A Fight to Save Urban Youth from Dogfighting," *USATODAY.com.* September 29, 2008. http://usatoday30.usatoday.com/news/nation/2008-09-29-dogfighting_N.htm.

Peterson, Brenda. "Who Will Speak for the Whales? – Elders Call for a Spiritual Dialogue on Makah Tribe's Whaling Proposal." *Seattle Times.* December 22, 1996. http://community.seattletimes.nwsource.com/archive/?date=19961222&slug=2366339.

Peterson, Brenda and Linda Hogan. *Sightings: The Gray Whales' Mysterious Journey.* Washington, DC: National Geographic, 2002.

Pew Research Center. "Animal Testing." July 9, 2009. http://www.people-press.org/2009/07/09/section-5-evolution-climate-change-and-other-issues/.

Pew Research Center. "Michael Vick Case Draws Large Audience: Blacks Say Press Treated Vick Unfairly." August 28, 2007. http://www.people-press.org/2007/08/28/michael-vick-case-draws-large-audience/.

Pew Research Center. *The Rise of Asian Americans.* June 19, 2012.

Philo, Chris. "Animals, Geography, and the City: Notes on Inclusions and Exclusions." *Environment and Planning D: Society and Space* 13, 1995, 655–81.

Philo, Chris and Chris Wilbert. "Animal Spaces, Beastly Places: An Introduction" in *Animal Spaces, Beastly Places: New Geographies of Human-Animal Relations*, eds. Chris Philo and Chris Wilbert. London: Routledge, 2000, 1–34.

Reference

Philo, Chris and Chris Wilbert, eds. *Animal Spaces, Beastly Places: New Geographies of Human-Animal Relations.* London: Routledge, 2000.

Pieterse, Jan. *White on Black: Images of Africa and Blacks in Western Popular Culture.* New Haven. CT: Yale University Press, 1992.

Pilgrim, David. "The Brute Caricature." November 2000. http://www.ferris.edu /jimcrow/brute/.

Piquero, Alex et al. "Race, Punishment, and the Michael Vick Experience." *Social Science Quarterly* 92, 2, June 2011, 535–51.

"Pit Bulls and Euthanasia Rates." *SFExaminer.com.* May 13, 2011. http://www .examiner.com/article/pit-bulls-and-euthanasia-rates.

Platt, Kym. "Michael Vick: Racism versus Responsibility." *Africanpath.com.* July 29 2007. http://www.africanpath.com/p_blogEntry.cfm?blogEntryID=1786.

Plumwood, Val. *Environmental Culture: The Ecological Crisis of Reason.* New York Routledge, 2001.

"Integrating Ethical Frameworks for Animals, Humans, and Nature: A Critical Feminist Eco-Socialist Analysis." *Ethics & the Environment* 5, 2, 2000, 285–322 *Feminism and the Mastery of Nature.* London: Routledge, 1993.

"Position Statement on Breed-Specific Legislation." American Society for the Prevention of Cruelty to Animals. n.d. http://www.aspca.org/about-us/policy-positions/breed -specific-legislation-1.aspx.

Potter, Will. *Green Is the New Red: An Insider's Account of a Social Movement Under Siege.* San Francisco, CA: City Lights Publishing, 2011.

Primm, Eric, Summer DuBois, and Robert Regoli. "Every Picture Tells a Story: Racial Representation on *Sports Illustrated* Covers." *The Journal of American Culture* 30, 2, June 2007, 222–31.

Proceedings and List of Delegates, California Chinese Exclusion Convention. San Francisco, November 21–2, 1901. San Francisco: The Star Press.

"Public Lukewarm on Animal Rights." Gallup News Service. May 21, 2003. http://www.gallup.com/poll/8461/public-lukewarm-animal-rights.aspx.

Putting Meat on the Table: Industrial Farm Animal Production in America. A Report of the Pew Commission on Industrial Farm Animal Production. n.d. http://www .ncifap.org/_images/PCIFAPFin.pdf.

Pyenson, Nicholas and David Lindberg. "What Happened to Gray Whales during the Pleistocene? The Ecological Impact of Sea-Level Change on Benthic Feeding Areas in the North Pacific Ocean." *PloS ONE* 6, 7, July 6, 2011. http://www.plosone.org /article/info%3Adoi%2F10.1371%2Fjournal.pone.0021295.

Raab, Barbara. "The Unfinished March on Washington? MLK's Dream of Jobs and Justice." *In Plain Sight.* August 27, 2013. http://inplainsight.nbcnews.com /_news/2013/08/27/20153493-the-unfinished-march-on-washington-mlks-dream -of-jobs-and-justice?lite.

"Race in the Court of Public Opinion." *News & Notes.* National Public Radio. August 6, 2007. http://www.npr.org/templates/story/story.php?storyId=12533203.

"Race Played Factor in Vick Coverage, Critics Say." *Talk of the Nation.* National Public Radio. August 28, 2007. http://www.npr.org/templates/story/story.php?storyId =14000094.

"Racist Obama Email: Marilyn Davenport Insists It Was Satire." *Huffingtonpost.com.* April 20, 2011. http://www.huffingtonpost.com/2011/04/20/racist-obama-email -marilyn-davenport_n_851772.html.

Ramirez, Michael. "'My Dog's Just Like Me': Dog Ownership as Gender Display." *Symbolic Interaction* 29, 3, 2006, 373–91.

Randour, Mary Lou and Tio Hardiman. "Creating Synergy for Gang Prevention: Taking a Look at Animal Fighting and Gangs." *Proceedings of Persistently Safe Schools: The 2007 National Conference on Safe Schools.* Washington, DC, October 29–31, 2007.

Ranlet, Philip. "The British, the Indians, and Smallpox: What Actually Happened at Fort Pitt in 1763?" *Pennsylvania History* 67, 3, Summer 2000, 427–41.

Rauch, Andrew and Jeff Sharp. "Ohioans' Attitudes about Animal Welfare: A Topical Report from the 2004 Ohio Survey of Food, Agricultural and Environmental Issues." 2005. http://ohiosurvey.osu.edu/pdf/2004_Animal_report.pdf.

Rawls, James. *Indians of California: The Changing Image.* Norman: University Of Oklahoma Press, 1984.

Razack, Sherene. *Looking White People in the Eye: Gender, Race, and Culture in Courtrooms and Classrooms.* Toronto: University of Toronto Press, 1998.

"Recent Whaling." www.makah.com. n.d. http://www.makah.com/whalingrecent.html.

"Refuting the Racist Rhetoric." Sea Shepherd Conservation Society. August 20, 2010. http://www.seashepherd.org/commentary-and-editorials/2010/08/20/refuting-the-racist-rhetoric-73.

Regan, Tom. *The Case for Animal Rights.* First edition updated with new preface. Berkeley: University of California Press, 2004.

Renker, Ann. "Whale Hunting and the Makah Tribe: A Needs Statement." May 2012.

Renteln, Alison. *The Cultural Defense.* Oxford: Oxford University Press, 2004.

"Report of the Aboriginal Subsistence Whaling Sub-Committee." International Whaling Commission/64/Rep 3, Agenda Item 7. June 27, 2012.

"Report of the Aboriginal Subsistence Whaling Working Group." International Whaling Commission/64/Aboriginal Subsistence Whaling 5 Rev1, Agenda Item 5.1. May 28, 2012.

"Report to Congress on the Extent and Effects of Domestic and International Terrorism on Animal Enterprises." U.S. Department of Justice and U.S. Department of Agriculture. September 1993. http://old.furcommission.com/resource/perspect2.htm.

"Report to the California Assembly Committee on Water, Parks and Wildlife/Submitted in Opposition to AB 238." San Francisco Society for the Prevention of Cruelty to Animals. March 10, 1999.

Rhoden, William. "Portrait of Reality, as Told by Vick." *The New York Times.* January 30, 2010. http://www.nytimes.com/2010/01/30/sports/football/30rhoden.html.

"Richard Cebull, Montana Federal Judge, Admits Forwarding Racist Obama Email." *Huffingtonpost.com.* March 1, 2012. http://www.huffingtonpost.com/2012/03/01/richard-cebull-judge-obama-racist-email_n_1312736.html.

Ritvo, Harriet. *The Platypus and the Mermaid: And Other Figments of the Classifying Imagination.* Cambridge, MA: Harvard University Press, 1998.

"Race, Breed, and Myths of Origin: Chillingham Cattle as Ancient Britons." *Representations* 39, Summer 1992, 1–22.

"The Animal Connection" in *The Boundaries of Humanity: Humans, Animals, Machines,* eds. James Sheehan and Morton Sosna. Berkeley: University of California Press, 1991, 68–81.

The Animal Estate: The English and Other Creatures in the Victorian Age. Cambridge, MA: Harvard University Press, 1987.

Roberts, David and Minelle Mahtani. "Neoliberalizing Race, Racing Neoliberalism: Placing 'Race' in Neoliberal Discourses." *Antipode* 42, 2, March 2010, 248–57.

Roberts. J. A. G. *China to Chinatown: Chinese Food in the West.* London: Reaktion Books, 2002.

Rogers, Paul. "Mountain Lion Photo Exposed Major Cultural Shift in California." *Mercurynews.com.* March 3, 2012. http://www.mercurynews.com/news/ci_20095676.

Roghair, David. "*Anderson v. Evans*: Will Makah Whaling under the Treaty of Neah Bay Survive the Ninth Circuit's Application of the MMPA?" *Journal of Environmental Law & Litigation* 20, 2005, 190–211.

Rudolf, John Collins. "Doom Feared as Asian Carp Advances." *Associated Press.* July 12, 2010. http://green.blogs.nytimes.com/2010/07/12/doom-feared-as-asian-carp-advances/.

Russell, Denise. *Who Rules the Waves? Piracy, Overfishing and Mining the Oceans.* London: Pluto Press, 2010.

Russell, Dick. "Tribal Tradition and the Spirit of Trust: A Makah Elder Speaks Out for the Gray Whale." *The Amicus Journal.* Spring 1999, 29–32.

Russell, Edmund. "'Speaking of Annihilation': Mobilizing for War against Human and Insect Enemies, 1914–1945." *The Journal of American History*, March 1996, 1505–29.

Russell, Sue. (a) "Animal Research's Changing Equation." *Miller-McCune.com.* December 19, 2011. http://www.miller-mccune.com/science/animal-researchs-changing-equation-38445/.

(b) "Should Animals Be Considered People?" *Miller-McCune.com.* December 20, 2011. http://www.miller-mccune.com/legal-affairs/should-animals-be-considered-people-38481/.

Rutmanis, Renada. "The Rise of Ecoterrorism." www.animallaw.info. 2006. http://www.animallaw.info/articles/ddusecoterrorism.htm#_ftnref20.

Saad, Lydia. "Four Moral Issues Sharply Divide Americans." *Gallup News Service.* May 26, 2010. http://www.gallup.com/poll/137357/Four-Moral-Issues-Sharply-Divide-Americans.aspx.

Sabatini, Joshua. "San Francisco's Asian Community Might Greatly Impact Mayoral Race." *SFExaminer.com.* March 15, 2011. http://www.sfexaminer.com/print/local/2011/03/san-francisco-s-asian-community-might-greatly-impact-mayoral-race.

"Pak Would Be Mayor if Daly Is Her Chief of Staff." *SFExaminer.com.* January 7, 2011. http://www.sfexaminer.com/print/blogs/blogs/2011/01/pak-would-be-mayor-if-daly-her-chief-staff.

Sachs, Wolfgang. "The Blue Planet: An Ambiguous Modern Icon." *The Ecologist* 24, 5, 1994, 170–5.

Sacks, J. et al. "Breeds of Dogs Involved in Fatal Human Attacks in the United States between 1979 and 1998." *Journal of the American Veterinary Medical Association* 217, 2000, 836–40.

Sagoff, Mark. "Exotic Species Are Not as Bad as We Fear." *Chronicle of Higher Education* 46, 42, June 23, 2000, B7.

San Francisco Society for the Prevention of Cruelty to Animals (SFSPCA). "Statement of the SFSPCA Pursuant to Proposed Regulatory Action: Enactment of a Ban on the

Importation of Live Turtles and Bullfrogs for Human Consumption." Submitted to the State of California Fish and Game Commission. April 2, 1999.

an Francisco Society for the Prevention of Cruelty to Animals (SFSPCA). "Report to the California Assembly Committee on Water, Parks and Wildlife: Submitted in Opposition to AB 238." March 10, 1999.

an Francisco Society for the Prevention of Cruelty to Animals (SFSPCA). "Import of Live, Non-Native Turtles and Frogs for Food: Supplemental Report #2." Submitted to the State of California Fish and Game Commission. January 15, 1999.

an Francisco Society for the Prevention of Cruelty to Animals (SFSPCA). "Supplemental Report on Live, Non-Native Turtles & Frogs Imported for Food." Submitted to the State of California Fish and Game Commission. October 1, 1998.

an Francisco Society for the Prevention of Cruelty to Animals (SFSPCA). "Statement Regarding Live Animal Markets." September 29, 1998.

an Francisco Society for the Prevention of Cruelty to Animals (SFSPCA). "Statement on the Import of Live Turtles and Bullfrogs for Food." Submitted to the State of California Fish and Game Commission. January 23, 1998.

an Francisco Society for the Prevention of Cruelty to Animals (SFSPCA). "Statement on San Francisco Live Animal Markets." Submitted to the San Francisco Animal Control and Welfare Commission. September 12, 1996.

anders, Robert. "Gray Whales Likely Survived the Ice Ages by Changing Their Diets." UC Berkeley News Center. July 6, 2011. http://newscenter.berkeley .edu/2011/07/06/gray-whales-likely-survived-the-ice-ages-by-changing-their -diets/.

Santos, Carla, Yaniv Belhassen, and Kellee Caton. "Reimagining Chinatown: An Analysis of Tourism Discourse." *Tourism Management* 29, 2008, 1002–12.

Savage Rumbaugh, Sue and Roger Lewin. *Kanzi: The Ape at the Brink of the Human Mind*. Reissue edition. New York: Wiley, 1996.

Saxton, Alexander. *The Indispensable Enemy: Labor and the Anti-Chinese Movement in California*. Berkeley: University of California Press, 1975.

Schaffer, Michael. *One Nation under Dog: America's Love Affair with Our Dogs*. New York: Henry Holt and Company, 2009.

Schlosser, Eric. *Fast Food Nation: The Dark Side of the All-American Meal*. Reprinted edition. Chicago. IL: Mariner Books, 2012.

Schmidt, Sarah. "The One That Got Away." *Saturday Night* 114, 2, 1999, 78–84.

"Documents Show Makah Eyed Commercial Whaling: Only at First, But Tribe Keeps It as an Option." *Globe and Mail*. October 24, 1998.

Schmidt, Steve. "Cougar Hunt Flap Adds Ammo to Culture War." *UT San Diego*. March 18, 2012. http://www.utsandiego.com/news/2012/mar/18/tp-cougar-hunt-flap -adds-ammo-to-culture-war/.

Schneider, J. and D. S. Eitzen. "The Perpetuation of Racial Segregation by Playing Position in Professional Football" in *Sport in Contemporary Society: An Anthology*, ed. D. S. Eitzen. New York: St. Martin's Press, 1984.

Schreiber, Dan. "Mayor Ed Lee Dominated 8 of 11 San Francisco Districts." *SFExaminer. com*. November 11, 2011. http://www.sfexaminer.com/blogs/under-dome/2011/11 /mayor-ed-lee-dominated-8-11-san-francisco-districts.

"Vote-By-Mail Popular With Asians Who Helped Ed Lee Win." *SFExaminer.com*. November 10, 2011. http://www.sfexaminer.com/local/sf-mayoral-race/2011/11 /vote-mail-popular-asians-who-helped-ed-lee-win.

"Leland Yee Robo-call Warns Voters about Ed Lee Campaign Workers." *SFExaminer. com.* October 28, 2011. http://www.sfexaminer.com/blogs/under-dome/2011/10 /leland-yee-robo-call-warns-voters-about-ed-lee-campaign-workers.

"Mayhem Breaks Out between Yee, Lee SF Mayoral Campaigns." *SFExaminer.com* October 26, 2011. http://www.sfexaminer.com/local/2011/10/mayhem-breaks-out -between-yee-lee-sf-mayoral-campaigns.

Scully, Matthew. *Dominion: The Power of Man, the Suffering of Animals, and the Call to Mercy.* Reprinted edition. New York: St. Martin's Griffin, 2003.

"Sea Shepherd has 12 Primary Reasons for Opposing the Plan to Slaughter Whales by the Makah." Sea Shepherd Conservation Society. n.d. http://www.seashepherd.org /whales/makah-tribe.html.

"Sea Shepherd Report to Makah Hearing October 11th." Sea Shepherd Conservation Society. October 12, 2005. http://www.seashepherd.org/news-and -media/2008/11/03/sea-shepherd-report-to-makah-hearing-october-11th-939.

Semencic, Carl. *The World of Fighting Dogs.* Reprinted edition. Neptune, NJ: TFH Publications, 1992.

Sepez, Jennifer. "Treaty Rights and the Right to Culture: Native American Subsistence Issues in US Law." *Cultural Dynamics* 14, 2, July 2002, 143–59.

Sexton, Jared. *Amalgamation Schemes: Antiblackness and the Critique of Multiracialism* Minneapolis: University of Minnesota Press, 2008.

"People-of-Color-Blindness: Notes on the Afterlife of Slavery." *Social Text* 28, 2 Summer 2010, 31–56.

Shafer, Holley. *Chinese American Voters Education Committee Chinese Newspaper Readers Poll.* Public Research Institute, San Francisco State University. September 1999.

Shaffer, Ralph. "Implementing the Fifteenth Amendment in California: 1870" in *California and the Coming of the Fifteenth Amendment* (Volume II), Sheila Skjeie and Ralph Shaffer. 2005. http://www.csupomona.edu/~reshaffer/books/black /shaffer/intro3.htm.

Shah, Nayan. *Contagious Divides: Epidemics and Race in San Francisco's Chinatown.* Berkeley: University of California Press, 2001.

Sheehan, James and Morton Sosna. *The Boundaries of Humanity: Humans, Animals, Machines.* Berkeley: University of California Press, 1991.

Sherbert, Erin. "Gavin Newsom Demands Fish and Game President Resign after Shooting Mountain Lion." *SFWeekly.com.* February 27, 2012. http://blogs.sfweekly.com /thesnitch/2012/02/gavin_newsom_dan_richards.php?print=true.

Shih, Gerry. "Behind-The-Scenes Power Politics: The Making of a Mayor." *The New York Times.* January 6, 2011. http://www.nytimes.com/2011/01/07/us/07bcmayor .html.

Shukin, Nicole. *Animal Capital: Rendering Life in Biopolitical Times.* Minneapolis: University of Minnesota Press, 2009.

Siebert, Charles. "The Animal-Cruelty Syndrome." *The New York Times.* June 13, 2010. http://www.nytimes.com/2010/06/13/magazine/13dogfighting-t.html?pagewanted =all&_r=0.

"What Are the Whales Trying to Tell Us?" *The New York Times Magazine.* July 12, 2009, 26–35, 44–5.

Simberloff, Daniel. "Confronting Introduced Species: A Form of Xenophobia?" *Biological Invasions* 5, 2003, 179–92.

Simmonds, Mark Peter. "Into the Brains of Whales." *Applied Animal Behaviour Science* 100, 2006, 103–16.

Simpson, Doug. "Dogfighting Culture Thrives Amid Crackdown." *Los Angeles Times*. February 8, 2004. http://articles.latimes.com/print/2004/feb/08/news /adna-dogfight8.

Singer, Peter. *Animal Liberation: The Definitive Classic of the Animal Movement*. Reissue edition. New York: Harper Perennial Modern Classics, 2009.

Skjeie, Sheila. "California, Racism, and the Fifteenth Amendment: 1849–1870" in *California and the Coming of the Fifteenth Amendment* (Volume I), Sheila Skjeie and Ralph Shaffer. 2005. http://www.csupomona.edu/~reshaffer/books/black /skjeie/v1_chap5.htm.

Smith, Michael David. "Warren Moon Sees Biases Hurting Black Quarterbacks." *ProFootball Talk*. April 24, 2013. http://profootballtalk.nbcsports.com/2013/04/24 /warren-moon-sees-biases-hurting-black-quarterbacks/.

Snyder, Deron. "Black Quarterbacks' Intelligence Still Scrutinized?" *The Root*. May 20, 2011. http://www.theroot.com/print/52555.

Soper, Kate. *What Is Nature? Culture, Politics and the Non-Human*. Oxford: Blackwell, 1995.

Spelman, Elizabeth. *Inessential Woman*. Reprinted edition. Boston, MA: Beacon Press, 1990.

Spiegel, Marjorie. *The Dreaded Comparison: Human and Animal Slavery*. New York: Mirror Books, 1997.

Spoehr, Luther. "Sambo and the Heathen Chinee: Californians' Racial Stereotypes in the Late 1870s." *Pacific Historical Review* 43, May 1973, 185–204.

Spurr, Stephen. "Wilderness Concepts." *Idaho Law Review* 16, 1980, 439–48.

Steiner, Gary. *Anthropocentrism and Its Discontents: The Moral Status of Animals in the History of Western Philosophy*. Pittsburgh: University of Pittsburgh Press, 2005.

Stepan, Nancy. "Race and Gender: The Role of Analogy in Science" in *Anatomy of Racism*, ed. David Theo Goldberg. Minneapolis: University of Minnesota Press, 1990, 38–57.

Stienstra, Tom. "PEER Survey of the California Department of Fish and Game: Alarming Answers to the DFG Survey." *San Francisco Examiner*. April 7, 1999.

Stoett, Peter. "Of Whales and People: Normative Theory, Symbolism, and the IWC." *Journal of International Wildlife Law & Policy* 8, 2–3, 2005, 151–75.

Stringer, David. "Iceland Says Whalers Can Hunt Hundreds More Whales per Year for Next 5 Years." *Associated Press*. January 27, 2009.

Strouse, Kathy with Dog Angel. *Bad Newz: The Untold Story of the Michael Vick Dogfighting Case*. Dogfighting Investigation Publications LLC, 2009.

Sturgeon, Noël. *Ecofeminist Natures: Race, Gender, Feminist Theory and Political Action*. New York: Routledge, 1997.

Subramanian, Banu. "The Aliens Have Landed! Reflections on the Rhetoric of Biological Invasions." *Meridians: Feminism, Race, Transnationalism* 2, 1, 2001, 26–40.

Sullivan, Robert. *A Whale Hunt: How a Native American Village Did What No One Thought It Could*. New York: Simon & Schuster, 2000.

"'Supporting Our Own': Blacks Split on Michael Vick." *Tell Me More*. National Public Radio. August 22, 2007.

Swan, James. "Indians of Cape Flattery." *Smithsonian Contributions to Knowledge*. Vol. XVI. Washington, DC: Smithsonian Institution, 1869.

Swartz, Steven. "Gray Whale Migratory, Social and Breeding Behavior." Report of the International Whaling Commission (Special Issue 8). 1986, 207–29.

Takaki, Ronald. *Iron Cages: Race and Culture in 19th-Century America.* New York: Oxford University Press, 1990.

Tallbear, Kim. "Why Interspecies Thinking Needs Indigenous Standpoints." *Fieldsights – Theorizing the Contemporary, Cultural Anthropology Online.* April 24, 2011. http://culanth.org/fieldsights/260-why-interspecies-thinking-needs-indigenous -standpoints.

Tam, Pui-Wing. "Chinatown Elders of SF are at Odds over Taiwan; Mainland's Economic Clout Persuades Daniel Hom to Make a Flag Switch." *The Wall Street Journal.* April 20, 2004, A1–A10.

The Department of Fish and Game/The 1990's and Beyond/A Vision for the Future. Administrative Report No. 93-1. January 28, 1993. Recompiled August 2011.

"The Economic Importance of Hunting." California Department of Fish and Wildlife. http://www.dfg.ca.gov/wildlife/hunting/econ-hunting.html.

"The Makah Indian Tribe and Whaling: Questions and Answers." Makah Tribal Council and Makah Whaling Commission. www.makah.com. January 2005. http://www .makah.com/pdfs/makahwhalingqa.pdf.

"The Whales' Navy." Sea Shepherd Conservation Society. n.d. http://www.seashepherd .org/whales/.

Thomas, Keith. *Man and the Natural World: Changing Attitudes in England 1500–1800.* London: Allen Lane, 1983.

Thompson, Wright. "A History of Mistrust." *ESPN.com.* n.d. http://sports.espn.go.com /espn/eticket/story?page=vicksatlanta.

Tinkham, George Henry. *California Men and Events: Time 1769–1890.* 2nd edition. Haverhill, MA: Record Publishing Company, 1915.

Tizon, Alex. "Makah Whale Hunt Spurs Racist Comments." *The Ecotone,* Fall 1999, 10–12.

Tizon, Alex and Jack Broom. "McCaw Trying to 'Buy Off' Whale Hunt? – Aide to Billionaire in Talks With Makah Tribal Leaders." *Seattle Times.* November 12, 1998. http://community.seattletimes.nwsource.com/archive/?date=19981112&slug =2783071.

"Top Ten Dog Fighting Questions." American Society for the Prevention of Cruelty to Animals. n.d. http://animal.discovery.com/tv/animal-witness/michael-vick /dog-fighting/.

Touré. "What if Michael Vick Were White? Since the Day He Was Arrested, People Have Asked. The Answer Isn't What You Think." *ESPN The Magazine.* September 5, 2011. http://espn.go.com/espn/commentary/story/_/id/6894586/imagining-michael -vick-white-quarterback-nfl-espn-magazine.

"Treaty Right to Hunt Grey Whales Splits B.C. Native Groups." *Vancouver Province.* September 11, 2007. http://www.canada.com/theprovince/news/story .html?id=d925e70a-85b8-4980-82c6-abe15838fbb7.

"Treaty with the Makah, 1855." [Treaty of Neah Bay]. http://www.fws.gov/pacific/ea /tribal/treaties/MAKAH_1855.pdf.

"Tribe's Whaling Commission Didn't Authorize Shooting of Gray Whale in Washington State." *Associated Press.* September 9, 2007.

Tsai, Luke. "Chinese-language Newspapers Having Unprecedented Impact on SF Mayor's Race." *SFExaminer.com.* October 16, 2011. http://www.sfexaminer.com/local /sf-mayoral-race/2011/10/chinese-language-newspapers-having-unprecedented -impact-sf-mayors-race.

Tsui, Bonnie. *American Chinatown: A People's History of Five Neighborhoods.* New York: Free Press, 2009.

uan, Yi-Fu. *Dominance and Affection: The Making of Pets*. New Haven, CT: Yale University Press, 2004.

Tucker Carlson: Michael Vick 'Should Have Been Executed.'" *Huffingtonpost.com*. December 29, 2010. http://www.huffingtonpost.com/2010/12/29/tucker-carlson -michael-vi_n_802192.html.

Turtles in Trouble Have a Defender in Annie Lancaster." *The Wall Street Journal*. April 16, 1998.

Twain's Frog Gets Reduced Living Space." EarthJustice. April 13, 2006. http://earthjustice.org/news/press/2006/twain-s-frog-gets-reduced-living-space.

Twining, Hillary, Arnold Arluke, and Gary Patronek. "Managing the Stigma of Outlaw Breeds: A Case Study of Pit Bull Owners." *Society & Animals* 8, 1, March 2001, 25–52.

United States of ALEC." *BillMoyers.com*. September 28, 2012. http://billmoyers.com /segment/united-states-of-alec/.

United States Facts." Food & Water Watch. n.d. http://www.factoryfarming.org /states/us.

Van Ginkel, Rob. "The Makah Whale Hunt and Leviathan's Death: Reinventing Tradition and Disputing Authenticity in the Age of Modernity." *Etnofoor* 17, 1/2, 2004, 58–89.

Vialles, Noëlie. *Animal to Edible*. Cambridge: Cambridge University Press, 1994.

Vick, Michael with Brett Honeycutt and Stephen Copeland. *Finally Free: An Autobiography*. Brentwood, TN: Worthy Publishing, 2012.

Wagner, Diana. "Competing Cultural Interests in the Whaling Debate: An Exception to the Universality of the Right to Culture." *Transnational Law and Contemporary Problems* 14, 2004–5, 831–64.

Wagner, Eric. "Savage Disobedience: A Renegade Whaler Rocks the Boat in the Makah Struggle for Cultural Identity." *Orion Magazine*. November/December 2009. http://www.orionmagazine.org/index.php/articles/article/5101/.

Walker, Peter. "Makah Whaling Is Also a Political Issue." *The Ecotone*, Fall, 1999, 8–10.

Walsh, Bryan. "Asian Carp in the Great Lakes? This Means War!" *Time*. February 9, 2010. http://www.time.com/time/printout/0,8816,1962108,00.html.

Walzer, Michael. *The Revolution of the Saints: A Study in the Origins of Radical Politics*. Cambridge, MA: Harvard University Press, 1965.

Wang, L. Ling-chi. "Symbolism Characterizes Lee's Appointment." *SFGate.com*. January 30, 2011. http://www.sfgate.com/cgi-bin/articl.cgi?f=/c/a/2011/01/30 /INQA1HE7UU.DTL.

Warren, Charles. "Perspectives on the 'Alien' Versus 'Native' Species Debate: A Critique of Concepts, Language and Practice." *Progress in Human Geography* 31, 4, 2007, 427–46.

Warren Moon: Black Quarterbacks Still Victims of Prejudice." *SIWire*. April 24, 2013. http://tracking.si.com/2013/04/24/warren-moon-black-quarterback-prejudice/#.

Wassener, Bettina. "Attitudes Shifting on Shark Fin Soup." *The New York Times*. April 24, 2011. http://www.nytimes.com/2011/04/25/business/energy-environment/25green .html.

Waterman, T. T. "The Whaling Equipment of the Makah Indians." *University of Washington Publications in Anthropology* 1, 1, June 1920, 1–67.

Watters, Lawrence and Connie Dugger. "The Hunt for Gray Whales: The Dilemma of Native American Treaty Rights and the International Moratorium on Whaling." *Columbia Journal of Environmental Law* 22, 1997, 319–52.

Weaver, Harlan. "'Becoming in Kind': Race, Gender, and Nation in Cultures of Dog Rescue and Dog Fighting." *American Quarterly*. Special issue "Species/Race/Sex," eds. Claire Jean Kim and Carla Freccero. 65, 3, September 2013, 689–709.

Weller, David et al. "Movements of Gray Whales between the Western and Eastern North Pacific." *Endangered Species Research* 18, September 2012, 193–9.

Wenzel, George. *Animal Rights, Human Rights: Ecology, Economy and Ideology in the Canadian Arctic*. Toronto: University of Toronto Press, 1991.

Westneat, Danny. "Washington's 19th-Century Man – Jack Metcalf's Days in Congress Are Numbered, Along With the Spirit of an Older Northwest." *Seattle Times* September 5, 1999. http://community.seattletimes.nwsource.com/archive/?date=19990905&slug=2981040.

"Whaling Tradition." www.makah.com. n.d. http://www.makah.com/whalingtradition.html.

Whatmore, Sarah. *Hybrid Geographies: Natures Cultures Spaces*. Thousand Oaks, CA Sage, 2001.

"Who We Are: Sea Shepherd's Mission Statement." Sea Shepherd Conservation Society n.d. http://www.seashepherd.org/who-we-are/.

Wildermuth, John. "S.F. Mayor Ed Lee Declares Victory." *SFGate.com*. November 10 2011. http://www.sfgate.com/cgi-bin/article.cgi?f=/c/a/2011/11/10/MNBT1LSR24.DTL.

Willis, James, Jerry Habib, and Jeremy Brittan. "Census Data Analysis." San Francisco Planning Department. April 19, 2004. http://www.docstoc.com/docs/78947606/san-francisco-planning-department-census-data-analysis.

Winograd, Nathan. "The Indictment of Wayne Pacelle." August 9, 2011. http://www.nathanwinograd.com/?p=6510.

Wise, Steven. *Drawing the Line: Science and the Case for Animal Rights*. New York: Basic Books, 2003.

Wolch, Jennifer and Jody Emel, eds. *Animal Geographies: Place, Politics, and Identity in the Nature-Culture Borderlands*. London: Verso, 1998.

Wolfson, David and Mariann Sullivan. "Foxes in the Hen House: Animals, Agribusiness and the Law: A Modern American Fable" in *Animal Rights: Current Debates and New Directions*, eds. Cass Sunstein and Martha Nussbaum. Oxford: Oxford University Press, 2004, 205–33.

Wong, Bernard. *Ethnicity and Entrepreneurship: The New Chinese Immigrants in the San Francisco Bay Area*. Boston, MA: Allyn and Bacon, 1997.

Wong, K. Scott. "Chinatown: Conflicting Images, Contested Terrain." *Melus* 20, 1, Spring 1995, 3–19.

Wong, Morrison. "Chinese Americans" in *Asian Americans: Contemporary Trends and Issues*, ed. Pyong Gap Min. Newbury Park, CA: Pine Forge Press, 2006, 110–45.

Woods, Mark and Paul Moriarty. "Strangers in a Strange Land: The Problem of Exotic Species." *Environmental Values* 10, 2001, 163–91.

Woodward, J. R. "Professional Football Scouts: An Investigation of Racial Stacking." *Sociology of Sport Journal* 21, 2004, 356–75.

"An Examination of a National Football League College Draft Publication: Do Racial Stereotypes Still Exist in Football?" October 13, 2002. http://physed.otago.ac.nz/sosol/v5i2/v5i2_1.html.

Worden, Amy. "Anti-dog Fighting Bill Vick Lobbied for Passes U.S. Senate." *Philly.com*. December 5, 2012. http://www.philly.com/philly/blogs/pets/Anti-dog-fighting-bill-Vick-lobbied-for-passes-US-Senate.html.

Wright, David. *It Takes a Neighborhood: Strategies to Prevent Urban Decline.* Albany, NY: Rockefeller Institute Press, 2001.

Wu, Judy Tzu-Chun. "'Loveliest Daughter of Our Ancient Cathay!': Representations of Ethnic and Gender Identity in the Miss Chinatown U.S.A. Beauty Pageant." *Journal of Social History* Fall 1997, 5–31.

Yamamoto, Eric. *Interracial Justice: Conflict and Reconciliation in Post-Civil Rights America.* New York: New York University Press, 1999.

Yang, Jeff. "A Taste of Racism in the Chinese Food Scare." *The Washington Post.* July 15, 2007. http://www.washingtonpost.com/wp-dyn/content/article/2007/07/13/ar2007071301712.html.

Yeh, Chiou-ling. *Making an American Festival: Chinese New Year in San Francisco's Chinatown.* Berkeley: University of California Press, 2008.

York, Geoffrey. "Chinese Taste for Exotic Flesh." *Toronto Globe & Mail.* June 28, 2003.

Young, Miles. "Investigative Report on the Sale of Live Turtles and Frogs as Food Items in California Markets." Prepared for Eric Mills and Action for Animals. August 22, 2006.

"A Challenged Environment: Let's Not Delude Ourselves about Environmental Protection." *San Francisco Chronicle.* December 29, 2004. http://sfgate.com/cgi-bin/article.cgi?f=/c/a/2004/12/29/edgdiai7ph1.dtl.

Zhan, Mei. "Civet Cats, Fried Grasshoppers, and David Beckham's Pajamas: Unruly Bodies after SARS." *American Anthropologist* 107, 1, 2005, 31–42.

Zhong, Nanshan and Guangqiao Zeng. "What We Have Learnt from SARS Epidemics in China." *British Medical Journal.* August 19, 2006, 389–91.

Zhou, Min. "Contemporary Chinese America: Immigration, Ethnicity, and Community Transformation." www.chinausfriendship.com. May 1, 2011. http://www.chinausfriendship.com/article2.asp?mn=255.

Chinatown: The Socioeconomic Potential of an Urban Enclave. Philadelphia, PA: Temple University Press, 1992.

Zhou, Min and Guoxuan Cai. "Chinese Language Media in the United States: Immigration and Assimilation in American Life." *Qualitative Sociology* 25, 3, Fall 2002, 419–40.

Zieralski, Ed. "Dan Richards Out as Fish and Game President." *UTSanDiego.* August 8, 2012. http://www.utsandiego.com/news/2012/Aug/08/dan-richards-out-president-fish-and-game-commissio/.

Zizza, Tony. "Take Race out of the Michael Vick Dogfighting Case." *The Reality Check.* August 26, 2007. http://www.therealitycheck.org/GuestColumnist/tzizza082607.htm.

Zu, Shuxian, Peter Li, and Pei-Feng Su. "Animal Welfare Consciousness of Chinese College Students." *China Information* 19, 1, 2005, 67–95.

ndex

Abernathy, Kwame, 253, 263, 276–8
abolitionism
  animal liberation and trope of, 283–7
  dogfighting history and, 256–63
  Negro as beast imagery and, 38–9
aboriginal subsistence whaling (ASW)
  defined, 222–4
  whale hunting moratoriums and exceptions
    for, 218–20, 228–32
aboriginal women, sexual violence
  against, 197–9
accommodation theories, cultural differences
  and, 8–12
accountability, gender politics and, 197–9
Action for Animals (AFA), 76–7n.35
advertising, Chinese cultural stereotypes
  in, 103–4
advocacy anthropology, Native animal use
  and, 13–14
Affiliated tribes of Northwest Indians, 241
Africa, Negro as beast images and colonialism
  in, 35–6
Agnos, Art, 134–6
agribusiness
  food libel laws and, 66–8, 67n.12
  instrumental use of animals and growth
    of, 64–72
  lobbying activities of, 69, 91–3
ahistoricity, Indian savage concept and, 43–52
Akeley, Carl, 43
alcohol
  impact on Makah people of, 211–12
  introduction of North American Indians to,
    29–31, 30n.9
Al-Hibri, Azizah, 193
American Civil Liberties Union (ACLU),
  71–2n.26

American Dog Breeder's Association, 272n.49
American exceptionalism, savage Indian
  paradigm and, 49
American Federation of Labor (AFL), 56–7
American Indians. *See* Native peoples
American Kennel Club (AKC), 272n.49
American Legislative Exchange Council
  (ALEC), 71–2n.26, 71–2
American Pit Bull Terrier (APBT), 272n.49
American School of anthropology, racialized
  hierarchies in, 39–41
American Society for the Prevention of Cruelty
  to Animals (ASPCA), 63–4, 82, 256
American Staffordshire Terrier, 272n.49
American Temperament Test, 274
American Tortoise Rescue, 76–9, 185–8
amphibian species, global threats to, 160n.61
anachronistic space, Chinese culture and, 53–4
analogization, ethics of avowal and, 283–7
Anderson, Virginia, 31
Anderson v. Evans, 224–6, 231–2
animal capital, instrumental use of animals
  as, 64–72
"Animal & Ecological Terrorism in
  America," 71–2
Animal Enterprise Protection Act
  (AEPA), 68–72
Animal Enterprise Terrorism Act (AETA),
  71n.25, 71–2n.26, 71–2
animal escape movies, popularity of, 64–5
Animal Fighting Prohibition Enforcement Act,
  257, 257n.7
animal husbandry
  colonial encouragement of Indians
    in, 45–7
  slave ownership using technologies
    of, 38–9